Housing Policy and Practice

Fifth Edition

Peter Malpass and Alan Murie

palgrave

First edition 1982
Second edition 1987
Third edition 1990
Fourth edition 1994
Fifth edition 1999

Published by
PALGRAVE
Houndmills, Basingstoke, Hampshire RG21 6XS and
175 Fifth Avenue, New York, N.Y. 10010
Companies and representatives throughout the world

PALGRAVE is the new global academic imprint of
St. Martin's Press LLC Scholarly and Reference Division and
Palgrave Publishers Ltd (formerly Macmillan Press Ltd).

ISBN 0–333–73188–3 hardcover
ISBN 0–333–73189–1 paperback

This book is printed on paper suitable for recycling and made from fully managed and sustained forest sources.

A catalogue record for this book is available from the British Library.

10   9   8   7   6   5   4   3
08   07   06   05   04   03   02   01

Copy-edited and typeset by Povey–Edmondson
Tavistock and Rochdale, England

Printed in China

Public Policy and Politics

Series Editors: Colin Fudge and Robin Hambleton

Public policy-making in western democracies is confronted by new pressures. Central values relating to the role of the state, the role of markets and the role of citizenship are now all contested and the consensus built up around the Key   elfare state is under challenge. New social movements are enterin   olitical arena; electronic technologies are transforming the natur   ployment; changes in demographic structure are creating heigh   nands for public services; unforeseen social and health problems   merging; and, most disturbing, social and economic inequalities are ir   ng in many countries.

Ho   nments – at international, national and local levels – respond to this   ing agenda is the central focus of the Public Policy and Politics serie   ed at a student, professional, practitioner and academic readership, i. a. s to provide up-to-date, comprehensive and authoritative analyses of public policy-making in practice.

The series   s international and interdisciplinary in scope, and bridges theory and practi   b relating the substance of policy to the politics of the policy-making p

Please

Wol

Public Policy and Politics

Series Editors: Colin Fudge and Robin Hambleton

PUBLISHED

FORTHCOMING

Public Policy and Politics
Series Standing Order
ISBN 0–333–71705–8 hardcover
ISBN 0–333–69349–3 paperback
(outside North America only)

You can receive future titles in this series as they are published. To place a standing order please contact your bookseller or, in the case of difficulty, write to us at the address below with your name and address, the title of the series and the ISBN quoted above.

Customer Services Department, Macmillan Distribution Ltd
Houndmills, Basingstoke, Hampshire RG21 6XS, England

Contents

List of Tables and Figures

Tables

Figures

Preface to the Fifth Edition

This new edition of *Housing Policy and Practice* represents an updating of the fourth edition, which was very extensively rewritten and revised from its predecessors. The changes made now are less extensive but the book has been updated throughout and Chapters 5 and 13 rewritten to take account of Labour's electoral victory in May 1997 and its consequences for housing policy. The end of eighteen years of Conservative government provides an ideal opportunity to look back over a period of rapid change in housing policy, and to provide an assessment of the achievements and failures of policy in that period.

In the years since the appearance of the first edition much has changed, not only in housing but also in housing studies, which has emerged as a distinct and thriving area of academic activity in Britain and elsewhere. In the midst of the proliferation of research and commentary, set against a changing policy background, it can be difficult to retain a clear grasp of continuities and linkages. The role of a book of this kind is to provide both a framework for analysis and a concise account of the main themes in the development of housing policy and practice in Britain. Over the years students have found the book to be useful in approaching housing for the first time, and we trust that this new edition will continue to be as helpful.

September 1998   7PETER MALPASS
ALAN MURIE

Guide to Reading the Book

The aim of this book is to provide a distinctive and up-to-date analysis of British housing policy and practice in which an examination of national policy is linked to studies at the local level, and to contemporary academic debates about housing and public policy. Since the early 1970s a large number of researchers in different social science disciplines have contributed to an expanding literature on housing policy and the housing system. Some writers have been concerned with developments at national level, but a lot of work has been done in the form of local studies, often dealing with the impact of national policy. The approach adopted here is based on the fact that housing policy and practice involve both central and local government in significant but different ways, and that, therefore, it is necessary to transcend the national or local focus in order to see what is going on. Not only are both central and local government involved in housing, but they are engaged in complex relationships with each other as well as with other state, private and voluntary institutions involved in the provision of housing.

The book does not attempt to be comprehensive; it is increasingly apparent that comprehensive accounts of housing policy and practice cannot be contained within one volume without sacrificing essential analysis and discussion. Instead the approach is thematic and selective. A main theme is the distinct contributions of central and local government in housing policy and practice, and the importance of the relationship between these two levels of state activity. As an analytical device, this focus provides a framework on which to build an understanding of the involvement of other state institutions and private interests. A very important idea underpinning the analysis and presentation is the need to avoid a tenure-by-tenure approach. A basic assumption in this book is that tenure divisions can often obscure more than they reveal, and that changes affecting the different tenures have to be understood as being closely interrelated.

Another theme is the importance of history in any understanding of contemporary housing issues, and the need to avoid seeing history as just one thing after another. In other words, the historical account presented here is located within a coherent explanatory framework, giving shape to the sequence of events and recognising the importance of both continuity and change.

Later chapters present a different perspective built around notions of policy-making, implementation and evaluation. Drawing extensively on empirical research in a variety of localities, the discussion focuses on the way decisions are produced, how such decisions are translated into action (questioning whether policy-making and implementation can be neatly separated into sequential activities), and how the benefits of policy action are distributed.

Chapter 1 presents an introduction to housing and the housing problem, looking at the scope and content of housing policy, and putting forward a particular perspective on tenure restructuring and the modernisation of the housing market. This part of the book is an important precursor to the more detailed historical account developed in Chapters 2–5. Chapter 2 looks at the nineteenth-century origins of housing policy and the factors which inhibited its growth before 1914. Chapter 3 deals with crucial events of the years during and immediately after the First World War, when state housing policy developed very rapidly. It also traces the course of events up to 1939. Chapter 4 takes the narrative on to 1979, showing how the notions of residualisation of the public sector and centralisation of control over local authorities emerge as important factors for an understanding of the changing emphasis of housing policy. Chapter 5 brings the story up to date, looking at the rapidly changing housing situation since 1979. Each of the historical chapters contains a summary guide to housing legislation.

Chapter 6 looks at the social and economic context within which housing policy is located. The discussion is focused on the current situation and contemporary trends, providing up-to-date evidence on issues such as residualisation and polarisation within the British housing system. There is also discussion of housing and the economy and the importance of the Treasury in housing policy.

Chapter 7 sets up the later discussion by explaining the administrative framework of housing policy. This includes reference to the structure of the central government administrative apparatus, and the powers of central and local government. The chapter also considers the roles played by the new towns, the Housing Corporation, the housing associations and the building societies.

Chapter 8 is an introduction to housing finance at the local level, from a policy point of view. It explains the importance of concepts such as capital and revenue in understanding housing finance, and also terms such as 'historic-cost pricing', 'current-value pricing' and affordability. The discussion then moves on to consider the financial frameworks within which local authorities and housing associations work.

Chapter 9 looks at different perspectives within the policy analysis literature, drawing out the differences between the 'top-down' and 'bottom-up' approaches, and seeks to apply some of the insights from policy analysis to housing policy processes.

Chapter 10 concentrates on aspects of policy-making; it looks first at work on roles and relationships within local government and then turns to policy-making in housing associations. The second half of the chapter presents evidence from four studies of policy-making, two where the local authorities were confronting problems which they had themselves identified, and two where the local authorities were responding to policies imposed on them by central government. One of these case studies is based on research carried out specifically for this book.

Chapter 11 is about the translation of policy into action and presents a discussion of housing management, beginning with a cross-tenure perspective which identifies ways in which owner-occupied housing is managed. The chapter then moves on to look at social housing and draws on evidence from major studies of housing management in England and Wales.

Chapter 12 is concerned with distributional issues arising from the implementation of housing policies. It illustrates aspects of the evaluation of policy and issues raised in evaluation through a focus on the sale of council houses and on the effectiveness of housing management initiatives.

Chapter 13 draws the book to a close by looking back over the eighteen years of Conservative government and forward to the prospects for housing under a Labour government beyond the end of the twentieth century.

Finally, there is a guide to further reading, indicating under a variety of headings the range of available sources on housing issues.

1

Introduction: Analysing Housing Policy

Policy is but one element in the scope of housing studies and by way of introduction it is appropriate to refer to the breadth of the subject. Housing provides a rich and varied field of study, beginning with the basic human need for shelter. There are approaching 24 million dwellings in Britain, and because of the durability of the structures built to withstand the rigours of the British climate, the houses now in use include some that are hundreds of years old and many (a quarter) that are over 80 years old. The form and type of housing tend to reflect its age. Most people live in conventional (for Britain at least) two-storey houses, but of course there is immense variation in what people's homes consist of, from the palatial residences of the rich and famous to the sometimes damp and overcrowded dwellings of the least well off. Housing conditions represent a key indicator of quality, and Britain in the 1990s still has over half a million dwellings lacking in basic modern amenities, and over 2.5 million that are considered to be in serious disrepair.

Houses occupy land and so there is a spatial dimension to housing studies; this means at one level recognising the distinctive forms and layouts found in different parts of the country (for example, Edinburgh is very different from Bristol), and at another level it is about the way in which the location of housing influences access to other things, such as jobs, shops, schools and sports facilities. Housing is therefore important as both a reflection and generator of social inequality. A house is more than a home – it is an address, and addresses are indicators of social position.

Social inequality is also reflected in the tenure of housing. Nearly 70 per cent of households in Britain own (or are buying) their homes, while the remainder rent from local authorities, housing associations or private landlords (see Table 1.1, p. 11). These different tenure categories are basic to an understanding of the British housing system, and one of the key dimensions to this is the extent to which socioeconomic status is reflected in housing tenure; the specific point here (and it is discussed in more detail later in the book) is the concentration of people on very low incomes in rented housing and the virtual absence of people on high incomes.

Housing studies also embraces the range of institutions responsible for the construction, financing and management of housing. This book concentrates on the role of central government, local authorities and housing associations, but other key players are the mortgage lenders and private construction firms. The market provides much of the framework within which these institutions have to operate, and links between the housing market and the wider economy are now acknowledged to be of great importance. Housing has links to and provides a way into a number of contemporary academic debates, including the direction of social change and the notion of an underclass, gender relations and the way they are reflected in housing form and provision systems, and aspects of race and ethnicity.

These debates are pursued in a number of disciplines and theoretical perspectives: sociology, economics, geography, politics and social policy all provide different ways into understanding aspects of housing provision. Different disciplines generate distinctive formulations of the problems to be understood and apply different analytical tools to the tasks of describing and explaining why housing is like it is and why it is used as it is. The scope of housing studies, then, is much wider than housing policy, but policy represents a powerful magnet for those who wish to understand the nature of housing provision. State housing policy is designed to deal with perceived problems and before attempting a definition of housing policy it is appropriate to consider the nature of the housing problem.

The housing problem

When housing students are asked to discuss the housing problem their initial suggestions are usually about homelessness, high prices and disrepair. It is not surprising that homelessness should be the first indicator to come to mind because it is the most visible and extreme form of housing problem. House prices, too, are much discussed in the media and mortgage interest rate changes attract widespread coverage. The problem of disrepair is perhaps less well understood by most people, but they are aware of the problems faced by low-income, highly mortgaged home owners, and they hear reports of huge backlogs of repairs in the public sector.

In the absolute sense the basic human need for shelter defines the housing problem in terms of quantity and quality: is there enough housing to go round, and is it of a satisfactory standard? The answers to both questions are contingent upon wider social and cultural factors but quantity and quality are essential components of the housing problem. Historically the British housing problem consisted of the fact that there were far more households than dwellings, and a significant proportion of the dwellings of the working class were of such low quality as to be damaging to health. Underpinning problems of quantity and quality, however, was the issue of price. In the unfettered market of the nineteenth century housing became a commodity to be produced for profit, for its exchange value rather than its use value. This meant that the standard of housing enjoyed by a family depended on what it could afford rather than what its members could build for themselves.

The underlying cause of the housing problem, then, was that there was a significant gap between the price of decent accommodation and the rent that could be afforded by a large proportion of the working class (Great Britain, 1977b: 7).

It remains true today that most housing in Britain is distributed through the market mechanism, with the result that the amount, quality and location of housing which consumers can obtain depend upon their ability to pay. The questions of price and affordability remain central to the housing problem. However there is another element which has emerged in modern times: ownership. One way of looking at this issue is to say that when there is a grave shortage, when the number of households exceeds the number of dwellings, as was the case in Britain until the late 1960s, then the issue of ownership is of secondary importance. But as conditions improve so consumers become more concerned about who owns their home. Ownership can be seen as a second-order problem, emerging only after progress has been made towards meeting more basic requirements. Successive governments (Great Britain, 1977a: 2) and some academic commentators (Saunders, 1990; Power, 1993) have interpreted the emergence of ownership issues as a demand-led phenomenon, reflecting an inherent human desire for property ownership and the sense of security which it is alleged to bestow.

An alternative perspective on home ownership is to see it as essentially a supply-side problem, and to interpret the growth of owner-occupation as a response to the problems of housing providers rather than consumers. This represents part of a broader alternative to the consumption-oriented approach which has been presented so far in this discussion. The term 'consumption-oriented approach' was introduced by Michael Ball in a major contribution to ways of thinking about housing (Ball, 1983, 1986a). He argued that housing problems and policies are conventionally seen in terms of the difficulties faced by consumers in securing satisfactory accommodation, with the state intervening to deliver solutions to consumer problems.

Ball called for a wider perspective on housing, embracing issues of production as well as consumption. There are two points to make here. First, Ball's work leads to the observation that the precise forms taken by the housing problems of consumers in different times and places reflect the prevailing supply-side mechanisms. Thus price is an issue in market-based systems but in societies where people build their own houses using raw materials which they collect and process themselves, price is not a determinant of housing consumption. Where mud is baked into bricks, trees are felled for roof timbers and grass is collected for thatch, the quality of housing may be limited by the availability of materials and the skills of self-builders but homelessness is unlikely to be a problem. It is the commodification of housing which elevates the issue of price to such a dominant position. When land, labour and materials all have to be paid for in cash, and dwellings are produced as commodities for sale, then obviously access to housing is determined by ability to pay, and the supply of accommodation will reflect effective demand rather than need.

Second, although political debate tends to be conducted in terms of the housing problems of consumers, the supply side has problems of its own, and policy responses are as likely to reflect a concern with these problems. Writing about the United States, Achtenburg and Marcuse say:

> Government policies affecting housing, which supposedly serve the common good, systematically operate to reinforce the profitability of the housing sector and of the business community. Such improvement in housing as has occurred historically has come about only when it has served the interests of private capital, or when pressures from below (both political and economic) have forced it to occur. (Achtenburg and Marcuse, 1986)

For the suppliers of houses in a market context the basic problem is how to make a profit from a product which consumers need but cannot afford to pay for outright. Historically it can be seen that the private rented system was the solution generally adopted in capitalist countries but this was not sufficient to produce good-quality housing and an adequate return on capital at a time of low real wages, hence low standards, overcrowding and continuing shortages. In contemporary Britain owner-occupation has largely replaced private renting but still supply-side problems remain. One of the main issues since the early 1970s has been the instability of the housing market, with periods of rapid house price inflation and excessive demand followed by falling real prices and low demand. Even the biggest house-builders have suffered from the problems of market instability and recession (Ball, 1986b, 1988; Balchin, 1989).

All this demonstrates that perceptions of housing problems vary according to the standpoint of the beholder. Different interests and perceptions generate different analyses and policy proposals. It is here that the essentially political nature of the housing problem is located. The political parties ground their policy proposals in their own perceptions of the problem, and in their critiques of their opponents' policies. Thus on the left there is the view that housing problems of homelessness, overcrowding, disrepair and so on stem from the fundamental inability of the market mechanism to deliver satisfactory accommodation in sufficient amounts to satisfy basic needs, especially amongst the poorer sections of society. The market tends to establish a close link between poverty and poor housing, even if it works rather more satisfactorily for the better off. This analysis points towards state intervention to ensure that there is an adequate supply of suitable accommodation available at a price that the poorest can afford.

The right-wing alternative, which has been dominant in Britain and the United States since the early 1980s, argues that state intervention is the cause of housing problems rather than the solution to them. Rent control in the private sector has long been blamed for the decline of this form of provision, and more recently council housing has been manoeuvred from its position as a central plank in any attempt to tackle British housing problems into one in which local authorities are blamed for housing problems and council housing is seen as part of the problem to be solved.

These opposed perspectives on the housing problem and its causes naturally tend to reflect more broadly-based ideological differences about the ability of the market to provide for all consumer needs and the appropriate role of state intervention. The next section goes on to look at what housing policy consists of, and how it fits into the wider housing system.

Housing policy and the housing system

The term 'housing policy' is used in different ways and covers a multitude of activities. The word 'policy' is notoriously difficult to define with any precision (Hill and Bramley, 1986: 1). A starting point is to say that it generally implies action in relation to a particular problem which it is intended to solve or ameliorate in pursuit of some objective. In this sense policy implies some kind of change, and in particular it implies change which is consciously planned and brought about with some end in view. It is in this context that politicians present their policies for dealing with problems whether they be economic, social, environmental or any other type. Policy therefore implies a process, involving an initial formulation of a problem and a planning or policy-making stage, followed by execution or implementation of the policy, which may itself be followed by an appraisal or evaluation of the success of the policy.

The notion of a policy process underpins the approach and structure of this book, although it must be said that the simple model of policy-making, implementation and evaluation which provides the basis of Chapters 10–12 is merely a convenient device and, as Chapter 9 makes clear, there is a considerable literature debating different perspectives on policy processes. In addition to the connotations of process and change attached to the word 'policy' the term is also used in a more static way, to describe how things are done as a matter of routine. Thus references to a rents policy, lettings policy or lending policy place the emphasis on the rules or conventions which govern the way that rents are set, dwellings are allocated and loans are made. To use the term 'policy' in this way is to reflect the existence of an established position or stance, as distinct from decision-making in the absence of any guidelines. This usage of policy is very important for the day-to-day operation of housing organisations, in two respects. First, the existence of a policy means that staff have a framework to guide and limit their discretion, although not necessarily ensuring equitable treatment of members of the public using housing services. Second, there is a well-established convention that elected members of local authorities and the members of housing association committees of management have ultimate control over policy, while it is the task of the professional staff to carry out agreed policy. This distinction is not watertight because it is widely accepted that officials influence policy-making as well as implementation, but it does help to distinguish the roles of different actors, and it also acts as a means of protection for officials who come under pressure from individual members to bend the rules to favour particular tenants or applicants.

All kinds of organisations have policies, although they may not be explicit or formally set out in writing. In the field of housing it is common to hear of the lending policies of building societies, the marketing policies of house-builders or the rents policies of housing associations. However housing policy itself is usually thought of in terms of state housing policy, at both national and local levels, and this is the usage adopted here (Hill and Bramley, 1986: ch. 1). This does not mean that the policies and practices of the building societies, housebuilders or housing associations are unimportant or ignored, just that they are dealt with in the context of a focus on state intervention. The term 'housing system' is used here in preference to 'housing market' because of the extent of state intervention in the provision of housing in Britain. There is no clear distinction between a free housing market on the one hand and state-supported housing on the other. State intervention in one form or another pervades the system, regulating and supporting important aspects of the market, such as new housing developent, improvement of older houses and neighbourhoods and the financial burden of house purchase. Equally, state-owned housing (council housing) is not entirely free from the influence of the market: local authorities have acted as developers to produce the existing public sector stock, but the great majority of the dwellings were built by private contractors, with privately produced materials on land bought from private owners with capital borrowed from private financial institutions. In effect the emergence of council housing left the production side firmly in private hands, even though it was initiated by the municipality, and it was only the consumption and exchange aspects of council housing that were taken out of the market.

The concept of tenure provides a conventional starting-point for analysis of the housing system. There are four main tenure categories in Britain: owner-occupation, council renting, housing association renting and private renting. These are convenient and often useful labels, which assume huge importance in political debate about housing but which have great analytical limitations. The first problem to be aware of in using tenure categories is that these are simple labels for highly varied phenomena. Each tenure is in fact far more heterogeneous than the labels imply: for instance, the heavily mortgaged recent purchaser of an older terraced house in an inner urban neighbourhood is in a very different position from an outright owner of a modern detached suburban property. Equally, council housing has very different meanings for a tenant living in a flat at the top of a tower block on a run-down estate in inner London and a tenant of a spacious stone-built cottage, with a large garden, in a village or small town where housing estates as such are rare.

The second problem inherent in a tenure analysis is that tenure is a mere consumption label: it tells us something about the terms on which households occupy their homes, but beyond that its utility is limited. There is no necessary link, for instance, between tenure and methods of financing and producing housing: although in practice owner-occupied housing in Britain is normally produced by speculative builders, this is not exclusively the case and both local authorities and housing associations are also increasingly involved in building for sale.

Housing policy can be defined in terms of measures designed to modify the quality, quantity, price and ownership and control of housing. These four elements cover the scope of policy as represented in the very general statements which have been made by British governments from time to time. For instance, a Conservative White Paper in 1971 set out the following objectives: 'a decent home for every family at a price within their means, a fairer choice between owning a home and renting one, and fairness between one citizen and another in giving and receiving help towards housing' (Great Britain, 1971). In the same vein, Labour's Green Paper of 1977 stated that 'the traditional aim of a decent home for all families at a price within their means must remain our primary objective' (Great Britain, 1977a). Few people could disagree with these general statements; the political aspect arises in the way they are interpreted and translated into specific programmes of action. The importance attached to the various components of policy and the role accorded to the state varies over time, reflecting changing political and economic circumstances and changes in the housing system itself. In theory, at least, a wide variety of quite different means could be put forward in pursuit of agreed objectives, and it is possible for profound disagreement to exist as to what could constitute fulfilment of these objectives. Conceptually the main differences in means are those between marketed and non-marketed, or individual and collective forms. In practice, successive British governments over many years have presented policies with differing emphasis as between the public and private sectors, but they have agreed on the need to work within the framework of the capitalist economic system. No political party in Britain with a realistic chance of forming a government has developed a socialist housing policy in which the profit motive was removed in respect of production, consumption and exchange. Policy differences between the major parties have tended to be ones of emphasis rather than of fundamental principle.

Housing policy pervades the housing system, and the structures through which policy is made and implemented increasingly involve private sector agencies. This is a reminder that state intervention is not necessarily state *interference*. Indeed it is increasingly the case that central government is choosing to pursue its objectives through support for the private sector, and interference is becoming confined to the public sector as local authorities experience continuing erosion of their freedom to determine the ways in which housing policy is interpreted at local level. The notion of local authorities as enablers rather than providers encapsulates the supportive objectives of state intervention, both emphasising the role of local authorities in facilitating private sector provision and indicating the change of policy direction for local authorities.

The term 'housing policy and practice' is used in this book to draw attention to the need to look at both the central government level and the local level. The role of the centre is to make policy and to provide a framework of powers and opportunities for policy to be implemented. But it is at the local level that implementation takes place: local authorities, housing associations, building societies, builders and others constitute the plethora of organisations through which policy is implemented. Much of the fascination of studying housing policy resides in the fact that these various organisations are not mere agents of central government; they are policy-making bodies in their own right and therefore they are likely to modify central government policy to some extent in the way that they interpret it in their particular situation. This will reflect both the different meaning of central policy for different organisations and localities, and the varying objectives of different organisations. Local authorities often occupy explicitly different political positions from those of central government and this is a source of tension in the central–local relationship. However it can also be argued that central and local government have quite distinct roles, which represents an additional source of tension, irrespective of ideology and party politics.

Central and local government have different aims, objectives and pre-occupations in relation to housing, because the centre is concerned with economic regulation, capital accumulation, investment and taxation con-sequences; local government, on the other hand, is concerned with need, territorial defence, local political pressure, management of the stock and costs (rent and council tax) falling on local residents. Several significant policy developments affecting council rents, rebates, sales, new building and homelessness, all involving reduction in local autonomy, can be explained against this background. From the point of view of local councillors, a residualised public sector has little appeal and few political advantages, though at the same time it carries political risks. Over many years, local councils have demonstrated their preference for 'respectable' working-class families of the sort who pay their rent regularly and take good care of their homes and gardens. They have been much less willing to welcome the poorest and those defined as 'undeserving' and as 'problem families'. It was to overcome these local preferences and prejudices that legislation on home-lessness was eventually necessary after years of central government encour-agement to local authorities to accept responsibility for a wider range of people.

In the same way, housing associations and mortgage lenders can be seen to have objectives which may differ from those of central government. Building societies are obviously independent financial institutions, operating in com-petitive markets and motivated by commercial considerations rather than social, economic or housing policy objectives.

Finally in this section, it is important to recognise that housing is affected by policies in a number of different areas. Economic policy is one of the most significant of these. In 1981, for example, the British government's mon-etarist stance deepened the recession in the construction industry, leading to a 25-year low point in private sector housing production. More recently, the use of interest rates as the main instrument of economic management led to housing being used as a means of reducing consumer expenditure. It is arguable that, in 1988–9, mortgage interest rate increases (from under 10 per cent in May 1988 to 14.5 per cent by October 1989) made far more impact than formal housing policy on the housing market, despite the major reforms contained in the Housing Act 1988. Personal taxation policy is another area which has important implications for housing. Again 1988 provides a good illustration: the Chancellor's decision, announced in the spring budget, to end so-called double tax relief in August, led to frenetic activity in the housing market, fuelling rapid price increases, only to be followed by a major slump in market activity.

While recognising the impact of other policies on housing, it is also necessary to question the impact of state policy on the overall rate of change in the wider housing system. Having previously stressed the pervasive nature of housing policy it would be a mistake now to overemphasise the potency of state intervention. There are three distinct points to be made in this context. First, in liberal democracies like Britain, governments have to take into account the power of capital to resist policies which threaten its position. As already mentioned, although housing problems are usually presented in terms of consumer difficulties, the state in a capitalist society is also concerned with maintaining private sector profitability. This means that there are supply-side constraints on the radicalism of policies which govern-ments can bring forward. But there are also demand-side constraints: governments have to pay attention to public opinion, and electoral con-siderations clearly exercise some influence over policy. Failure to act on the reform of mortgage interest tax relief is usually attributed to the voting power of home owners. The general point here, then, is that some issues are kept off the policy agenda because of constraints on the power of the state.

Second, as Donnison and Ungerson pointed out some years ago, 'Past experience in the housing field – with the Rent Act 1957, the half-million housing programme of 1966 and the Housing Finance Act 1972, for example – suggests that the impact of new policies is rarely as dramatic as either their advocates hope or their critics fear' (Donnison and Ungerson, 1982: 161). Why should this be? Part of the explanation is probably that crusading politicians get carried away by their own rhetoric and enthusiasm into making claims which go beyond the terms of their legislation, while opposition groups have a natural tendency to describe the implications of new policies in the most colourful terms in order to mobilise support for their cause. Another factor is likely to be that, although governments can usually dominate parliamentary proceedings and the making of legislation, at the implementation stage they are much less powerful and much more reliant on agencies which they do not fully control. Implementation is therefore much less predictable and more open to variation at the local level.

Third, given the power and dominance of private interests in housing production, consumption and exchange, it is likely, to say the least, that these interests will be a major force in bringing about change. It should not be assumed that change is led by policy; it may be the other way round, and the main engines of change in housing may reside in the market rather than in housing policy. This last perspective underpins the following section, which attempts to set out a cross-tenure framework for comprehending change in housing provision during the twentieth century as a whole.

The state and the modernisation of housing tenure

Since 1979, there has been a rapid increase in home ownership in Britain, fuelled to a large extent by government policies designed to exalt the private sector, to cut back investment in new council house building and to promote the sale of existing council houses. In this context, there has been much discussion of the 'residualisation' of local authority housing, involving speculation about the limits of reduction in the public sector and the impact of social polarisation which concentrates the least well-off and least powerful sections of the population in the remaining, least desirable, parts of the publicly rented stock (Forrest and Murie, 1988; Malpass, 1990; Page, 1993; Willmott and Murie, 1988). The focus of debate has tended to be on recent and current developments, linking temporary changes in the housing system to wider processes in the labour market and the economy as a whole. While it is important to make these links outwards from an analysis of housing, it is also necessary to develop a longer-term historical perspective, and in

Table 1.1   *Housing tenure in England and Wales, 1914–96*

	Owner-occupied %	Rented from local authorities and new towns %	Rented from private landlords landlords %	Rented from housing associations %
1914	10	Negligible	90	
1951	31	17	52	
1971	52	29	19	
1996	67.8	17.5	10.2	4.5

Note: In Scotland the pattern of change has been significantly different, and by 1995 owner-occupation stood at only 57.9 per cent while local authority renting was 31.1 per cent (Wilcox, 1997: 84).

particular to avoid overemphasising the impact of particular government policies or economic recession since 1979.

Changes in the pattern of ownership of housing in the 1980s and 1990s must be set against the background of 60 years of restructuring in the tenure system, as indicated in Table 1.1.

Accounts of housing in Britain generally refer to the decline of private renting and the emergence of owner-occupation and local authority renting as if these were three virtually unrelated processes. The purpose of this section is to put forward a perspective on change in the housing market and housing tenure which links all three tenures together. This is designed both to indicate the deep roots of contemporary processes such as residualisation, and to provide a framework within which to set the historical narrative set out in the next four chapters.

Private renting can be seen as a mode of provision which was devised in the nineteenth century as an appropriate form for that early phase of capitalist economic and urban development. At a time when the new urban working class on the whole earned low wages and had little scope for saving, renting enabled people to obtain access to an essential commodity which they could not afford to buy. Private renting also allowed investors and builders to realise profits from housing, even though most consumers could not buy outright. The decline of this system reflects its economic obsolescence in the twentieth century. Donnison (1967: 287) long ago identified private landlords as typical and successful representatives of the local capitalism of the nineteenth century, but as victims of change to a more national and international phase of capitalist development. Private renting can be seen as giving way to home ownership as a form of housing provision that is more appropriate to the capitalism of the twentieth century. Harloe has suggested that owner-occupation represents the modern form of the private housing market, and that this is the most effective form from the point of view of capital (Harloe, 1985). It is therefore useful to conceive the restructuring of housing tenure over the period since the First World War as a process of modernisation of the housing market. There has been a long transitional period (which is not yet over) from the overwhelming predominance of private renting to the new predominance of owner-occupation. The process of modernising the housing market necessarily took many years, since it required the growth and development of new mechanisms and institutions; in particular its pace was contingent upon a substantial and sustained growth in the real incomes of consumers.

However there was nothing inevitable about the transition to owner-occupation; the development of alternatives to private renting was a matter to be determined politically. Housing has long been an issue of class conflict, and it is significant that historically the demands of organised labour were for control of the private landlord and for municipal housing provision, not for individual home ownership. Important gains were made on these demands during and just after the First World War when the disruption of the housing market and a shift in the balance of class forces in favour of the working class forced the state first to introduce rent control and then to undertake a major programme of subsidised municipal housing construction. It is essential to remember that the high quality and relatively high rents of council houses in the 1920s meant that the beneficiaries were mainly the better-off skilled workers, rather than the poor, and that this was no accident or economic inevitability. In this respect, state housing was more a response to a political problem than a housing problem, reflecting the political power of organised, mainly skilled, labour. As Byrne and Damer have argued, 'For the state the *housing* problem at the level of physical reproduction was the housing conditions of those who were *worst* housed. The *political* problem in terms of articulated political pressure came from the *better* housed in the working class who wanted cheap high quality council housing' (Byrne and Damer, 1980: 68).

In the 1930s, when housing market conditions favoured the construction of houses in the private sector, and the power of labour was weakened by the recession, the state withdrew to a more confined role, concentrating on slum clearance. The abandonment of general needs housing construction by local authorities was specifically to remove competition with the private sector and to enable the market to expand, recolonising an area of demand from which it had withdrawn before the First World War. The private housing boom of the 1930s was ended by the outbreak of the Second World War, which again disrupted the housing market and tilted the balance of power in favour of the working class. After 1945, there was a decade in which housing policy concentrated on the production of local authority housing, of a high standard, before a reassertion of private-sector interests once more led to the local authorities being confined to a more specialist role, complementary to the market rather than in competition with it.

What this means is that in the political struggle to determine how housing needs should be met in the twentieth century, private sector interests have generally been predominant, with local authority housing achieving only temporary ascendancy after the two world wars. The development of council housing has reflected a focus on different sections of the working class at different times, as a result of changes in political and economic conditions. The important point to be established here is that council housing did not develop primarily as housing for the least well off. In analysing housing policy in the twentieth century, the differentiation of the working class into two broad groups, the better off and the less well off, is of considerable significance. During the first four decades of the modernisation of the private housing market, council housing played a crucial role in meeting the demands of organised labour (the better off) for decent accommodation at times when the market could not respond. For the rest, there was still a huge stock of less adequate but generally cheap private rented housing, although of course some did find their way into the public sector, principally through slum clearance.

Over the years the position changed. On the one hand, the continued growth of owner-occupation (fuelled by the long period of postwar economic growth and prosperity, and by 13 years of Conservative government, 1951–64) drew in more and more working-class purchasers. The continued growth of this modernised form of private housing provision depended on the maintenance of demand from a widening range of working-class consumers. This in turn implied the adoption of policies to favour home ownership and to discourage demand for council housing (by poorer standards, higher rents and other devices). On the other hand, the contraction of the private rented sector, which greatly broadened the social base of owner-occupation, nevertheless increasingly meant that the least well off had no alternative but to seek council accommodation. And to facilitate their entry to council housing a different set of policies were required, to give them priority in allocation procedures and to enable them to afford the rent.

This way of conceiving the restructuring of housing tenure represents an attempt to integrate developments in each tenure. Council housing emerged as a political response to tensions set up in the early phases of the modernisation of the private market, which were exacerbated by the effects of warfare. Local authorities could have developed as the main providers of housing, replacing the private landlords but, from the vantage point of the present day, it can be seen that their role has been quite different, reflecting the outcome of wider economic and political conflicts. Council housing originated and grew mainly as housing for the better-off working class, but over the past 30 years or so, it has been subject to gathering pressures to transform it into a residual tenure for the least well off. This now looks like being its long-term future role.

Looking at tenure restructuring in this way not only produces an integrated explanation, but also indicates how the residualisation of the public sector has been in progress for many years, and how the forces behind the process are quite fundamental. It is therefore a mistake to explain residualisation as such (as distinct from its pace) in terms of the policies of Conservative governments in the 1980s or to assume that some future swing of the political pendulum will inevitably lead to a return to a more even-handed approach to housing tenure.

The manipulation of public housing into a residual role has been a process of a quite different kind from the way in which home ownership has grown. In the case of home ownership, growth has meant a continuing broadening of the social composition of the tenure, whereas in council housing, residualisation has meant not just drawing in more of the less well off, but also dislodging and deflecting the sorts of tenants who were previously in the majority on council estates until relatively recently. Residualisation of council housing should be seen in terms of those two flows, drawing in the sorts of households who were previously not well-served by local authorities and removing the more traditional sorts of council tenants. Housing policy has been specifically designed to bring about a situation in which local authorities increasingly, if not yet exclusively, provide for those who must rent, whose economic status and housing market position excludes them from home ownership. Reinforcing this process is a wider set of changes in the economy as a whole which are enlarging the marginalised section of the working class (Forrest and Murie, 1991). Britain's long-term economic decline, relative to the rest of the industrialised world, together with the impact of industrial obsolescence and new technology, is producing a larger pool of people who are permanently or semi-permanently unemployed, living on the margins of the formal economy. While the marginalised poor can be found in all tenures, they tend to be concentrated in public housing.

Tools for analysis

This chapter has sought to introduce housing policy and practice by reference to the housing problem, the housing system, the content of housing policy and the changing role of policy in the housing system. Throughout the discussion a number of concepts and analytical categories have been used, either explicitly or implicitly. In any subject the level of understanding which can be achieved is highly dependent upon the conceptual framework that is used and the questions that it generates. In this final section the objective is to bring together some relevant conceptual tools for analysing housing policy and practice.

What has been emphasised in preceding pages is the breadth of perspective needed, and the wide range of factors which contribute to explanations for housing provision being as it is, and why it changes in the ways that it does. It is also relevant here to ask why the rate of change is not faster than it is – what holds the system together is just as fascinating an issue as what makes it change. Stress has been placed on the need to avoid attributing unreasonable influence to housing policy, and on the importance of recognising that policies in other programme areas can have considerable impact on housing.

The point was made earlier that analysis of housing policy and practice should include both demand- and supply-side issues, and in this context it is appropriate to refer to the value of the concepts of class, race and gender. These are the basic social cleavages, which generate a whole set of questions about the distribution of power and resources in the housing system. The sorts of questions raised here are, for example, about whose interests predominate in the ways that housing is produced, distributed and con-sumed, and about the sources and deployment of the political or economic power of different groups in society.

The state is sometimes presented as being somehow above conflicts to do with class, race or gender. In this perspective the state is seen as a kind of neutral umpire, acting in the best interests of society as a whole. The alternative perspective is based on the view that the state cannot exist separately from the various interests which constitute society and that, therefore, the state has to be seen as reflecting the interests of dominant groups. Thus in capitalist society the state is viewed as acting generally in the interest of capital. The nature of the state in advanced capitalist societies is a contentious issue, which has been widely debated in the academic literature (Dunleavy and O'Leary, 1987; McLennan, Held and Hall, 1984; Dearlove and Saunders, 1984). The position taken in this book is that the state is not best understood as a neutral arbiter; nor should it be seen as a single entity. The state is more than the government and it has complex relationships with various other institutions and interests. The focus in this book is mainly on central and local government, and on the links with key institutions in the housing system, including housing associations, the Housing Corporation and building societies.

To understand the state in relation to housing policy and practice it is important to recognise the distinct, but interdependent, roles of central and local government. The centre establishes the overall policy and the legislative framework for its implementation, but it is largely dependent upon other institutions in the public and private sectors to carry out the implementation activities. In the past local authorities were acknowledged as the main institutions through which housing policy was implemented, but in the 1980s their position was challenged by a government which displayed a strong commitment to developing private sector alternatives, and which was deeply sceptical of local government in general. Nevertheless local authorities retain their important role in delivering housing services, and are encouraged to develop an enabling role in relation to private and voluntary providers.

Although local authorities are responsible for a considerable amount of policy implementation, they are not merely the agents of central government. They are also democratically elected bodies, accountable to the local electorate, which in itself implies that they have some sort of policy-making role of their own. This raises two interesting issues, accountability and autonomy. Local authorities in Britain are elected by universal adult franchise within specified boundaries, and the elected members have responsibility for a range of services. This means that they are accountable to a wider constituency than the direct recipients of a particular service, such as housing. In most parts of Britain council tenants represent a relatively small proportion of voters, and it can be argued that in many authorities the local policies in relation to council housing are decided by councillors elected mainly by owner-occupiers. On the other hand, it can also be argued that local housing policy is wider than council housing, and in any case all voters have an interest in the quality of housing services. The point here is that local elections every three or four years represent a rather indirect form of accountability, especially in an era with an increasing emphasis on a customer orientation in service delivery. A related issue concerns the notion of professionalism in housing services. As increasing numbers of housing workers acquire professional qualifications and are encouraged to adopt a customer orientation, the issue of their accountability is sharpened. Are they primarily accountable to their formal employers or to the consumers of housing services? This question is equally relevant in the housing association sector, where the members of the management committee are generally not elected by tenants.

On the issue of autonomy, local authorities in Britain have a tradition of commitment to protecting their right to make policy, albeit within the general framework established by Parliament. Housing is a policy area in which local authorities have conventionally enjoyed considerable autonomy, but, as in other areas, this autonomy has been subject to erosion over a long period. During the 1980s the relationship between central and local government was marked by heightened tension and mutual suspicion, which gave rise to a considerable outpouring of academic analysis (Stoker, 1988; Elcock, 1986; Hampton, 1987; Stewart and Stoker, 1989; Blunkett and Jackson, 1987; Gyford, Leach and Game, 1989; Lansley, Goss and Wolmar, 1989). Local autonomy implies central government tolerance of local variation and deviation from its overall policy. This is more likely during periods of growth in public services, but when government policies emphasise cuts and contraction then local autonomy is less easy for the centre to countenance with equanimity. A key theme in much of what follows is that in British housing policy there has been a marked tendency in recent years for the autonomy of local authorities to be eroded by increasingly assertive interventions by the centre. Much of this can be linked to policies of tenure restructuring.

Turning to the question of tenure, it is appropriate to reiterate the point made earlier in this chapter that tenure is a basic and useful concept, but one which should be used as a tool for opening up understanding of the housing system, rather than as a taken-for-granted framework. It is important to take account of the ways in which tenures change over time, and therefore how tenure labels have different meanings at different times. For instance, council housing used to be predominantly a modern, high-quality tenure, occupied mainly by the better-off working class; it is now necessarily much less uniformly modern, problems of disrepair have emerged and the social composition of tenants has changed. Similar sorts of contrasts could be produced for the other main tenures, and inter-tenure comparisons would also highlight changes over time. For example, the distinction between 'public' and 'private' in relation to housing tenure used to be more clear-cut than it is now, given that council housing is increasingly self-financing and owner-occupation rides on a substantial raft of financial support from public funds.

This points to the need for some sort of historical perspective in housing analysis. The dynamism in the system requires an understanding of the forms and directions of change, and the reasons for them. In developing a historical perspective it is important to aspire to going beyond a view of the past as just one thing after another, and to avoid perceiving housing policy as a succession of Acts of Parliament. Subsequent chapters do provide lists of the major housing legislation, but, as this chapter has already argued, some overall understanding of the shape of policy development is also necessary. In this context it is appropriate to look for the continuities in policy as well as the changes, and to look for key turning-points, which may not be expressed in legislation. Continuity does not necessarily imply sameness; it is possible to refer to continuity in support for owner-occupation since the early 1950s, but the form and intensity of that support has varied over time. In general, the concepts of change and continuity can be very helpful in understanding the development of housing policy, as can the related notions of consensus and conflict. Perspectives on political developments in Britain since 1945 generally refer to the postwar consensus, and its gradual collapse, particularly since the mid-1970s, as politics have become more polarised.

The notion of the modernisation of housing provision has been put forward in this chapter as a way of conceiving and explaining housing restructuring in the twentieth century. Linked to that perspective are three other useful ideas which have been discussed in the housing literature in recent years. First, 'residualisation' is a term which has become quite widely used to refer to developments in local authority housing (Malpass, 1990). It describes the way in which council housing has become increasingly the tenure of the least well off. Residualisation is a process embracing changes in the social composition of council housing as well as the related policy changes. But it is not just to be explained in policy terms; it is a trend influenced by the wider restructuring of the housing market, and is also affected by developments in the labour market.

It is in this context that the term 'marginalisation' has come to be used (Forrest and Murie, 1991). Marginalisation refers to the decreasing demand for living labour as machines and computers take over many routine tasks. The emergence of a substantial population of people without skills in current demand (including those whose skills have become obsolete) has led to the notion of the marginalised poor. These people, subsisting on state benefits and occasional earnings, have to be accommodated somewhere in the housing system but they are in a weak position in the housing market, and they have turned increasingly to the local authorities, as the providers of housing for people in need. Marginalisation links explanation of changes in housing to wider processes of economic restructuring. In this respect it differs from residualisation, which focuses on changes driven from within housing itself.

A third useful concept for describing contemporary trends in housing is privatisation (Forrest and Murie, 1991). This is a word which has entered the language in recent years in the wider context of the sale of public assets. In relation to housing, privatisation refers most obviously to the sale of council houses, but it is important to see beyond the transfer of ownership from local authorities to individual owners: the sale of council houses also results in the privatisation of housing management, in the sense that once houses have been sold they are then maintained by private builders and subsequently resold through private estate agents. Privatisation can also penetrate the public sector itself, to the extent that property maintenance activity is subject to competitive tendering and private contractors in practice secure a proportion of the work. In a broader sense it can be said that during the 1980s the government's whole housing strategy was built on the view that public housing is both unnecessary and unsuccessful, and that it is possible to develop a housing system which is almost wholly based in the private sector.

Finally, this chapter concludes with a set of headings for thinking about housing policy and practice: objectives, content, structures and processes. This suggests an analysis centred upon the idea that:

1. policy is consciously directed towards some end or ends;
2. it consists of an identifiable set of principles and actions which can be distinguished from other policy areas;
3. it involves a set of actors, institutions and relationships which determine objectives, content and delivery; and
4. there are certain processes through which housing policy is made, implemented and received.

This generates questions, first, about what housing policy is for, whose interests it serves and how problems and solutions are formulated. Second, there are questions about content. What does housing policy consist of? How are its boundaries to be defined and how does it interact with other policy areas? On structures, the focus of questions is upon the mechanisms for making and delivering policy. What is the role of the state in relation to the market? How does central government relate to local authorities and housing associations? What is the relationship between elected members and salaried officials? What role do tenants play in decision-making? Lastly the idea of policy processes invites questions on the way policy is made and implemented. How are decisions made about policy objectives and how are different solutions evaluated? How is building maintenance carried out in different tenures? How is housing financed and paid for? And how is it decided who will live where?

The title of this book, *Housing Policy and Practice,* reflects the approach indicated above, and subsequent chapters embrace policy-making, implementation and evaluation. The objective is to link central and local, policy and practice.

2

The Origins of Housing Policy

Housing is a subject in which history is very important. First, and obviously, this is because houses have a long life: roughly a third of the housing stock now in use is more than 60 years old; at least 90 per cent of the dwellings built between 1871 and 1918 were still standing in 1975 (Great Britain, 1977b: 4) and most remain in use today. Dwellings are the enduring artefacts from earlier periods of social and economic organisation, and can only be fully understood by reference to the conditions prevailing at the time of their construction.

Second, contemporary housing policy is inevitably heavily influenced by the past, in the sense that dwellings inherited from earlier periods represent both a resource to be utilised and a problem to be dealt with. A significant component of housing policy in the twentieth century has necessarily been a response to the stock of dwellings bequeathed by nineteenth-century builders. Third, and of greatest relevance in the present context, is the fact that it is not just dwellings but also policy mechanisms and institutional traditions which have been inherited from the past. Housing policy in the 1990s is the outcome of a process of accretion over a long period; the shape and structure of policy, including the distribution of powers and responsibilities amongst the main branches of the state, largely represent sedimented accumulations from the past.

Housing policy has its origins firmly rooted in the nineteenth century, but in examining those origins it is necessary to bear in mind the question as to why development of a coherent policy was so slow, given the severity of the problem. Amongst the factors to be considered are the need for a clear understanding of that problem as a prerequisite for policy, the resistance of vested interests and the nature of the institutions of the state at the time.

Urban growth and civic decline

Britain in the 1840s was what is now referred to as a developing country. The economic base was changing from agrarian to industrial production, and at the same time the population was increasing with unprecedented rapidity.

The Census of 1841 recorded 18.5 million people in the United Kingdom, an increase of no less than 76 per cent in 40 years. A characteristic of this rapid growth was its concentration in the manufacturing towns of the north of England, but also in cities such as London, Glasgow, Birmingham and Bristol (Ashworth, 1954: ch. 1). Britain was being transformed into a predominantly urban society by the concentration of trade and manufacturing in the towns, and consequential movements of population away from the countryside.

The growth and concentration of industrial production was in itself damaging to the local environment, as smoke and fumes filled the atmosphere and noxious effluent drained into the rivers. Whereas towns had previously been thought of as havens of culture and civilisation, they now quickly became grossly congested, polluted and unhealthy places to live and work. Thus, ironically, the very centres of wealth production in the world's richest country were themselves squalid and insanitary. They seemed to prove not only that where there was muck there was brass, but also that where there was brass there was muck.

Nevertheless people continued to flock to the towns in search of work and shelter. In so doing, they added considerably to the environmental problems caused by industrialism. Two essentials of healthy human settlements are a supply of pure water and an adequate system of waste disposal. In the small-scale communities characteristic of pre-industrial society, the needs of the population were more in balance with nature's capacity to supply the water and dispose of the waste. The *concentration* of large numbers of people, and the *speed* with which the towns grew, completely overwhelmed the existing services. Unfortunately, this problem was compounded by the general inadequacy of the established local government institutions. Their deficiencies were exposed by the challenge of urban growth, for it was not just the physical services but also the municipal authorities which were geared to the demands of an earlier period.

As a rule, the process of town growth involved the virtual abandonment of the old central area as a place to live by those who could afford to leave. In the face of increased congestion and squalor, they departed to new lower-density suburbs and the poor crowded into the vacated dwellings. Open spaces such as gardens and orchards were quickly built on (Gauldie, 1974), adding to the congestion and the strain on essential services. In addition, of course, it was necessary to build new houses beyond the existing built-up area for the working class as well as the rich. Wholly new neighbourhoods were established, but these were often grossly insanitary places because of the lack of adequate services. For the great majority of urban dwellers, there was no escape from the horrors of squalor and overcrowding because of their need to be close to work in the period before the development of cheap public transport. If industry was concentrated in the towns, then the labour force must concentrate there too.

The generally low level of wages paid to the working class at this time was reflected in their poor standard of living. Poverty and bad housing conditions were inextricably linked, or as Merrett (1979: 4) puts it, 'The working class lived in slums because they could afford nothing else.' Thus, in addition to the serious health hazard of overwhelmed and underdeveloped water and sewerage services, the poor also had to make do with dwellings which were small, damp, badly ventilated, deprived of daylight and sometimes structurally unstable. To make matters even worse, in areas of high demand (near to places of work), rents were driven up, which led to considerable overcrowding as people sublet their already inadequate accommodation in order to meet the rent.

Defining the problem

The world's leading industrial nation was by the 1840s also the location of some of the world's worst slums. It was clear that capitalism generated extremes not only of wealth and comfort, but also of poverty and deprivation. But in what sense, and for whom, was this a problem? Was it a situation which required state intervention in defiance of property rights and the conventional wisdom? The slums were obviously a problem for the people who lived there, but that fact alone was unlikely to bring about attempts to improve their circumstances, although the danger of their misery and disaffection manifesting itself in rebellion or revolution was sufficient to unsettle the ruling class. (A deep distrust and fear of the brutalised masses was a theme running through the whole Victorian period.)

Perhaps a more important factor in the developing definition and recognition of the urban problem was that the lack of adequate sanitation represented a real threat to the health of all classes. Epidemics of infectious diseases quickly spread amongst the teeming population of the towns; cholera in particular affected the middle classes as well as the poor, for as a water-borne disease it easily reached into their well-plumbed homes.

The development of social statistics and a series of investigations of conditions among the poor revealed that their rates of morbidity and mortality were significantly higher than in the better-off classes. In the smoky, damp and generally unhealthy atmosphere of the slums, infectious diseases such as typhus and tuberculosis were rampantly endemic. Perhaps the best known of the studies at this time was Edwin Chadwick's *Report on the Sanitary Condition of the Labouring Population of Great Britain*, published in 1842. Chadwick was then secretary to the Poor Law Commissioners and he had realised that illness and early death, especially in the case of breadwinners, had important consequences in terms of the level of demand for poor relief (Klein, 1984). He therefore argued that preventive measures should be taken to deal with disease as a way of reducing the cost of the Poor Law. At a more general level, employers gradually came to realise that sickness amongst the labour force held down productivity and profits.

These three factors formed the basis of the public health problem as it was comprehended by Victorian society. It was clearly in everyone's interest to remedy the situation, but there was considerable opposition to state intervention. The prevailing theory of *laissez-faire* emphasised the importance of individual responsibility and freedom, and a minimum role for the state. Wealth and prosperity for all, it was believed, stemmed from free individuals pursuing their own self-interest.

However the consequences of the unrestrained pursuit of profit in the case of housing were set out quite clearly by the reformer James Hole in 1866:

> Social and sanitary considerations do not sufficiently weigh with the capitalist builder if they involve increased outlay without a corresponding return. The smaller the house, the larger is his percentage of profit . . . [And he went on to say] If by any ingenuity he [the builder] can cram a cottage or two more on the land, and thus increase his percentage, he will be only too glad to do it; and if there are no municipal regulations enforced he will do it. If by a little contrivance he can let off the cellar as a separate dwelling, he largely increases his profits. He has no difficulty in finding tenants for the worst places. There are always some so poor that the most wretched den seems to them better than to be homeless. (Hole, 1866: 5–9)

The free market system (incorporating low wages and high-price housing) was the cause of the problem and could not easily, if at all, produce the remedy. Even strong supporters of *laissez-faire* could see that complete freedom was anarchy, and they readily acknowledged that the state had certain important functions in a capitalist society in relation to the establishment of the conditions necessary for continued accumulation.

The argument was about whether the state should properly intervene in an issue such as public health, where this would mean, to a greater or lesser extent, a reduction in the rights of property. It was the formulation of the problem in terms of public health, and the threat posed to society as a whole by insanitary conditions, which in the end justified state intervention.

It should be realised that there was also a housing problem alongside the genuine problem of public health in the towns. This housing problem was not articulated until much later in the century. The market failed to supply a sufficient number of dwellings; those that were built were often of poor quality and rents were high in relation to working-class wages (hence much of the overcrowding). The provision of piped water and sewerage systems would have little impact on this aspect of the condition of the working class and, if anything, were likely to make matters worse by driving up costs and, in turn, rents.

The structure of the state

By the end of the 1840s, public health had been established as a major problem and, by the passage of the Public Health Act in 1848, the state had begun a preoccupation which was to dominate local government for much of the next half-century. This book has as one of its main themes the question of relations between central and local government, and it was from the 1830s and 1840s onwards that the continuing arguments about the proper roles of each governmental tier began to be hammered out. It is important to remember that the state did not exist in a highly developed form, ready to intervene as the urgent problems of urbanisation were revealed. New institutions had to be established and new mechanisms developed.

In terms of the electorate, Marx's judgement that the state was a committee for the management of the affairs of the bourgeoisie (Marx and Engels, 1967: 82) was substantially true, until working-class men gained the vote towards the end of the century. The Reform Act of 1832 gave the vote to middle-class males, but the urban and rural labourers did not achieve the vote until 1867 and 1884 respectively. Women, of course, were denied the right to vote until after the First World War. At the local level, elected councils were established by the Municipal Corporations Act 1835 (Fraser, 1979: ch. 1). The new councils replaced the old corporations, those snug oases of privilege (Smellie, 1969: 30) based on the historic powers of the Freemen, but the Act was not an attempt to go beyond borough reform towards the establishment of a coherent and comprehensive system of local government. The Act applied to only 178 boroughs, leaving out London, because it was a special case, and large towns like Manchester, Birmingham and Sheffield, because they had no corporation to reform:

> So between 1832 and 1888, while there was for the whole of England and Wales a special system of elected Boards of Guardians to deal with paupers and a form of town government in certain urban areas for problems other than the poor law, it was necessary, outside those municipal areas, either to use the non-elected Justices of the Peace, the rear guard of an agrarian oligarchy . . . or to create special *ad hoc* authorities to deal with urgent problems as they arose. (Smellie, 1969: 25)

An important feature of local government in the nineteenth century was the proliferation of *ad hoc* bodies with specific and limited responsibilities. As a device the *ad hoc* authority developed before 1835 because of the corruption and ineffectiveness of the old corporations, and it continued to be used not only in the unreformed areas, but also in the reformed boroughs. This inevitably led to very considerable administrative confusion; there were improvement commissions, highways boards, health boards and sanitary authorities often not operating with common boundaries and frequently disputing with each other and the councils for the responsibility for specific tasks. A further cause of confusion was that there was no uniformity of powers across the country, because it was usual for each locality to proceed by promotion of its own local Acts of Parliament, bestowing specific powers.

This brings in a second important theme, the resistance to control by central government. Hostility towards central interferences in local affairs was particularly strong in the middle of the nineteenth century. The opposition to centralisation was led by propagandists such as Joshua Toulmin Smith who fiercely argued for the historic right to local self-determination. On the other hand, people like Edwin Chadwick believed that the problems of government in modern urban society required strong central administrative organisation. Chadwick was influential in framing the 1848 Public Health Bill, which proposed to create a General Board of Health, and some local authorities petitioned against the Bill, not because they denied the need for action, but because the price to be paid in lost local autonomy was too high. Despite the weight of evidence in the form of the dreadful urban squalor, in the end Chadwick was defeated by the opposition, for, although the Bill was passed and the Board set up, the Act was on the whole a failure. This was for two reasons which were commonly the downfall of nineteenth-century legislation of this kind. First, the Act was an enabling measure; it conferred on the localities the power, but not the duty, to establish local boards of health to carry out sanitary reforms under central supervision. The General Board of Health could only compel a town to establish a local board in circumstances of exceptional death rate. Second, in order to avoid the indignity of central control, local communities could promote their own legislation, and many of them did so.

'The hostility to centralisation thus not only delayed and restricted the growth of central administrative bodies, but also accelerated the proliferation of local Acts that spread increased powers throughout the municipalities' (Fraser, 1979: 166). However, from the early 1870s, a process of rationalisation was begun in which the creation of new *ad hoc* bodies declined, a more coherent and uniform structure of local government was pulled together, and Parliament began to assert more authority over the local councils, in the sense that it began to confer on them duties rather than powers.

In 1871, the Local Government Board was set up to oversee local affairs, and in the following year the Public Health Act required the formation of sanitary authorities covering the whole country. Increasingly it was the local council which took over the tasks which had been the *raison d'être* of the *ad hoc* bodies. Two major Acts, in 1888 and 1894, completed the construction of local government. The Local Government Act of 1888 set up the county councils, the London County Council and the county borough councils. In 1894 the final pieces were fitted into the system when the urban and rural district councils were formed to take over from the old urban and rural

Table 2.1   *Principal housing and public health legislation, 1848–1914*

1848	*Public Health Act.* Established the General Board of Health and enabled local boards to be set up.
1851	*Labouring Classes' Lodging Houses Act.* First Act to permit local authorities to provide housing, but very widely ignored. Common Lodging Houses Act (amended in 1853). Provided for control and monitoring of private common lodging houses.
1866	*Labouring Classes ' Dwelling Houses Act.* Permitted local authorities and model dwellings companies to borrow at cheap rates from the Public Works Loans Commissioners.
1868	*Artisans' and Labourers' Dwellings Act (Torrens Act).* Authorities given the power to demolish individual unfit houses. No compensation for owners and no municipal rebuilding. (Amended to provide compensation in 1879.)
1872	*Public Health Act.* Created urban and rural sanitary authorities across the whole country.
1875	*Artisans' and Labourers' Dwellings Improvement Act (Cross Act).* Permitted local authorities to purchase and clear areas of unfit housing. LAs permitted to build on cleared sites, but had to sell within 10 years. (Amended in 1879 to limit compensation.)
1875	*Public Health Act.* Established principles for the purchase of land by local authorities and set up the framework for extension of local building by-laws.
1885	*Housing of the Working Classes Act.* Consolidating Act.
1890	*Public Health Act.* Extended 1875 Act.
1890	*Housing of the Working Classes Act.* Consolidated and amended earlier legislation. Part I dealt with areas of unfit and insanitary housing and rebuilding powers. Part II dealt with individual unfit houses. Part III dealt with local authority powers to build housing for general needs.
1900	*Housing of the Working Classes Act.* Amended 1890 Act to give London metropolitan boroughs powers to use Part III of the Act (in addition to the LCC).
1909	*Housing and Town Planning Act.* Ended obligation on authorities to sell houses in redevelopment areas within 10 years. Provided powers for authorities to prepare town planning schemes.

sanitary authorities. This structure remained virtually intact until the major reorganisation of 1974. Table 2.1 shows the principal housing and public health legislation during the period 1848–1914.

From nuisance removal to town planning

Modern housing policy consists of two major components: the private and the public sectors. Policy towards the private sector includes, amongst other things, the specification of minimum standards and measures to be taken in relation to dwellings which breach these standards. This represents a definite housing strand in the refinement of sanitary policy, and has its origins in the mid-nineteenth century. The development of public housing came later and was a logical progression from environmental control measures, as will be explained below.

The first Nuisances Removal Act was passed in 1846 in an attempt to enable authorities to deal with urgent threats to public health, such as neglected middens. The Nuisances Removal Act of 1855 was noteworthy for introducing the words 'unfit for human habitation', which remains central to slum clearance legislation. The first housing Acts were the Shaftesbury Acts (after their promoter Lord Shaftesbury) of 1851: the Common Lodging Houses Act and the Labouring Classes' Lodging Houses Act. The latter remained almost totally ignored because the authorities were not ready to use the power to build, but the former, as amended in 1853, did prove useful, for it was concerned with the inspection and supervision of lodging houses. The powers of inspection were vested in the police, and Gauldie suggests that they were used to promote law and order rather than better housing (Gauldie, 1974: 245).

Public housing, as we understand it today, was not even on the horizon at that time; it was considered neither necessary nor desirable in the *laissez-faire* society. Economic theory which asserted that the market, free of restraints, would provide, popular attachment to the notion of private property, and the vested interests of the property owners who comprised the personnel of the local state, all militated against municipal housebuilding. However the *regulation* of standards of provision of privately owned housing did gain slow acceptance as an adjunct of sanitary policy. The development and, more important, the implementation of controls were strongly resisted by the local authorities. The reason, as James Hole pointed out, was largely that the authorities and the people who elected them were the very people most likely to have to foot the bill – the owners of the property to be affected by regulations. 'To ask them to close the cellar dwellings is to ask them to forfeit a portion of their income. Every pound they vote for drainage, or other sanitary improvement, is something taken out of their own pocket' (Hole, 1866: 25).

In the process of defining a distinct housing theme in sanitary policy, the Artisans' and Labourers' Dwellings Act 1868 (known as the Torrens Act after the man who piloted the Bill through Parliament) was something of a milestone. It gave authorities the power, not the duty, to demolish individual houses which were unfit for human habitation. There was no power to compensate owners of such houses, nor the power to rebuild on cleared sites (although the Act was amended in 1879 to give these powers). Torrens believed that housebuilding should be left to private enterprise, but he also realised that it was in the interests of employers to have a workforce which was made fit, happy and healthy by state intervention to deal with slum housing. His original Bill had a very hard passage through Parliament and emerged much weaker for it. A further Bill promoted by Richard Cross, the Home Secretary, extended the power of local authorities to areas of unfit houses. This measure, the Artisans' and Labourers' Dwellings Improvement Act 1875, did require local authorities to arrange for rehousing on the site for numbers of people equivalent to those who were displaced by clearance, although amendments in 1879 and 1882 reduced and modified this obligation. The Act was definitely not designed to encourage public housing and any dwellings built by local authorities were to be sold within 10 years. Octavia Hill, a strong opponent of public housing, was a supporter of the Bill who advised in its drafting, because she had learned from experience that removal of slums required municipal intervention.

In practice, neither the Torrens not the Cross Acts, as amended, made any significant impact. One obvious reason was that, until it was made much easier and cheaper for local authorities to build houses, they would not do so, and private builders were uninterested in providing new dwellings for the displaced poor.

Clearance without adequate replacement was certain to make matters worse by increasing overcrowding in nearby areas. However Cross, like Torrens, believed that private enterprise could and should provide the necessary dwellings. The legislators' coolness towards an adequate replacement policy implemented by councils themselves meant that the local medical officers of health proved very reluctant to bring forward clearance schemes, because they knew very well that to do so would be to make matters worse elsewhere.

The second reason for the lack of use made of these Acts was the preference for local Acts. Fraser (1979: 165) has drawn attention to the need to consider not only resistance to central legislation, but also the positive approach to reform contained in the great number of local Acts. In this vein, Merrett (1979: 13) writes:

> It was the local Acts which were most important in the total impact of improvement. In their case we see basically a transformation in land-use from workers' housing to commercial development and social infrastructure which rarely benefited the manual working class directly. In a sense these specific schemes appropriated the city for the bourgeoisie.

The removal of unfit property, for whatever reason, was only part of the developing framework of environmental controls. Another equally important facet was the specification of regulations stipulating the standards to be achieved in new housing for the working class. Again, local Acts had anticipated this development, but the Public Health Act of 1875 remains a major landmark in the emergence of housing policy, in that it gave health authorities powers to make by-laws governing new buildings. These powers, which were extended in 1890, had a significant effect on the improving standards of new houses in the last quarter of the century. The most important of nineteenth-century housing Acts was the Housing of the Working Classes Act 1890. It was mainly a consolidating statute, bringing together the Cross and Torrens legislation on unfit housing, and simplifying the previously cumbersome administrative procedures. However the Act did not require authorities outside London to rehouse people displaced by slum clearance.

In 1866, James Hole had pointed out the value of preventive measures: 'The cheapest remedies . . . are those of prevention. An ill-planned town can never have all the errors of its first formation corrected' (Hole, 1866: 20). In this sense, then, the first Housing and Town Planning Act 1909 represents another important development. Tarn (1973) believes it to be 'one of the most important measures in the history of the whole housing movement'. The significance of the Act lay in the permissive powers given to local councils to declare Town Planning Schemes. Such schemes related to specific areas of new development, wherein the authority was given special powers to define such things as density, road widths and the zoning of land uses. 'These powers gave the local authority a unique opportunity to develop new districts in a balanced and organised manner; they gave them the means of control which had never before existed in this country' (Tarn, 1973: 180).

To sum up this section, it can be seen that there was a logical progression from the control of nuisances, through the removal of unfit dwellings, first individually and then in groups, leading to the emergence of the notion of town planning. Despite local opposition from property interests, there was an ever-widening definition of the problem, as it became clear that real improvement required further powers and more public intervention. The state developed its organisation and administrative expertise in order to be able to deal with the broader understanding of the problem.

However the dominant view of the state throughout the period was that it should play a minimal role, designed to set the framework within which private enterprise could fulfil its function of meeting consumer demand. The unquestioned capacity of the market system to provide adequate housing for all only came under close scrutiny towards the end of the century.

'Philanthropy at five per cent'

Various semi-charitable attempts were made to tackle the housing problem, at least partly motivated by a desire to counter the case for state intervention, but even collectively they made very little impression on an enormous problem. From the 1840s onwards there developed what became known as 'philanthropy at five per cent' (Tarn, 1973: 179), in recognition of the investors' willingness to accept a less than commercial rate of return on their money. Model dwellings companies, like the Improved Industrial Dwellings Company, made valiant attempts to put into practice the ideals of enlightened entrepreneurs such as Sir Sidney Waterlow. They were assisted by the Labouring Classes' Dwelling Houses Act 1866, which enabled them to borrow cheaply from the Public Works Loan Commissioners, but despite this access to cheap capital it proved impossible to provide new housing of a decent standard at rents affordable by the poor.

In addition, there were charitable housing trusts, endowed by rich capitalist benefactors such as Peabody, Guinness and Rothschild (White, 1981). The Peabody Trust, established in 1862, was endowed with £150 000 for the purpose of providing housing for the working class, but it, too, was accused of failing to reach those in greatest need. The conflicts between high cost and the desire to maintain standards by avoiding overcrowding, on the one hand, and on the other the low rent-paying capacity of the poorest, meant that the beneficiaries of Trust accommodation were likely to be those who were anyway rather better placed in the housing market. It may also have been the case that the rather disciplined, authoritarian approach to housing management by the Trusts also worked against the poorest.

An alternative approach was that developed by Octavia Hill (Malpass, 1984; Darley, 1990) who set out to reach those she described as being 'as low a class as have a settled abode'. Even she did not attempt to help those who lived on the streets. In order to keep costs, and therefore rents, to a minimum she concentrated on improving the management of *existing* housing. In a method which combined housing management and social work, Octavia Hill aimed simultaneously to rehabilitate slum properties and slum tenants. She was able to show that, by an authoritarian, labour-intensive system of management, using trained middle-class women managers and rent collectors, it was possible to make profits out of housing the poor in decent conditions. Octavia Hill's initial small-scale operation grew very large and provided the inspiration for others, but it is to be doubted whether she deserves her reputation as the founder of modern housing management practice. It can be argued that, whereas she emphasised the social work aspect of housing management as an activity carried out by women with the intention of moral improvement in the tenants, the growth of council housing after the First World War effectively redefined housing management as a bureaucratic–administrative activity done by men, with very little emphasis on social work aspects.

The scale and intensity of the housing problem in Victorian Britain was such that these various approaches were overwhelmed and, instead of demonstrating that enlightened private enterprise could cope with the situation, their failure tended to enhance the case for municipal intervention.

The emergence of council housing

So far, it has been shown that it was a long, hard battle for the sanitary reformers to establish even a regulatory role for the local authorities. It was much more difficult to gain acceptance for a positive approach to housing in the form of direct public provision. All the familiar arguments against further state intervention were deployed, with greater vigour, against house building. Even those who could see the economic wisdom of the state setting a framework of regulations in order to limit the workings of the market drew back from the idea of the state doing anything further. The dominance of *laissez-faire* ideas was such that for much of the century direct state provision of dwellings was not on the agenda; it was to most people a wild and ridiculous notion. The idea of council housing was ridiculed by those who argued that if the state should provide housing, then why not clothing and food and all the essentials of life? It was self-evidently the job of private capitalist enterprise to provide housing.

One line of reasoning, derived from writers like Adam Smith, was that *any* state intervention was state *interference* with the smooth working of the market. The imposition of regulations which specified minimum standards in housing was seen as damaging to the market, in the sense that costs would be raised and, unless wages also rose, then the supply would fall, thus making the situation worse for the poor.

Another important theme in nineteenth-century thinking about social policy was the view that state provision made people dependent. The notion of less eligibility, which underpinned the Poor Law Amendment Act of 1834, was an expression of this idea that people should be coerced into self-help, and actively discouraged from accepting help from the state. The pauperising effect of indiscriminate charity was taken for granted by reformers such as Octavia Hill and her colleagues in the Charity Organisation Society. Merrett (1979: 20) quotes Sir Richard Cross (of the Cross Act) saying in 1882: 'To provide such necessaries [as housing] for any class is not the duty of the State, because, if it did so, it would inevitably tend to make that class depend, not on themselves but what was done for them elsewhere.'

The 1880s were a period of important developments in the emergence of council housing. In 1883 a searing polemic, *The Bitter Cry of Outcast London* by Andrew Mearns, gave wide publicity to the continuing problem of housing for the poor. Recognition of the situation by Parliament was reflected in the appointment of a Royal Commission on the Housing of the Working Classes in 1884.

By now a *housing* problem, as distinct from a sanitary problem, was the focus of official attention. It was becoming understood that the poor lived in slums because they could not afford the rent for decent housing. The Royal Commission gathered a mass of evidence which 'demonstrated that through poverty, the failure of local authorities to protect their interests and the success of the landlord class in exploiting their need, the working people in Britain were as a class ill-housed to the point of destitution' (Gauldie, 1974: 289).

At around this time, too, the working class was making real political gains and, having secured the franchise, they were able to begin electing advocates for their cause. The revelation of the failure of both free enterprise and charitable endeavour strengthened the hand of the labour movement. Wohl (1977: 317) explains that 'Mounting discontent with housing conditions and the growing strength of left-wing opinion combined in the late-Victorian period to produce the first specifically working class housing reform movement. For the first time the working man himself emerged to take a leading part in the agitation for better housing'. However he goes on to suggest that the activists had difficulty in stimulating interest amongst the slum dwellers.

Bodies such as the Workmen's National Housing Council and the Social Democratic Federation campaigned for better housing. Wohl says that the SDF wanted council housing, but also fair rent courts and stricter enforcement of the sanitary and building laws. Byrne and Damer (1980) argue that housing provided the issues around which working-class activists could organise local pressure groups. They refer to Tenants' Defence Associations and the role of the Independent Labour Party branches.

Demand for state-provided housing obviously met fierce opposition from the property lobby. The local authorities also resisted these demands, partly because of the implications for the rates, and partly because property owners were well-represented on town councils:

> there was systematic resistance from the urban bourgeoisies who controlled the local states to any initiative involving the mandatory construction and subsidisation of working class housing. This resistance was compounded by the fact that in many local states, the dominant local bourgeoisie were landlords of such housing and municipal housing conflicted *directly* with their interests. (Byrne and Damer, 1978)

In addition to resistance to the building of municipal houses was the resolute determination on the part of most local authorities that there should be no subsidy from the rates for any working-class housing. The idea of a rate subsidy was anathema to the property-owning classes in general, and perhaps even more so amongst the ranks of middle-class councillors. At the levels of central government, the continuing belief in private provision militated against any central grant in aid, such as was already available for education. However there remained a gap between the cost of new housing and the rent-paying capacity of substantial numbers of the working class; subsidies were essential if the historic link between poverty and poor housing was to be broken.

It was the Housing of the Working Classes Act of 1890 that provided the legislative basis for the development of local authority housing before the First World War. It was in part a consolidating Act, bringing together much of the earlier legislation on slum clearance, but in Part III it gave local authorities powers to build for general needs. However there was no *obligation* to build, and no financial help from central government to help bridge the gap between costs and the rents that working-class tenants could afford. The importance of the Act lay more in its timing than its content. It made few changes in the legislative position (although it did simplify the financial procedures affecting municipal housing), but it was passed at a time when the political pressures on local authorities were building up and there was in existence a coherently structured local government system capable of reflecting popular demands and carrying out the functions of a housing authority. The recently established London County Council was particularly active in building under this Act and did much to promote a tradition of high-quality design in municipal housing. Elsewhere, cities such as Sheffield, Liverpool and Glasgow were also leading the development of public housing, but most authorities built no houses at all, and the majority of authorities that did build before the First World War did not do so until after 1909. In all, only about 20 000 council dwellings were produced in England (Great Britain, 1977b: 7), and about 24 000 in Great Britain (Merrett, 1979: 26) as a whole, before 1914, representing an insignificant proportion of the total stock.

The beginning of housebuilding, even on this very limited scale, can be seen as a triumph for the power of working-class political pressure and, indeed, it seems highly unlikely that councils would have moved this far had it not been for the emergence of such a force. On the other hand, it is not fair to assume that the development of collective provision for housing, and other needs, at the end of the nineteenth century represented a definite trend towards socialism. The Conservative politician Balfour said in 1895:

> Social legislation, as I conceive it, is not merely to be distinguished from Socialist legislation but it is its most direct opposite and its most effective antidote. Socialism will never get possession of the great body of public opinion . . . among the working class or any other class if those who wield the collective forces of the community show themselves desirous to ameliorate every legitimate grievance and to put Society upon a proper and more solid basis. (Hill, 1976: 28)

The Liberal government which assumed office in 1906 was responsible for laying a number of foundation stones in the construction of the welfare state, but it did not advance the housing cause, apart from the measures contained in the 1909 Housing and Town Planning Act. Nevertheless, during the period up to the outbreak of the First World War, pressure continued to accumulate for a more radical housing policy, especially as the slump in private housing gathered pace after 1905/6. The first parliamentary Bill to propose state aid to local councils as a way of overcoming their general reluctance to build was brought forward in 1912. It failed; similar Bills were introduced in 1913 and 1914, again without success (Wilding, 1972). The housing situation in Scotland was particularly serious, and in 1912 a Royal Commission was set up to investigate and make recommendations. Its report in 1917 was to be an important factor in the development of new policies to meet the new postwar world.

The Garden City movement

Before concluding this discussion of the origins of housing policy, it is necessary to refer briefly to the Garden City movement, not because of any great impact achieved before 1914 but because of the considerable influence which it exerted on the design and layout of municipal housing between the wars. Underpinning the Garden City idea was a rejection of the congestion, squalor and lack of planning in Victorian cities in which workers' housing was packed in among factories, mines and mills. The vision set out by Ebenezer Howard in his book *Tomorrow: A Peaceful Path to Real Reform* (1898) (republished as *Garden Cities of Tomorrow,* 1902) proposed new low-density settlements of limited size protected by permanent green belts, but linked in groups to form larger cities of 250 000 people.

The main designers who collaborated with Howard in establishing the first Garden City at Letchworth, Hertfordshire, in 1904 were Raymond Unwin and his partner Barry Parker. These two architects had previously been commissioned by Joseph Rowntree to design a small garden suburb at New Earswick, near York, and from this small beginning, Unwin, in particular, went on to become the leading influence behind the design and layout proposals contained in the Tudor Walters Report of 1918, which provided the basic architectural framework for the development of interwar municipal housing (see Chapter 3, pp. 43–6). Unwin was a strong opponent of the high-density, gridiron developments typical of by-law housing built in the last quarter of the nineteenth century, and his main contribution was to devise an alternative approach to the design and layout of working-class housing.

Letchworth itself was not an immediate success as a development project (Miller, 1979). It relied mainly on private capital and private housing, with very little local authority provision at first. However, in 1907, the concept was taken up in another scheme at Hampstead Garden Suburb in London, and the company behind Letchworth later moved on to establish Welwyn Garden City in 1920. Numerically, these developments were even less significant than the various attempts at 'five per cent philanthropy', but in the context of the emerging town and country planning movement and the gathering demands for municipal housing they assumed historic importance.

Conclusion

This chapter has shown that it was only towards the end of the nineteenth century, and even then only very tentatively and reluctantly, that the state began to recognise a need for action to deal with the supply of decent housing for the working class. For most of the period, resistance to any form of state intervention to influence the supply of housing was dominant, leading to the conclusion that 'No real reform in housing was achieved by legislation during the nineteenth century' (Gauldie, 1974: 240). The only effective action concerned questions of public health. However, in a sense, the case for a public housing policy was strengthened by the demonstrable failure of public health measures alone to resolve the problem. In addition, the state came under increasingly organised pressure from the working class, whose demands were expressed partly through the ballot box and partly through organisations such as the Workmen's National Housing Council. They demanded controls on the activities of private landlords and the development of a subsidised municipal housing service to break the market links between poverty and bad housing. The response at local level was highly variable, so that by 1914 a few authorities were already substantial landlords, others had a small housing stock and most had built nothing at all.

In 1914, there remained extensive areas of very poor-quality, insanitary and overcrowded urban housing, together with serious rural housing problems. Despite the accumulation of unassailable evidence on the scale and intensity of the housing problem, a coherent policy response was slow to develop. Central government provided local authorities with certain *powers* but gave them few *obligations* in respect of housing. In particular, the refusal by the Exchequer to provide financial assistance for local authority housing was the major reason for the low levels of municipal housebuilding. In this context, it is important to recognise not only local authority resistance to becoming housing landlords but also the extent to which some authorities that were enthusiastic about building were prevented from fulfilling their ambitions by central government's parsimony.

The main point to emerge from this chapter is that, although the roots of housing policy clearly lie in the Victorian period, nothing effective was done before 1914 to confront the key issues of the overall supply of accommodation and the rents that people had to pay. And on the question of standards very little was done to remove existing slum areas (as distinct from by-law controls over new building). It can therefore be argued that authentic housing policy is essentially a twentieth-century phenomenon. Chapter 3 shows how the questions of quantity and price were at last confronted during the upheaval of the First World War, and how the third key issue, quality, was not tackled until the slum clearance campaign in the 1930s.

3

Housing and the State, 1914–39

Before 1914, there was barely a recognisable housing policy as such, but the events of the next four years were to bring about major changes in housing, as in so many other aspects of British society. The First World War weakened resistance to change, helping to undermine long-established class and gender divisions (for instance, the war helped to secure votes for women). In the case of housing, the war produced conditions in which the state could no longer resist working-class demands. As a result, the period 1914–19 represents a historic turning-point in the development of housing policy, leading to far more state intervention than had seemed possible before 1914, and in the years up to the outbreak of the Second World War it proved impossible for this intervention to be completely withdrawn, despite considerably altered political and economic circumstances.

An overview of housing policy, 1914–39

As Chapter 2 made clear, there was a serious decline in the level of housing production for most of the decade before 1914, and new building fell still further during the war itself. The result was that by 1918 there was a severe housing shortage which for economic reasons private enterprise could not tackle effectively, especially in the short term, and which for political reasons the state could not ignore.

During the interwar period, housing policy consisted of two main elements: rent control in the private sector and the development of the public sector, which can itself be separated into two distinct activities, provision for general housing need and provision for need arising from municipal slum clearance programmes. A feature of the period was the *lack* of direct intervention designed to encourage the growth of home ownership.

Rent control covering most private rented housing was introduced in 1915, ostensibly as a temporary wartime measure, but the shortage made it impossible for control to be lifted when peace was restored in November 1918, and restrictions continued in modified form right up to the Second World War. Legislation in 1920 permitted certain rent increases, but continued extensive control, again for a limited period. However, in 1923, an element of decontrol was introduced: sitting tenants continued to be protected from eviction and subject to controlled rents, but there was automatic decontrol at the next change of tenant. Thus decontrol was planned to spread gradually through the stock, at a pace determined by the movement of tenants. Unfortunately, this did not lead to the anticipated revival of new investment in private rented housing, especially of the cheaper variety, and in 1933 further legislation introduced a system whereby the highest-value properties were completely decontrolled immediately, those in the middle range continued to be subject to decontrol at the next change of tenant, and the cheapest dwellings were once again subject to continuing control. All these Acts applied only to houses built before 1915; rent control did not affect new housing, but in September 1939, at the outbreak of the Second World War, controls were extended to cover virtually the whole of the private rented sector. One effect of rent control policy was to create a pattern of variation in rents which meant that identical houses could have very different rents, reflecting changes of tenancy at different times. For instance, in 1939, where the same tenant had been in occupation continuously since 1915 the rent of all but the highest-value houses was related to the rent charged in August 1914, but where there had been changes of tenant then the rent that became controlled in 1939 was the rent that had been determined by the market.

Rent control was a rather blunt instrument, in the sense that although it dealt with the problem of the high price of rented accommodation, it led to the sorts of anomalies referred to above and it raised problems of under-investment affecting both the quality of existing housing and the supply of new dwellings. The development of local authority housing can be seen as a positive response to the negative effects of rent control. At first, local authorities mainly built relatively high-quality houses, at lower densities than had been the norm for private working-class housing before 1914. Throughout the 1920s, local authorities concentrated on reducing the housing shortage and at a time of high costs their contribution represented the main source of supply of housing for the working class.

However the combination of high costs, high quality, low density and relatively low subsidy inevitably led to rents which were above controlled rents at the lower end of the private market. In other words, during the 1920s when housing policy was concerned with reducing the overall shortage, the public sector emerged as a tenure serving mainly the rather better-off workers and tending to exclude the least well off.

After 1930, and more especially after 1933, however, local authorities were pushed towards a quite different role, abandoning general needs housing in favour of slum clearance and redevelopment. For a decade after the war there was virtually no slum clearance. One reason for this was arguably that, until the shortage was reduced, it made little sense to demolish existing houses, even if they were unsatisfactory. In 1930, local authorities were required to draw up plans for slum clearance, and from 1933 they were encouraged by the subsidy system to concentrate their new building on the needs generated by the clearance programme. The standard of new local authority housing was reduced, partly in order to produce rents that could be afforded by poor families rehoused from slum property. Another factor was probably the desire to make council housing less attractive to people who could afford to secure private accommodation.

It is important to locate changes in policy in the public sector in the context of changing housing market conditions. When costs were high, councils ensured a supply of housing that private enterprise could not have provided, but when costs fell, the local authorities withdrew from general needs construction, thereby opening up the market for private builders, who had been arguing that subsidised municipal activity was preventing them from meeting the demand. The expansion and contraction of local authority activity can be seen as directly complementary to the needs of the private sector.

The abandonment of general needs housebuilding by local authorities coincided with a massive boom in private housebuilding. A feature of the interwar period as a whole was the high level of new building in both public and private sectors. Private sector output was above 100 000 dwellings every year after 1925, and above 250 000 per year in the five-year period 1934–8. Local authority output averaged a little more than 50 000 per year throughout the interwar period, which was very high compared with pre-1914 municipal building rates, but it was overshadowed by the scale of private construction, especially in the 1930s, as Figure 3.1 shows. It is interesting that, although Exchequer subsidies were available for private housebuilding in the 1920s, the highest rates of construction came several years after their removal. It is important to appreciate that the 1930s' building boom was a product of market conditions, specifically low costs of land, labour and materials, and low interest rates, coupled with rising living standards in the more prosperous southern half of the country, where most of the new building was located. The boom was largely unsubsidised and occurred without the sort of state support for home ownership that has become such an integral part of housing policy in more recent years.

The majority of new private houses built in the interwar period were sold to owner-occupiers, but as many as 900 000 dwellings were added to the private rented sector (Great Britain, 1977b: 39). Despite this level of building for renting, the private rented sector declined quite rapidly as a proportion of

Figure 3.1 *Dwellings completed annually in England and Wales, 1920–39*

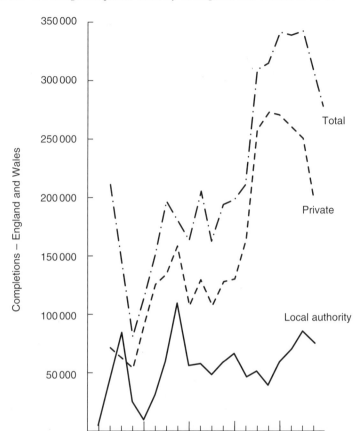

Sources: House of Commons Debates, Written Answers, cols 161–2 (11 March 1946). Quoted in Cullingworth (1966).

all housing because of slum clearance and the transfer of over 1 million existing rented houses into owner-occupation. The net effect was that private renting lost about half a million dwellings, whilst owner-occupation gained 2.9 million from new building and transfers. It was the sale of previously rented houses that enabled home ownership to expand so rapidly between the wars, despite the absence of direct state support. By the outbreak of the Second World War, the pattern of housing tenure had been significantly redrawn (see Table 1.1, p. 41) and the process of tenure restructuring which has continued apace since 1945 was well under way.

Rent control

One type of housing reform demanded by the labour movement before the First World War was the introduction of 'fair rent courts', as a way of regulating the market for rented housing. The state, however, showed no signs of intervening to control rent levels until forced to by a famous example of mass political action by the working class. When the war began, housing production fell away from already low levels, thereby exacerbating the shortage, especially in areas of high demand resulting from concentrations of extra labour brought in to manufacture munitions. Some landlords exploited this situation by raising rents, and others felt justified in levying increases because they themselves faced higher rates of interest on borrowed capital. During 1915, working-class resentment of higher rents as an accompaniment to the slaughter in the trenches built up into a wave of rent strikes across the country. The centre of resistance was in Glasgow, where a combination of existing bad housing conditions, a large influx of munitions workers and a well-organised labour movement led to particularly solid and effective strike action. In the context of a war, civil unrest of this sort, involving court cases, evictions, mass demonstrations and the use of force against the civilian population, obviously put considerable pressure on the government. The problem was resolved by emergency legislation at the end of 1915: the Increase of Rent and Mortgage Interest (War Restrictions) Act fixed the rents of most houses at the level operative in August 1914 (only dwellings of high rateable value were excluded). Mortgage interest rates were also fixed at August 1914 levels. (For a summary of principal housing legislation in the period 1915–39, see Table 3.1.)

The Glasgow rent strikes have been the subject of considerable interest among students of housing policy (Damer, 1980; Melling, 1980; Orbach, 1977), and their significance in the long-term development of policy is a matter of much argument. However, for present purposes, it is sufficient to note that, in the peculiar conditions created by the war, direct action by the working-class movement was for the first time able to bring about an immediate change of housing policy. The introduction of rent control was intended to be a temporary wartime expedient, but the significance of the action in 1915 is that it brought into existence a form of intervention from which no government has been able to extricate itself completely. The final point to make here is that rent control made state subsidies for new building inevitable. As Marian Bowley (1945: 9) succinctly put it: 'Increases in rents staved off in deference to public opinion during the war could scarcely be regarded as an appropriate form of peace celebration.' Private builders who had virtually abandoned working-class housing as an unprofitable undertaking before the war would not return to it unless it could be made to pay, which meant higher rents or state subsidies. The logic of the situation led directly towards some sort of state subsidy after the war, and for this reason

Table 3.1 *Principal housing legislation, 1915–39*

1915	*Increase of Rent and Mortgage Interest (War Restrictions) Act.* Fixed rents and interest rates at their August 1914 levels.
1919	*Housing and Town Planning etc. Act (Addison Act).* Introduced Exchequer subsidies for local authority houses. Local liability fixed at 1 penny rate; Exchequer met any remaining deficit. Withdrawn in 1921.
1919	*Housing (Additional Powers) Act.* Extended subsidy to private builders of working-class housing.
1920	*Increase of Rent and Mortgage Interest (War Restrictions) Act.* Continued principle of control but permitted certain increases.
1923	*Housing Act (Chamberlain Act).* Introduced a new subsidy with fixed Exchequer liability and no mandatory rate contribution. Intended mainly to stimulate private builders. Withdrawn in 1929.
1923	*Increase of Rent and Mortgage Interest Restrictions Act.* Introduced decontrol of rent at next change of tenancy.
1924	*Housing (Financial Provisions) Act (Wheatley Act).* Introduced a new, higher subsidy with mandatory rate contribution. Withdrawn in 1933.
1930	*Housing Act (Greenwood Act).* Intended to promote slum clearance; new subsidy calculated on the number of people rehoused from clearance areas. Permitted local authorities to operate rent rebates.
1933	*Housing (Financial Provisions) Act.* Withdrew subsidy for all new housing, except that for slum clearance replacement. All authorities required to produce five-year clearance plans.
1933	*Rent and Mortgage Interest Restrictions (Amendments) Act.* Extended decontrol.
1935	*Housing Act.* New subsidies to help with the relief of overcrowding. Local authorities required to operate one Housing Revenue Account, and permitted to pool rent and subsidies.
1936	*Housing Act.* Major consolidating Act.
1938	*Housing Act.* Introduced a single subsidy of £5 10s for slum clearance and relief of overcrowding.
1939	*Rent and Mortgage Interest Restriction Act.* Reintroduced rent control on all but the highest-value properties.

rent control and the subsequent introduction of subsidies must be seen as closely linked. By achieving their goal of rent control the rent strikers made certain of achieving the other goal of subsidies.

The struggle over Exchequer subsidies

For some years before 1914 pressure had been building up for the introduction of state financial assistance for working-class housing. In particular, the demand from such bodies as the Workmen's National Housing Council (WNHC) and the recently formed Labour Party was for subsidised council housing. Unsuccessful private members' Bills were introduced in 1912, 1913 and 1914 in an attempt to obtain some sort of subsidy (Wilding, 1972).

There has been some debate as to whether the war hastened or delayed the introduction of subsidies. Wilding (1972: 15), for instance, has argued that there is evidence of government proposals in 1914 to provide a subsidy. Byrne and Damer (1980), however, deny that there was any intention to develop public housing until the state was forced into it by the political situation that developed during the war.

Whatever the intentions of the prewar Liberal Government it was generally accepted by 1916 that some sort of state aid would have to be made available. Disputes about the nature of such a subsidy remained among government departments, and between them and the local authorities. Indeed, it was not even evident that the local authorities were to be the main recipients of assistance. Alternatives were available, and in view of the subsequent development of public housing the choice to be made among them was obviously an important one. A straightforward grant to private builders would have been a simple solution, avoiding the creation of a distinct public sector stock and its associated bureaucracy. This, however, was ruled out as politically unacceptable to the majority of the electorate. On the other hand, a precedent was set during the war for direct provision by central government; the Ministry of Munitions and the War Office built houses for their civilian workers (Swenarton, 1981: 19–62). However an extension of this was considered impractical for the needs of a nationwide housing programme in peacetime. The local authority option was commended by the fact that it was what the labour movement demanded, and there was the well established tradition of local responsibility for local services. Against it of course was the equally well established reluctance of local authorities to use ratepayers' money to build houses.

Within the cabinet, Addison, who headed the Ministry of Reconstruction, was the chief advocate of decisive state action. He wanted a duty to be placed on local authorities to build houses, and in this he was supported by the Salisbury Committee (Gilbert, 1970: 140–1). Addison was, however, opposed by the Local Government Board (LGB). Until he became President of the LGB in early 1919, and later the first Minister of Health, Addison was unable to make substantial progress in planning the housing programme. The result was that by the general election in November 1918 agreement had still not been reached with the local authorities on the nature of the proposed subsidy.

Government policy was to build half a million dwellings in three years, but the achievement of such a target required the cooperation of the local authorities, and they were insistent that their financial liability should be strictly limited. The local authorities were in a particularly strong position in relation to the government at this time. Fear of revolution and the salience of the housing question forced the government to act, but success was dependent upon the local authorities (Swenarton, 1981: 77–87). The authorities' cooperation was obtained by limiting their annual liability to the product of a penny rate. The balance between the income from rents and the cost of providing the houses was to be made up by the Exchequer. For once, the opposition of the Treasury was subordinated to what was perceived as the overriding need to preserve the country from Bolshevism. Fear, according to Orbach, acted as the constant stimulus directing government policy on housing at this time (Orbach, 1977: 49).

The Housing and Town Planning Act which introduced subsidies became law in July 1919. For the first time, local authorities were given a clear responsibility for housing provision, and also financial support by central government. The key government relationship in public housing, which was to last for more than 60 years, was forged in the turbulent days at the end of the First World War. This was not seen by those who passed it as implying a long-term subsidy policy. In 1918–19, government ministers saw the introduction of subsidies as a way of dealing with problems created by the war, and the form of assistance as a reflection of policy-making under difficult wartime conditions. The dominant view was that subsidised housebuilding was necessary only on a limited scale and for a limited time.

The main beliefs underlying this view of the policy were: (i) that the housing shortage was a by-product of the war, and therefore capable of being solved by a short concentrated burst of investment; (ii) that subsidies were necessary only to cover the expected period of inflation and readjustment before the return to normal market conditions; (iii) that improved housing was one specific demand by the working class which would have to be met by state intervention during the critical period of social and political instability after the war, but not permanently.

In practice, successive governments retained housing subsidies of one sort or another, so that by 1939 local authorities had built over 1 million dwellings, about 10 per cent of the total housing stock. The introduction of subsidies was important because it made possible this scale of building, and because it set the pattern of roles in which central government provided financial assistance and local authorities built and managed the dwellings. However no government has ever been, nor could ever be, content *merely* to provide financial support, leaving the authorities free to make all the decisions about what sort of service municipal housing was actually going to be. Throughout the period since 1919 council housing has been subject to continued attempts by central government to influence various aspects of policy and practice at the local level.

Housing standards and costs

The question of the standard of housing and costs incurred by the Exchequer was obviously a matter of concern to central government, especially at first when the subsidy system meant that local authorities' liability was fixed and the Exchequer was committed to bearing any additional deficit. In stark terms the local authorities had no incentive to economise; indeed, they were under pressure from the spokesmen and women for the working class in their areas to produce higher-quality housing than had normally been available before the war. On the other hand, the Treasury wanted to keep its expenditure down to a minimum.

However, the quality of houses produced at this time was distinctly better than the norm which operated before the war. Demands were articulated by the WNHC and others for three bedrooms, parlours, separate bathrooms and piped hot-water systems. Another important influence, which resulted in the marked changes in housing design and street layouts, came from the Garden City movement, and particularly from the architect Raymond Unwin. He was an established advocate of low-density housing, and as a leading member of the Tudor Walters Committee his ideas were incorporated into its report in 1918. This committee was set up by the LGB to examine ways of producing quickly and economically after the war. Unlike the LGB, however, the committee took a progressive line and produced recommendations based on the views that postwar housing should be built to improve standards. Its report was 'the first comprehensive treatise on the political technical and practical issues involved in the design of the small house, and in the housing debates of 1918/19, its authority became almost unquestionable' (Swenarton, 1981: 137). The Tudor Walters Report contained recommendations about estate layout and model house plans which were to become the basis of an official Housing Manual issued to local authorities in 1919. Guidance was given to local authorities on minimum room sizes as well as provision of cooking and heating arrangements and general design matters. The message of the Tudor Walters Report was that careful design was a better way of saving money than lowering standards, but most local authorities had no substantial experience in housing design and construction. An elaborate administrative apparatus was quickly set up within the newly created Ministry of Health to guide and regulate activity at local level. There were 11 regional housing commissioners appointed to oversee the programme in England and Wales alone, and authorities had to obtain approval at several stages in each scheme. Swenarton (1981: 93) comments that 'whereas before 1914 Whitehall had exercised only a limited influence over the provision and design of municipal housing, under the system adopted for the implementation of the 1919 Act a local authority had to obtain the approval of the Ministry of Health (either at central or regional level) for every aspect of its housing scheme'.

The cost of housing turned out to be a major problem immediately after the war. Before 1914 working-class houses had been built for under £250 each, but by 1920 average tender prices for council houses reached £930 (Swenarton, 1981: 129), with actual completion prices of £1200 (Swenarton, 1981: 122). After October 1920 prices began to fall, but they remained high for all Addison Act houses. Prices were high generally as a result of inflation during a brief postwar economic boom, and local authorities were required to compete in the open market for scarce materials and skilled labour. Central government intervention was restricted to provision of subsidy and did not extend to control over the use of resources. Although public housing had a high political priority the government took no effective steps to ensure that councils had priority access to bricks and bricklayers.

A further problem concerned access to capital. Progress with building projects and the number of houses to be built was determined by the authorities' ability to borrow the necessary money. High prices meant more borrowing, but again the government failed to help. If the Treasury had supplied the funds by borrowing on behalf of local authorities it would have ensured a more even flow of capital at lower interest rates, but such help was firmly withheld. In general, local authorities were left to raise capital as best they could, although this resulted in delays and high interest rates. The rapidly escalating cost of housing inevitably led to charges of extravagance on the part of local authorities, and the problem of costs was used as the pretext for cutting short the housing programme in July 1921. A Departmental Committee on the High Cost of Building Working Class Dwellings reported in 1921, and it is worth quoting Marian Bowley's comments on it:

> It seems clear . . . from the Report that the Ministry of Health failed to exercise sufficient control over the types of houses built and the layout of estates. The Report pointed out that the Ministry had not prevented the local authorities selecting more elaborate models and more expensive layouts than seemed necessary . . . The local authorities on the other hand, were only too apt to make use of the freedom from effective control to select the expensive types of plans and layouts. Nor did they in general display any obvious interest in trying to secure economy in building either by insisting on the use of the cheaper type of materials or by general supervision of their contracts to secure cost reductions. The Committee absolved the local authorities of charges of spectacular extravagance or gross inefficiency. It seems that apart from the basic problem of lack of control of the market, the Ministry of Health did not display sufficient determination or imagination in exercising its powers in circumstances in which the type of subsidy made central control particularly necessary. It seems reasonably certain, however, that the lack of financial incentives to economy on the part of local authorities raised new and difficult problems of administration (Bowley, 1945: 34–5)

The ability of the Ministry to exercise detailed scrutiny and control was very severely weakened when in 1921/2 all the regional commissioners' offices were closed and total numbers of staff working on housing were substantially reduced. Thereafter, in the period up to the outbreak of the Second World War, the Ministry was much less able to intervene directly on a day-to-day basis, although its influence was keenly felt in other ways. For instance, Merrett quotes figures for the average floor area for three-bedroomed council houses, which show that the biggest dwellings were produced in the early part of the Addison programme, and that even before its demise standards had been cut (Merrett, 1979: 322). Throughout the rest of the interwar period average floor areas never approached the figures achieved in 1919/20. It was not just that overall floor areas fell. but also that more non-parlour houses and more two-bedroomed houses were built. Increased densities, lower standards of layout and design and cheaper finishes were all employed as ways of saving money. In 1927 and 1929 the Conservative Government issued circulars calling on all authorities to concentrate on building the cheapest type of house.

Nevertheless, the Chamberlain and Wheatley Act houses built in the 1920s were still good dwellings. It was later, after 1930, that standards really fell. Another circular in January 1932 renewed the government exhortation to local authorities to build small houses, and during the 1930s more blocks of flats were built. The standard of accommodation and general residential environment provided in these blocks of flats was reminiscent of the nineteenth-century model dwellings, and far inferior to the spacious, leafy cottage estates of the early 1920s.

It is a clear indicator of the political importance attached to housing in 1918–20 that despite high costs good-quality houses were produced. After 1920, in the long period of high unemployment which lasted until 1940, housebuilding costs were generally low, but compared with the years up to 1920 the power of organised labour was weak and, instead of low costs resulting in increased output and improved quality, the opposite happened. Whereas in 1920 the average tender price for a three-bedroomed house was nearly £900, by 1932 the figure had fallen to £295 (Merrett, 1979: 322). Falling costs encouraged central government to cut back the level of subsidies.

Subsidies and the function of council housing

In addition to the issue of quality, central government also had an interest in the quantity of local authority housing production. Local authorities were given considerable freedom to decide the levels of capital expenditure on housing. While there was no direct control over capital expenditure, central government was able to influence what local authorities did by raising or lowering subsidies. It is important to remember that local authorities have never been given extensive *duties* in relation to housing provision. From 1919 the duty placed on them was to review housing need in their area and to submit plans for building, but the local authorities have always had a high level of autonomy to decide how much housing they should provide. In general, if a local authority proposed to build houses and could show that design standards were acceptable, then central government automatically gave loan sanction and subsidy approval.

In the absence of direct controls over capital programmes, the manipulation of subsidy levels quickly assumed importance as the mechanism by which central government raised or lowered output, and by which it could channel local authority housing towards certain needs groups, such as people rehoused from slum clearance areas. It has already been mentioned that the generous 1919 subsidy reflected both the political situation and the insistence of the local authorities that to achieve a target of half a million houses they required that their liability be fixed at a 1*d* rate.

The Addison programme was aborted by central government refusal, in July 1921, to subsidise any more than 170 000 council houses, that is those that were already contracted to be built. The new subsidy introduced by the Conservative Government in 1923 avoided the open-ended Treasury commitment and gave the local authorities £6 per house per year for 20 years, with no requirement that there should be a rate fund contribution. This was really designed to limit municipal activity and to encourage private builders, who could also claim subsidy on houses that reached certain minimum standards and were defined as for the working class. In the case of this Act, it was necessary for a local authority that wanted to build houses first to demonstrate to the Ministry that private builders could not meet the need of the area (this provision was in fact removed by the 1924 Housing (Financial Provisions) Act).

Although the 1923 Act was not repealed until 1929, only 75 900 local authority dwellings were built, compared with 362 000 subsidised private houses. Whereas the 1923 Act set out to limit local authority housing, the 1924 Act was intended to establish a long-term high level of investment, and in fact some 505 000 council houses were built under its provisions. John Wheatley, the first Labour Minister of Health, hoped that ultimately municipal housing would completely replace private renting as the tenure for the working class; that is, he was operating with a long-term view of council housing, quite different from the ideas of the previous Coalition and Conservative governments that state provision was a temporary expedient. Accordingly, Wheatley sought to increase output, first by a 50 per cent increase in subsidy (to £9 in urban areas and £12 10*s* in rural areas) which would be payable for 40 years rather than 20. Local authorities were required to make a contribution from the rates of up to half the Exchequer subsidy (the rates contribution varied according to the level of private rents in the area, see below) so that in total the assistance given to tenants could be more than twice that available under the 1923 Act. Second, the Act set up aggregate production targets for the years up to 1936, and payment of subsidy to individual authorities could be withheld if total output fell below these levels.

Although the Labour Government of 1924 was quickly replaced by a Conservative administration which lasted until 1929, the Wheatley Act remained in operation and proved effective in stimulating local authorities to build in large quantities. Falling building costs and antipathy to public housing led the government to cut subsidy levels in 1927 and 1929, although the Wheatley subsidy was restored by Labour when the party returned to power in 1929.

During the 1920s the subsidy system was used to encourage local authorities to build houses that would increase the aggregate size of the stock. Very little was done to tackle the problem of unfit housing – only 11 000 slum dwellings were demolished in the period 1918–30. It was known too that housing subsidies had in practice helped the better-off workers because the rents of council houses built in the 1920s remained beyond the reach of the poor. In 1930, therefore, the Labour Government attempted to nudge local authorities into helping poorer families in bad conditions by introducing a new form of subsidy related to the number of people rehoused from slum clearance schemes. Associated with this policy was a requirement that all but the smallest housing authorities should produce five-year slum clearance programmes. The idea of making local authorities operate with a five-year programme of work was new, and represented an attempt by the Ministry to persuade authorities into a more organised approach, and it gave the centre a clearer picture of local requirements and progress.

The slum clearance subsidy in the 1930 Housing Act was to operate alongside the Wheatley subsidy and represented an additional element in housing policy, confirming Labour as the party of municipal housing. However the depression in trade and the formation of the National Government in 1931 foreshadowed a major change of policy. An official Committee on Local Expenditure reported in 1932 with a recommendation that the Wheatley Act subsidy should be withdrawn on the grounds that public expenditure should be cut, and that economic circumstances made it possible for private builders to provide for general housing need. New local authority building, except for slum clearance purposes, ceased to be welcomed by the Ministry, and in 1933 the Housing (Financial Provisions) Act repealed the Wheatley subsidy. In future, the only new local authority housing to receive subsidy would be that built to rehouse families from the slums, and again local authorities were to produce five-year plans for slum clearance. Bowley (1945: 47) comments that this was 'in practice the end of attempts to increase or improve the supply of houses for ordinary working class families' and that 'the Government had gone as near to rejecting responsibility for working class housing as it could' (Bowley, 1945: 140).

In terms of the analysis of central–local relations, the point here is that in 1933 central government took the effective measure of stopping the general needs subsidy as a way of imposing the view that the function of public housing should be to rehouse the poor, leaving the private market to provide for the rest of the population. By its control of this powerful lever on local authority practice, central government was able to limit the scope of public housing and to return to a pre-1914 type of sanitary policy, albeit with a subsidy which would ensure that some slum clearance and rehousing was actually carried out. As a result of this change of central government policy, council housing built in the 1930s was physically inferior and socially less respectable than the estates of the 1920s (Community Development Project, 1976: 16). Altogether, some 273 000 dwellings were built in the 1930s to rehouse people from clearance areas, and 24 000 were built after 1935 specifically to relieve overcrowding.

Rents and rebates

The question of rents was of course central to the whole development of public housing: the very reason that private builders had abandoned working-class housing was largely that the consumers could not afford economic rents. Exchequer subsidies were introduced in order to make it possible for new houses to be let at rents that the workers could afford. The decision as to just what tenants could afford to pay thus became an important one from the Treasury point of view. However local authorities had in practice a good deal of control over the levels of rent charged on individual houses.

To return the 1919 Act, the assumption was that subsidy would be necessary only until conditions returned to 'normal', and this was expected to come about by 1927. Until 1927, rents were to be fixed in relation to controlled rents of similar houses, bearing in mind the class of tenant for whom the houses were provided, the difference between that level and actual costs being made up by subsidy. After 1927 it was expected that rents could be set at a more economic level. In addition to scrutinising house plans the regional commissioners were responsible for approving rent levels. This involvement in rent levels was presumably made necessary because of the deficit subsidy system in the 1919 Act. (Under later Acts, when the subsidy level was fixed, central government had less interest in rent levels.) Despite the high level of subsidy, rents were set which tended to preclude low-income families. Swenarton (1981: 175) quotes 11s per week for a three-bedroomed non-parlour house in London at Old Oak, and 15s 6d at Roehampton, both exclusive of rates. Both figures were well above average controlled rents in urban areas.

In the case of the Chamberlain Act, rents were again relatively high, because although prices had fallen from the peak in 1920 the subsidy was low and fixed. Under the Wheatley Act the situation was rather more complicated: the rates subsidy was to be related to the amount needed to keep average rents down to the equivalent of controlled private rents, but the rents of individual houses were decided by the local authority. As costs continued to fall it was possible to reduce the rents of new houses, despite cuts in subsidy, but nevertheless Bowley (1945: 129) concludes that:

There is really no doubt about how rent policy worked out in practice. The market for local authority houses was largely confined to a limited range of income groups, that is, in practice the better-off families, the small clerks, the artisans, the better-off semi-skilled workers with small families and fairly safe jobs. Right up to the economy campaign of 1932, and even later, it was these families who absorbed most of the houses.

Attempts by central government to persuade local authorities to build smaller, cheaper houses represented one response to the rents problem in the late 1920s. In 1930, Greenwood's Housing Act required local authorities to set 'reasonable' rents and gave them the power to operate rent-rebate schemes; that is, some tenants would pay less, at the expense of others who would pay more. Pressure on local authorities to operate differential rent schemes began to mount, and in 1932 the Committee on Local Expenditure argued that public money should not be 'wasted' on subsidies for tenants who could afford an economic rent. The Committee believed that subsidies should be concentrated on providing lower rents for the poor. Circulars to local authorities in 1933 urged them to adopt this policy, but, 'a very large proportion of local authorities ignored the Ministry of Health's advice on the rent problem' (Bowley, 1945: 125). Why? First, it was not really in the interests of local authorities to seek out the poorest families in the population to occupy their houses; from the point of view of a landlord, better-off tenants are an easier proposition. Second, differential renting was highly unpopular among tenants, many of whom saw it as quite unfair that their rents should be increased to help others, whom they probably regarded as less deserving anyway. Third, an essential ingredient of such schemes was the use of means tests, even on tenants who were proud to be able to avoid the hated means test applied by the Public Assistance Board.

Local authorities had wide discretion in the area of differential rents; they were free both to decide whether to have a rebate scheme or not, and to devise the details of any scheme that was introduced. The available evidence suggests that large urban authorities with major slum clearance programmes were most likely to operate differential rents, but in only a few cases were rebates available to all tenants, the majority being confined to families from clearance areas (Parker, 1967: 40). In Leeds, for example, a comprehensive rebate scheme was introduced in 1934, with higher rents for some but allowing that the poorer tenants would pay no rent at all, whereas most other schemes required a basic minimum payment (Ravetz, 1974: 36–9). The Leeds initiative met fierce opposition from Conservatives on the council and from tenants themselves, resulting in the threat of rent strikes and defeat for Labour in the 1935 municipal elections (Finnegan, 1980). However it was a Conservative rebate scheme that in Birmingham in 1939 caused the largest and most successful council tenants' rent strike in the interwar years (Schifferes, 1976: 64–71). Here the intention was to raise basic rents, to induce better-off tenants to leave the public sector, and to provide rebates for the poor. The rent strike and the approach of the war resulted in the postponement and ultimate abandonment of the scheme.

In 1935 the government pursued its interest in rent-rebate schemes by introducing an important change in the rules covering council housing accounts procedures. Hitherto the accounts related to houses built under each Act had to be kept separate, and each account had to balance. The 1935 Housing Act required that, in future, authorities should consolidate all accounts into one Housing Revenue Account, which must balance annually. One advantage in this change was that rents could be related to use-value rather than being tied to the highly varied actual production costs. In the long run this was to become very important as a way of keeping down the rents of new houses, which could be subsidised by surpluses generated on cheaper, old houses, but this particular benefit resulted from inflation and was certainly not foreseen at the time. The real reason for the measure was consolidation of subsidies as a way of facilitating rebates: subsidies could be pooled to form a resource to fund rebates to poorer tenants, the rest paying full economic rents. Nevertheless local reluctance to introduce rebate schemes persisted, and by 1939 only a small proportion of authorities were operating them.

The rebates issue is an important one in that it illustrates how local authorities resisted central government policy, and it points up the question of whether it is better to subsidise houses or tenants. From the point of view of central government, beset by the perpetual Treasury preoccupation with public expenditure, it was obviously better to withdraw subsidy from the more affluent tenants – in effect to make them subsidise the poor rather than taxpayers doing so.

Conclusion

This chapter has demonstrated the importance of the period 1914–39 in establishing a housing policy that was concerned with aspects of quality, quantity and price. Local authorities played a key role in the implementation of policy throughout the period, within the framework of objectives established by central government. Those objectives changed considerably over time, reflecting developments in the political and economic context, and it is important to understand how council housing in the 1930s was developing in quite different directions to those that had been dominant in the first postwar decade. Local authorities were being manoeuvred towards a more residual role, leaving general needs provision to the private sector.

However, despite central government's attempt to influence local authority behaviour, there were key aspects, such as housing allocation and management, and rents policy, in which there remained substantial local discretion.

4

The Changing Emphasis of Housing Policy, 1945–79

By 1939, Britain had a framework of housing policy in a recognisably modern form, and state intervention of various kinds was beginning to look permanent, if not enthusiastic. Housing conditions were on the whole substantially better than they had been at the end of the First World War; the stock of dwellings, for instance, had increased by more than 40 per cent, largely as a result of new building for home ownership and municipal renting, the emergent tenure forms of the twentieth century. The building boom of the 1930s meant that by the outbreak of war there was a crude numerical balance between households and dwellings. However, over the next six years, there was a marked worsening in the situation. Mobilisation for the war effort meant an immediate halt to slum clearance, and after completion of schemes already under construction in September 1939 there was virtually no new building for the duration of the war (Merrett, 1979: 320). The existing stock suffered badly from the effects of bombing and neglect. Altogether, some 450 000 dwellings were destroyed or made uninhabitable in the air raids, and a further 3 million were estimated to be damaged to a lesser extent. Labour and materials for housing repair and maintenance were in short supply and priority was given to work on war-damaged property. This shrinkage and deterioration of the stock took place alongside a growth of about 1 million in the population, and must be seen against the wider background of a burgeoning popular demand for social reform which gained strength from the summer of 1940 (Addison, 1977: 104) and culminated in Labour's massive election victory in July 1945. Thus the war ended with the new Labour Government facing a serious housing problem, amongst all the other difficulties of social and economic reconstruction. It is from this point that this chapter takes up the development of housing policy. The account begins with an overview, followed by consideration of some key elements in the central–local relationship, as a way of focusing the analysis.

An overview of housing policy, 1945–79

There are several points that need to be made to sketch in the overall shape of developments in housing and housing policy since the Second World War. First, throughout the period, housing has rarely been far from the centre of domestic political debate. A series of issues have maintained the salience of housing in British politics, and both Conservative and Labour governments have been vigorous legislators on housing; there has been at least one major housing Act in every Parliament since 1945 (see Table 4.1). In some ways there have been substantial areas of broad interparty consensus. For example, the significant role of public housing was generally accepted by Conservative governments until after the 1979 election, and Labour has come to accept that owner-occupation is now the dominant form of tenure, catering for large numbers of households in all levels of society. On the other hand, Labour governments have tended to encourage building by local authorities and to rely more on the public sector to achieve policy objectives, while Conservative governments have run down local authority production and emphasised the contribution of the private sector.

Second, for almost 25 years after the war, there was general agreement that there was a need for high levels of housing construction, in order to eliminate shortage, to remove the slums and to provide for a growing population. Estimates varied quite widely as to the precise dimensions of the housing problem, but governments of both parties were intent on reducing it by major building programmes. Production targets and 'the numbers game' became a familiar part of the politics of housing in the 1950s and 1960s. It is a sign of changing political and economic circumstances that housebuilding targets have ceased to be a measure of ministerial virility, and have therefore disappeared altogether.

An important feature of the period of high production was the contribution made by the local authorities (Figure 4.1). Whereas in the 20 years between the wars local authorities in Great Britain built just over 1.3 million dwellings, well under half the total achieved in the private sector, in the 20 years after 1945 they built over 2.9 million dwellings, approaching a million *more* than the private sector. Thus, after the Second World War, the local authorities consistently built at a much higher level numerically than they had been accustomed to up to 1939, and overall their contribution was proportionately significantly greater. In addition to local authority construction at a high level, the postwar period was notable for the development of new towns, in which non-elected new town development corporations built substantial proportions of public housing.

However within this period of high-output policy there were three distinct phases. From 1945 to 1953 the dominant objective was to increase the supply of dwellings, and slum clearance was held in abeyance. This was also a period when, as a result of the Labour Government's policy, local authorities

Table 4.1   *Principal housing legislation, 1945–77*

1946	*Housing (Financial and Miscellaneous Provisions) Act.* Raised level of subsidies and rate fund contributions.
1949	*Housing Act.* Removed statutory restriction which limited public housing to 'the working classes'. Introduced improvement grants.
1952	*Housing Act.* Raised subsidies.
1954	*Housing Repairs and Rents Act.* Restarted slum clearance and encouraged private sector improvement. Introduced '12 point standard' for improvement.
1956	*Housing Subsidies Act.* Reduced subsidies for general needs housing. Rate fund contributions made optional. Subsidy structure encouraged high-rise building.
1957	*Housing Act.* Major consolidating Act.
1957	*Rent Act.* A measure to begin decontrol of rents at next change of tenancy.
1958	*Housing (Financial Provisions) Act.* Consolidating Act for financial matters.
1959	*House Purchase and Housing Act.* Extended improvement grant system. Encouraged local authority mortgage lending.
1961	*Housing Act.* Reintroduced subsidy for general needs housing, but at two rates.
1964	*Housing Act.* Extended improvement grants. Established the Housing Corporation
1965	*Rent Act.* Introduced 'fair rents'.
1967	*Housing Subsidies Act.* Introduced a new subsidy system. More generous to local authorities.
1968	*Rent Act.* A consolidating Act.
1969	*Housing Act.* Raised level of improvement grants and introduced 'general improvement areas'.
1971	*Housing Act.* Increased rate of improvement grants in assisted areas.
1972	*Housing Finance Act.* Introduced fair rents for council tenants and replaced all existing subsidies with a new deficit subsidy system. Housing revenue accounts now permitted to generate a surplus. Introduced a mandatory rent-rebate scheme.
1974	*Housing Act.* Introduced housing action areas and expanded the role of the Housing Corporation.
1974	*Rent Act.* Gave security of tenure to tenants in furnished dwellings.
1975	*Housing Rents and Subsidies Act.* Fair rents abandoned in the council sector. Rebate scheme retained. New interim subsidy arrangements to replace 1972 Act provisions.
1977	*Housing (Homeless Persons) Act.* Placed a duty on local housing authorities to provide accommodation for homeless households in certain priority needs groups.

dominated housing construction: in 1945–51 over 80 per cent of all new dwellings were built by local authorities. The Conservatives continued with encouragement for local authority housing only until their target of 300 000 houses per year was achieved in 1953. The second phase began in 1954 and lasted until 1964. Within the continuing objective of high output, the Conservatives inverted the contributions made by the public and private sectors. Local authority completions in Great Britain fell by more than 50 per cent between 1954 and 1961 from 223 731 to 105 529, and, as private production expanded, council housing was maintained at roughly the level needed to achieve a total of 300 000 dwellings per year (Merrett, 1979: 248).

In the overall context of postwar housing policy in Britain, the mid-1950s represent the most important period of reorientation, in which the private sector was set free and given the dominant role in housing provision, while the local authorities were set on a course towards a much more limited role. In 1954, the government finally removed the licensing system which had constrained private building since the outbreak of the Second World War. It also introduced legislation relaunching the slum clearance programme, which had been in abeyance since 1939. This clearly signalled that private builders were expected to meet general housing need, while local authorities concentrated on slum clearance and associated rehousing. In 1956, the subsidy system was changed so as to reinforce the local authority focus on slum clearance; henceforth there was to be no subsidy for general needs housing, except for one-bedroom dwellings for the elderly. In 1955, the government changed its approach to local authority rents and urged adoption of 'realistic' (i.e. higher) rents, especially for older, interwar dwellings. Alongside the general increase in rents, local authorities were exhorted to introduce or extend rent-rebate schemes, designed to channel subsidy towards the least well off tenants. This change in rent policy marked the beginning of a trend towards council rents more closely related to market rent levels, with greater reliance on means-tested assistance, which has continued since that time (Malpass, 1990). The final element of policy reorientation in the mid-1950s was the relaxation of rent control in the private sector, introduced in the 1957 Rent Act. Like the 1923 Act, this immediately decontrolled rents at the top of the market and introduced creeping decontrol lower down.

Housing policy from 1945 to 1964 was very similar to policy between the wars. In the first decade after each world war there was concentration on reducing the severe housing shortage which was partly created by the war. Only after a period of about 10 years in each case did the question of slum clearance reemerge, at which point the local authorities were edged out of general needs housing, leaving the field clear for the private sector. Another striking similarity is that, in the years immediately after each war, when the shortage was most severe and the economy was most disrupted, the quality of new local authority housing was highest. In both periods, the quality of new public sector output fell as policy shifted away from general needs

Figure 4.1 *Dwellings completed in the United Kingdom, 1945–80*

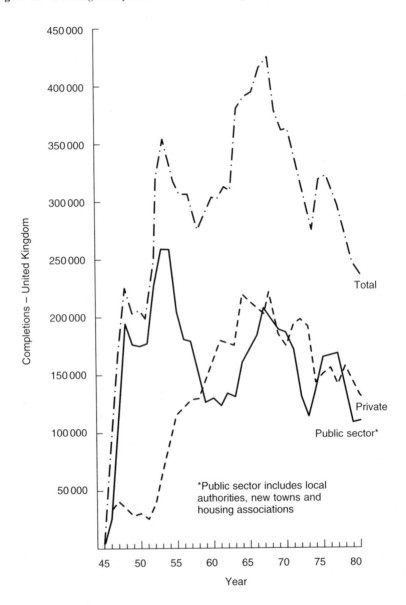

Sources: *Annual Abstract of Statistics* and *Housing and Construction Statistics*.

towards slum clearance replacement. This raises the very interesting question of why governments should choose to build the best houses at the most difficult times, and to reduce standards later on, when the position had eased. The explanation lies in the way in which the two world wars disrupted the economy, creating an aftermath of very difficult market conditions from the point of view of capital, while at the same time giving a considerable, if temporary, political advantage to the working class. After each war there was a demand for more and better housing, at reasonable rents, a demand which private enterprise could not satisfy. In these circumstances, the state intervened to ensure a supply of new housing. The quality of this housing reflected the political and economic power of organised skilled labour – the better-off working class, as distinct from the poor.

The third phase of the high-output period lasted only from 1964 to 1968, covering the years when the Wilson Government aimed for half a million houses per year by 1970. This level of production was to be achieved by expansion of the public sector, but only to a situation of broad parity of output with the private sector. There was to be no return to the policy of the 1940s, and the extent to which Labour housing policy had changed was revealed in the 1965 White Paper:

> Once the country has overcome its huge social problem of slumdom and obsolescence and met the need of the great cities for more houses to let at moderate rents, the programme of subsidised council housing should decrease. The expansion of the public programme now proposed is to meet exceptional needs: it is born partly of a short-term necessity, partly of the conditions inherent in modern urban life. The expansion of building for owner-occupation on the other hand is normal; it reflects a long-term social advance which should gradually pervade every region. (Great Britain, 1965)

For a brief period total output did expand, exceeding 400 000 in both 1967 and 1968, but wider economic problems led the government to cut back the building programme as part of the package of public expenditure reductions which followed the devaluation of sterling in November 1967. Public sector completions fell away sharply after 1968, reaching a low of 88 000 in 1973. Along with the decline of public sector housebuilding there was a run-down in slum clearance activity (English, Madigan and Norman, 1976: ch. 2), foreshadowed in the White Paper of 1968, *Old Houses into New Homes*, which really marked the end of the period of high levels of construction and the beginning of a shift towards rehabilitation and improvement of existing dwellings. The new emphasis on improvement rather than redevelopment was reflected in the 1969 Housing Act which introduced general improvement areas, and the 1974 Housing Act which added housing action areas. In these areas, systematic rehabilitation and environmental improvement were to be carried out, stimulated by higher levels of grant aid, in order to prevent the need for demolition and rebuilding. Although presented as a switch of resources, it has been shown subsequently that the new policy represented a major reduction in public investment in housing over the next five years or so (Merrett, 1979).

The retreat from the aspirations of 1965 and the abandonment of high-output policy can be explained in terms of wider economic problems, but it was a policy change the implementation of which was lubricated by a genuine easing of the overall shortage. As Table 4.2 shows, the total number of dwellings was broadly equivalent to the number of households by the late 1960s, and ministers were able to present the national housing shortage as over; what remained was a series of 'local shortages'.

In addition, there was growing public resentment of the damage that large-scale redevelopment was inflicting upon settled urban communities (Dennis, 1970, 1972), and the new high-rise industrialised housing was being revealed as expensive, unsatisfactory and unpopular (Gittus, 1976). In these circumstances a slowing down of new housing production was not a serious political liability. Labour did engineer a revival of public sector building in 1974–6, but, since then, completions have dropped to the lowest levels since the 1920s.

During the 1970s, issues of finance came to replace production in dominating the politics of housing. The main reason for this development was the impact of inflation and rising interest rates on government assistance with housing costs in both the public and owner-occupied sectors. The level of subsidy on new council houses had been raised in 1967, and in the owner-occupied category assistance in the form of tax relief on mortgage interest tended to rise as a result of growing numbers of mortgagors. But, in particular, public attention was focused on the cost of tax relief by the unprecedented rise in house prices in 1972/3 (Boddy, 1980: 181), and by the increase in the mortgage interest rate from 8 per cent in 1971 to 11 per cent in 1973. In the period 1967/8 to 1976/7 total relief to mortgagors rose by 146 per cent in real terms, and on the same basis subsidies in the public sector rose by 107 per cent (Lansley, 1979: 144). These increases, which took place against the background of falling completions of new houses, not surpris-

Table 4.2   *Households and dwellings in England and Wales, 1951–76 (thousands)*

	1951	1961	1971	1976
Total dwellings	12 530	14 646	17 024	18 100
Total households	13 259	14 724	16 779	17 600
Deficiency (−) or surplus (+)	−729	−78	+245	+500

Sources: 1951–71: *Housing Policy Technical Volume Pt 1* (HMSO, 1977) p. 15, table 1.5; 1976: *Housing Policy,* Cmnd 6851 (HMSO, 1977) p. 10.

ingly raised questions about the wisdom of the Exchequer paying out larger and larger sums on what was seen as unproductive expenditure.

The Heath Government's Housing Finance Act of 1972 attempted to deal with the problem of subsidies in the public sector, but left assistance to owner-occupiers untouched. When Labour returned to power in 1974, this Act was largely repealed, but the continuing need to reform housing finance was recognised in the establishment of a housing finance review, later broadened into a housing policy review. This review eventually led to the publication of the Green Paper on housing policy in June 1977 (Great Britain, 1977a). The outcome of two years' study was widely regarded as an insipid document (Harloe, 1978), reflecting perhaps the weakness of the government's parliamentary position at the time. The nettle of thorough-going reform of housing finance was not grasped; no major changes were proposed for the private sector, although a new system of council house subsidies was outlined and included in the Housing Bill which fell with the Labour Government in May 1979.

An important factor inhibiting reform of financial assistance for owner-occupiers is the fear of the electoral consequences, given that more than half of all households are now in this form of tenure. This brings us to the third point, which is to note that the restructuring of the tenure system which began in the 1920s has continued since 1945, as Table 4.3 makes clear.

This way of looking at the postwar period highlights the secular decline of the private rented sector, largely due to redevelopment and sale for owner-occupation, despite attempts such as the 1957 Rent Act to revive investment by progressive rent decontrol. The public sector just about doubled as a proportion of the total stock in the period 1945 to 1956, but its rate of growth has been much lower since then, and council house sales now exceed new completions, causing a net loss to the sector as a whole.

The restructuring of the tenure system is closely related to government policy which, over many years, has shown strengthening bipartisan support

Table 4.3 *Housing tenure in Great Britain, 1945–79 (percentages of all households)*

	Public rented	Owner-occupied	Private rented*
1945	12	26	62
1951	18	29	53
1961	27	43	31
1969	30	49	21
1971	30.8	52.7	16.5
1979	31.9	54.6	13.5

Note: * Including housing associations.
Sources: 1945–61. M. Boddy, *The Building Societies* (Macmillan, 1980); 1969–79: *Housing and Construction. Statistics 1969–79* (HMSO 1980).

for owner-occupation. There has been systematic encouragement to households to become owner-occupiers, specifically in the form of ways of reducing the cost of home ownership for low-income families (for example, the option mortgage introduced in 1967, the savings-bonus-and-loans scheme in 1978, and the 'right to buy' for council tenants in 1980). More generally, home ownership has been presented as 'normal', 'natural' and 'deeply satisfying'. On the other hand, council housing has been manoeuvred into an increasingly residual role by measures designed to restrict investment and to concentrate on the needs of those groups not catered for by the private sector. Rising rents and inducements to buy have also contributed to the residualisation process.

A feature of changes in the tenure system since 1974 has been the development of housing associations as a 'third arm' of housing, an alternative for people unable or unwilling to enter the two main tenures. Housing associations received their biggest boost in 1974 when the Housing Corporation was expanded and given more resources to fund their activities. For several years housing associations grew rapidly, providing new and renovated accommodation to let at fair rents. Completions of new dwellings rose from 8800 in 1973 to 25 000 in 1977, but fell away again by 1979.

Finally, it is necessary to set all this against the background of real improvements in housing conditions generally (Great Britain, 1977a: ch. 3) and worsening economic difficulties in the decades since the war. Attempts to explain changes in housing policy, in particular the growing unwillingness of successive governments to continue to support high levels of investment and subsidy in the public sector, need to take these factors into account.

Housing standards and costs

One of the most visually striking features of postwar public housing is its variety. Compared with prewar estates there is much greater variation in layout, form, density and finishing materials. Standards of space and amenity within the dwellings also vary according to the date of construction. One factor that helps to explain this variation is that local authorities have made greater use of architects to design housing schemes, and have been encouraged to do so, at least since the early 1960s (Great Britain, 1961: 7).

However, over time, the major influence on standards and form has been changes in central government policy. Whereas the Tudor Walters Report set the standards for local authority housing between the wars, it was the Dudley Report of 1944 that provided local authorities with guidance as to the minimum acceptable standards after the Second World War. The Dudley Report (a product of the Central Housing Advisory Committee) followed the same basic approach that had been adopted in the Tudor Walters Report, and framed its recommendations about house design in terms of minimum room sizes and adequate circulation space. By adopting these recommendations as the minima to be achieved if houses were to qualify for subsidy, central government was able to raise standards and exert its influence over local authorities, while leaving them free to have their own schemes designed within this framework.

In practice, the Dudley Committee's recommended minimum of 900 square feet for a three-bedroomed house was on average comfortably exceeded during the whole of the period of the Labour Government up to 1951. The council houses of the 1940s were much more expensive than those built in the 1930s, partly because of inflation and partly because of improved standards; a quarter of the increased cost was attributed to higher standards (Cullingworth, 1966: 113). These dwellings remain the most spacious council houses ever built, averaging over 1000 square feet, compared with 800 square feet in 1939, and just over 900 square feet in the 1950s. In defence of the emphasis on quality during the difficult period of postwar reconstruction, the Labour Minister of Health, Aneurin Bevan, is quoted as saying in 1946, 'While we shall be judged for a year or two by the *number* of houses we build, we shall be judged in ten years' time by the *type* of houses we build' (Foot, 1973: 82).

In the 1990s the houses built in the Bevan era remain considerably more popular with tenants and less trouble to local authorities than a lot of the dwellings built later when central government pursued cost savings through reduced standards. The Conservatives in 1951–3 moved towards the overall production target of 300 000 dwellings by maintaining high output in the public sector. However costs were rising and the balance of payments was in difficulty, and lower standards were specified for council houses. Government circulars and Supplements to the Housing Manual urged local authorities to economise by building smaller houses at higher density. The so-called 'people's house' produced by this new attitude was achieved by what Merrett calls a 'brutal reduction in standards' (Merrett, 1979: 246). Unit costs fell as a result of this policy throughout most of the 1950s, and by 1959 the average floor area for a new three-bedroomed house had fallen to 897 square feet.

In 1959 the Central Housing Advisory Committee appointed a Committee under Sir Parker Morris 'to consider the standards of design and equipment applicable to family dwellings and other forms of accommodation whether provided by local authorities or by private enterprise, and to make recommendations'. The Parker Morris Report, *Homes for Today and Tomorrow*, published in 1961, took the increase in living standards since 1944 as the main reason for revising the specification of new housing. The report's main proposals referred to space (including storage) and heating within the home. Criticising current practice, the Committee said, 'Homes are being built at the present time which not only are too small to provide adequately for family life but also are too small to hold the possessions in which so much of the new affluence is expressed' (Great Britain, 1961: 2).

A large number of recommendations were made with the intention of improving the size, comfort and convenience of new houses, but in one important respect this committee departed from its predecessors; whereas both the Tudor Walters and Dudley committees had specified minimum room sizes, the Parker Morris approach was to state minimum overall floor areas, leaving the designer greater freedom in devising plans to meet particular needs.

Houses built to Parker Morris standards were obviously going to be more expensive, and although the Ministry commended the Report to local authorities there was at first no move to make the new standards mandatory. However, by 1965, about half the new local authority houses then being designed incorporated either the space or heating standards or both (Great Britain, 1965). It was not until after the 1967 Housing Subsidies Act that Parker Morris standards were required as a qualification for subsidy, and this part of the Act did not come into effect until 1969. Nevertheless average overall floor areas rose consistently during the 1960s, but then fell back slightly after 1970, and at no time did they approach the level achieved in the 1940s although in other respects Parker Morris houses represented a real advance in specification (Merrett, 1979: 322).

It was made quite clear in *Homes for Today and Tomorrow* that the proposed standards were minima, to be exceeded wherever possible. However, when these standards became mandatory, it was in conjunction with a new device, the Housing Cost Yardstick, which specified expenditure ceilings. To obtain sanction and subsidy, a local authority had to demonstrate to the central department that its proposed dwellings conformed to both Parker Morris standards and the Housing Cost Yardstick. The designer was thus in a situation where he had to achieve certain rather exacting, minimum standards, within the limits imposed by the Yardstick, and at a time when rising inflation was beginning to make Yardstick figures obsolete very quickly. There was a pincer effect in which the designer was squeezed from both above and below. What happened as a result was that, first, Parker Morris standards soon ceased to be minima but became maxima to be aimed at within limited resources, and second, in order to escape the pincer some most unsatisfactory design solutions were produced to what was a highly artificial problem.

The chief targets of criticism have been high-rise blocks of flats and dwellings produced by industrialised building systems. From 1956 to 1967 flats in high-rise blocks attracted additional subsidy. It was already known that high-rise housing was expensive to construct but central government chose to encourage local authorities to develop this form, largely because higher densities could be achieved. There was a rapid increase in the construction of flats as a proportion of local authority output in the period up to the mid-1960s. Throughout most of the decade flats constituted at least half of all local authority dwellings built each year and, as Gittus (1976: 138) has shown, in 1966, 25.7 per cent of dwellings in tenders approved by local authorities in England and Wales were to be built in blocks of five or more storeys. However from this peak there was a rapid reduction in the number of high flats under construction. On the high costs of tall flats Gittus reports that 'It appears . . . that the cost differential between low-rise flats and houses has remained of the order of 30 per cent, and rather higher since 1969 than previously. That between high-rise and houses has been more variable, but was still, in 1971, near 60 per cent for industrialised schemes and 70 per cent for the rest' (Gittus, 1976: 113).

Despite the high cost of flats, the quality of this accommodation in use has often been quickly revealed as inadequate (Bryant, 1979). One of the emergent problems of the 1970s was posed by the existence of a large stock of recently built housing which was expensive to build, yet socially and technically deficient. In the face of this problem, new building has shown a reversion to traditional materials and two-storey terraced forms at rather lower densities.

Subsidies and the function of local authority housing

Before the Second World War central government used the subsidy system to raise or lower the rate of local authority housebuilding and to direct output towards either general need or slum clearance rehousing. The same technique continued to be used after 1945, although the situation has changed quite substantially since 1970 as subsidy alterations have been increasingly related to rent policy.

Accounts of social policy legislation in the 1940s often omit to mention the 1946 Housing (Financial and Miscellaneous Provisions) Act, but it was an important measure because it trebled the money value of subsidies compared with 1939, and in so doing provided the stimulus for local authorities to build to a high standard, on a large scale. The new subsidy was similar to the model established by the Chamberlain and Wheatley subsidies in the 1920s; the standard rate was £16 10s per house per year for 60 years, plus a mandatory local rate fund contribution (RFC) of £5 10s. Even allowing for inflation since the 1930s this was a generous level of assistance, which proved effective in encouraging local authorities to build.

The Conservatives raised the level of subsidy to £26 14s, plus a rate fund contribution of £8 18s, in 1952, as a means to even higher levels of production. Once the target of 300 000 houses per year was reached, the subsidy was cut to £22 19s (plus £7 7s RFC), to take effect in April 1955. The following year, the Housing Subsidies Act slashed the subsidy by more than 50 per cent, but by the end of 1956 even this subsidy had been removed (by executive order rather than legislation) on all general needs housing other than one-bedroomed flats for the elderly. Subsidy continued to be available, at the rate of £22 1s, for dwellings built to replace those lost in slum clearance areas. The amount of subsidy was higher for dwellings in blocks of flats above three storeys in height. In this way the 1956 Act was clearly designed to direct local authorities to build for certain categories of need and to do so at high density. The subsidy system was used as a lever of control over local authorities to give effect to the slum clearance policy begun in 1954, and to remove councils from general needs family housing, which was to be left to the private sector.

Until 1961 the government continued with this policy of a limited and focused role for local authority housing. However, in the 1961 Housing Act, a general needs subsidy was reintroduced, and the rate of council house construction began to recover from its downward trend. Despite this recovery, housing was a major issue in the 1964 general election which brought Labour to power for the first time for 13 years. The new government planned a 'housing drive', to consolidate its rather tenuous hold on power, and higher subsidies were to be made available, again to stimulate local authorities to build. Legislation was, in fact, delayed by the 1966 election, but in due course the 1967 Housing Subsidies Act was passed.

The fixed subsidies introduced in 1961 had by then declined in value by 20 per cent; the new Act not only raised the level of assistance but also entirely altered the basis on which subsidies were calculated. Fixed annual payments were abandoned on all new houses (existing subsidies remained operative on completed houses) and, instead, the Exchequer contribution was calculated on the basis of the difference between loan charges at 4 per cent interest and the actual prevailing interest rate. That is, the local authority bore the cost of repaying loans on an assumed rate of 4 per cent, and the difference between that amount and the actual cost of repayment was borne by the Exchequer.

The effect of this was to relate subsidy to the cost of construction and debt repayment, in a way that had not been used since the abandonment of the Addison programme. The government's objective was to increase local authority production and to raise the quality of new dwellings to Parker Morris standards; the price to be paid was measured in the much higher subsidy bill resulting from the 1967 Act. The immediate effect of the new system was to raise average basic subsidy from about £24 to about £67 per dwelling completed, with a further threefold increase to £187 per dwelling by 1971, as both construction costs and (up to 1970) interest rates rose (Great Britain, 1977c: 48–9). Nevertheless local authority housing completions fell each year after 1967 until 1973; higher subsidies helped to meet higher costs and achieve higher standards, but did not result in more building, as had been the case in the past. Since 1970, subsidy changes have been replaced by different ways of controlling the level of construction, involving direct capital allocations for each authority.

It is clear, then, that the subsidy system had been used since the war to determine the function of new local authority housing in the sense that at some times councils have been encouraged to build for a wide range of needs, while at other times they have been forced to concentrate exclusively on slum clearance replacement. This sort of leverage on local authorities has only a marginal, though cumulative, effect, because it leaves out of account the existing stock. Since the 1950s, various (Conservative) governments have taken steps to change the function of the stock as a whole by developing the relationship between subsidies and rents.

Subsidies, rents and rebates

It is important to remember that, for many years, before and after the Second World War, council housing catered mainly for the better-paid sections of the working class, largely because, despite government subsidy, rent levels were relatively high and tended to exclude poorer families. The level of rents in the public sector reflected the comparatively high quality of the stock. In broad terms, the effect of subsidised public housing was to create a privileged tenure, in which financial assistance was channelled into providing good-quality accommodation for people who were better placed to meet the full cost of their housing than many of those who remained in the poorer parts of the unsubsidised private sector. The case for helping the lower-paid to obtain access to council housing was recognised by the government as early as 1930, when local authorities were urged to introduce rent-rebate schemes. However it was not until the mid-1950s that central government began to develop more effective policies designed to channel subsidy to the poor, and to withdraw assistance from the better-paid tenants.

In the 1956 Housing Subsidies Act the requirement that local authorities should contribute to the Housing Revenue Account (HRA) from the rate fund was removed. This was an attempt to encourage what were called 'realistic rent policies' and the logic was to give councils an incentive to raise rents; hitherto, local authorities had had an obligation to subsidise housing from the rates in fixed amounts, whatever the total level of rent income. With compulsion removed councils could raise rents generally, while providing rebates for the needy, and increase their total income, thereby reducing the need for a rate fund contribution. Realistic rents therefore meant higher rents for those who could afford to pay the full economic cost of their housing, and lower rents for the poor. This required a redistribution of subsidy away from better-off tenants; subsidising the rents of tenants who could afford to pay the full cost was seen as a misuse of public money. It was also intended that higher rents would increase the attractiveness of home ownership and encourage some tenants to buy their council houses or move on to owner-occupation elsewhere. The policy of realistic rents, facilitated by the restructuring of subsidy within the authority, was designed to increase the proportion of low-income tenants and to decrease the proportion of high-income tenants.

The freedom to reduce rate fund contributions was exercised by many authorities, although less frequently among the large urban authorities, and Parker (1967: 44–5) has shown that 'the most significant and drastic cutting back in rate subsidy occurred very soon after the opportunity was first provided in the 1956 Act . . . Rent increases were widespread and often considerable between 1956 and 1957.' A further step towards realistic rents was taken in 1961 when the Housing Act introduced a two-tier system of subsidies, granted according to an assessment of the need in individual local authorities. Authorities were entitled to the higher rate of £24 per house per year if their total HRA expenditure was more than twice the rateable value of the whole stock. Where HRA expenditure was less than twice the rateable value a lower subsidy of only £8 was provided. The system of differential subsidies was designed to put pressure on low-cost authorities to raise their rents and to introduce or extend rebate schemes.

Although local authorities were formally free to fix rent levels, the evidence is that central government's realistic rent policies had a marked impact on local practice. In 1949 a survey of 64 per cent of all housing authorities found rebate schemes in only 5 per cent of cases, but by 1964 such schemes were operating in almost 40 per cent of authorities (Parker, 1967: 42). Nevertheless it is true that there was no compulsion until the Conservatives' 1972 Housing Finance Act. It must be said here that, although the Labour governments of 1964–70 had done nothing to make rebate schemes mandatory, there was strong support for them in principle (Merrett, 1979: 184). The 1972 Act was a definite development from the earlier realistic rents approach and set out to convert the 'reasonable' rents of council houses into 'fair rents'; that is, local authorities were required to raise rents in stages until they were equivalent to the fair rents charged in the private sector under Labour's 1965 Rent Act. The 1972 Act was a radical measure, which broke with established practice in four main ways. First, always in the past when subsidy levels or arrangements had changed only new houses were affected and existing payments continued to be made; the 1972 Act abolished all previous subsidies and introduced what was known as the 'residual' subsidy (in effect the tapering-off of the old subsidies) and the 'rising cost' subsidy which quickly became the most significant. Second, local authority freedom to set rents was removed and a timetable was set up for the progression towards fair rents. Third, local authorities were for the first time permitted, and even expected, to show a surplus on the HRA. Any surplus above £30 per dwelling was to be paid to the Secretary of State. Fourth, a national rent-rebate scheme became mandatory on all authorities.

The system introduced in 1972 was yet another form of subsidy, this time based on a proportion of any deficit on the HRA arising from 'reckonable expenditure' exceeding income. In principle, one major advantage of deficit subsidy in terms of equity is that it is flexible enough to channel greatest assistance into the neediest areas, that is, authorities with extensive recent building and high loan charges. In the specific case of the 1972 Act it was also a system that allowed for the orderly withdrawal of assistance from authorities as rents were raised to fair rent levels and HRAs no longer required subsidy. The rent and subsidy policies in the Act were therefore closely interrelated.

For the record, the arrangements were that in the first year the Exchequer would pay 90 per cent of any approved deficit and the rate fund would meet the balance. In reality the Exchequer contribution was somewhat higher because rate support grant was payable on the local authority component. There was to be a gradual transition to a stage where the Exchequer paid 75 per cent and the local authority paid the rest. It is interesting to note here that, whereas before 1972 local authorities were encouraged to channel subsidies towards poorer tenants, that is, to use subsidies to finance rebates, after 1972 a *separate* rebate subsidy was introduced, made up of 75 per cent Exchequer and 25 per cent local authority contributions. The impact of the national rebate scheme was dramatic: an estimated 270 000 tenants received rebates in England and Wales in 1972 before the scheme became fully operational, but by 1976 the figure was 945 000 (Great Britain, 1977c: 10). Together with over a million tenants receiving supplementary benefit to help with their rents, this meant that an estimated 44 per cent of all tenants were paying less than the full rent.

The clear intention behind the 1972 Act was, by raising rents, to reduce the total cost of Exchequer subsidies, and to remove subsidy altogether in many areas. By tying rents to fair rents in the private sector the government for the first time broke the link between rents and the cost of providing council houses; henceforth aggregate rents could, and were intended to, exceed the costs of providing the dwellings. The benefits of historic costs were to be denied to the public sector as a whole (though individuals could benefit). In practice, however, what happened was that 'the combination of sharply rising land prices, construction costs and interest rates produced a growing HRA deficit in virtually all authorities, despite the increase in rents' (Great Britain, 1977c: 51). Thus a measure designed to reduce subsidies proved to be flexible enough under pressure of rising costs to permit an increase in the total subsidy burden. The Act was never given a chance to work as intended because of the acceleration in the rate of inflation and the return of a Labour government in February 1974. Council rents were frozen in March 1974, as part of counter-inflation policy, and as a step towards redemption of the party's pledge to repeal the contentious provisions of the Act. The mandatory rebate scheme was retained but freedom to set reasonable rents was restored in the 1975 Housing Rents and Subsidies Act, which also introduced a set of temporary subsidies, pending the outcome of the housing finance review.

There were five new subsidies: (i) the basic element, which was a consolidation of all subsidies received by a local authority in 1974/5 and fixed in money terms in future years; (ii) a new capital costs subsidy of new investment equivalent to 66 per cent of loan charges; (iii) a supplementary element equivalent to 33 per cent of any increase in loan charges on existing debt due to increase in the pooled interest rate; (iv) a special element for 1975/6 and 1976/7 only, to help authorities faced with the need to increase rents sharply at the end of the rent freeze; (v) a high-cost element paid to authorities with exceptionally high costs.

This temporary subsidy regime operated until it was replaced by the 1980 Housing Act. However, as early as the 1977 Green Paper, the Labour Government had outlined its ideas on a more permanent system of assistance, and these had been written into the Housing Bill which fell with the government in May 1979. The Green Paper (Great Britain, 1977a: 83) set out the basis of a new deficit subsidy, one to be distinguished from the Tories' 1972 version by the commitment to the preservation of local rights and duties restored in the 1975 Act. The proposal was that each year the rate of subsidy would be negotiated, with the previous year's subsidy as the starting-point. There would then be a calculation of extra expenditure for the coming year, compared with an 'appropriate level of increase' in the 'local contribution' (rents and rates). Where admissible costs rose more than the local contribution then subsidy would increase, and vice versa.

Under this system, the rate of increase in the 'local contribution' rents and General Rate Fund contribution would be perhaps the most important decision to be taken annually. It would be the predominant factor in determining the total Exchequer subsidy bill and it would also be likely to influence the size of local authority rent increases, although the balance between rents and General Rate Fund contributions, and the fixing of individual rents, would remain a matter for local discretion (Great Britain, 1977a: 83).

Access, allocation and control

As the previous section has indicated, local authorities have, since the 1930s, received increasing encouragement to provide housing for low-income families, but the authorities have remained free to decide who shall be eligible to join their waiting-list and to allocate dwellings according to their own priorities. Under Section 113 of the 1957 Housing Act local authorities must give reasonable preference to persons who are occupying insanitary or overcrowded houses, have large families, or are living under unsatisfactory housing conditions. Beyond these constraints they have almost complete autonomy.

The management of council housing has also been an area of substantial freedom from central government intervention, illustrated, for example, by the great diversity of administrative arrangements across the country: increasingly local authorities are adopting unified housing departments, responsible for all housing functions, but in the past it was common for rents to be the responsibility of the treasurer, and for repairs to be handled by the surveyor's or engineer's department. However a number of changes have occurred that have reduced local autonomy in this respect, and it is necessary to refer to these briefly. In particular, the Housing (Homeless Persons) Act of 1977 and the 1980 Housing Act require consideration as indicators of growing central government control over access, allocation and management.

Before the Second World War, when private renting was still the major form of tenure, the rules adopted by local authorities for determining access to, and allocation of, their housing stock were relatively unimportant: the number of dwellings involved was comparatively small, and households excluded from the public sector could expect to secure some sort of privately rented accommodation. In the years since 1945 the supply of privately rented housing has diminished so considerably that for most families in most parts of the country council housing is the only real alternative to owner-occupation. In this situation the criteria upon which local authority waiting-lists and lettings procedures are based become much more important.

Reflecting the non-interventionist style of the old Ministry of Housing and Local Government, local authorities were advised and exhorted to liberalise their housing policies in a number of reports produced by a quango, the Central Housing Advisory Committee (which was replaced by the Housing Services Advisory Group in 1976, itself abolished in 1980). Of these reports the best known is the Cullingworth Report (Great Britain, 1969) which endorsed the view expressed in the Seebohm Report on local authority social services that local authorities should take a wider view of their responsibilities, including the most vulnerable families in the community and those households who in the past would have been housed in the private sector. The report made a large number of other recommendations, of which perhaps the most important concerned the widening of access by the abolition of residential qualifications, and the use of points schemes based on housing need in the allocation of dwellings. In concluding that all restrictions on admission to local authority waiting-lists should be abolished, the Cullingworth Committee was repeating the advice of earlier inquiries in 1949 (Great Britain, 1949) and 1955 (Great Britain, 1955).

The Seebohm Committee (which did not, in fact, have housing as part of its brief) and the Cullingworth Committee both contributed to the development of a wider role for local housing authorities in terms of, first, the range of households eligible for public housing and, second, the responsibility of local authorities for the satisfaction of housing need beyond the provision of council houses, that is, within the private sector. This notion of a 'comprehensive housing service' has been slow to be implemented, although during the 1970s the introduction of housing strategies and investment programmes was an attempt by central government to ensure that local councils took a wider view. On the whole, local authorities have proved reluctant to broaden their activities, and ultimately their refusal to make adequate provision for the homeless led to legislation creating a duty to provide for certain categories of homeless people (Richards, 1981). The Housing (Homeless Persons) Act of 1977 was a Liberal private member's measure, supported by the government and assisted by the existence of the Lib–Lab Pact at the time. It established a definition of homelessness and of priority needs groups; local authorities have a duty to provide accommodation for any applicant who is both homeless within the meaning of the Act, and in a priority group (for example, a family with children, a pregnant woman or an elderly person). Although homelessness was defined in a way that has been criticised for its restrictiveness, and although the opposition to the Bill was able to weaken it in Parliament, the Act represents an important landmark in housing policy, in that it gives statutory recognition to the view that local authorities must accept responsibility for households in urgent need of accommodation, even where these are people that they would rather not have as tenants under other circumstances. The Act also represents an erosion of local autonomy, and is a reminder that councils' freedom of action is ultimately contingent upon their willingness to keep within the central government policy framework; where they refuse advice, guidance and exhortation, legislation is always likely.

Another more recent example of central government resorting to Act of Parliament in an area previously left to local determination is the 'tenants' charter', and in particular the 'Right to Buy'. Local authority housing has always been, and remains, outside the Rent Acts and the body of landlord and tenant law covering the private sector. As a consequence, council tenants have been denied the protection and formal rights enjoyed by private tenants. They have also come to be seen in recent years as disadvantaged by comparison with owner-occupiers, not just in relation to the acquisition, or non-acquisition, of capital assets, but also in relation to the terms on which they occupy their accommodation. The notion of a tenants' charter to remedy this situation, and to reduce the paternalistic style of housing management, developed in various forms from the late 1960s onwards. Conservative spokesmen took up the idea in Opposition after 1974, and the Labour Government's Green Paper on housing in 1977 made only a brief reference to its intention to introduce a tenants' charter which would give security of tenure, improved tenancy agreements and an extension of tenants' rights (Great Britain, 1977a: 100–3).

Capital programmes and investment control

In general, local authorities were, until the mid-1970s, substantially free to set their own capital programmes of housing expenditure. Throughout most of the period since 1919 central government has exercised only indirect influence, via the operation of the subsidy system, as already discussed. From the point of view of the individual authority it was necessary to obtain 'loan sanction' for each capital project, but if the scheme met the cost limits and design standards then approval could be regarded as almost a certainty. Central government planning control was at the level of setting overall targets, or ceilings, in terms of the number of dwellings to be built or approved in the year. In times of crisis or transition, these have operated as constraints as, for instance, in 1947 when the poor state of the pound led to attempts to cut back on public expenditure. Whereas hitherto the problem facing the Ministry of Health was to raise the level of building, Foot says that 'Henceforth, Bevan's instrument for house building had to be used in reverse; instead of stimulating the laggard authorities into action, it became a main function of the Ministry to stop local authorities building too much' (Foot, 1973: 95). The chief mechanism used for this purpose was a system of controls which enabled the Ministry of Works to set earliest starting dates for building projects – a form of capital allocation. A similar device was used again in 1953–5 when the Conservative Government aimed to scale down local authority production and expand the private sector.

There were also controls on permitted sources of capital, which operated to affect the cost of borrowing. During the period of the Labour Government 1945–51, a cheap money policy was pursued and local authorities were free to borrow at very low interest rates from the Public Works Loans Board. When the Conservatives returned to power they increased the interest rate charged by the Board, and later required authorities to borrow on the open market, using the Board only as a last resort (Merrett, 1979:155–6).

Later, after the devaluation crisis in 1967, the government announced a package of public expenditure cuts in January 1968, which included a cut of 16 500 local authority dwellings in both 1968 and 1969, but this sort of reduction in a projection only had limited impact at the level of individual local authorities, which were at that time slowing down their building programmes for political rather than economic reasons. It was not until the public expenditure crisis of the mid-1970s that local authorities began to be affected individually and directly by a tightening of central government control over capital spending.

In an attempt to control public expenditure at a time of high inflation and high, volatile interest rates, successive governments have used cash limits to fix the maximum level of spending by each authority. A system of annual local authority 'bids' and central government 'allocations' began under the 1974 Housing Act in relation to improvement expenditure. In 1976, the Secretary of State for the Environment announced that this system would be extended to all capital spending on housing in Housing Investment Programmes (HIPs), beginning in 1977/8. The HIPs system was explained in the 1977 Green Paper as a way of giving flexibility to local authority investment. Four specific advantages to central and local government were claimed:

> It will provide a means of controlling public expenditure while allowing resources to be allocated selectively with regard to variations in local housing requirements. Within the context of national policies and standards it will increase local discretion by putting greater responsibility for deciding the right mix of investment on the local authorities. For instance, they will be able to decide for themselves the right balance to be struck between acquiring and if necessary renovating existing houses and building new ones.
>
> It will give authorities an incentive to seek the most cost-effective mix of spending programmes to meet their requirements. It will encourage local authorities to adopt a comprehensive approach to housing provision including provision for those in special needs. It will provide some flexibility to alter spending within a financial year and from one year to another as circumstances change, thus improving the use of time resources and cash when unforeseen opportunities or problems arise. (Great Britain, 1977a: 77)

The idea was that each year all local authorities would prepare an investment programme for the next four years, and there would be an annual capital allocation, initially in three blocks for different purposes, but later in just one block, which the authority would be free to spend with much less detailed scrutiny of individual schemes by the centre. Once the annual allocation was made, the local authority would have complete control over its capital spending within the cash limit.

Although presented as an increase in local autonomy, and generally welcomed as such, it has become clear in practice that the HIPs system in fact represents an extension of central control which has been used to bring about substantial cuts in investment right across the country. Previously, as indicated above, individual authorities could effectively set their own investment programmes, but under HIPs the Department of the Environment sets a maximum sum to be spent by each authority; that is, the decision about the appropriate level of investment locally has been taken over by Whitehall. Although local authorities submit their bids, their estimates of necessary spending, it has become clear that Ministers no longer regard these as a reasonable basis for deciding allocations. Whitehall now decides not only the total amount available for housing investment but also how it is to be distributed amongst the authorities.

Housing associations

Especially because of the subsequent importance of housing associations the policy developments which affected housing associations in the 1960s and 1970s merit some attention. It was developments in this period which enabled public funds to be channelled to associations, established the modern framework for their operation and provided the basis for later growth.

Public support of voluntary housing effort is by no means new. Since the passing of the Labouring Classes Dwelling Houses Act of 1866, voluntary housing bodies had been borrowing money from the Public Works Loan Board. Following the Housing and Town Planning Act of 1909, public utility societies were eligible for such loans and also for Exchequer housing subsidies on the same basis and through local authorities. Under the Housing Acts 1935 and 1936, central government paid an annual grant to the newly created National Federation of Housing Societies (NFHS). In addition, the North Eastern Housing Association Limited (1935), the Scottish Special Housing Association Limited (1937) and the Northern Ireland Housing Trust (1945) were established directly through central departments. However, none of this support for voluntary housing was on a major scale. The emphasis in public housing policy before the early 1960s was firmly on local authority and new town activity. Local authorities themselves were disinclined both to lend to housing associations and to encourage them to undertake developments which would qualify for Exchequer subsidy.

The first of the modern generation of housing associations were the co-ownership and cost rent societies set up following the Housing Acts of 1961 and 1964. The government initially made £25 million available under the Housing Act 1961 to provide loans to non-profit-making housing associations to provide new housing for letting at cost rents. The loans were provided through the National Federation of Housing Societies. This arrangement was developed under the Housing Act 1964 which set up the Housing Corporation as a 'quango' to work with housing societies, building societies and government to provide loans – taking over the task from the NFHS. A major element in the approach was the involvement of building societies in funding and the Act of 1964 provided that two-thirds of the mortgage finance on cost rent schemes would come from building societies, with the remainder from the Exchequer. The Housing Corporation was empowered to register all societies seeking finance under the Act and to administer the available funds.

Cost rent and co-ownership schemes did not involve any direct public subsidy. After an initial upsurge of activity, however, the number of dwellings built under these schemes fell dramatically. The use of building society finance was made difficult by shortages of funds, unfamiliarity and rising interest rates which pushed up costs and rents. Only some 1600 cost rent dwellings were completed before these pressures halted progress. Co-ownership was more viable and the 35 000 completions benefited from tax relief. By 1974, these too had been affected by rising interest rates and were unattractive compared to owner-occupation. The political acceptability of housing associations could only be used to contribute to the housing programme by encouraging other developments.

Between 1960 and 1970 the membership of the NFHS rose from 638 to 1912. Only 300 of the new members were societies operating under the Acts of 1961 and 1964. The increased bipartisan political support and the close relationship with the strong charitable lobby had increased their political acceptability, especially in a period of reaction against local authority clearance policies and management style and the continuing decline and controversy surrounding private renting. Church organisations, including the Catholic Housing Aid Society and the British Churches Housing Trust, sponsored housing associations and provided housing aid centres. The five voluntary groups involved in the foundation of Shelter in 1966 included the Housing Societies Charitable Trust, the charitable arm of the NFHS. Shelter used the Trust to channel the funds which it raised to associations in inner city areas. It also sponsored the formation of new associations in a number of other cities.

In the late 1960s the level of local authority support for housing associations in rehabilitation and conversion work had also begun to increase. In 1967 the Greater London Council (GLC) had begun a major initiative in this area and by 1983 had funded the provision of over 20 000 dwellings, the majority of which stemmed from the rehabilitation of existing properties. Two-thirds of the dwellings were located in inner London, and almost 200 housing associations received funding. In addition to Exchequer subsidy, the GLC provided a rate fund contribution. It also encouraged associations by making sites available for development, transferring completed estates and passing over GLC-owned dwellings to housing associations for rehabilitation.

The key steps in further developing the role of housing associations involved providing new subsidy arrangements for rented housing. Housing associations were included in new financial arrangements under the Housing Finance Act 1972. Fair rents and rent allowances were extended to housing association tenancies (excluding 1961 and 1964 Act housing societies) and the Housing Corporation was given powers to lend to all housing associations meeting the 1957 Housing Act definition for new construction. It also introduced a deficit subsidy based on assumptions of steep rent rises which would eliminate the need for subsidy on schemes within 10 years.

The significance of the 1972 Housing Finance Act for housing associations is often underestimated and overshadowed by political conflicts between the government and local authorities. Indeed the introduction of fair rents was welcomed by the National Federation of Housing Societies. Nevertheless the Act was the first major breach in the local authority monopoly of provision of *subsidised* rent housing, and paved the way for an effective deficit subsidy to enable such a development. The new legislation to provide this was the Housing Act 1974. This provided a deficit subsidy system to enable associations to engage in new activity and to help associations struggling with past deficits. It was the Act of 1974 which, through both a generous new subsidy system and new policies for older housing, provided the basis for the enormous subsequent growth in the role and output of housing associations. The new subsidy system recognised the particular financial structure and vulnerability of associations during the development process, and their lack of a pool of older properties to cross-subsidise rents on new schemes. In order to take advantage of funds for development, associations had to be registered with the Housing Corporation. The Corporation was given powers to establish a register of housing associations and all future loans by itself or local authorities were to be restricted to registered housing associations. Other distinctions (for example, between charitable and non-charitable associations) became, for a period at least, less significant. The Corporation was also given powers to require compliance with procedures and the submission of accounts in a particular format, powers to restrict the disposal of land, powers to investigate suspected mismanagement, malpractice or misdemeanour, and powers to replace committee members or transfer property.

To finance housing association activity, a new set of subsidies was introduced. The main one – Housing Association Grant (HAG) – was a deficit subsidy and applied to new building and acquisitions, improvement works and conversions. It has always been administered as a capital grant rather than as an annual contribution to debt charges. HAG covered the difference between the mortgage which could be supported by the income from a scheme in the first year at fair rent levels, after deduction of DoE-determined allowances for management and maintenance and the total scheme costs. As well as being paid on Housing Corporation-funded schemes, HAG was also to be paid on schemes administered by local authorities, thereby eliminating the need for rate fund contributions from them, except on existing schemes. The 1974 Act also introduced a Revenue Deficit Grant (RDG) to cover a wide range of circumstances in which associations could not balance their income and expenditure. This was a discretionary grant, payable annually on an association's revenue expenditure, and only where deficits were deemed to be due to circumstances beyond the control of the association. Nevertheless this proved a lifeline for many associations, especially those reliant on rate fund contributions for pre-1974 subsidised dwellings. Hostel Deficit Grant (HDG) was also introduced as a similar revenue subsidy in relation to hostel schemes.

The initial emphasis of housing associations' investment following the 1974 Act was on general needs building for rent. After 1976, the balance shifted to acquisition and improvement. Local authority lending to associations grew up to 1976, but declined in the 1980s. By 1983, 87 per cent of funding was channelled through the Housing Corporation. The Housing Corporation, in the period of growth after 1974, was preoccupied with internal expansion and organisation, with registration and with developing approaches to its tasks. Throughout this period active, investing associations were becoming more dependent on the state and those working within such associations were dependent on a continuing flow of funds and consequently under pressure to respond in the ways wanted by government. Criticism of the way the voluntary sector worked led to a subsequent tightening up of Housing Corporation control and supervision (and a relaxation of dual controls involving the DoE).

Conclusion

This chapter has dealt with the changing emphasis in postwar housing policy. Over the years it is inevitable that some changes will occur in response to a variety of factors, including the overall quality and supply of accommodation in relation to developing needs and aspirations. Political priorities will vary as governments come and go and as the broader economic background alters. It is quite clear that in Britain since 1945 the social, economic and political context of housing policy has changed considerably. This may be seen to be reflected in different dominant policy objectives over time: the early postwar years were a period of high output, followed by a growing preoccupation with the problem of replacing old and unfit property, which itself gave way to a policy of rehabilitation rather than redevelopment as financial problems came to dominate the debate. Throughout much of the postwar period, especially since 1951, the rise of home ownership has been highly influential, producing a considerable degree of interparty consensus. As a corollary of this trend, council housing has been subject to a strong residualising tendency.

A feature of postwar housing policy has been the adoption of measures designed to effect a gradual narrowing of the scope of local authority provision, while at the same time state housing policy, often working through the local authorities, has widened and increased the amount of direct support for the private sector. This represents a marked contrast to the interwar period when, as Chapter 3 has shown, housing policy consisted mainly of rent control and local authority production. In the post-1945 era, policy has become much broader and more positive in support of private housing, especially home ownership. Looking back over the period as a whole, it is useful to think in terms of the residualisation of public sector housing policy and the widening of private sector policy as two separate, but linked and mutually reinforcing, processes.

It is necessary also to remember that along with changes in the content and direction of policy have gone changes in the relationships among the institutions responsible for that policy. In particular, stress has been laid on the progressive loss of local autonomy as central government has taken increasing powers to achieve its objectives against local opposition. The shift into a period of economic crisis in the mid-1970s, when high public expenditure was seen to be part of the problem to be tackled, no doubt added to central determination to curb local freedom. In addition, it is appropriate to refer to the closer relationship between the state and the private sector. As governments in the 1960s and 1970s relied increasingly on a policy of expanding home ownership, the behaviour of the institutions managing that sector moved into sharper focus. The emergent issue here was the extent to which private sector institutions, such as building societies, were prepared to be incorporated into housing policy. The question was the degree of fit that could be achieved between the fulfilment of housing policy objectives, which had a social and political content, and the essentially commercially motivated operations of the institutions. At the local level, too, there was a growing involvement of housing authorities with housing associations, building societies, developers and builders (especially in improvement and housing action areas). It is important to see both the narrowing of municipal housing and the broadening of local authority support for the private sector as at least partly the outcome of pressure from central government. That pressure intensified and the range of support for the private sector increased considerably in the 1980s, as the next chapter demonstrates.

5

Housing under the Conservatives 1979–97

The period of Conservative government between 1979 and 1997 saw major changes in housing policy and provision in the United Kingdom epitomised by privatisation and deregulation and an anti-municipal approach. There were, however, important continuities in policy too. It is widely argued that the downturn in public expenditure on housing commenced in 1976 and the concern to keep public expenditure under control was already embedded in housing policy under the previous Labour administration. Rather than developing a coherent financial framework for the provision of housing, the Conservative Government continued to operate very different financial arrangements for different parts of the housing system. The lack of a coherent approach to public expenditure is evidenced by the substantial growth of housing benefit expenditure and the growth of tax relief expenditures associated with home ownership. By the end of the period of Conservative government, the tax advantages associated with home ownership had come under attack and the ideological drive which marked the earlier years of the government with encouragement of home ownership associated with electoral and political, as well as other advantages, had been modified. Deregulation of the private rented sector had not resulted in any marked increase in supply or investment in this sector but the rising rents which resulted considerably increased housing benefit expenditure. At the same time, a crisis in the home ownership sector following the boom period of 1986–9 left a series of questions about the sustainability of home ownership in a different economic and labour market context than had applied years earlier.

Eighteen years of active legislation, of centralisation of housing policy and of diminution of the importance of housing policy left a more fragmented housing system with more dramatic differences between tenures, between urban and rural areas, between estates and between communities. Increasing concern about concentrations of deprivation, about marginalised council estates and about low income and low-quality home ownership was not all attributable to the effects of housing policy but housing policy was part of the problem.

The period of Conservative government saw a decline in local authority new building to its lowest peace time level since 1920; a programme of council house sales which represented the largest single privatisation programme of the government and the largest single source of capital receipts; a decline in the stock of council housing for rent for the first time since 1919; the termination of any significant role for new towns in the provision of housing; a dramatic fall in Exchequer subsidies to council housing; a real increase in rents in all tenures; substantial replacement of general subsidies by housing benefit with a significant impact on the poverty trap; the erosion of the rights of tenants in the private rented sector; and significant changes in the nature of housing associations, their finance and their role in the housing market.

Privatisation took a variety of forms, including the Right to Buy and large-scale voluntary transfers. By 1997 some two million council houses had been transferred to owner-occupation and more than fifty local authorities had transferred their total housing stock to housing associations. Between December 1988 and March 1997, 54 local authorities in England transferred their housing stock of around 250 000 dwellings. These transfers, as well as the changed financial environment for housing associations generally, contributed to the growth of the housing association sector. It was another element in the use of private finance to achieve policy objectives related to rental housing. These developments contributed to a greater diversity in housing governance within the UK. At one extreme there were still local authorities with very large council housing stocks, at the other extreme there were local authorities with no council housing whatsoever and where the local authority's role in housing was purely one of strategic enabling. In the early 1990s housing associations became the preferred vehicles for the provision of new rented housing. However the new financial regime for housing associations produced higher rents and new housing association tenants had fewer rights. Over time the housing market structures, housing choices and rights available to residents diverged. While the dominant language of government had shifted towards that of choice and charters, this increasingly was associated with exit from council housing, through the Right to Buy or stock transfers. At the same time the significance of problems of homelessness, the growth of mortgage arrears, negative equity and repossession suggested that some of the rights and certainties in the housing system were limited.

An overview of housing policy

The principal housing legislation of the period since 1979 is summarised in Table 5.1.

Table 5.1   *Principal housing and related legislation, 1979–96*

	Legislation	Main housing policy elements
1980	*Housing Act* and *Tenants' Rights, etc. (Scotland) Act*	Introduced 'Right to Buy', tenants' charter, new housing subsidy system and changes to rent Acts
1980	*Local Government Planning and Land Act*	Changes to local government finance (England and Wales)
1982	*Social Security and Housing Benefits Act*	Established housing benefit system
1984	*Housing and Building Control Act* and *Tenants' Rights etc. (Scotland) Amendment Act*	Extended and tightened 'Right to Buy'
1984	*Housing Defects Act*	Obligations placed on local authorities in respect of sold defective dwellings
1985	*Housing Act*	Consolidating
1985	*Housing Associations Act*	Consolidating
1985	*Landlord and Tenant Act*	Consolidating
1986	*Building Societies Act*	Enabled building societies to own and invest in housing directly and to compete with other financial institutions
1986	*Housing and Planning Act* and *Housing (Scotland) Act*	Increased 'Right to Buy' discounts (but Lords' amendment excluded dwellings suitable for the elderly). Facilitated block sales of estates
1986	*Social Security Act*	Modifications to the housing benefit scheme

Housing policy in this period has moved through five phases:

1. The vigorous implementation of policies worked out in Opposition in the late 1970s.
2. A period of consolidation in housing policy and financial deregulation.
3. Following 1986/7, there was 'a fundamental and much needed review of housing policy' (Young, 1991) and the development of a rental housing strategy.
4. A period, following 1989, when economic problems and unplanned changes in the housing sector competed with the implementation of earlier policy
5. A final review resulting in a new White Paper and a new framework for stock transfers.

	Legislation	Main housing policy elements
1987	*Housing (Scotland) Act*	Consolidating
1987	*Landlord and Tenant Act*	
1988	*Housing Act*	Deregulation of private renting. New financial arrangements for housing associations. Tenants' Choice and Housing Action Trusts introduced (England)
1989	*Local Government and Housing Act*	New local authority rent and subsidy systems. Changes to urban renewal policy (England and Wales)
1990	*National Health Service and Community Care Act*	New arrangements for care in the community as alternative to institutional/residential care
1992	*Local Government Act*	Extended compulsory competitive tendering to housing management, introduced performance measurement
1993	*Leasehold Reform, Housing and Urban Development Act*	Enabling leaseholders to acquire freehold interest in their property. Rent to Mortgage scheme
1996	*Housing Act*	New regulatory framework for 'Registered Social Landlords'. Amendments to housing benefit, tenants' rights and homelessness.
1996	*Housing Grants, Construction and Regeneration Act*	Amendments to improvement and repair grant systems. Abolition of mandatory grants

The first phase: privatisation and home ownership

The Conservative Manifesto 1979 referred to housing under the heading 'Helping the Family' and devoted one and a half pages to housing – more than to social security, or education, or health and welfare, or the elderly and disabled (Conservative Party, 1979). The manifesto emphasised 'Homes of Our Own', 'The Sale of Council Houses', and 'Reviving the Private Rented Sector'. While the primacy given to home ownership was not new, the specific policies designed to achieve it marked a break with previous policy and with local autonomy. The absence of reference to the homeless or policies for the council sector (other than sale) is striking. Housing was not an area of policy to be developed in relation to evidence of need but was principally about extending home ownership and the role of the market.

Through this it provided an opportunity for government both electorally and fiscally. The Conservative Manifesto in 1979 and ministerial statements since demonstrate a consistent disrespect for planning and projection of need and for the language of the housing lobby – of housing shortage and crisis. They referred to 'what the country can afford', to underused resources (especially empty housing) and to the capacity of the private sector to provide both what people need and what they want (see Murie, 1985).

When the Conservative Party won the general election of 1979 they regarded housing policies, and the 'Right to Buy' in particular, as constituting one of the factors contributing to their electoral success. The expansion of owner-occupation remained the key element in policy and became part of an approach to a property-owning democracy and popular capitalism which emphasised the merits of ownership of capital rather than seeing home ownership as a means of achieving housing policy objectives. Throughout the subsequent period the government continued to regard its initial policy stance as an electoral asset. It had achieved the added attribute of being advantageous fiscally – of delivering the largest capital receipts of any privatisation programme. The government showed few signs of wishing to change policy.

The Housing Act 1980 in England and the Tenants' Rights, etc. (Scotland) Act 1980 introduced the Right to Buy to enable public sector tenants to buy their homes, introduced new tenancy arrangements for public and private tenants and introduced new arrangements for subsidy of council housing. The latter facilitated the reduction of general assistance Exchequer subsidy. Consolidation of the rent-rebate system into a new housing benefit system in 1982 formed the other part of a strategy to shift away from general 'bricks and mortar' subsidies towards individual subsidies targeted on the basis of household needs and incomes.

The second phase: consolidation and deregulation

The Conservative Government formed after the general election of 1983 did not have major new housing policy proposals but introduced legislation to consolidate earlier measures; to extend discounts available to council tenants under the Right to Buy; to deal with the problems of people who had bought defective council houses; to enable block sales of council estates to private developers and other landlords; and to modify the housing benefit scheme. New and radical legislation related to financial deregulation and the role of building societies. These measures were principally driven by considerations about the operation of the finance market but the desire to enable private sector institutions and building societies in particular to take a more active role in housing provision was also important. The Building Societies Act 1986 was partly a response to arguments that building societies should be able to compete equally with the clearing banks in the personal finance sector and to be able to offer unsecured loans and a full home-buying service, including estate agency, conveyancing and insurance. This legislation did alter the range of services offered by building societies and subsequently a number of the larger societies used it to change their status. Only the Abbey National Building Society converted itself to a bank in the period immediately following this legislation. However by 1994 a more striking pattern of mergers and flotations commenced. Lloyds Bank took over the Cheltenham and Gloucester Building Society, Northern Rock and the North amalgamated and subsequently became a bank. The Halifax and the Leeds merged and subsequently became a bank. The National and Provincial Building Society was taken over by the Abbey National and the Bristol and West and Birmingham Midshires Societies both embarked upon flotation policies.

The third phase: a rental housing strategy

By 1987 criticisms of housing policy were increasingly apparent. The failure of the 1980 solution to housing finance was evident well before 1987. The dog's breakfast of the 1970s had been recreated and the system was neither equitable nor effective. It neither encouraged new building, investment in repair and maintenance, nor facilitated mobility and exchange. These failings had been the subject of comment in an enquiry established by the Archbishop of Canterbury (1985) and in another enquiry chaired by the Duke of Edinburgh (NFHA, 1986).

It was against this background and in the run-up to the general election of 1987 that ministers presented a new agenda. This did not abandon the commitment to home ownership but signalled a renewed concern with the availability of rented housing. This related both to a Right to Rent and to choice of landlord. New legislation and new financial arrangements for housing associations were designed to increase the supply of rented housing. The emphasis on choice of landlord involved procedures to enable local authority tenants to choose an alternative landlord and other measures to break the 'monopoly' control of local authorities through Housing Action Trusts and the termination of a major role for local authorities in providing new rented housing.

The Housing Act 1988 embodied the manifesto commitment to revive private renting. The government introduced assured tenancies (already existing in England and Wales but not in Scotland) and shorthold (England and Wales) or short (Scotland) tenancies. For all new lettings from 15 January 1989, landlords could either let on an assured tenancy basis, with rents freely negotiated between landlord and tenant, but with security of tenure protected, or let on a shorthold or short tenancy basis, with no security beyond the period of the tenancy but with the right for either party to seek registration of an appropriate rent. The legislation also included detailed adjustments to the Right to Buy, a changed financial regime and changes in tenancy arrangements for housing associations, the introduction of Tenants' Choice for local authority tenants and power to establish Housing Action Trusts. Although there was now a rental housing strategy it remained consistent with continued demunicipalisation and did not mean a swing back to local authority provision. Local authorities' future role would be as enablers rather than direct providers of housing and rents generally would move towards market rents.

The fourth phase: housing in recession

The policy concerns of the 1990s were not restricted to this package but related to problems arising from the economic recession and associated with the deregulation of housing finance following the Building Societies Act 1986. Following this legislation there was a pronounced shift from mortgage rationing towards lending on demand and loans related to a high proportion of property value. Lenders were willing to advance much higher multiples of income sometimes with only cursory scrutiny of ability to meet payments and security of jobs. This situation was further fuelled by the ending of the system under which two persons buying the same house could each qualify for tax relief in respect of interest payments on the first £30 000 of any loan. In 1988 this system was replaced and the limit applied to the property rather than the person. The Chancellor of the Exchequer gave some three months' notice of the change and generated substantial housing market activity among households seeking to qualify for double tax relief before the system ended. Many of these households may have been premature entrants to the home ownership sector and overextended themselves financially at a time of rapidly rising house prices and interest rates. The consequences of deregulation are bound up with other changes. At that stage employment and incomes were rising and government embarked on a taxation strategy which added to the explosion of consumption, credit and house prices. A boom in house prices had commenced in 1986 and spread outwards from the overheated economy of the south-east. The booming market was also evident in the rise in private sector housing starts (from 180 000 in Great Britain in 1986 to 216 000 in 1988). Measured against total personal disposable income, mortgage debt rose steeply throughout the early to mid-1980s and began to level off in 1988. The explosion in borrowing had wider impacts on interest rates and inflation and contributed to the conditions in which rising unemployment and economic recession deepened the home ownership crisis.

After August 1988 the private housing market faltered and Britain entered a sustained period of depressed housing market activity. Building society interest rates on new mortgages rose from around 9.5 per cent in 1988 to 15.4 per cent in February 1990 and remained at that level – the highest on record – until October 1990, when they fell to some 14.5 per cent. The impact of these changes on individual owners varied. For those (often higher-income households) who had taken out substantial mortgages in that period, payments were substantially higher than expected. Not surprisingly, mortgage arrears and repossessions increased.

Although interest rates fell, mortgage arrears, as with unemployment and repossessions, became more important. Table 5.2 illustrates the extent of problems in the home ownership sector. The number of transactions fell considerably. House prices were in decline and the volume of repossessions was much higher than had previously applied. The trend in mortgage arrears followed a similar pattern. This combination of factors was self-reinforcing. High levels of repossession depressed house prices. Declining house prices made it more difficult for people to sell at the price they wanted on the open market and depressed the number of transactions. The problem of being able to achieve a rapid sale further depressed the market. These factors contributed to a problem of negative equity in which households could find that the value of their property declined to a point where it was less than their outstanding mortgage. For these households, selling the property would not even clear the debt outstanding on it. In 1989 there were estimated to be 230,000 households in the United Kingdom with negative equity and this rose to 1 768 000 in 1992. It remained at over 1 000 000 until 1996. The most significant problems of negative equity were in the south of England, with Scotland and Northern Ireland largely escaping. In 1996 there were 465 000 households in negative equity, representing some 3 per cent of all home owners (Wilcox,1987).

The weakness of the housing market affected the construction industry, building materials producers and those producing consumer durables purchased on moving house and estate agencies, insurance companies and

Table 5.2   *Problems in the home ownership sector, 1986–96*

	Number of residential property transactions (000s)	Average house prices[1] (1990 = 100)	Repossessions during year
1986	1600	57.2	24 090
1987	1744	66.7	26 390
1988	1990	83.8	18 510
1989	1467	101.3	15 810
1990	1283	100	43 890
1991	1225	98.7	75 540
1992	1032	95.0	68 540
1993	1114	92.5	58 540
1994	1168	95.4	49 190
1995	1047	96.0	49 410
1996	1122	99.6	42 560

Note: [1] Mix adjusted index.
Source: Wilcox (1997).

building societies all experienced problems (see Forrest and Murie, 1994). All of these changes contributed to policy responses. Building societies, local authorities and housing associations developed mortgage rescue packages and in 1991 the Council of Mortgage Lenders sought to develop new arrangements to enable social security payments of income support in respect of mortgage interest to be paid direct to lenders. Ministers expressed concern at rising repossessions (in contrast to earlier statements) but wanted a solution with no cost to the Exchequer. The package which emerged involved building societies and others establishing mortgage rescue schemes. The funds would be used in various ways but mostly would enable housing associations or others to purchase repossessed properties and relet them. The government's part of the package was, initially, only to allow direct payment (that is, from the state to the lender rather than the borrower) of the £750 million of income support paid for mortgage interest. This was quickly followed by the suspension of stamp duty associated with house purchase. A further initiative was introduced in the Chancellor of the Exchequer's Autumn Statement in 1992. This involved some £750 million to be made available in 1992/3 to help promote activity in the housing market especially by enabling housing associations to acquire unsold properties before the end of 1992/3 and reduce problems of vacant and repossessed housing which were delaying recovery.

This whole episode represented a dramatic unplanned intervention in the operation of the home ownership market but the costs of these developments to government and lenders were very small and the immediate impact limited (Foster, 1992; Ford and Wilcox, 1992).

In the general election of 1992 the Conservative Party Manifesto referred to housing in the context of the right to own and the Citizen's Charter. The main proposals were included in a one-page statement headed 'Home Ownership' reasserting support for the further expansion of home ownership and the encouragement of a strong private rented sector. New proposals were for a new 'rents to mortgages' scheme and 'commonhold' legislation giving residential leaseholders living in blocks of flats the right to acquire the freehold of their block. Other commitments included maintaining mortgage interest tax relief. The manifesto was 'meeting housing need' and referred to increasing the supply of affordable housing for those in housing need. This referred to introducing more choice, and creating new rights – as part of the tenants' charter. References were made to housing management, large-scale voluntary transfers and to rough sleeping.

The last Acts

In June 1995 the Conservative government published a White Paper *Our Future Homes*. This 60-page document set out the government's housing policies for England and Wales. It highlighted three things: choice, opportunity and responsibility and its general approach was to pursue the agenda which had dominated since 1979. This involved the focus on the promotion of home ownership, the revival of private renting and the transfer of public sector housing to other landlords. The expressed aim was to expand home ownership by 1.5 million over the next decade. Grants would be made available to enable housing association tenants to buy their homes and future grants to housing associations would be conditional upon them agreeing to sell to tenants on request. Private companies would be able to compete with housing associations for funds to provide social housing at below market rents or for shared ownership for people in housing need. Legislation to introduce Housing Investment Trusts would be designed to encourage financial institutions to invest in the private rented sector, which would also be assisted by further deregulation and the introduction of pre-tenancy determinations of rent eligible for housing benefit. Encouragement of the continued transfer of local authority housing to new landlords included the possibility of setting up local housing companies – companies which included on their controlling board local authority representatives, as well as tenants and other interests. Such companies would be in the private sector and therefore outside the public expenditure control system.

Other elements in the White Paper included measures to reduce the proportion of empty housing, to transform the remaining large-scale poor-quality public estates, to support innovative schemes to create mixed communities in the heart of cities, to reform renovation grant legislation and change homelessness legislation to amend the duty related to the housing of eligible homeless applicants. The subsequent Housing Act 1996 incorporated many of these measures. It introduced the term 'Registered Social Landlord' (RSL) to embrace housing associations, local housing companies and, potentially, other organisations. It established a new regulatory framework for these bodies. It introduced registration schemes for houses in multiple occupation and made a number of detailed changes to landlord and tenant law, particularly in relation to assured tenancies and leasehold reform. It extended Right to Buy provision (right to acquire) to tenants of RSLs where dwellings had been provided with public funds. It introduced introductory tenancies for local authorities and gave councils new powers to tackle anti-social behaviour. It gave the Secretary of State powers to regulate who may or may not appear on local authority waiting lists and how housing should be allocated. Finally, it amended the existing duty of local authorities to provide suitable accommodation to homeless people. A separate Housing Grants, Construction and Regeneration Act amended the systems for repair and improvement grants in 1996.

These final Acts marked continuity with earlier policies pursued by the Conservatives in government, but embodied a significant change with acknowlegement of the need for a social rented housing sector. The White Paper referred to social rented housing as the most cost-effective way to provide long-term housing for those with low incomes and stated that this was because providing a subsidy to a social landlord to charge a below-market rent was cheaper over time than paying housing benefit on a market rent, that it reduced dependency on benefits and improved work incentives and therefore that it increased the prospect of breaking out of benefit (p. 26). To this extent there was some evidence of an adjustment of long-established policy positions. It is also apparent that the policy package was not being adopted unthinkingly by territorial departments. With the exception of the housing benefit measures, legislation did not apply to Scotland. Even more significantly the Northern Ireland Office's proposals, *Building on Success*, did not envisage a major change in the approach to housing policy there, and represented a statement of confidence in the record and achievements of the public sector and a rejection of approaches which would destabilise and undermine those achievements (DoE, NI, 1996).

Measures of change

Table 5.3 indicates how the structure of the housing market in the United Kingdom changed in the period 1980–96. The housing stock increased by almost three million dwellings but the balance between tenures changed much more dramatically. The owner-occupied sector expanded by 10 percentage points while the local authority sector declined from housing

Table 5.3   *Dwellings by tenure in the United Kingdom, 1981–96*

	All dwellings	Owner-occupied	Local authority	Housing association	Private rented
	(000s)	%	%	%	%
1981	21 586	56.4	30.4	2.2	11.0
1982	21 761	57.7	29.3	2.2	10.8
1983	21 956	58.7	28.3	2.3	10.7
1984	22 165	59.6	27.6	2.4	10.5
1985	22 378	60.5	26.8	2.5	10.2
1986	22 598	61.5	26.1	2.5	9.9
1987	22 794	62.6	25.3	2.6	9.5
1988	23 036	64.0	24.2	2.7	9.1
1989	23 263	65.2	23.0	2.8	9.0
1990	23 464	65.8	22.1	3.0	9.1
1991	23 671	65.9	21.4	3.1	9.5
1992	23 845	66.1	20.8	3.4	9.6
1993	24 028	66.4	20.3	3.7	9.7
1994	24 217	66.6	19.7	4.0	9.7
1995	24 394	66.8	19.2	4.3	9.7
1996	24 568	67.0	18.8	4.5	9.7

Sources: DETR (1997); *Housing and Construction Statistics.*

almost one in three households to housing less than one in five. Housing associations increased their share of the market, although they remain very small. Finally, the private rented sector continued its decline through to 1989 and has seen a small recovery in size since that date. These bald statistics of changes to the structure of the market obscure a more complex set of changes. More than half of the growth of the owner-occupied sector has been associated with the transfer of public sector housing stock, especially through the Right to Buy. The owner-occupied sector has altered more than just in size and now includes properties not originally built for sale and in locations not normally associated with home ownership. These are also older properties and where they have been bought under the Right to Buy their purchasers, although classified as first-time buyers, are older than first-time buyers in general and have benefited from substantial discounts on their house purchase. The evidence related to the Right to Buy suggests that there are distinctive characteristics and that these properties will, in many cases, form a separate submarket, not fully absorbed into mainstream home ownership (Forrest, Gordon and Murie, 1996).

The Right to Buy and stock transfers have also affected the local authority sector. With very limited new building of local authority housing the disproportionate sale of more attractive and better-quality stock has left the tenure with a greater proportion of flats and non traditional dwelling types. Large-scale voluntary transfers have implications for the ownership and control of rented housing and for rent levels and tenants' rights. In general those who were tenants at the time of transfer experienced relatively little change but the next generation of tenants will not have the same rights as their predecessors and will be exposed to higher rents. Housing associations in general have seen a change in their financial basis and the higher rents which had developed in that sector are an important feature. Finally, the private rented sector has been significantly deregulated. In 1988 59 per cent of lettings in the private rented sector had been regulated. By 1995/6 this figure was 12 per cent. Assured tenancies over the same period had risen from 4 per cent to 59 per cent. There are implications here in terms both of rents and of tenants' rights. The development of the housing benefit system since 1982 had protected tenants against rising rents. However this protection was only partial. There had always been rent caps which could be applied and these were more significant following changes in the mid-1990s. Furthermore it is argued that higher rents and the housing benefit regime had increased the significance of the poverty trap and left a larger group of tenants with no problems in paying their rent but with severe problems of changing their overall social circumstances. If their incomes, through employment, rose, so their benefit entitlement fell to almost an equal extent. Only if their income rose dramatically and in a way that was inconsistent with remaining in the same area of employment would someone escape the clutches of the poverty trap.

The key indicators of the housing changes in the period 1980 to 1995 are presented in Figure 5.1 and Table 5.4. These show a dramatic decline in public sector housing completions from over 88 000 in 1980 to only just more than 3000 in 1995. While housing association completions increased dramatically after 1990, this increase and changes in private sector investment were not sufficient to sustain the 1980 level of housing completions.

General government expenditure on housing remained relatively stable in cash terms but the dramatic decline in expenditure is shown by the figures which take inflation into account. Housing's share of government expenditure fell to just over 2 per cent in 1995. In real terms social housing investment declined over the period and this is evident, particularly in relation to investment in new building and acquisitions which had fallen to a negligible level for local authorities in 1995/6. In spite of the increasing evidence of a backlog of disrepair in the council housing stock, there was no sustained increase in Housing Revenue Account (HRA) stock renovation. The figures show a decline since 1985 and a more dramatic one since 1990. In real terms total gross investment has fell by some 47 per cent of its 1980 figure.

Figure 5.1 *Dwellings completed and council house sales in Great Britain, 1979-96 (thousands)*

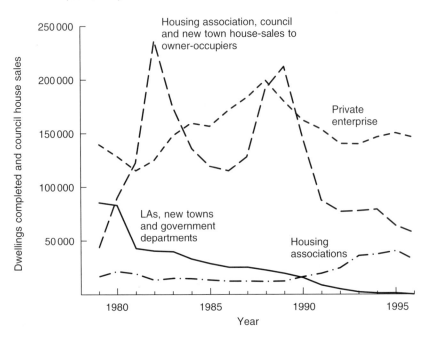

Source: Housing and Construction Statistics (HMSO).

Table 5.4   *Housing performance and expenditure in Great Britain, 1980–95*

	1980	1985	1990	1995
Housing completions				
Public sector	88590	30422	17931	3218
Housing associations	21422	13648	17911	39178
Private sector	131974	163395	166798	156293
All dwellings	241986	207465	202640	198689

	1980/1	1985/6	1990/1	1995/6
General government expenditure on housing				
(£billion cash)	5.6	4.1	4.8	4.9
£billion 1995–6 prices	12.1	6.5	5.7	4.9
Gross social housing investment				
in GB (£billion 1995–6 prices)	8733	7274	6837	5260
Housing capital investment 1995–6 prices: England (£m)				
LA new build and acquisitions	2187	1121	648	71
HRA stock renovation	1453	2094	2049	1550
Total gross investment	7382	6041	5274	3908
Total net investment	5054	2850	2198	2486
Mortgage interest tax relief (£m)	2188	4750	7700	2700
Net subsidies for LA housing (GB) (£m)	2130	9161	213	(483)
Housing benefit				
Rent rebates: number	1330	3710	2944	2917
Rent rebates: average payment				
per person (£ per annum)	240	606	1030	1763
Rent allowances: number	240	1150	1044	1867
Rent allowances average payment				
per person: (£ per annum)	1996	19	1323	2621

	1980	1985	1990	1995
Homeless acceptances				
England	62920	93980	145800	125500
Scotland	7976	11972	15813	16700
Wales	5446	5371	9963	9001
Great Britain	76342	111323	171576	151201

Source: Wilcox (1997).

Real spending on new local authority and new town construction fell continuously but spending on the renovation of existing council dwellings increased. Local authority investment was increasingly channelled towards renovations to local authorities' own housing stock and improvement grants. Since 1983 these two programmes accounted for over two-thirds of local authority capital investment. The majority of investment in the renovation of local authority stock relates to the purpose-built council stock. The demand for investment has mushroomed in this area, not only as a result of government initiatives such as the Housing Defects Act, the Priority Estate Projects and the Urban Housing Renewal Unit (renamed Estate Action in 1986) but also as awareness of the scale of problems in the traditionally built stock, the 'non-traditional' stock of the 1950s and 1960s and the industrialised and system-built dwellings of the 1960s and 1970s has grown. In many authorities the condition of the council-owned stock has become a political issue of equal or greater significance than more traditional inner city problems and the condition of the older private sector stock. These circumstances focused attention on the availability and use of capital receipts.

The rules governing the use of capital receipts have varied between the different countries of the UK. They have been more restricted and have changed more in England and Wales. The restrictions on use of receipts became the subject of increasing criticism although government protested that unspent receipts had been taken into account in public expenditure calculations. In both Scotland and Wales restrictions on the use of capital receipts have differed from England. Capital allocations in Scotland have been made in two blocks (HRA and non-HRA) after making assumptions about the level of capital receipts. Apart from some negative allocations local authorities were able to make full use of receipts. In Wales 50 per cent of council house sales receipts and 30 per cent of others were taken into account. Processes in connection with capital programmes also differ with Housing Strategy and Operational Programmes in Wales and Housing Plans in Scotland, both involving different time-scales and procedures than Housing Investment Programmes (HIPs) in England. Wilcox (1993) indicates that Scotland and Wales have maintained or even increased their public expenditure on housing investment in real terms since 1979/80 and the brunt of reduced housing investment has been felt in England. In Northern Ireland housing public expenditure was explicitly regarded as a high priority until the late 1980s (Murie, 1992). In Northern Ireland, with the Northern Ireland Housing Executive the only public sector landlord, processes of determining and allocating public expenditure involve direct and close consultation. Moving on from local authority expenditure, there have been important changes for new towns and particularly for housing associations. The post-war new town experiment had been terminated by 1985 and proposals to dispose of new town dwellings to the private or voluntary sector had become the major feature of housing policy in the new towns. New towns by

1990 generated more than twice as much in capital receipts they spent on housing.

By 1986/7 spending on new housing association housing exceeded that on new council housing. And the new emphasis in government policy meant that housing association spending on housing for rent rose considerably in the early 1990s to a level which was three times that of local authorities in 1991/2. The new financial regime for housing associations also drew in substantial amounts of private finance. In 1992/3 some 25 per cent of housing association gross investment involved private finance (Wilcox, 1993).

While these changes in conventional housing expenditure and in housing investment were taking place, mortgage interest tax relief rose to a peak in 1990 and housing benefit costs increased. These increases were most marked in the private sector. The figures for 1980 pre-date the introduction of the housing benefits scheme and are not strictly comparable. However the 1995 figures show a considerable increase in the number of rent allowances, compared with 1990 or 1985. More significantly the average payment per annum had almost doubled in each five-year period. This meant that they had significantly over taken the average payment of rent rebates associated with the public sector. The changes in the financing of council housing meant that in aggregate local authority housing in Great Britain had moved into surplus. In 1980 £2130 million was spent on subsidy to local authority housing and in 1990 £1213 million. However, in 1995 there was a surplus of £483 million. In effect general assistance subsidy had been eliminated and this figure should be offset against the costs of rent rebates. By 1995/6 total housing benefit expenditure in Great Britain was £11 901 million. Although investment in housing and housing subsidy had been cut and tax relief had fallen, it could be argued that the total housing expenditure bill remained above that of 1980. Rather than a cut in expenditure, what had been achieved was a growth and reorientation.

Interpreting these data is complicated. Where local authority housing stock has been transferred to housing associations, so any housing benefit entitlements have also been transferred. Notwithstanding this, it is evident that increasing rents and housing benefit entitlements in the private rented sector do not represent good value for money for the taxpayer. They have not resulted in significant new investment in the private rented sector, either to increase the supply or the quality of that tenure. In the six years 1988/9 to 1993/4, 4527 Business Expansion Schemes were established in the UK for housing. The total investment associated with these was almost £3 billion and they generated 75 100 lettings. Eighty per cent of the investment under these schemes was in London and the south-east. The value of the income tax relief associated with them was in excess of £1 billion or £16 450 per letting (Wilcox 1997).

If the Right to Buy and large-scale voluntary transfers had been the most effective ways of achieving the demunicipalisation of housing, their greatest weakness had been in the extent to which they had penetrated urban Britain. The Right to Buy was taken up much more in the Shire districts and more affluent towns and regions. Large-scale voluntary transfers, in the majority of cases, involved smaller landlord authorities with a similar locational spread. It is against this background that the strategy of the Conservative Government developed towards one designed to engineer transfers of urban housing stock. This involved the further turn to the financial incentive structure that had been applied throughout the period of government. The stark choice for local authorities was increasingly one of being unable to improve and maintain a deteriorating stock with a backlog of disrepair or transfer that stock in order to produce a formula that was more acceptable to Labour-controlled local authorities. Proposals related to local housing companies were promoted. These would produce registered social landlords in the private sector but retaining a significant degree of local authority control and accountability. The initial attempt to develop this proposal involved the establishment of an Estates Renewal Challenge Fund in 1995, with the first-round bids for this fund in 1996. This Challenge Fund was renewed in 1997 and at the same time the indications were that allocations under the Housing Investment Programme would increasingly depend on stock transfers.

Rents and subsidies

The period since 1979 saw a new approach to rents and subsidies. There had been concern about the balance of spending between investment and subsidy over a long period and the government in 1981 stated its commitment:

> To reduce the overall level of housing subsidies over a period of years so as to enable a greater proportion of the resources available for public expenditure on housing to be devoted to capital rather than current expenditure. (Treasury, 1981)

This concern was focused on the narrow area of subsidies to local authority housing revenue accounts rather than subsidies generally. The rising council housing subsidy bill in the early and mid-1970s reflected a combination of factors including rising investment levels and high interest rates. A new subsidy system for local authority housing, designed specifically to give central government more control over the total subsidy bill, was proposed in the 1977 Green Papers, but not introduced (under the Housing Acts of 1980) until 1981/2. The different systems introduced for Scotland and for England and Wales both gave central government unprecedented powers to force up council rents and left local authorities with limited room to manoeuvre. Rents initially rose rapidly. However, after the early 1980s, rent increases were more limited. This reflected political and electoral considerations and the failure of controls applied through the Rate Support Grant system. But in addition a large proportion of the reduction in general subsidy to local authority housing was matched by an increase in expenditure on income-related housing benefit in the Social Security budget.

Proposals to unify assistance with rent and rates in a scheme administered by local authorities went forward in the Social Security and Housing Benefits Act 1982. Under the new housing benefit scheme the previously separate schemes for rent rebates, rent allowances and rate rebates were integrated, as were the supplementary benefits associated with these costs. The Act gave local authorities little more than the powers they needed to operate the scheme and details of the scheme were left to DHSS regulations. The new scheme was introduced partially in November 1982 and fully in April 1983 (November 1983 in Northern Ireland).

The problems experienced in implementing the new scheme were considerable. The determination to avoid any cost increase meant that some of those on benefit experienced a cut. However government was unwilling to respond to arguments about gainers and losers beyond confining losses by paying a transitional addition. Subsequent revision of the tapers used to determine level of benefit involved further real cuts in benefit for individuals and contributed to an increasingly severe poverty trap for tenants in receipt of benefit while the overall expenditure continued to soar.

One view of this is that passing a welfare service to local authorities places them in the front line in explaining and implementing cuts and represented a sensible distancing strategy for central government. For local authorities and housing authorities in particular, the income maintenance and means test role involved a significant change in relationships, especially with their own tenants. The implications for workloads, staffing, organisation and training in housing were considerable.

The subsidy schemes established under the Housing Acts of 1980 operated alongside the housing benefit scheme until 1 April 1990. In England and Wales, the rules governing subsidies to local authority housing were replaced on that date by a new scheme established by the Local Government and Housing Act 1989 (for more detail see Chapter 8 below). In Scotland the operation of Housing Support Grant (HSG) involved similar elements with ministerial judgements about management and maintenance costs, interest rates, rent losses, rent income, general fund contributions and other elements determining HSG. In practice the formula has been used to steadily reduce HSG. By 1992/3 only seven authorities were entitled to make general fund contributions (GFCs) and these only totalled £1.5 million. In the same year 32 authorities qualified for HSG but 11 only received an element in respect of hostels. The total of HSG was £47.5 million and the bulk of this was distributed to a small number of authorities.

Table 5.5 indicates that the combined costs of rent rebates and rent allowances had increased from £3.4 billion in 1986/7 to over £10 billion in

1994/5. This increase could be attributed both to the effects of recession and widening social inequality but even more so, it was the result of government policies relating to rents and subsidy. The formula which saw a shift away from bricks and mortar subsidy and increasing rents towards market levels as a sounder basis for an effective housing system meant that housing public expenditure had fallen but the social security bill had increased dramatically. What suited the Department of the Environment did not suit the Department of Social Security.

The situation was most extreme in the private rented sector where rents had increased more rapidly than elsewhere. The hope that this would lead to an increase in private investment and in rented housing and an improvement in the quality of the private rented stock was not fulfilled. The incentive structures, rather than encouraging investment, encouraged profit-taking. At the same time higher rents and housing benefits added to the poverty trap and an adverse incentive structure for lower income households living in rented accommodation. The formula was not working from a housing market point of view, from an economic point of view or from a public expenditure point of view, and it is likely to be this aspect of the Conservative Government's housing policy which will prove most easy to ridicule. Not surprisingly, government began to institute reforms of housing benefit to provide tenants and landlords with incentives to economise on rents and meaning that housing benefit would not be calculated to meet a 100 per cent of rents charged in all cases. Rather benefit entitlement would be linked to regional average rents.

Table 5.5   *Housing benefits in Great Britain: outturn expenditure, 1986–96 (£ millions)*

	Rent rebates (council and new town tenants)	Rent allowances (private and housing association tenants)	Income support with mortgage costs
1986/7	2419	996	351
1987/8	2506	1030	335
1988/9	2718	1055	286
1989/90	2940	1359	353
1990/1	3368	1779	539
1991/2	4068	2426	925
1992/3	4617	3284	1141
1993/4	5025	4188	1210
1994/5	5246	4874	1040
1995/6	5440	5445	1016
1996/7 (estimated)	5636	5887	867

Source: Wilcox (1997)

In the environment of economic recession in the early 1990s, government's first priority was to hold down public expenditure and its attention shifted away from housing public expenditure and towards social security expenditures which were directly connected with housing. In addition to housing benefits, income support payments associated with mortgage costs had also increased significantly and they became the new target for government's attention. Following the 1991 package under which government had allowed income support for mortgage interest to be paid directly to lenders, government shifted its stance dramatically. It proposed that private insurance cover should be used to protect home owners, so that income support would not be required. While building societies were unhappy with this arrangement, the changes were introduced in 1995.

The final element in this picture relates to the treatment of mortgage interest tax relief. The value of this had expanded enormously with rising house prices and interest rates in the late 1980s, although the ceiling on the amount of mortgage qualifying for relief had been retained at the figure introduced in 1983 – £30 000. The government ended the opportunity for double tax relief and linked the ceiling on tax relief to the dwelling rather than the person in 1988. Government continued to identify an important part of its housing policy as being to support the growth of home ownership through mortgage interest tax relief and other measures. However, subsequently there were signs that the wide challenges to tax reliefs were having an impact. In 1991 tax relief was limited to the basic rate of tax. In 1993 (and in spite of the 1992 manifesto commitment) the Chancellor announced that mortgage interest tax relief would be reduced from 20 per cent to 15 per cent with further reductions to be made at a rate of 5 per cent a year. In a period of extended depression in the private housing market, the Chancellor came under pressure to modify this position and in June 1994 he announced that mortgage interest tax relief would not be reduced below the 15 per cent rate in the life of the current Parliament.

These developments and falling interest rates eroded the sums associated with tax relief and reduced its most regressive aspects. At the same time house prices in many parts of the country meant that new mortgages were increasingly in excess of the £30 000 maximum eligible for relief. Mortgage interest tax relief was no longer so important to affluent purchasers or to lenders and its reduction had not aroused fierce opposition. The environment was more favourable for further erosion or removal.

Homelessness

The changes outlined previously in this chapter involved a reduction in the stock of rented housing. Nevertheless the supply of new lettings fell relatively slowly. In England lettings to new tenants fell from some 275 100 in 1980/1 to 247 000 in 1985/6, 239 600 in 1990/1 and 248 900 in 1995/6. These figures reflect an increasing turnover (ratio of new letting to dwelling stock) in the council stock: from 5 per cent per annum to 7 per cent per annum – an increase of 33 per cent. This and the changing profile of new tenants reflect the changing nature and role of the council housing sector. The increase in housing association lettings did not make up for this decline in lettings. The consequence of the restricted supply of housing to rent was that an increasing proportion of new tenants became homeless before being allocated a local authority tenancy. In England in 1979/80, 15 per cent of new secure council tenancies were let to homeless households. In 1991/2, the comparable figure was 34 per cent and in 1995/6 28 per cent. For London the percentage had increased in these years from 26 per cent to 42 per cent and 51 per cent. Between 1980/1 and 1995/6 the share of new local authority lettings made to homeless households in Wales rose from 10.9 per cent to 14.4 per cent and in Scotland from 13.6 per cent to 20.4 per cent. In 1979, 70 232 households were accepted as homeless by local authorities in Great Britain. By 1991, the number had risen to 178 867. By 1996 there had been a fall to 131 139 Just as significant as this was the rising number of homeless households housed in temporary accommodation. Such accommodation, especially that in bed and breakfast hotels, was insecure, substandard, unsafe and expensive. At the end of 1980, 1330 households in England were in bed and breakfast hotels and a total of 4710 in some form of temporary accommodation. At the end of 1991 these figures were 12 150 and 20 140 and in 1996 4020 and 13 610.

The two main reasons for acceptance as homeless were the breakdown of sharing arrangements with relatives and friends or the breakdown of a relationship with a partner. Social and demographic trends are key elements in homelessness. The characteristics of those allocated housing as homeless was very similar to those at the top of general waiting lists. Homelessness legislation was wrongly portrayed as giving special priority to single parents and others and was increasingly associated with attacks on the structure of the welfare state. A review of homelessness legislation concluded in 1989 recommended that the law should remain unchanged and new Codes of Guidance issued in relation to homelessness emphasised prevention and performance monitoring. Nevertheless in 1993 the then Housing Minister Sir George Young announced another full-scale review of homelessness legislation. The government's proposals published in 1994 were more re-strictive than expected and claimed that homelessness had become a 'fast track' into social housing. Following this and in spite of strong opposition to legislative change, Part VII of the 1996 Housing Act replaced existing homelessness law and came into effect on 20 January 1997. The new legislation identified similar categories of people in priority need but changed the entitlements of many people from abroad. It removed the duty to house homeless people where suitable accommodation (including private rented housing) was available in the area, limited the duty to secure accommodation and introduced a new duty relating to the provision of advice and information about homelessness.

This new framework was closely linked to the new law on the allocation of social housing. This required every authority to maintain a housing register, but only 'qualifying persons' were allowed to be placed on it – excluding many people from abroad. Homeless people were allowed to join the register, but were no longer to be given 'reasonable preference' in the allocation of tenancies. The overall effect of these changes was to give homeless people less chance of obtaining long-term housing from local authorities and housing associations. Private landlords were to play a much larger role in housing homeless people. However, this was often not a realistic option given the high levels of rents, restrictions on housing benefit and the reluctance of many landlords to house people with children or those who were vulnerable. The Labour party in opposition promised to: 'restore a clear, strong framework based on the principles of the 1977 Act, which will require local authorities to secure permanent accommodation for homeless people in priority need'. The legislation to protect some households from homelessness placed duties upon local authorities to assist households which were homeless or threatened with homelessness and were deemed to be in priority need (provided that they had not become homeless intentionally and had a connection with the local authority area). The priority categories are households which include children, a pregnant woman or someone who is otherwise 'vulnerable' and households made homeless as a result of an emergency such as fire or flood.

People generally falling outside these priority categories are single persons and couples without children and are widely referred to as single homeless people (Anderson, Kemp and Quilgars, 1993). Single homeless persons were affected by a number of policy decisions in the 1980s. First, government's 'hostels initiative' to improve the standard of temporary accommodation for single homeless people involved closing down very large traditional hostels, including the resettlement units run by the DHSS, and replacing them with a more diverse range of accommodation mainly through housing associations. Second, government's reform of social security in the late 1980s involved the replacement of previous board and lodging allowances by income support and housing benefit. It also provided a lower rate of income support for those aged under 25 and removed entitlement for most aged under 18. It is generally accepted that these factors had contributed to a growth of single homelessness and government's recognition of this was apparent in the development of a series of initiatives relating to homelessness. In June 1990, £96 million was made available for 1990–3 to tackle the problem of people sleeping rough in central London by providing extra hostels and longer-term accommodation. Some additional funds (£6 million in 1992/3) were given in grants to organisations and projects providing advice and assistance to single homeless people. The 'rough sleepers initiative' was further extended subsequently both in and beyond London.

Tenants' charter and tenants' choice

The tenants' charter introduced in the Housing Act 1980, while not as radical as the proposals contained in the Labour Government's Housing Bill in 1979 (especially in respect of tenants' involvement in management and of mobility) did change the conditions and rights associated with public sector tenancies. The principal development in the tenants' charter was to place tenancies in the public sector within a precise legal framework. This included definition of security of tenure and procedures and grounds for obtaining possession. Rights of succession for widows, widowers or members of the family who have been resident in the property were laid down. Rights to take lodgers or to sublet, to carry out improvements (subject to a landlord's permission) and apply for improvement grants and rights to consultation and provision of information were also specified. In addition to these rights for tenants, the wider public was given rights to information about rules and procedures on housing allocations and transfers, rights to information on consultation procedures and rights to check details which they had provided in making an application for housing.

While it was an important development to clarify and back these areas by the law, the tenants' charter often did not require significant changes in local practice. In some localities where management practice was less enlightened, major policy changes were required. However, in certain respects, the tenants' charter required a change in the way policy was carried out, but not in the substance of policies. The local authority was still able to gain possession in a wide range of circumstances although the process and justification for possession changed. Other rights in the tenants' charter were circumscribed by the need to obtain permission or the council's concern over issues of overcrowding. The rights involved do not involve crucial areas of rents or mobility and transfer opportunities and there has been little monitoring of how they are being implemented in practice. Furthermore other policy developments have reduced the resources available to tenants and applicants as a group and exacerbate the lack of self-determination and choice. The tenants' charter has not fundamentally altered the position of the council tenant and remedied problems of 'serfdom' associated with the tenure. Nor has central government hesitated to erode these rights by extending the grounds for possession (under the Housing and Planning Act 1986) in order to facilitate other policies concerned with privatisation of estates. Similarly changes to the legislation on homelessness and the introduction of probationary tenancies appeared to go against the spirit of previous concern to establish rights.

In 1987, a new phase of discussion of tenants' rights commenced. The Conservative Manifesto 1987 introduced the idea of a Choice of Landlord scheme under the heading 'Rights for Council Tenants'. Where many council estates were badly designed, vulnerable to crime and vandalism and in bad repair and, in many areas, rent arrears were high it was often difficult for tenants to move: 'If they are ever to enjoy the prospect of independence municipal monopoly must be replaced by choice in renting.' Two key paragraphs outlined what this involved:

> We will give groups of tenants the right to form tenant co-operatives owning and running their management and budget for themselves. They will also have the right to ask other institutions to take over their housing. Tenants who wish to remain with the local authority will be able to do so.
>   We will give each council house tenant individually the right to transfer the ownership of his or her house to a housing association, or other independent, approved landlord. (Conservative Party, 1987)

The Housing Act 1988 included provisions to give tenants a right to choose their landlord. Subsequent guidelines set out the criteria under which government would consent to Tenants' Choice transfers. These gave a considerable role to the Housing Corporation in England and to Scottish Homes and Housing for Wales in approving, scrutinising, regulating and monitoring prospective landlords and proposals for the process of transfer.

While government presented Tenants' Choice as an unproblematic extension of tenants' rights, controversy centred on the procedures for balloting tenants and the long-term effects on tenants' rights. By the end of 1993 Tenants' Choice had not resulted in the transfer of a single property but transfers had taken place under parallel arrangements for landlord-initiated large-scale voluntary transfers. The Housing Act 1988 included provisions to set up Housing Action Trusts (HATs). Subject to tenants' views and to parliamentary approval, the Trusts were intended to tackle the problems of run-down, predominantly public sector housing by taking over responsibility for local authority housing in designated areas. They would be responsible for securing its repair and improvement, improving management and diversifying ownership, and encouraging local enterprise and employment by cooperation with bodies concerned with economic development. Trusts would have a limited life and would pass their housing on to other forms of ownership and management. Initial proposals to set up HATs in Lambeth, Southwark, Tower Hamlets, Leeds, Sandwell and Sunderland were either abandoned or delayed because of tenant consultation and ballots and the HATs which were set up in Hull, Waltham Forest, Liverpool, Birmingham, Brent and Tower Hamlets had local authority support and separate earmarked funds.

The language of tenants' rights and the tenants' charter reemerged in the context of the government's wider Citizen's Charter proposals. The new tenants' charter established as part of this approach only applied to council tenants and tells tenants how to exercise their rights on matters such as security of tenure, exchanges and the freedom to take lodgers. Annual reports to tenants providing information on key issues including empty properties, rent levels and arrears, lettings, housing benefit administration, homelessness and management costs were intended to increase accountability to tenants and improve standards of service.

This approach was complemented by new measures introduced in the Leasehold Reform, Housing and Urban Development Act 1993, which introduced an improved 'Right to Repair' enabling tenants to get urgent repairs done and a Right to Compensation for Improvements under which tenants moving out of a home could be compensated for improvements they had carried out. This legislation also extended opportunities for council house purchase through the Rent to Mortgage scheme. With the Right to Buy continuing (but with the removal of rights to shared ownership and to a mortgage) the rights of council tenants were wider than ever before and more extensive than elsewhere in the rented sector.

In line with the principles of the Citizen's Charter the government made available grants to enable the development of Tenant Management Organisations for the management of their estates. At the same time, the extension of compulsory competitive tendering (CCT) into housing management was indicated in 1992 through a consultation process. Pilot projects for CCT were set up and local authorities were developing procedures for CCT although the exact timing of its introduction was affected by plans for local government reorganisation. One final element in the approach to tenants' rights is the proposal to set up an ombudsman to act for housing association tenants. The emergence of this proposal can be taken as a tacit admission that the arrangements for regulation and scrutiny of housing associations are insufficient to ensure tenants' rights. They signalled some modification of the post-1988 honeymoon period in which housing associations were regarded as favoured agencies with inherent strengths.

Economic regeneration

The development of the Estates Renewal Challenge Fund and the increased interest in run-down and deprived urban housing estates reflected a wider agenda than that traditionally associated with housing policy. In this wider agenda housing problems contributed to other social and economic difficulties and at the same time these wider circumstances contributed to housing problems. The conventional wisdom increasingly moved towards a view that the approach to housing and other urban problems should be a holistic one which involved different levels of government, different agencies in the public, private and voluntary sector and different programmes, departments and disciplines. What was needed was a coherent and systematic approach which brought together a range of different resources to focus upon problems which had multiple origins.

While the evidence of the residualisation of council housing and the increasing concentration of lower-income groups within council housing made it clear that residents' problems would rarely be restricted to housing, a major shift in approach is associated with the review of urban policy completed in 1994 (Robson *et al.*, 1994). Areas of deprivation were increasingly seen as a drag on the economy, damaging recovery and restricting its impact. Against this background there was a renewed interest in how to achieve economic regeneration in neighbourhoods with high levels of unemployment. As these neighbourhoods included many with high levels of council housing the role of housing in urban regeneration was being reassessed. Out of this review in England new Government Offices in the Regions and a new Single Regeneration Budget (SRB), which included major former housing programmes (including Estate Action and HATs), were presented as the vehicles for the new approach to regeneration. Housing expenditure would increasingly be absorbed within broader strategies linked with employment, training, education and other elements to achieve sustained recovery. Expenditure on improving the housing stock was not sufficient unless it was part of a more broadly-based regeneration strategy.

In 1995 the first round of operation of the Single Regeneration Budget marked a significant departure in policy. Its direct effect would mean that once existing committed programmes had terminated, there would be fewer programmes that were properly described as housing programmes. New approaches to regeneration also applied in other parts of the United Kingdom. Taken together they represent a significant shift in the thinking about urban problems and could herald the end of an era of housing policy. At the same time the reduced expenditure associated with these programmes suggested that concerns to constrain and target a declining budget played an important role in overall thinking. In the first years of the SRB it was evident that there was considerable innovation and fresh thinking. However, the share of housing within the SRB declined as the previous programmes began to diminish (Hall *et al.*, 1998). While housing expenditure alone would be unlikely to remedy urban problems, there remained some fear that policy makers at local or national levels believed that economic regeneration could be achieved through actions which did not include housing investment.

Conclusions

The 18 years of Conservative government between 1979 and 1997 are associated with important changes in housing policy and the housing market in Britain. It is impossible to satisfactorily assess what would have happened without these changes and how much is attributable to the particular policy stance and ideological position of the Conservative Party in this period. There are continuities with earlier phases and the fiscal and public expenditure context would have restricted the options for any government. In this sense it is wrong to attribute everything that happened in the period to Thatcherism. At the same time there are distinctive features of policy as housing, more than any other part of the welfare state, saw significant changes in the level and direction of expenditure. If it has become the conventional wisdom among social policy analysts that the period of Conservative government did not really have such a dramatic effect upon the welfare state, this view is incorrect as far as housing is concerned. The reduction and reorientation of expenditure, the shift to the private sector, the continuing ideological opposition to municipal activity and the rewarding of home ownership and private provision are distinctive features. If comparisons are made with other countries facing the same global economic pressures during this period, it is difficult to find another example pursuing the same policy so vigorously. While the direction of change has been to increase the role of the private sector, to reduce subsidies, to target assistance with housing costs through rent allowance and rebate schemes, only Ireland has adopted a Right to Buy policy comparable with that in the United Kingdom. The levels of discount and financial support associated with the Right to Buy are not consistent with global economic pressures but with ideological positions. In a similar way the deregulation of the private rented sector has gone further and faster in the UK and the consequences in terms of housing benefit expenditure are more apparent than elsewhere. To the extent that the UK is out of step, its policy directions cannot be attributed to global economic pressures.

Many of the changes associated with the period, including the residualisation of council housing and the changing role and balance of tenures, have been reinforced rather than initiated in this period. Others have not been as dramatic as is often represented and some reflect changes of pace rather than policy direction. Some of the most significant influences on policy have been associated with economic and fiscal policies rather than housing policy change. For example, low inflation and high interest rates have affected housing subsidy and other expenditures and costs. Rates of house price inflation and the impact of economic recession and rising unemployment have had effects on individual problems of meeting housing costs, of mobility, maintenance and repair. Especially in the 1990s they overwhelmed the housing policy set out by government.

Traditional views of the housing problem of the consequences of reduced investment in housing and of increasing housing and social inequality did not significantly influence policy. Secretaries of State quite explicitly rejected planning and projection techniques until towards the end of this period. The determinants of policy were 'what the country could afford' and it was desirable to reduce public intervention and encourage the private sector. But in order to do this the distinctions between public and private sectors were obscured and the state increasingly sponsored and supported independent provision. Government encouraged the 'market' by subsidy and special treatment as well as by deregulation. Views that there is a needs-related or politically-related level below which state provision cannot fall may not have been disproved. Homelessness, mortgage arrears and repossessions rose to levels incompatible with a view that the previous pattern of provision had emerged because it was necessary for the maintenance of the political and economic system. The politics of housing are not so one-dimensional.

By the end of the period housing had declined from a major to a minor capital programme. While social security, education, health and social service expenditure grew in real terms, there was more public debate on real and threatened cuts in these services than there was on housing which had much more marked cuts in total expenditure. It may be argued that the most important issue is why housing proved so easy to cut: why issues of need and welfare were so easily bypassed; why pressure groups were so ineffective; why new and increased inequalities were so easily introduced. 'Technical' arguments may be advanced showing that it is easier to cut capital programmes or that demographic or economic (unemployment) factors lead expenditure in other policy areas more than in housing. It may also be argued that council housing had less public support than other areas of the welfare state. There are other factors which are at least equally worthy of reference. The development of a dual tenure system may have divided or confused political opposition to cuts in public expenditure and to privatisation. Cuts in housing investment do not have an immediate or easily identifiable impact on a particular group and there are time lags before the reduction in housing is felt. There are also turnover and other processes affecting who experiences changes and when.

In considering this period it is worth noting those policies which achieved much less than was expected of them. The relative failure of low-cost home ownership initiatives (not including the 'Right to Buy') are attributable to cost and affordability factors as well as to local implementation (Forrest, Lansley and Murie, 1984). The variable response of private sector output in a new 'climate' was attributable to aspects of commercial judgements and opportunities for profit, as was the slump in activity following 1988. The failure of Tenants' Choice, Housing Action Trusts, the Right to Repair and the Rent to Mortgage scheme relates to consumer responses and resistance. The experiment over private renting is of more fundamental interest. The policy makers largely did what the theoreticians said was needed to revive the sector. Removing rent regulation and reducing tenants' rights put the incentive structures in place to trigger a transformation of rental housing provision. Landlords took advantage of the opportunity to raise rents and change tenancies but did not significantly increase the supply or quality of the sector. Increased costs to the Exchequer through housing benefit payments to meet higher rents did not generate increased investment. The experiment appears to have been based on poor premises and an inadequate appreciation of incentive structures.

The lack of coordination between the policies and budgets of the Department of the Environment and the Department of Social Security, illustrated by the apparently unanticipated explosion of housing benefit expenditure and subsequent attempts to stem this, illustrate a deeper-seated problem. Within government, policies towards housing development do not appear to have been strongly influenced by considerations about transport, the environment or energy. The development of community care policies illustrates the problem from another angle. In this case, the consequences of community care have fallen significantly upon housing and are reflected in homelessness and other statistics and yet there appears to have been very little real exploration of cross-departmental interests. Taken together it is easier to portray the policy package as a contradictory fragmented and incoherent series of initiatives and experiments often built upon prejudices and poor information, rather than a coherent sustainable strategy for the development of cities and regions. Perhaps it is the recognition of this tendency generally that explains the adoption of more broad-based holistic regeneration strategies at the end of the period – albeit without the resources or wider policy changes which would suggest a real rethinking of policy.

By the end of its period in office, the Conservative Government's policy reflected the same concerns as in 1979. Privatisation and public expenditure control dominated the agenda. However, the agenda had been significantly affected by what had happened to the home ownership sector, by economic problems and by its own inconsistencies – especially relating to the burden imposed on the social security budget. By 1997 government was talking about sustainable home ownership, about the continuing need for social rented housing and about regeneration. The growing awareness of the interconnections between housing circumstances, economic opportunity and local economic regeneration were being recognised in urban policy and in other ways. The concern expressed over where to house the 4.4 million additional households forecast for England between 1991 and 2016 involved a reengagement with the traditional concerns of housing policy with forecasts of need and demand and debates about planning and the provision of housing in different tenures and different locations. The agenda which had been pursued since 1979 was no longer sufficient and, indeed, had not provided the climate in which the market could flourish and the need for state intervention could be eliminated. Nor had it provided a continuing formula for electoral success.

In the early years of the Conservative government much emphasis was placed on the extent to which its housing policy was influenced by the view that council tenants were more likely to vote Labour and that home owners would be natural supporters of the Conservative Party. By 1997 there was a much-expanded number of home owners – expected by some to be natural Conservative voters. In the event neither attitudes to party, to politics, to neighbourhood problems or to a wide range of issues divided along housing tenure lines nor the expansion of home ownership was sufficient to secure the Conservatives in government. It is unlikely that governments of the future will regard housing tenure in the same way.

6

The Policy Context

Accounts of the development of housing provision and housing policy in Britain lend little support to assumptions that housing policy has emerged as a natural response to economic development or changing housing needs. There has normally been disagreement over what constitute the needs which should be addressed through policy and over the best ways of responding to need. And in any case, there have been other important pressures and concerns which have influenced policy – concerns about the spread of disease; civil disorder and threats to the political status quo; the creation of employment, reflation of the economy, or control of inflation; the reduction of public expenditure and electoral calculations. British experience is no different from that of other countries in this respect and accounts of the development of housing policy in other countries illustrate the range of factors influencing housing strategies (see, for example, Harloe, 1995; Pooley, 1992). This wide range of influences continues to affect policy and action in housing. The housing agenda for those involved in the policy process at different levels is not a one-dimensional one in which the aims are straightforward, the mechanisms for achieving policy are uncomplicated and the task is simply to marshal resources, communicate what is wanted and control performance. In contrast, objectives are complex and often in conflict and the context which affects resources, methods and performance is a changing one. This policy context changes over time and according to place. The context for achieving objectives in relation to meeting housing need, improving housing conditions or achieving specified standards of performance differs between cities and districts and over time. In this sense, assessing what policies can achieve or what tasks have to be overcome involves a recognition that the task varies and is uneven and that the resources available differ. Policies which are effective in one context, say of full employment, moderate real interest rates and modest house price inflation, may be less effective when interest rates are high or house prices fall or unemployment is high.

This chapter addresses the key elements in the environment affecting housing policy. It focuses on the nature of housing and goes on to consider five major areas affecting housing policy. These are demographic change, the economic context, social change, the political context and the wider structure of the welfare state. The chapter then considers issues of residualisation and social exclusion where the different elements referred to previously come together with important implications for housing policy and housing management.

Housing and the legacy of previous policy

The provision of shelter is fundamentally about the production and use of a high-cost, durable, fixed investment. Making additions to the stock is a long and expensive process involving land assembly and the provision of infrastructure (roads, water, sewerage, gas, electricity and other services). New building in Britain added less than 1 per cent of dwellings to the housing stock each year in the early 1990s and the length of time from starting on-site to completion of a dwelling was between 15 and 20 months. This understates the length of time involved because it leaves out earlier stages of land acquisition, designing schemes, financing development, gaining planning approval and organising the construction process. In this environment, a central feature of the housing policy process relates to time-scales and time-lags. In some areas, such as housing benefit, changes can be made and be effective almost immediately. But where policies are concerned with the size, condition and even ownership of the housing stock the time-scale for achieving change is much lengthier. Thus, for example, reforms of the social security system, decisions to introduce a new housing benefit scheme or to uprate benefits or change tapers for benefit can be taken and implemented rapidly. The time-scale for implementation of measures to eliminate housing poverty in the sense of ensuring that no household lives in dwellings that are substandard or unfit for human habitation is very different. Dealing with these issues of housing condition in the postwar period required more than legislation or the development of a system of transfer payments, it required significant capital investment and sustained planning and programming of major works.

Although dwellings have a long life they require repair and maintenance and are subject to processes of social and physical obsolescence. An ageing housing stock will not provide the same standard of accommodation if there are no expenditures to maintain and improve it. At some point the fabric and structure of dwellings are so far obsolete as to require replacement. In other cases the lack of demand for dwellings indicates that replacement or conversion would be appropriate. Examples of the latter may range from poorly designed flats in peripheral locations to bedsitters in sheltered housing schemes. Thus the process of adjusting the housing stock to meet demand and need involves not only planning additions to the stock but also responding to changes in the existing stock. In both cases the time-scales are considerable and the way the housing stock changes may reflect circumstances in the past. Thus, for example, housing in some areas may have been neglected because it was in areas blighted by plans for road-widening or slum clearance or because its owners did not have the desire or the resources to maintain it. Although current plans or current owners may not be associated with these problems, the consequences of previous circumstances are apparent in a backlog of disrepair.

Finally, the legacy of previous policies and circumstances may be illustrated in another way. The impact of policy changes may take a very long time to work through. Households do not move house in response to every shift in relative advantage. However, households entering the housing market for the first time or those moving house for job reasons or because of changing family size and structure are likely to move to tenures and dwellings which provide the best combination of attributes taking into account both the need for housing (size, design, etc.), locational factors (schools, jobs, etc.) and investment aspects. Thus the decline of private landlordism in Britain has been a long-drawn-out slow process, heavily influenced by the rate at which tenancies were vacated and therefore by the age and mobility (or immobility) of tenants. Similarly the impacts of the Right to Buy on council housing stocks, the availability of housing for letting and the changing nature of neighbourhoods are slow to accumulate and emerge. To pursue this example, at the point of sale to a sitting tenant, there is no change in who lives in the house, in the social make-up of the neighbourhood or in the supply of housing to the homeless or households on the waiting list. The sitting-tenant purchaser may move at any point thereafter and the evidence shows a slow turnover in the early years after initial purchase. As initial purchasers move on, so there is a change in neighbourhood and, as time passes, there is a loss of direct housing opportunities for the homeless and others seeking to rent as the houses are sold on the market rather than relet. At the same time, the fact of transfer from, say, public sector control to home ownership will affect the pattern of maintenance and repair. But all of these changes will work through incrementally over a long time period. The momentum for change is established when the properties are sold but the consequences (adverse or otherwise) will emerge at different stages. Taking stock of the situation at any point in time involves recognising the changes which are still working their way through the system and the processes of change which will continue to affect what services are available.

As mentioned in Chapter 1, the implication of this kind of discussion is that the central resource for providing housing – the dwellings themselves – is the product of a long history and continues to be affected by past policies. Policy-makers do not start with a blank sheet and cannot easily reshape the housing stock in the short term. A fundamental constraint on policy and policy development is the legacy represented by the housing stock. Presented in a different way this housing stock represents the key resource for housing the population. The older housing stock plays a much more important role than new additions to it both in terms of stock and the flow of vacancies or opportunities for households to obtain housing for the first time or to move house. Both new housing and the older stock vary considerably in size, design and layout. Suitability and desirability vary: issues of overcrowding, barrier-free housing or dwellings suitable for persons with mobility problems, energy efficiency and heating costs relate directly to the dwelling. Issues of tenure, security of tenure, dwelling condition, housing costs, access and affordability are not intrinsic to the dwelling but are of fundamental importance at any stage. Furthermore there are issues of location and proximity to local services such as schools, shops and transport, and issues of safety which are generally associated with neighbourhood rather than dwelling. These dimensions of housing resources are affected both by past and present policies and the wider social and economic environment. While it is possible to present housing stock statistics for specific places at specific dates the pattern of opportunity that they represent involves understanding the interaction between these different dimensions. In the British context it is generally acknowledged that rather than a national housing market being at work, regional and local elements are of great importance. It is also clear that the workings of the housing market have not been effectively analysed by attempts to convert the different dimensions of housing into some combined measure of housing service. Consequently, while it is clear that the existing local housing stock and its characteristics are a key ingredient of the context for housing policy and practice, summarising and measuring local differences are not straightforward.

Demographic change

Housing, unlike health services or education, is used continuously by all persons at all stages of their lives. It enables people to develop independent and private lives and is an essential element not just at points of crisis in relationships, employment or health. In view of this the basic demand for housing relates directly to the size and structure of the population and judgements about the adequacy of housing supply may be upset by changes in the population. It is important to recognise that this is a two-way process with the availability of housing influencing when and whether new households form and, for example, how long people continue to live in the parental home. Where housing is available and what its characteristics are, as well as a range of economic and other factors, also affect patterns of migration and local demographic change. In this context, whether housing is 'available' relates to costs and incomes. Demographic changes reflect the risks and opportunities existing in a particular society as well as attitudes, habits, circumstances and choices, and housing conditions and are one of the elements affecting both risks and opportunities.

Discussions of demographic changes in Britain in recent years emphasise the changes in family structures – the rise in birth rate from the mid-1950s created new young households from the mid-1970s. This increase in households coincided with higher divorce rates and increased numbers of persons of retirement age with a greater tendency to continue to live independently (Coleman and Salt, 1992). For housing, while total population size and structure are fundamental, it is households and families which more directly relate to housing provision. This is especially so if it is the population living in private households which is referred to as relating to the task of those developing housing policy or a measure of those competing for housing. Household is a wider definition than family and in official definitions refers to a person or persons living in a single dwelling unit and sharing meals and household costs.

Changes in the size and structure of households in Britain have had a direct impact on housing problems and requirements. A number of key elements are normally identified in this (see Coleman and Salt, 1992). Average household size has declined significantly. In 1901 average household size in England and Wales was 4.6; in 1939, 3.5; in 1961, 3.1; and in 1989, 2.5. The decline in household size means that the number of households has grown much more rapidly than the population as a whole. Equally important, it is this change which has done most to reduce problems of overcrowding. The older housing stock can house smaller households with a lower rate of overcrowding and the decline in fertility from a five or six child family to a two child family is important, even though its impact on overall household size has been reduced by declining mortality. The elements contributing to reduced family size in addition to lower fertility are the reduction in non-related people such as servants and lodgers living with families and the increased numbers of people, young and old, living alone. In 1989, 1 in 4 households were of one person compared with 1 in 20 in 1911. In 1911 there were more unmarried adult men and particularly women, more younger widows living alone but almost no divorced persons. This contrasts with the present situation. As Coleman and Salt state:

> Now people are most likely to live alone in old age (mostly through widowhood) and to a lesser extent at younger ages. Only 7 per cent of single-person households are under age 35, about three-quarters are over 60 years of age. In 1981, 5 per cent of people aged 25–44 lived alone, 29 per cent of people aged 65–74, and 47 per cent of those aged 75 and over. Beyond that age, an increasing proportion (19 per cent aged 85 and over) live in institutions. (Coleman and Salt, 1992: 225)

The life cycle of the household has direct implications for competition for housing. The ability of young people to leave the parental home and set up an independent home relates to income and other resources or willingness to share. Young married couples and lone parents living with their parents are often regarded as concealed households which would live independently if they could negotiate access to housing and this can also be argued to apply to some single adults living with their parents.

Partly because of the growth of one person households since the 1960s, married or cohabiting couples with dependent (under 16) children formed only 24 per cent of all households in 1995/6. Married or cohabiting couple households without children or without dependent children formed 35 per cent of all households and 7 per cent of households consisted of one parent with dependent children. The increase in divorce, relationship breakdown among cohabiting couples and illegitimacy have led to a considerable increase in this latter with divorce much the most important element. Finally 28 per cent of households in 1995/6 consisted of one person. Over two-thirds of households consist of one or two persons and it is this group rather than families with children which dominate housing need and demand. Some of these households are at a stage before family growth and some are beyond this phase.

The other element of demographic change which has most impact on housing is the increasing importance of older persons in the population. Discussions of older people in Britain usually refer to people above the age when state retirement pensions have been available (60 for women and 65 for men). In 1901 this elderly population accounted for some 6 per cent of the population. In 1951 this had risen to 14 per cent in 1981 and 1991 it was 18 per cent. Population projections show some increase in future years (19 per cent in 2011; 22 per cent in 2025), however it is evident that the most dramatic growth has already occurred. In the period of relative stability which is anticipated the numbers aged over-75 will increase. This group has risen from some 26 per cent of all old people in 1951 to 32 per cent in 1981 and 38 per cent in 1991. It is expected to rise to 41 per cent in 2001. This over 75 age group makes the greatest demands on health and social services. Levels of disability and dependency on residential institutions tend to increase with age. Women significantly outlive men and in 1989 3.9m of the 6.9m people of retirement age were women. Women were 1.4m of the 2 million persons aged over 80. Older people are most likely to live with their spouse or to live alone. The likelihood of living alone increases with age and has increased since the 1960s. Generally this appears to reflect the preference of older people and previously achieved independent housing is crucial in that. It also relates to the smaller size of families. The role of family networks in caring for or housing older people is limited by this.

Older people have benefited from the general improvement in housing circumstances which has resulted from public and private investment in housing through the years since 1945. Public sector housebuilding both for general needs and to replace slum housing eliminated the crude shortfall of houses compared with households by the mid-1970s and had almost eliminated dwellings regarded as unfit, those lacking amenities and those unsuitable for modern living. While older people benefited from this general improvement in housing they also benefited from specific policies directed at elderly people. There are over half a million sheltered housing units in Britain (5 per cent of older people) and these involve dwellings with some communal facilities and a warden available for emergencies. Other provision includes very sheltered housing with extra facilities, hostels, granny annexes and assistance or adaptations to enable people to continue to live in their present home.

These general improvements have not eliminated housing problems. Elderly people remain more likely than others to be in dwellings lacking basic amenities, and in dwellings which are unfit and in poor repair. But most older people are in substantial self-contained dwellings with modern amenities. They are usually living in what was the family home (whether they own or rent the house) and more than one in four elderly households live in houses with two or more spare bedrooms. This is not in itself a problem and enables family contacts to be better maintained through extended visiting but it may contribute to problems over the costs of heating and maintaining dwellings. These problems have become more prominent as the proportion of older people who are home owners has increased.

In the current policy framework the proportion of elderly persons who are home owners will continue to rise. Privatisation since the 1980s has not directly affected the elderly as much as other groups. For example the 2 million households which bought their dwellings under the Right to Buy were generally in their 40s and early 50s. As these householders age they will be part of a cohort with very high levels of home ownership. Some of these households will have low incomes and limited savings and problems of maintenance and repair are likely to be as common as now if not more common. In this way future developments, especially if they are to accord with people's wish to remain in their own home, are likely to include policies related to these problems. One policy which continues to operate has sought to reduce the population living in state residential institutions and to enable people to remain in the community. The growth of private residential homes has been facilitated by social security payments to meet costs.

The current environment of fiscal and public expenditure constraint limits the development of plans to deal with the outstanding problems of older people in housing, health and social security. Reduced levels of public expenditure in the 1980s have affected various programmes including those to provide sheltered housing. One argument in this context is to influence the design of newly built housing to introduce 'barrier-free' or 'lifetime houses' design features which mean that rather than building houses specially for older or disabled persons the general housing stock is suitable for continued use by those with health and mobility problems. The situation of older people depends on the interaction of a number of key policy areas. In particular these relate to the provision of medical care, income maintenance, housing policy and specialist welfare services. The failings of any one have implications for others.

The demographic changes outlined above have altered the number, size and types of household seeking housing. A key element in the whole process is ability to compete for housing but, for example, the increased numbers of divorced persons often involve people already in home ownership and with sufficient resources to obtain independent housing after separation. Demographic changes relating to a more affluent population with savings and accumulated wealth translate into increased demand for housing and demonstrate capacity to obtain such housing. Policy-makers concerned to provide sufficient housing, say for households with children, cannot ignore the competing demands coming from other groups. Policies which on one scenario would achieve objectives could be overtaken or overwhelmed because they have not taken sufficient account of competition from other groups. In this sense the effectiveness of policy in the past and future is crucially affected by the opportunities available to people and the choices which people make in relation to independent housing and household fusion and fission. Recent debates about housing and planning in Britain have attached considerable attention to projections suggesting a growth in the number of households. In England these projections were of a growth from 19 215 000 households in 1991 to 23 598 000 in 2016. The projections showed an increase in one person households from 27 per cent to 36 per cent and a decrease in couples with or without children from 61 per cent to 49 per cent. With concern about the impact of new housebuilding on the countryside these figures sparked a major debate about city living, the reasons for movement away from the cities and whether single persons would choose different types of housing and different locations than couples. The significance of demographic change for housing and related policies was evident.

The pattern of demographic change introduces other factors into the housing situation. The growth of lone-parent households, of elderly persons and of young single-person households has been a major element in the growth of low-income households and those dependent on social security benefits. This has been exacerbated by the high unemployment of the 1980s and 1990s. However, in a situation where two incomes are increasingly necessary to gain access to home ownership – especially in areas of high house prices – households with, at most, one wage earner are likely to be unable to buy. The level of demand for rented housing and the characteristics of households being housed in the rented sector reflect this. Local authorities and housing associations in the 1990s are operating in a context where the types of household seeking housing differs from 40 years before. The pressures on them and the management task involved is fundamentally affected by the changing demographic situation.

The economic context

The development of housing in the postwar period until the late 1970s took place against a background of full employment. The growth of home ownership in that period was in a context of stable, secure employment with rising incomes. For much of the period from the 1960s, rising house prices and a more general inflation, at times rising to high inflation, provided an environment favourable to home ownership. At some stages and significantly in the 1970s negative real rates of interest applied and those who were borrowing money for house purchase were subject to interest rates which fell below the rate of inflation. These most favourable circumstances did not continue throughout the 1980s as lower inflation and higher interest rates produced positive real rates of interest. The 1980s and 1990s saw a major restructuring of the British economy with the decline of key sectors of manufacturing industry and the growth of the service sector. A different occupational structure and higher levels of unemployment contributed to a wider disparity of earnings and incomes. The uneven geographical pattern of economic change meant that there were significant regional and local differences which affected demand and affordability. This chapter restricts its attention to employment and the development of a flexible labour market. Key aspects included:

- The rise of unemployment and long-term unemployment.
- Changing patterns of employment with the decline of skilled employment in manufacturing alongside a growth of lower-paid insecure and unskilled work in the service sectors.
- Uneven patterns of economic restructuring with declining job opportunities in different regions (the north in the early 1980s) related to the industrial structure of the area and with the growth of service sector employment.
- The growth of atypical working such as that without conventional contracts and conditions of work.
- The expansion of women's employment.

These long-term changes in the structure of employment have direct implications for both the stability and level of household incomes. They have generally contributed to a widening of income inequality in Britain. Although this view was widely resisted for some time the evidence is no longer in serious dispute. The most definitive evidence is contained in a statistical analysis for 1979–88/9 published by the Department of Social Security: *Households Below Average Income* (1992). This analysis shows that in the period concerned average income rose by around 30 per cent in real terms. Real income rose in each income decile (10 per cent group) in the lower half of the population except for the bottom 10 per cent. For the bottom 10 per cent, income in 1988/9 was 2 per cent higher than in 1979 (before housing costs) and 6 per cent lower after housing costs. The bottom 50 per cent of the population had some 5 per cent less of total income in 1988/9. In 1988/9 there were more unemployed families in the bottom 10 per cent of the income distribution and fewer pensioners. Single parents were over-represented in the bottom 10 per cent. The proportion of the population with incomes below the average income for each year was 59 per cent in 1979 and 62 per cent (61 per cent after housing costs) in 1988/9. And the proportion of the population with incomes below half the average income for each year was 8 per cent in 1979 and 19 per cent in 1988/9 (before housing costs). The comparable figures after housing costs have been taken into account were 9 per cent and 22 per cent. These figures indicate that lower-income groups had not shared in the growth of income over the period concerned and demonstrate wider inequality and social polarisation. Key elements in this wider inequality have been the growth of unemployment and labour market restructuring and the rate at which welfare benefits have been increased.

In the late 1980s and early 1990s the impact of economic change on housing was particularly dramatic. Indeed the history of housing policy between 1987 and 1994 can reasonably be portrayed as one in which changes in the national economic situation overwhelmed housing policy and generated a new agenda with problems associated with mortgage arrears, repossessions and negative equity. These issues have been outlined in Chapter 5.

The housing market does not operate in isolation from the wider economy but is both affected by and affects economic change. At its simplest the demand for housing and the availability of resources for housing from the public and private sectors are fundamentally affected by the pattern of growth of the economy. At the same time the capacity of individual households to negotiate access to housing and to achieve satisfactory housing relates fundamentally to whether they are in employment and to the security and level of remuneration associated with that employment. This situation has become more true as home ownership has become the dominant tenure in Britain and as access to credit and ability to maintain mortgage payments have become the key elements in secure housing for a larger section of the population. How the economy changes has an impact on household budgets and the ability to enter and sustain home ownership.

These same economic changes also affect the whole environment in which decisions about taxation, benefits and public expenditure are made. These include decisions about housing public expenditure but also about the other major public expenditure programmes which impinge on housing – social security benefits, expenditure on health and social services including care in the community, expenditure on regional and urban policies. While the options related to public expenditure are crucially affected by the economic context, the decisions are about priorities and political stances.

The political context

Housing policy and practice can be seen as direct expressions of political processes. Policy aims and mechanisms and the ways in which policy emerges through the range of policy action is constantly affected by the wider political system. Much of this is apparent from the account of the development of the housing system presented in earlier chapters of this book. As was emphasised in Chapter 2 the key precondition for the dominant role of local government in housing policy in Britain was the development of a strong and effective local government system in the nineteenth century. In other countries where the role of local government has been less important in housing policy this has partly been because of the absence of a system of local government which could undertake such a role. Local authorities provided a political and administrative structure which was suitable for the tasks identified. In the words of Aneurin Bevan as Minister of Health immediately after the Second World War:

> If we are to plan we have to plan with plannable instruments and the speculative builder, by his very nature is not a plannable instrument . . . we rest the full weight of the housing programme upon the local authorities, because the programmes can be planned. (House of Commons Debates, vol. 420, col. 451, March 1946)

The capacity of local government to deliver policy outputs has remained. However the new framework provided for housing associations after 1974 began to create an alternative vehicle for tasks which the private sector would not undertake. This together with the increasing disenchantment of the Conservative Party with local government represented important changes in the political context for housing policy.

In view of the key role of local government in housing policy the respective roles of and relationships between central and local government in housing have been and continue to be of considerable importance. Key elements of the organisation and structure of both central and local government and the nature of the relationship between them are discussed in Chapter 7. An additional factor is the membership of the European Union and the effect of this on the economy and various areas of regulation. Even though housing is not a competence of the European Union, legislation and regulation affect housing, and the indirect effects of membership of the EU are apparent both in the wider development of the economy and in a range of measures. These include, for example, measures relating to procurement, safety and employment and in the use of structural funds and development of initiatives which interact with housing. At this stage it is important to acknowledge that changes in the structure and organisation of government and relationships between different parts of the machinery of the state have repercussions on housing policy. The structure and resourcing of both central and local government, of quasi non-governmental organisations and of the voluntary and private sectors are affected by a history and pattern of power and interest which have an independent effect on housing. The interests which are able to have most impact on policy will partly reflect the nature of these political and institutional arrangements. Thus, for example, there is a long-standing debate in Britain about the power and influence of civil servants rather than ministers or of Parliament and a similar debate about the respective roles of local government officers and councillors. A new set of issues will emerge with greater devolution to Wales and Scotland and the emergence of stronger regional bodies in England.

These debates have been particularly apparent in periods of consensus politics and limited policy change. They have been less apparent in the more ideological and confrontational phase which marked the 1980s. In this period the adoption of certain policies (although less so in housing than some other areas of policy) implied an increased power and influence for a 'new right' ideology and organisations associated with that ideology and linked with the Conservative Party. In this phase of policy to a greater extent than in the past the nature of the dominant political ideology was a key element of the political context. Various institutional and ideological factors affect how priorities and policies are determined. Whatever the demographic and economic context, and whatever the legacy of past policy is, there are choices of priorities. How these are arrived at will reflect institutional and ideological factors, electoral and party political judgements and negotiation and bargaining between key actors and agencies. Judgements about what the country can afford to spend on housing, about taxation and public expenditure more generally, involve political decisions and are not inevitable outcomes of other factors.

Although some of these issues are picked up in Chapter 7 they are not extensively developed in this book. The crucial points for this chapter are to recognise, first, that the political system is not static and that the balance of power and influence shifts over time and, second, that differences in local politics and local political traditions have been and continue to be important. While the tendency is to focus on formal political processes it is equally important to recognise that key negotiations and policy processes take place elsewhere. In all of this the key questions are about who exercises power and influence at the different stages of the policy process and what interests they represent. Accounts of the British political system do not conclude that the system is either pluralistic with a sharing of power between a wide range of interest groups or a simple command system controlled by an economic or political elite. In the housing context accounts identify the role of a range of organisations involved in housing finance, production and exchange processes. They also identify formal roles for government and the voluntary sector and for those involved variously in electoral, representative and bureaucratic capacities.

In general and especially in recent years, housing has not often been an important factor in elections, especially in general elections. Nor does it appear that housing pressure groups have had a significant impact on the development of housing policy. Perhaps just as important, it is not easy to demonstrate that the potential users of services are able to exercise a major influence over housing policy. The literature referring to tenant participation and influence over housing indicates a lack of effective power and the absence of a strong unifying collective interest expressed by tenants. The position of households on local authority waiting lists or of those which are homeless, in temporary housing or living in inadequate housing is, arguably, one of even less power especially where they are regarded as undeserving. In the 1990s increasing reference is made to exclusion and to an underclass. The coincidence of exclusion from employment or adequate independent income, lack of an effective political voice and limited ability to influence housing policy is evident. At the same time the importance of quangos in housing and the power of patronage and co-option should not be ignored. The commissioning, independence and use of research and the orchestration of debate around housing issues is connected to power, interests and politics as well as the direct experience or observation of housing.

The wider welfare state

Fundamental to housing problems are issues of poverty and ability to meet the costs of housing of adequate standard. Both the task faced in developing policies to affect housing access and conditions and the types of policies used reflect the fact that other welfare state interventions affect levels of employment and income distribution. At one extreme it could be maintained that full employment and an income guarantee could form a housing policy. If people had sufficient income to obtain adequate housing specific housing policy measures would be unnecessary. Such a view is simplistic and takes too little account of aspects of the production, supply and pricing of housing in different locations and of different sizes, suitability and quality. Nevertheless it is undoubtedly true that the nature and extent of wider welfare state provision affects the options for housing policy and vice versa. It may be argued that rather than rendering a housing policy unnecessary the existence of an effective redistributive welfare state is an important precondition to developing a housing policy which involves security of tenure, choice of dwelling and social integration. In particular it is other welfare arrangements (provided direct, or through fiscal and occupational welfare provided by public, private and voluntary sectors), which will affect the ability of households to cope with changes in income and family composition associated with the life cycle, age, ill health, unemployment and other crises affecting the level, continuity and adequacy of income.

The most important elements of the wider welfare state for housing policy are those relating to fiscal measures and occupational welfare provision as well as the direct service provision made by the state, the voluntary sector and the private sector. Some of these elements have received wide attention in the housing literature where they relate directly to housing. The clearest examples of this are the arrangements for mortgage interest tax relief and the importance of a range of taxation and subsidy measures for the development of home ownership, and policies relating to provision of persons with learning difficulties, mobility problems or disabilities. Other elements of the wider welfare state tend to be neglected or taken for granted even though they have a direct relevance to the development and effectiveness of housing policy. However in the 1980s the significance of these arrangements became more apparent through a number of examples relating to homelessness. Accounts of the increase in homelessness in Britain in the 1980s identified a range of contributory factors. Some of these related directly to welfare services beyond housing. Three examples were the effect of reductions in the entitlement to social security benefits among those aged below 25 and particularly below 18; the position of young people who had been in the care of the local authority and whose care status ended on achieving age 16; and the high representation among homeless persons of those whose last address had been in some form of institution. In each of these cases the adequacy of services provided and of aftercare and resettlement services impinges on housing. If different arrangements existed in relation to these other services these would be reflected in the homelessness situation.

Other examples relate to more general provisions for social security, health care, employment rights and citizenship rights in general. The effectiveness of anti-discrimination measures and equal opportunities policies will influence the extent to which households from minority ethnic groups are disadvantaged. The extent and effectiveness of commitment to full employment is of critical importance for the extent of social inequality and therefore for the degree of income inequality which will be reflected in housing access. The general level of social security benefits and the extent to which they enable households to sustain the same pattern of housing expenditure in periods of interruption of earnings is of fundamental importance for housing. For the housing debate in Britain it is important to recognise that benefit income is low related to current earnings. Countries such as Denmark and The Netherlands have much higher levels of benefit for unemployed persons and in general the UK performs badly in comparison with other EU member states. Some countries have established a minimum level below which social insurance payments may not fall and this obviates the need to claim supplementation through means-tested assistance (see Townsend, 1987). In contrast, in Britain the level of benefit is such that supplementation is generally required especially to meet housing costs. The implications for housing policy are very different in these different situations.

The importance of the provision made through the wider welfare state can be illustrated through reference to the position of older persons. The housing situation of older people and problems faced in older age do not relate simply to housing policy and provision. Housing policies operate within a wider framework of welfare provision and both affect and are affected by that framework. In Britain the welfare state which emerged in the 1940s embraced two fundamental services for older people and a range of more specific provisions. The first of these fundamental provisions was the development of a national health service providing medical care for all persons irrespective of age, income, or any insurance status. The service was initially free at the point of consumption and although user charges developed in relation to prescriptions, dental and optical treatment, these have rarely recovered full costs and waivers exist for key groups including older people.

The second fundamental provision was the establishment of a national social security system providing retirement pensions and a safety net social assistance scheme. Since the key legislation of the 1940s, the groups which did not qualify for retirement pensions have become less significant. Unfortunately, the level of benefit provided in this scheme has been low relative to earnings. The rate of benefit for state pensions was originally intended to be sufficient to meet average rent payments as well as other expenditure requirements. However, the variation in rent levels between regions and properties is substantial and, in practice, pensions were increasingly insufficient to meet rents and other requirements. Where pensioners had no other source of income and paid high rents they qualified for supplementary pensions. In effect there was a means-tested entitlement in which rents were taken into account in determining benefit. This safety net subsequently developed into the system of housing benefit. Under this system all tenants (in the public or private sectors) are entitled to assistance with housing costs and the level of entitlement relates to household composition (needs) and income (resources). The scheme is more generous for pensioners than other (younger) households and effectively ensures that inability to meet rent payments will rarely arise for older people. The limitations are that some rents can be identified as excessive and that there is a problem of non-take-up. The problem of non-take-up mainly affects those whose incomes are sufficient to reduce but not remove their entitlements.

In view of these social security provisions it is probable that, among older people, the problems of meeting housing costs are now more associated with heating costs and the lack of energy efficiency and with the costs faced by older home owners. Almost all of these have completed the purchase of their dwelling and where they have not done so housing benefit is not available to help. Other social security regulations mean that little help is likely to be available with the final payments on a mortgage and only limited assistance is available for repairs and maintenance.

The final elements of wider welfare state provision are a range of services available to older people in their homes or in residential accommodation. Domiciliary welfare services include meals on wheels, home help, and other services which enable people to continue to live in their own accommodation. Assistance with transport costs and other services are also important. This wider welfare state provision is the base on which housing provision for older people has developed. However, it is wrong to overstate its generosity or comprehensiveness. The British research literature has always referred to two nations in old age and the welfare state has failed to eliminate gross differences in living circumstances. Moreover, in recent years, public expenditure controls and fiscal constraints have squeezed the budgets associated with provisions in older age. Households which are wholly dependent on public services generally receive a lower standard of provision in many areas and especially in relation to pensions.

Residualisation and social exclusion

The various factors outlined above interact to form the environment for housing policy. This environment changes over time and differences between regions, cities and localities are important. In the 1990s one way in which these elements come together relates to debates about marginalisation and residualisation in housing and broader processes of social exclusion. All of these debates are about changing patterns of poverty and social inequality. They form the essential background to housing policy. Policies which are designed to have an effect on the supply, location, condition or means of access to housing operate against the backdrop of existing patterns of housing inequality. This is not to assume that distributional issues lie at the heart of policy objectives or that housing policy has developed or will develop as an attempt to meet needs. Nevertheless what impacts housing policy will have are circumscribed by patterns of inequality and access to resources generated outside the housing sector. And the nature and operation of the housing sector itself affects other spheres in which opportunities and inequalities are generated.

The end of full employment, changes in the labour market, changes in the welfare state and changes in the demographic structure have generated much greater inequalities in incomes and wealth than have applied in the postwar period (see, for example, Hills, 1997). The costs of social security and unemployment are both seen as a major burden upon the economy and the development of policies to bring young people, the long-term unemployed and older workers back into the labour market is the focus of policy. Policies in these areas relate to housing in two ways: first, housing policy contributes to the pattern of incentives and opportunities which are associated with the poverty trap, the work incentives trap and the savings trap through the operation of housing benefits and the interaction between housing finance and the social security system. Second, concentrations of poor people are associated with a spiral of decline and exacerbate other problems of low income and employability. These concentrations are the product of interaction between housing and other factors. The housing research literature has for a considerable time identified a systematic process of sorting of the population between different tenures according to income and employment (see, for example, Murie, Niner and Watson,1976). The policies pursued since the mid-1970s speeded the process of tenure polarisation and what has become known as residualisation – referring to the increasingly residual or welfare role of council housing. Changes in rents and housing subsidy systems and the operation of the Right to Buy added to the well-established trend for the social rented sector to increasingly cater for households with the fewest resources.

In the period of full employment before the mid 1970s it was apparent that households with different characteristics moved to different parts of the housing system. Data from 1970/1, referring to households moving house, showed that those with economically inactive heads of household and those in semi-skilled and unskilled manual occupations were more concentrated in council housing after moving. The social segregation between tenures was more marked after moving than before (Murie, Niner and Watson, 1976: 43–9). The economic and demographic changes since then affect the pattern of distribution between tenures but there is consistent evidence that the social rented sector caters disproportionately for households with fewest resources. In 1977/8 39 per cent of households moving into the council sector were not in employment. In 1993/4 and 1996/7 the comparable figures were 73 per cent and 64 per cent respectively. There has been a tendency for working households to move out of the social rented sector and to be poorly represented among those moving in. This pattern appears to have particularly affected the housing association sector in recent years and higher rents in that sector have made the pattern more pronounced. The ageing of the tenants in the social rented sector and the differential uptake of the Right to Buy (with middle-aged tenants in the best properties most inclined to buy) has contributed to the changing social profile of the tenure. Compared with the past the sector today has proportionately more younger and older tenants and there has been a hollowing out of the middle. The proportion of tenants in work appears to have declined up to 1984 but has remained consistent since (Holmans, 1993). Those in work are more likely to be in low-paid work or experience periodic unemployment. While individual household circumstances may change, the social and economic role of the tenure has become one of housing those outside the labour market or in weak employment situations moving in and out of poverty. This residual role is increasingly associated with high mobility and turnover reflecting the changing circumstances of tenants and the position of much of the sector in the hierarchy of choice.

By the end of the 1990s the image and reality of council housing is very different from 50 years earlier and this itself influences choices and preferences. Rather than the activities of local authority and other gatekeepers, the direct advantages associated with home ownership, especially through tax reliefs, changes in the wider housing market, changes in how the social rented sector is perceived and the higher rent regime associated with social rented housing, have worked to diminish the attractiveness of social rented housing. Households which did not qualify for housing benefits were likely (except sometimes in the short term) to prefer home ownership. With the operation of the Right to Buy the range of choice offered within the local authorities sector also declined. The best properties have been disproportionately sold and the backlog of disrepair has become more apparent. The attractiveness of the sector has been affected. As the social base of the council sector became narrower so this itself altered perceptions and aspirations. Increasing social inequality, the operation of the Right to Buy and changes in rents and subsidies speeded the pace of change from the mid-1970s onwards. The available data suggest that where tenants in employment will be financially disadvantaged by accepting high-rent properties in the social rented sector they will reject them. The interaction between rents and benefits and the different levels of rents within the social rented sector influence housing decisions. The rented sectors house a disproportionate number of people not in employment and new tenants continue to be drawn disproportionately from those without work. This picture is most pronounced where rents are highest – especially in the higher-rent housing association market. These data are also consistent with the evidence that where households' circumstances improve (perhaps directly as a result of regeneration initiatives) they are likely to move away from the social rented sector. Rather than experience the impacts of the poverty trap as it operates within the sector they move on and the household replacing them in the social rented sector is likely to be unemployed and on benefit. The concentration continues.

The statistics of residualisation show that in 1967 45 per cent of all recipients of supplementary benefit (now income support) were council tenants. In 1979 the comparable figure was 61 per cent. In the same period council housing had increased from housing 29 per cent of households to 32 per cent. The concentration of lower income households had increased. Family Expenditure Survey data show that in 1963 council tenants accounted for 26 per cent of households in the bottom three income deciles. The comparable figures for 1972 and 1979 were 41 per cent and 47 per cent (Murie, 1983). Between 1980 and 1991 the proportion of tenants who were in the lowest three income deciles rose from 44 per cent to 65 per cent.

Some other features of the changing social profile of council housing have been identified, as follows:

- A decline in the proportion of economically active heads of households.
- A decline in the proportion of multiple-earner households.
- A decline in the proportion of higher-income households.
- A declining level of car ownership.
- A declining family housing role.
- An increase in the proportion of households with no earners.
- An increase in the proportion of unskilled manual workers.
- An increase in the proportion of non-married households.
- An increase in the proportion of female-headed households.
- An increase in the proportion of households with older persons and single elderly households.
- An increasing role in housing persons aged under 25.
- An increasing role in housing those on income support.
- An increasing role in housing those on lowest incomes.
- A declining dwelling stock and rate of new building.
- An ageing dwelling stock.
- A declining proportion of 3–4-bedroom houses in the stock and among newly built dwellings.
- An increasing proportion of flats and small houses.
- An increasing proportion of lettings to homeless persons. (Forrest and Murie, 1990a)

The consequences of this pattern of change are now widely accepted and the increasing concentration of low-income households in council housing represents a key element in patterns of urban social stratification in the UK (see, for example, Murie, 1983; Forrest and Murie, 1983; Malpass, 1990).

The changing role of council housing in Britain is fundamental to questions about the management of council housing, the development of social rented housing, and the broadening of choice, opportunity and empowerment among tenants and lower-income households. In its early and expanding years council housing consisted almost exclusively of modern, traditionally built dwellings with much higher standards (and rents) than applied in the private rented sector which dominated the housing market. In the 1990s council housing is much more mixed in age, design, type, condition and desirability and the alternatives to council housing are mainly in the home ownership sector. The structure of housing finance has changed to make council housing less attractive than home ownership for those who are in employment and in a position to buy. One consequence is that over time the characteristics of households in the council sector have changed from the affluent, employed working-class family to a low-income, benefit-dependent group including disproportionate numbers of elderly persons and lone-parent families. Thus housing is both a product and contributory factor in determining inequality. What is emerging is a compound, reinforcing pattern of multiple deprivation which is persistent over time and concentrated in particular areas because of the role of housing. It is resistant to traditional policy interventions and partly generated through public policy.

The process of residualisation has been associated with wider processes of social exclusion and this can be summarised as follows:

- Households entering the housing market have differential choices and bargaining power. Those without jobs and with family responsibilities and those with special needs and outside the labour market graduate towards the rented sectors.
- Those with least choice graduate towards the least desirable dwellings and areas.
- Households living in these areas are dependent on local facilities and low-demand housing areas tend to be poorly served by other services. Consequently those living in deprived areas are less able to build satisfactory homes or avail themselves of opportunities which could increase their incomes and bargaining power and enable them to move on.

The term 'social exclusion' is generally used to refer to more than income poverty and relate to a wider range of resources and citizenship rights; to emphasise the compound, persistent, resistant and concentrated nature of deprivation; to emphasise spatial processes; and to focus on the processes of exclusion and the roles of actors and agencies rather than simply on outputs. It is also a merit that the term social exclusion does not imply that the population is simply divided into the excluded and included but that there is a range of different communities and groups experiencing different processes and types of social exclusion. In this way the term is more flexible and useful than alternatives.

The adoption of the term 'social exclusion' by government has given a new impetus to this. The social exclusion unit refers to social exclusion as

> a shorthand label for what can happen when individuals or areas suffer from a combination of linked problems such as unemployment, poor skills, low incomes, poor housing, high crime environments, bad health and family breakdown.

Such a definition is relatively neutral but it begs questions about why individuals or areas suffer from such a combination of problems. Without a clear causal perspective responses may focus upon factors which are not the key causal factors. Housing is nevertheless included in this definition and identified in the initial remit of the unit both in relation to rough sleeping and the worst estates. Rough sleeping relates to the traditional housing agenda in which homelessness and the lack of adequate housing are seen as contributing to disadvantage and representing a threat to health and security. Homelessness, poor housing conditions and overcrowding represent direct challenges to full participation in society and are most easily seen as examples in the housing sphere how citizens do not participate in the same rights as the rest of the community. However the current debate involves a move from this traditional debate towards one also concerned with neighbourhood resources and instability.

To focus the policy agenda on the worst estates would appear to follow quite naturally from the picture discussed above. The disproportionate concentration of poor people in council housing and the social rented sector would suggest that if you wanted to target those experiencing social exclusion you would target council housing. The spiral of decline and stigma and adverse labelling clearly affects mass council estates. Research which has sought to map deprivation shows a strong link with housing tenure but does not show that it is safe to assume that mapping council housing is the same as mapping where the most disadvantaged live (Lee, Murie and Gordon, 1995). It is not safe to assume this in any city but it is particularly unsafe to do so in some cities. The structure of the housing market in London (with very high affordability thresholds for home ownership) and perhaps in Scottish cities (with peripheral council estates remote from employment centres) may mean that in these cities the most disadvantaged sections of the community are most likely to be found in council housing. However even in these cities they will also be found in mixed-tenure estates, in housing association housing and in the private rented sector. A more profound challenge exists in the Midlands and in the north of England where the proportion of all the housing stock which is in the private sector is much higher and where accessibility to home ownership is greater with house prices often much lower. As a result of this a significant proportion of low-income households are found in the private sector. This may be particularly true among ethnic minority communities where the early experience of discrimination in housing led to concentration of households in owner-occupation and where preferred areas of residence tend to be dominated by the private sector. An agenda which equates social exclusion with council housing will actively discriminate against significant proportions of disadvantaged groups in parts of the country where there is a considerable difference between the probability of deprived white households living in council housing and the proportion of equally deprived non-white households. Taking the same definitions of disadvantage a focus on council housing is likely to pick up white households to a greater extent. The extent to which this is true differs significantly between local authorities (Lee and Murie, 1997).

The conditions in private sector and mixed tenure neighbourhoods with deprived populations are comparable with those on council estates. They have differences, just as different council estates have differences, in terms of access to services, crime and the fear of crime and other factors. These neighbourhoods are more like council estates than they are like affluent enclaves of owner-occupation. The private rented sector continues to provide the poorest-quality housing and to house many of those with the least bargaining power in the economy and society. The owner-occupied sector, especially in some cities, has a disproportionate role in housing the elderly, low-income groups, ethnic minority groups and many of those who are in relative poverty.

The recognition that social exclusion is not contained purely within the social rented sector suggests that the solution to the problem does not simply rest in tenure diversification or privatisation. There would still be concentrations of people with least choice in the housing which is least desirable and the consequences of this are likely to be as damaging as at present. Instead we need a policy agenda which builds up from an analysis of cities and deprivation and adopts a more wide-ranging approach to housing interventions, including action in the private rented sector and in relation to urban renewal.

Much of the debate about social exclusion has emphasised the operation of the labour market and unemployment. However it is the interaction between labour market processes, training, education, discrimination on grounds of race or gender, housing, social benefit systems and a range of social resources and services which combine to trap people in disadvantaged situations. It is this interaction which is referred to as social exclusion. The emphasis is on multiple deprivation, regional and local exclusion and a causal process in which different elements in exclusion reinforce one another. In the British context in the 1990s, debates on poverty and disadvantage have tended to emphasise unemployment, differences in employment opportunities related to age, class, race and gender and to focus on social security benefits and the adequacy of rates of benefit and entitlement. Without denying the centrality of these elements there is a need to identify the role of housing in social exclusion. The 'passive' view of housing as the receptacle for inequalities created elsewhere gives too little weight to the extent to which where and what people live in affects their access to employment, education and other resources as well as their health, wealth and ability to change residence.

The new Labour Government elected in 1997 identified social exclusion as a key issue at an early stage and set up a Social Exclusion Unit reporting to the Prime Minister. Its early priorities included both rough sleepers and the worst estates. This focus reflects a concern with the processes which prevent people from participating in social and economic activity taken for granted by others. In discussing these processes where people live is both a factor reflecting differences in opportunity and choice and a factor contributing to these – it is both a cause and consequence of exclusion. The persistence and extent of exclusion are affected by a range of factors including where people live and what opportunities and resources are available. Obtaining employment or training, combating social isolation and accessing networks which assist in breaking out of poverty are widely accepted as relating to neighbourhood and community, as well as to family and friends and local economic circumstances.

People living in areas with concentrations of deprivation are not necessarily further disadvantaged by this. However the resources available to communities and the social relations within them are often damaged by continuing high levels of unemployment and poverty. In an environment in which state expenditure has been cut back and welfare benefits are reduced, it is no coincidence that areas with concentrations of poorer people have seen the quality of a wide range of services decline and have seen increased problems of crime and disorder.

An appropriate response to social exclusion and housing has to relate to more than housing management and more than the social rented sector. It has to relate to the structure of the housing market and of housing finance, as well as to the wider regeneration agenda about employment, training and incomes and the delivery of local services. In relation to the housing finance agenda, issues about rent levels, subsidy and the poverty trap are fundamental and suggestions include a shift from housing benefit expenditure to bricks-and-mortar subsidies in order to reduce rent levels and the impact of the poverty trap to make housing more genuinely affordable and put more expenditure choices in the hands of tenants. At the same time social exclusion relates to standards of housing and longer-term demand for different types of housing and tenures and locations. Clearance and urban renewal have a key part to play in strategic responses to social exclusion.

Conclusions

Housing policy and practice operate in a dynamic world. Priorities and ideologies change with time and place. But even if these elements were constant the effects of social, economic and demographic change and the working through of housing changes continue to alter the policy agenda. A dynamic policy area presents real difficulties. Any snapshot representation of the housing situation tends to ignore the established direction and pace of change and there is a possibility that desired changes will emerge in time without additional policy measures. At the same time a failure to recognise new elements of housing need or changing patterns of demand will render well-intentioned interventions inadequate. Unless a totally *laissez-faire* position is adopted the implications of this are that policy-making and planning involve setting targets (which take underlying changes into account) and monitoring and reviewing policy. A wide range of factors impinge on the housing sector and will affect its performance in relation to policy objectives. Some of these, including economic growth and change, are of fundamental importance but are difficult to predict. Others, including patterns of demographic change, can be anticipated to some extent. Yet others, such as the level of public expenditure or the activities of key public and private agencies, are likely to relate to economic and demographic patterns and alternative scenarios can inform policy-making.

These considerations are particularly appropriate to national and local estimates of levels of new housebuilding or investment in housing that is required to achieve objectives related to housing supply and standards. They are not only relevant in an active housing policy-making sense but are central to any explanation of the effect of policy. In considering the impact of policy it is an error to perceive policy and practice as acting on a static object and to conclude that if the effect of the policy is not as intended or expected the policy must be at fault. In reality, policy is not the only element introducing change and the changes arising from the loss of employment or from increased migration may have much more profound effects than those emanating from housing policy change. The residualisation of council housing or the concentration of lower-income and benefit-dependent house-holds among new council and housing association tenants is initially explained by changes in the labour market and by increasing social inequal-ity. These changes operate against a long-established pattern of housing tenure restructuring with the decline of the private rented sector and an increasing attractiveness of home ownership for all but the least affluent. In this way the tasks for housing management in the social rented sector are the products of long-established changes and the prospects for the sector reflect the continued working-through of these changes and how they interact with current policies in and beyond housing.

Addressing concentrations of poverty in the social rented sector requires more than changes to housing benefits housing finance and improved housing management. As with mixed-tenure and other deprived areas it also requires concerted and sustained activity to increase employability and the skills needed to command well-paid jobs; and it requires attention to be paid to local service delivery to ensure that neighbourhoods provide opportunity rather than entrapment. But the agenda does not stop there. Addressing concentrations of poverty in the social rented sector also requires sustained action to renew and redevelop social rented housing whether in the council housing sector or other ownerships. While central government and its concern with social exclusion has a role in this it is fundamentally to provide a framework within which local policy can develop. Even in a new financial framework the strategies required to rebuild social rented housing will be different ones in different parts of the country and will relate to an analysis of the operation of the local economy and housing markets and of households' needs and demand. What is required is a renewal which provides a supply of accommodation that keeps up with the aspirations of households.

Even with better management and better finance the existing social rented sector may not meet the aspirations of existing households, let alone new entrants to the housing system. Higher turnover suggests that the sector is increasingly regarded as providing emergency, recovery and short-term housing. This is a valuable function but is very different from the historical role of the sector and requires a different approach to management. If the situation where only those with no choice move into the social rented sector is to be avoided a more radical rebuilding of that sector is required and this involves a new look at the structure of housing markets and the range of choice offered in different parts of it.

7

The Administrative Framework

State intervention in housing has developed over many years and, as it has developed, the respective roles of central and local government have changed. For most of the history of active housing policy local authorities have been the favoured agencies for housing provision alongside the private sector. Latterly local authority housing provision has been in decline with sales to sitting tenants and large-scale transfers to registered social landlords occurring alongside low rates of new local authority housebuilding. The role of local authorities has shifted towards an enabling role with key roles for housing associations and their regulators alongside private provision. The powers and duties of local authorities and central government have expanded but the constraints, and in particular financial constraints imposed by central government, have increased considerably. Any attempt to describe or understand the operation of housing policy has to take account of the ways in which both public and private sector agencies involved in the housing market act in relation to housing. This chapter focuses on the framework for public sector administration relating to housing and on central and local government and housing associations. As was emphasised in Chapter 1, these institutions operate within a wider context in which there are a range of private sector agencies involved in the production of housing. In addition to builders and developers, others such as estate agents, solicitors, building societies and other financial institutions are involved in the production or consumption of housing.

Before considering the activities of these organisations it is important to acknowledge the legal aspects of state intervention in housing. Housing and public health legislation interfere with private property rights and place obligations on landlords and tenants irrespective of contractual arrangements. The courts, as a result, are important in interpreting the law and in adjudicating on the personal and property rights of individuals and between the rights of individuals and the powers of public and private corporations. The initial check on both central and local government in housing is the principle of *ultra vires*. Only where statute can be referred to show that relevant powers exist are activities legal. Consequently, legislation, Parliament and the courts (as interpreters of legislation) play crucial roles in establishing the framework for state action in housing. In many cases legislation empowers the appropriate government minister to issue regulations and determinations which are of very great importance. Thus, for example, under the Housing Act 1985 the Secretary of State is empowered to make and alter regulations (without new legislation) in relation to limitations on the effect of discount in reducing price of properties sold under the 'Right to Buy', prescribing the form and particulars to be contained in any prescribed notice under the 'Right to Buy'. Under the Local Government and Housing Act 1989, the Secretary of State is empowered to issue regulations relating to housing subsidy for local authorities. Under the Leasehold Reform, Housing and Urban Development Act 1993, the Secretary of State may prescribe by order aspects of the deed relating to rent to mortgage transactions, may make regulations relating to rights to have repairs carried out and may make regulations for imposing requirements on a local housing authority in any case where a tenant management organisation serves a written notice proposing a management agreement. The financial controls exercised by the Secretary of State under statute are of importance. In particular, these include powers in respect of loan sanction. In some cases, for example, those concerning housing subsidy, legislation has stated that, before making a determination for all local authorities, the Secretary of State shall consult the organisations appearing to him to be representative of local authorities. Such a requirement is not, however, a major constraint. Finally, the Secretary of State has certain broader powers laid down by legislation. These include, for example, powers to extend the 'Right to Buy' and to take various measures in relation to implementation of the 'Right to Buy', including powers of intervention.

Central government

Housing policy matters relate to the activities of a number of central government departments. The Treasury's interest in public expenditure and taxation issues can be argued to make it the most important influence on housing policy although its involvement in detailed issues of legislation and implementation is limited; the Department of Social Security has a key involvement in housing benefit and the interaction between housing and social security policy is important; the Department of Health has a major interest, especially in terms of care in the community policy; and other ministries involved in economic and social policies have various interests in housing. Various ministries also have responsibility for public sector landlords and although these landlords are of declining importance the ministries will continue to have an interest in housing matters which affect their operation.

Notwithstanding this broader picture, the prime responsibility for housing policy rests with the territorial departments: the Department of the Environment for England, the Scottish Office, the Welsh Office and the Northern Ireland Office. The Scottish Office, founded in 1885, administers a nation of almost 5 million with its own systems of law, local government and education, and employs over 13 000 people. In contrast, the Welsh Office is newer (1964), smaller (some 2400 staff in 1993) and regarded as dealing with a smaller nation more integrated with England than is Scotland and with fewer Members of Parliament reflecting a smaller population. With no separate system of law, legislation is more likely to mirror that for England (see Kellas and Madgwick, 1982). The Northern Ireland Office is an even newer department of the Westminster government (1972), arising with the demise of the previous devolved administration of Northern Ireland. In that devolved administration housing legislation and policy-making were wholly devolved and the legacy of independent administration and legislation remains (see Birrell and Murie, 1980). The territorial departments for Scotland, Wales and Northern Ireland have responsibility for a similar range of policy areas within one department. This is a distinct approach from the departmental distinctions which divide environment, industrial and regional development, agriculture, employment, roads and transport, education and health in England. The opportunities to develop coherent integrated policies are enhanced (but not guaranteed). They represent approaches to central government which emphasise the distinctiveness of territories rather than functions which represent special territorial interests and which stand between Whitehall and these territories. The territorial departments have different traditions, resources and ways of operating. In relation to housing, the Northern Ireland Office works closely with the Northern Ireland Housing Executive (NIHE) which took over responsibility for housing from local government in 1971. The NIHE replaced a total of 67 housing authorities and took over some 155 000 dwellings. The NIHE is widely regarded as having removed housing from the political and sectarian area and having significantly improved housing in Northern Ireland. The Board of the Executive is its key decision-making and executive body. Three of its 10 members are nominated by the Housing Council which has an advisory and consultative role and comprises one representative from each of the 26 district councils. The other Board members are ministerial nominees (Conway and Knox, 1990). The size and professionalism of the Northern Ireland Housing Executive has been an important feature of housing in Northern Ireland in recent years. Equally important is the fact that in Northern Ireland housing was declared to be government's main social priority in the 1980s and expenditure reflected this (Murie, 1992). In this situation the fact that the Executive has no capacity to raise funds and little financial autonomy was less critical. Nevertheless, in the view of one past Chairman, the limited degree of independence from government was one of a number of disadvantages affecting the NIHE (Brett, 1982).

The Scottish and Welsh situations differ strikingly from that for Northern Ireland. Relations with local authorities remain of key importance and the smaller number of local authorities than in England arguably enables a closer relationship. Local authorities in Scotland and Wales are also more united. The Convention of Scottish Local Authorities and the Welsh Association of District Councils have presented a more united front to central government than the fragmented English associations. Both Scottish and Welsh Offices have developed separate cultures and traditions and while Secretaries of State as cabinet ministers have followed government and party priorities, differences are more than just those of bureaucratic culture with different patterns of expenditure and differences in emphasis of policy. The Scottish Office is generally regarded as more independent and robust with a longer tradition of separate legislation, regulation and advice. In relation to housing the Welsh Office has become more distinctive since 1980 with higher levels of public expenditure a key feature. The establishment of Scottish Homes and Housing for Wales under the legislation of 1988 further strengthened the separate and distinct nature of housing policy and administration in these countries. These two government agencies accountable to nominated boards have developed distinctive policies and profiles. They are discussed more fully below in relation to housing associations. Secretaries of State for each of the territorial ministries represent their departmental interest at Cabinet. Public expenditure decisions relate to whole departments and the share going to housing will depend on internal discussions.

It is argued that Scotland, Wales and Northern Ireland have advantages compared with the English regions in having a cabinet minister with a wide territorial brief. They have developed different policies. In Scotland, for example, important differences have existed relating to finance, subsidy and improvement policies. Problems of coordination between different programmes are not eliminated in these territorial ministries but more coordination is internal to, say, the Scottish or Welsh Office rather than between separate ministries as in England. The potential benefits, say, in care in the community policy or developing coherent responses to urban renewal and regeneration are significant. Within the territorial ministries, and under the respective Secretary of State, junior ministers will have responsibility for different functions. Thus, in the Scottish Office in 1993, there was one Minister of State and three Parliamentary Under-Secretaries, one of whom was Minister for Home Affairs and the Environment; in Wales, there was only one Minister of State and one Parliamentary Under-Secretary of State.

Since the development of housing policy as a major interest of central government, responsibility for housing in England has rested with ministers associated with a succession of different departments. In 1919, housing was removed from the remit of the Local Government Board to that of the Minister of Health. It remained that minister's responsibility until 1951, when briefly a Minister of Local Government Planning and then a Minister of Housing and Local Government were established with responsibility for housing. In 1969, a Secretary of State for Local Government and Regional Planning was appointed, with a commitment to set in train the process of integration of departments with closely-related functional responsibilities. This process was consolidated in 1970 with the establishment of a Department of the Environment with a Secretary of State responsible for the duties and powers formerly residing with the Ministries of Housing and Local Government, Transport and Public Building and Works (Draper, 1977). The central reason for this reorganisation was the desire to strengthen coordination between related functions and the decision to reorganise can be partly attributed to the vogue for management rationality in public administration (Painter, 1980: 136). In another sense reorganisation can be seen as one attempt to strengthen the efficiency and effectiveness of central administration in implementing government strategy. This involved increasing the capacity to propose and implement that strategy and to control large resource-consuming programmes in a manner compatible with the overall financial, economic and political objectives of government. A separate Department of Transport was established again in 1976. In 1997 the new Labour Government reestablished the functional coordination through a new Department of the Environment, Transport and the Regions.

The Secretary of State works with a group of subordinate ministers with responsibilities for particular policy areas. While in some respects ministers work as a team the Secretary of State's position is 'akin to a presiding overlord with authority to take major transdepartmental decisions when they arose, and to interfere in the separate functional fields of his ministers' (Painter, 1980: 138). In housing, a subordinate minister (the Minister for Local Government and Housing in 1998) is in closest touch with executive, policy and political work including consultation and negotiation with pressure groups, professional bodies, local government and statutory bodies. While this minister will be involved in Cabinet committees, attendance at full Cabinet to present major policy submissions is rare (Painter, 1980: 139). The working of the central department in relation to housing will depend on the general direction of government policy, the role and effectiveness of the Secretary of State in Cabinet, the relationship between the Secretary of State and subordinate ministers and the relationship between ministers and civil servants. It should not be assumed that because the Secretary of State has responsibility for housing he will take a close or detailed interest in that service. For example, while Anthony Crosland between 1974 and 1976 took such an interest in housing finance and set up a major review of that area, his successor, Peter Shore, between 1976 and 1979 did not take the same view. Similarly, Geoffrey Rippon and his successor, Crosland, argued successfully in Cabinet for more housing expenditure, but did not press for equivalent increases in transport expenditure (Painter, 1980: 144). Michael Heseltine in 1980 explained the level of housing expenditure agreed in Cabinet in terms of 'what the country can afford' rather than a departmental brief arguing from a housing policy perspective (House of Commons, 1980). This latter stance is explicable in terms of a general desire to reduce state expenditure and intervention in housing and marks a shift away from the assumption that a minister in a period of expenditure restraint attempts to defend departmental budgets. Such a stance by the central department is not likely to find favour with local government. In the past differences have existed over what was the best use of resources and subsidy and other arrangements were used to persuade local authorities to adopt particular building techniques, to cater for particular needs or to increase emphasis on improvement rather than new building. However the stance of central government in the 1980s has led to a deeper division over how much state intervention is needed, and for what. The view expressed by a Treasury minister in 1979 that housing 'can, in the main, be better provided by the private sector' (Biffen, 1979) was not one generally held in local government or compatible with the tradition of state intervention in housing. This general change in central government's approach to housing is consistent with the change described by a former permanent secretary as 'the move out of a period of consensus into a period of controversial policies' (Heiser, 1992) and the conflicts with local government which arose.

Painter's conclusion from analysis of the experience of the operation of the DoE in the early 1970s is that attempts to enhance the rationality of the annual resource allocation process took second place to cutting back expenditure (Painter, 1980). Painter argues that there were additional reasons for the limited success of the DoE in providing a coordinated approach of the type envisaged in 1970. Different functional areas such as transport or housing generate separate problems and require separate political attention and management. In addition, in an area such as housing, the decentralisation of political and administrative power through the local government system is important. A coordinated rational 'central planning' approach was difficult to pursue where even ministerial views acknowledged the significance of local problems and local expertise in developing responses (DoE, 1976). As the concern of the central department has drifted from rational resource allocation towards control of expenditure, political and policy differences with local government also have become more apparent. At the same time, the development and effectiveness of the organisation of central government for housing can only be assessed in the light of changes in government and in the policies of government. As government has reduced expenditure on housing, restricted finance available to housing authorities and imposed policies which some authorities regard as running down the housing service, so the model of centralised rational policy-making has been adapted. In the period since 1988, the introduction of Housing Action Trusts, the development of Tenants' Choice, changes in housing finance and ministers' often-expressed low opinion of local authority housing management have all been elements in a centralisation of policy. The preference for housing associations as providers of social rented housing and the promotion of an enabling role as the main role of local authorities marks a final phase in the breakdown of central government's use of local authorities as the major instruments of housing policy.

In England in 1998, the DETR had, in addition to its headquarters in central London, some headquarters functions located in Bristol, nine regional offices and the Merseyside Task Force. The nine regional offices and the Merseyside Task Force are executive branches of the department administering inner cities and housing programmes, undertaking certain planning functions and providing the main local points of contact between the department and local authorities. They have had a considerable administrative role in connection with, for example, project controls, the Housing Investment Programme system, the Single Regeneration Budget and regeneration policy. The government's plans for the development of England's regions (DETR, 1997) proposed the creation in each region of a regional development agency to promote development and regeneration and coordinate regional and local partners. These proposals are likely both to change the system of governance and to change the way that housing is addressed and increase further its incorporation in regional and regeneration strategies.

The regional offices are part of a very large department in which there are unavoidable issues of communication. In 1993, there were seven ministers in the department – the Secretary of State, three Ministers of State including the Minister for Housing and Planning, and three Parliamentary Under-Secretaries of State as well as spokesmen in the House of Lords. The range of responsibilities in the DoE itself are organised in a series of divisions. The five housing divisions existing in 1979 were reorganised in 1981 into three divisions, each with an under-secretary at the head. The main responsibilities of these divisions changed to reflect shifting policy preoccupations (see Malpass and Murie, 1990). By 1991 housing was dealt with as part of a housing and urban group which included responsibility for private ownership and renting, the Housing Corporation, housing associations and local authorities along with inner cities, new towns and the European Regional Development Fund. In 1997 the new Department of the Environment, Transport and the Regions had a Minister of State for Local Government and Housing and a Junior Minister of State with responsibilities for housing. On the official side, under the Permanent Secretary, a Senior Director was responsible for Housing, Construction, Regeneration and Countryside. There were three Housing Directorates: Housing Policy and Private Sector (HPSS); Housing, Social Policy and Resources (HSPR); and Housing and

Urban Monitoring and Analysis (HUMA). HPSS had divisions responsible for housing policy coordination and home ownership, the private rented sector and housing renewal policy. HSPR had divisions responsible for local authority housing, homelessness and housing management, housing associations and housing transfers and private finance. HUMA had divisions of economists, researchers and statisticians.

In addition to the housing divisions of the DETR, other divisions had an interest in housing matters through their responsibilities, for example, for planning, rural affairs and water; local government; and construction. The Department employed almost 8000 persons directly but it delivers many of its policy aims mainly through sponsored bodies and local authorities, rather than directly. Other policy aims are achieved through regulation and monitoring. Sponsored bodies are executive non-departmental public bodies. Some of these have a direct and central housing role (Housing Action Trusts, the Housing Corporation); others have important roles linked to housing (the Audit Commission, Rural Development Commission, Commission for the New Towns, Urban Development Corporations, the Urban Regeneration Agency). By far the largest of all the department's expenditure on sponsored bodies relates to the Housing Corporation.

The DETR along with all the territorial departments expends considerable energy in consultation and liaison with other bodies and employs some professional advice within the department. Consultation with the local authority associations, which see the majority of government circulars affecting their members before they are published, is important. Some consultation, such as that through the Housing Consultative Committee, is formal and involves ministers but much more involves working parties (as with the Housing Act 1988 discussed in Chapter 9) and routine consultation between officials. The relationship between the DETR and the local housing authorities can be a two-way one and advice, ideas and even legislative proposals are sometimes based on practice developed by and within local authorities. However it would be wrong to give an impression that, because consultation exists, there is an equal relationship. It is not evident that in relation to housing the local authority associations have been powerful pressure groups. They have had a major influence on some measures. For example, the Housing (Homeless Persons) Act 1977 was affected by amendments prompted by Association of District Councils (ADC) – but arguably only because of the unusual political situation at the time (Richards, 1981). Claims that they have affected the Housing Act 1980 are less substantial and centre on a small number of amendments (McCulloch, 1980). The local authority associations in England have often been divided between and within themselves, and until the formation of a single organisation – the Local Government Association in 1997 – the failure to provide a united front to central government has been a factor in the centralisation of housing policy. In the face of clear policy preferences, backed by financial and economic stringency, it is doubtful if a united local authority lobby would have been effective. Nor is it clear in what way the party allegiances of the controlling groups on the local authority associations, and whether or not they coincide with those of central government, affect their lobbying performance and its impact.

The importance of other interest groups in the development of housing policy can briefly be illustrated with reference to the trade association of the building societies, the Building Societies Association (BSA). Boleat comments that, as building societies became more important, so government took a closer interest in their activities (Boleat, 1986: 3). The mortgage rate, the availability of funds for lending and fluctuations in rates of house price inflation were matters of political importance. Government activities in relation to these matters included provision of funds for on-lending and the establishment between 1975 and 1983 of a Joint Advisory Committee between government and the building society industry. The importance of monetary policy and of building societies in the financial system increased the importance of relationships between government and the societies in the 1980s. The Building Societies Act 1986 introduced changes to both the investment and the lending sides of the activities of societies. Reflecting the joint interest of government and societies to increase their role in the housing market, the Building Societies Act 1986 made it possible for societies to play a leading role in the restructuring of the organisation of owner-occupation. The Green Paper of 1984, which heralded new legislation, very closely followed the proposals of a Working Group of the Council of the BSA. The legislation itself reflected comments made by the BSA on the Green Paper. The BSA was actively involved in the legislative process and promoted a number of amendments with the assistance of members of the Standing Committee on the Bill (Hawes, 1986: 73). Important changes were achieved in that committee, where 'business had been conducted in an exceptionally good humour and constructive attitude with very few points being made for party political purposes' (*BS News*, 1986). Although some late amendments (especially relating to an approved ombudsman scheme) aroused some controversy, the legislation passed without major dispute – consistent with a view of consensus on home ownership and state support for building societies as the leading agencies in home ownership.

Within the context of a discussion about influences on policy-making it is relevant to refer to the role of parliamentary Select Committees. These committees are less strongly orchestrated by the leadership and party whips in Parliament and are a potential source of critical comment and investigation. A number of enquiries have been concerned with housing issues. For example, in the early 1980s the Environment Committee looked at council house sales, the private rented sector, the operation of the regional offices of the DoE and public expenditure plans for housing. The same committee has since then investigated the Housing Corporation, the need for housing and the Single Regeneration Budget. While these investigations raised the profile of issues it is not clear that they had any impact on policy or legislation. One view is that such an impact is most likely where investigations relate to areas in which government has not made strong commitments and where policy is still being developed through negotiation with a range of pressure and interest groups.

While the Secretary of State will not normally be swayed by local authority representations (and certainly has not been in recent years in relation to HIPs, acquisition, the moratorium on capital expenditure in 1980/1 or determinations affecting rents), the minister has not traditionally attempted to intervene directly in local housing policy implementation. Even before the minister's default powers were removed by the Local Government Act 1972, central government preferred to rely on advice, informal consultation and financial measures to influence local policy. The minister's powers mainly involve negative checks on local initiative. The most significant controls in the past have been in respect of compulsory purchase or clearance orders which require ministerial consent and of controls over capital expenditure (through project controls, cost yardsticks, cash limits, consents on council house sales, grants and subsidies and sanctioning of local authority borrowing). This latter area of control has in recent years been consolidated into the Housing Investment Programme system, through which the Secretary of State allocates permission to borrow and set restrictions on how capital expenditure can be used (Bramley *et al.*, 1979). Project controls have also been revised, but the value-for-money formula provides ample scope for scrutiny of local proposals (Bramley *et al.*, 1979). While some detailed controls have been relaxed (for example, on general improvement area declarations), the general tightening of financial controls represents a centralisation of policy-making.

A more important development is apparent in the increased scrutiny and control associated with the 'Right to Buy' clauses of the Housing Act 1980 (and the Housing (Tenants' Rights, etc. Scotland Act, 1980). Section 23 of the Housing Act (Section 164 of the Housing Act 1985) empowers the Secretary of State to issue a notice of intention to exercise powers to intervene and do all such things as appear to him necessary or expedient to enable secure tenants to exercise their rights. This is regarded as a very strong and unusual power. On the basis of this power, the central department engages in much closer monitoring and scrutiny of local authority performance and of complaints about performance. The department has also been willing to use the powers – notably in the case of Norwich City Council in 1981 (see Chapter 10). These powers do represent a considerable enhancement of central control and an uneven development of intervention – there is no equivalent power or scrutiny of performance in respect of, say, homelessness. The Housing Act 1980 and its successors is also notable again in relation to the 'Right to Buy' – in laying down precise timetables and prescribing forms and procedures which local authorities must pursue. In this respect the central department has become much more involved in the implementation of local policy (Forrest and Murie, 1985).

The final developments of this type are of more positive programmes directly controlled by central government. The Priority Estates Programme, the Urban Housing Renewal Unit and its successor Estate Action and Housing Action Trusts are examples of such programmes which together involved growing public expenditure allocated and managed separately and directly by the DoE or sponsored bodies rather than through the HIP. The increased role of housing associations also involved a greater role for the Housing Corporation and its equivalents in Scotland and Wales. These centrally appointed and accountable agencies exercise control over housing associations through a different process. Lastly, a series of Challenge Funds including the Single Regeneration Budget Challenge Fund have been used by central government to assess local projects and determine which should go ahead rather than allocate funds and leave local authorities to determine the action. A wide range of other urban policy measures includes City Challenge, Urban Development Corporations, Inner City Task Forces and City Action Teams.

The local authorities

In the period since 1919, and more particularly since 1945, local authorities have been the dominant organisations involved in developing housing policies. A legislative and financial framework provided by central government enabled local authorities to become, in turn, the major organisations providing new housing for rent and then providing rented housing. Local authorities have also had an important enabling role for a long period, providing the planning framework, physical infrastructure and social facilities which have enabled other agencies to provide housing. They have played a major role in the development of home ownership through the use of planning process, sale of land and dwellings, building for sale, provision of mortgage loans and operation of a range of policies which have facilitated private investment. The changes in policy described in Chapter 5 have changed this situation. Local authorities have been replaced by housing associations in having the dominant role in providing new housing to rent. In some areas, transfers of property have removed their role as landlord altogether.

Local authorities are elected, statutory bodies legally independent of central government, exercising considerable local discretion and power within the confines of statute and the principle of *ultra vires*. For a period of 80 years up to 1974, housing policy has been developed and implemented through a system of local government largely unaltered since the legislation of 1884 and 1894. Before 1 April 1974 the public provision of housing outside Greater London was the responsibility of county borough, municipal borough, urban district and rural district councils. County councils had some limited housing powers in providing accommodation for employees, making advances for house purchase and assisting housing associations. On 1 April 1965, when local government reorganisation in Greater London was completed, there were 1429 principal housing authorities in England and Wales. These varied tremendously in size, resources and departmental organisation.

In England and Wales the reorganisation of local government in 1974 (under the Local Government Act 1972) involved three major dimensions. First, responsibility for health and water was removed from local government and vested in new regional authorities. Second, the existing local authorities ceased to exist and were replaced by 426 new local authorities. Only London was unaffected by this. Third, a new division of responsibilities between two tiers of government meant that, outside the six metropolitan counties, responsibility for education and social services fell on the county authorities, leaving some former county boroughs with fewer responsibilities than before. The subsequent abolition of the GLC and six metropolitan counties left 36 metropolitan districts in England, 39 county councils and 296 county districts.

The distribution of functions to local authorities under the 1957 Housing Act, as amended by the 1972 Local Government Act, placed responsibility for housing with district councils. County councils have limited reserve powers in housing. The reorganisation of local government in 1974 substantially reduced the number of local housing authorities. The argument for maintaining housing as a district council responsibility was expressed in the Conservative Party's White Paper on Local Government reorganisation as follows:

> One of the most important functions of local government is housing. The government believe that the accurate assessment of housing requirements and the provision of housing and housing advice to the individual is of such paramount importance that the service should be operated as close to the citizen as possible. (DoE, 1971)

Such consideration automatically implied responsibility at district level. In the non-metropolitan districts, housing is by far the most important function as measured in current and capital expenditure and by employment. It consistently creates work for councillors and remains prominent in local elections.

The situation in London is very different from that of England and Wales. Prior to 1986, responsibility for housing was divided between the Greater London Council and the London boroughs (and the City of London). This had applied since the London Government Act 1963 which made each of the boroughs principal housing authorities and also established a strategic role for the GLC as coordinator of functions within the area and with a wide range of housing powers. Between 1979 and 1982, however, the GLC transferred its housing stock to the London boroughs and districts it was in. While it maintained a policy involvement in the allocation of housing through its mobility scheme, its management responsibilities were considerably reduced. With the abolition of the GLC in 1986, no equivalent strategic responsibility remained. However the local authority associations (LBA and ALA) and the London Residuary Body continued to provide certain central coordinated services including research and the London Area Mobility Scheme.

In Scotland, local government reorganisation took a different form from that in England and Wales by adopting a two-tier system of regions and districts everywhere except in the three remoter island areas. It was districts and island authorities which had housing powers. Scottish reorganisation also had the effect of creating large housing authorities, eliminating the smallest previous authorities but leaving authorities of very different sizes and with different housing stocks.

In Northern Ireland local authorities lost their housing powers in 1971. Since then the powers normally associated with local authorities have been carried out by the Northern Ireland Housing Executive. Local authority influence on the NIHE is exercised through a Housing Council, but this has no significant power.

Before the reorganisation of local government in 1995–8 came into effect the categories of local authorities with principal (rather than reserve) housing powers were as follows:

- England   36   Metropolitan districts
             32   London boroughs
                 The City of London
        296   Non-metropolitan districts
- Wales   37   Non-metropolitan districts
- Scotland   53   Districts
              3   All-purpose island authorities

The local government reorganisation of 1995–8 partially replaced the two tier local government structure in England and fully replaced it in Scotland and Wales. The resulting pattern of local authorities with housing powers was as follows:

- England   36   Metropolitan districts
             32   London boroughs
                 The City of London
        237   Shire districts
         39   Unitary authorities

- Scotland   32   Single-tier councils
- Wales   22   Single-tier councils

The range of differences which exist between the size and housing stock of these authorities is less than existed before 1974, but remains significant. The organisation of housing functions within the new local authorities after 1974 was no more uniform than had been true previously. The Institute of Housing *Annual Review* referred to three-quarters of all housing authorities in 1980 and indicated a wide variation in responsibilities. While over 90 per cent of housing departments were consulted about new building and were responsible for assistance to homeless persons, for lettings and for the general care of estates, only 68 per cent were responsible for rent collection, 50 per cent for administration of rent rebates, 37 per cent for rent allowances and for administration of house purchase schemes, 30 per cent for administration of grants to private tenants and landlords and 20 per cent for registration of multi-occupied premises (IoH, 1981). Subsequent policy changes have changed this situation (see Chapter 12). The transfer of local authority housing stock to housing associations also meant that some local authorities (62 by the end of 1997/8) retained duties in respect of housing without retaining a stock of housing to manage or a development programme.

While the great majority of authorities had a committee specialising in housing matters, departments other than housing took the lead or made major contributions to housing policy. The housing management profession and official reports have consistently recommended the development of a comprehensive housing service but this has rarely emerged in practice. However local authorities, especially in London and the larger metropolitan areas, have developed aid and advice services and activities relating to private sector housing, urban renewal and home ownership which go a long way beyond a narrow concern with the provision and management of council housing. To this extent many authorities had developed a facilitating or enabling role alongside other roles well before central government identified this as the key role for the future. The reorganisation of local government in 1974 produced larger housing authorities and facilitated the adoption of corporate planning, management and decision-making in local government. This and subsequent developments have affected housing, with a general increase in management sophistication. The case for adopting points schemes in allocation policy, making use of computer technology, developing research and intelligence and training activities and for clearer statements of objectives and policy reviews has been argued on housing as well as management grounds. There have been considerable, but by no means uniform, responses to these pressures. One of the consequences of this (partial) adoption of new approaches to management, occurring alongside greater central government scrutiny and more complex legislation and regulation, is a professionalisation and centralisation of the housing service. The complexities of financial arrangements in housing are often only appreciated by a small group of officers in various departments. It is more difficult for elected members or tenants or applicants to penetrate policy and identify key determinants or alternatives for action. In this sense developments at a local level increase the tendency deriving from central government's pressure. It is not evident that the problem is made worse by the size of authorities as such or would be relieved by creating a large number of smaller independent housing authorities. These and other aspects of the management of housing are discussed more fully in Chapters 11 and 12.

The powers and duties of local housing authorities are laid down in legislation. They are complex and relatively few duties are sufficiently precise to identify whether they are being carried out or not. It must be emphasised that, in addition to the management of their own houses, local authorities have responsibilities in relation to private housing, especially where it is unfit for habitation or in need of repair and improvement. Although there are differences in legislation between Scotland and England and Wales, this general view applies in all cases. The simplest way to indicate the range of activities is to list expenditure headings. Thus the major items of current expenditure are associated with the stock of dwellings owned by local authorities. They are management and supervision, repair and maintenance and the repayment of debt involved in capital expenditure. Other items accounted for in current expenditure include rent rebates and housing benefit, lending for house purchase and improvement, housing aid and advice, accommodation for homeless persons, gypsy caravan sites, expenditure on area improvement and contributions to housing associations. The major items of capital expenditure are land acquisition, new building, the acquisition of dwellings, slum clearance and municipalisation, improvements to the local authority's own dwellings, improvement grants and loans to housing associations and private individuals. In addition the disposal of land and dwellings must be accounted for. One expanding area is the management of leasehold properties and charging leaseholders for services, repairs and maintenance. Right to Buy sales of flats have led to a major growth in this area with some London boroughs having particularly large numbers of leasehold properties.

The policy package developed between 1987 and 1990 involved new measures to encourage private landlords and housing associations to take the dominant role in providing new housing to rent and also in acquiring parts of the existing council housing stock. The other side of the policy coin is the view that local authorities' role should diminish and change. In 1987, the Minister of Housing and Planning stated that he could see no arguments for generalised new building by councils and expressed the belief that there should not be much property in council ownership at all (Waldegrave, 1987).

The ministerial view was that the housing association movement would expand and become the main provider of new social housing. The role of local authorities would gradually change and become less concerned with the direct provision of housing. In the Secretary of State's view, 'there will be a need for authorities to act as facilitators to ensure that the markets work, that housebuilders, private landlords and associations meet the full range of local housing needs and that the three markets are operating efficiently in their areas and meeting the demands of the customers' (Ridley, 1988). The ways in which they will operate involve or could involve the following:

- Proper use of planning powers.
- Administration of the system of building regulations.
- Monitoring of housing condition and drawing up policies for private sector renewal.
- Assessing housing needs and conditions.
- Bringing together appropriate agencies to achieve improvement redevelopment and new building.
- Offering improvement grants.
- Providing assistance to schemes for private renting.
- Sponsoring housing association schemes.
- Acting as long-stop for homelessness.
- Cooperating with housing associations over their allocation of tenancies.
- Entering into contracts with landlords to enable the local authority to meet its statutory obligations.
- Working with housing associations, health authorities and other social services to make sure that housing is available for vulnerable groups.
- (Normally) retaining housing to let to elderly and disabled people and (occasionally) adding to this stock.

There are, inevitably, doubts about whether these components of an enabling role are sufficient to influence housing supply or to protect tenant interests. The past experience in British housing is that strategic bodies are easily ignored and that it is difficult to channel or direct resources which are not controlled by the agency concerned. Local authorities could find themselves in the position where they can only influence the pattern of housing opportunity by providing grants and loans. Restrictions on continuing nominations are important. One possible outcome is that their ambitions will become limited to a minimal residual role. Experience also suggests that dependence on planning powers (especially with declining land ownership) and legal enforcement is not a strong basis on which to operate a housing policy. The fear must be that maintaining minimum standards in housing and protecting tenants will be beyond the capacity of many local authorities.

Local authorities have not been the only public bodies involved in the provision of housing. Reference has already been made to the fact that other public bodies including the Ministry of Defence, health authorities, the police, the fire service and higher-tier local authorities which do not have general housing responsibilities have provided housing – mainly for their employees. It is only new towns which have had a more general role in the development and management of housing, comparable to that of local housing authorities. As New Town Development Corporations have been wound up their direct housing functions have mainly been transferred to local authorities.

Housing associations, the Housing Corporation, Scottish Homes and Housing for Wales

The Housing Act 1996 created a new official category of landlord – registered social landlord (RSL). This is now the generic term embracing the existing housing association sector and new local housing companies – non-profit-making private bodies set up by local authorities to facilitate stock transfers. In this section we will normally refer to RSLs as housing associations although some specific comments on local housing companies are made separately. Housing associations may be incorporated as friendly societies under the Industrial and Provident Societies Act; as charities under the Charities Act; as companies under the Companies Acts; or in some cases as trusts by Royal Charter or private Acts of Parliament. Under the definition in the Housing Act 1974, an association is a society, company or body of trustees with the objective of building, improving or managing houses and operating on a non-profit-making basis. As with many voluntary organisations, the label 'voluntary' applies only to the Committees of Management which control the activities of associations, and employ paid staff to carry out their functions. Hence methods of administration may be similar to those in statutory agencies. Since the Housing Act 1974, housing associations have increased their activity enormously and although they only own some 4 per cent of the national housing stock their contribution to the housing programme has been significant. Between 1977 and 1987 housing association new dwellings completed in the United Kingdom grew from 8 per cent of the public sector total to some 32 per cent and the number of dwellings rehabilitated by housing associations has ranged between 10 000 and 20 000 a year. This rediscovery of voluntary effort, following its less than overwhelming success in the nineteenth century, was initially fuelled by central government disillusionment with local authority housing. In this rediscovery and the subsequent development of policy towards housing associations, central government has used the voluntary sector to increase its direct control over housing programmes and by-passed local authorities with which it has a less simple relationship. This development of housing associations can consequently be seen as part of the wider centralising tendency evident in housing policy in recent years. By 1995 housing associations accounted for 20 per cent of all new dwelling completions in Britain (38 500 out of 190 000) and accounted for 20 times as many dwellings as completed by other public sector bodies.

In 1984, the National Federation of Housing Associations (NFHA) estimated that there were more than 4400 housing associations. Some 3447 societies were registered under the housing category of industrial and provident societies, compared with 4104 in 1975. This decline is partly accounted for by the winding-up of co-ownership societies. In 1997 there were some 2500 housing associations registered with the Housing Corporation, Scottish Homes and Housing for Wales (Table 7.1). In Scotland, Wales and Northern Ireland the housing association movement is relatively young and prior to the stock transfers carried out since 1988 there were very few large associations. The impact of stock transfers and the dominant role of new building for rent have been significant. Between 1991 and 1997 the numbers of dwellings in the housing association sector more than doubled in Scotland and increased by more than 50 per cent in both England and Wales. But in this period the number of associations declined slightly. Mergers and stock transfers were creating a significant group of large associations often with origins or strong partnerships with local authorities (or Scottish Homes). This group of associations may have little in common with many of the smaller more local organisations which also form part of the sector.

In 1991 in England only 541 associations had active development programmes but they accounted for 91 per cent of the total housing association stock in England. Comparable figures for Scotland were 169 (92 per cent)

Table 7.1   *Housing associations and dwellings, 1997*

Size of association	England	Scotland	Wales
Up to 100 dwellings			
Associations	1697	44	62
Dwellings	30200	1286	1040
101–1000			
Associations	238	120	15
Dwellings	78800	44822	8234
1001–2500			
Associations	103	31	11
Dwellings	176100	44206	15740
Over 2500			
Associations	112	6	7
Dwellings	704200	18201	27376
Total			
Associations	2150	201	85
Dwellings	989300	108370	52380

Sources: Housing Corporation; Scottish Homes; Tai Cymru.

and for Wales 35 (92 per cent) (Day *et al.*, 1993). Many of the remaining 2000 associations, including almshouse trusts and small charities, were long-established 'dormant' associations operating without assistance from public funds. A large number of associations have not progressed to the stage of building or owning property, have no continuing involvement in housing development or are solely management associations involved with established self-build or co-ownership schemes or almshouses. While the largest housing associations tend to have area offices, those with a dispersed housing stock are often unable to provide a local presence and, although they tend to be more intensively staffed than local authority housing departments, it would be misleading to assume that sensitive, local, uncomplicated management is a hallmark of all housing associations.

One of the more significant changes to the housing association movement has resulted from the transfer of local authority and new town housing and the housing stock of Scottish Homes. Over 250 000 dwellings were transferred from local authorities to new housing associations in the ten years up to the end of 1998. In addition a new set of transfers associated with the operation of the Estate Renewal Challenge Fund were beginning to take place. These involved the establishment of new organisations with greater direct accountability to tenants and to local authorities through representation at board level. In some cases new local housing companies were self-standing RSLs and in other cases new organisations formed part of a group structure with existing RSLs also involved. These various transfers have created a housing association stock and a significant number of associations which reflect their local authority origins but are able to adopt new approaches.

In Northern Ireland the former Northern Ireland Housing Trust (NIHT) was incorporated into the Northern Ireland Housing Executive in 1971 along with local authority housing and the legacy of the NIHT may be identifiable in the practices of the NIHE. The housing association movement has been associated with the provision of accommodation for special needs and had a stock of about 15 000 in 1996 with 43 active 'building' associations (DoE, NI 1996). In Scotland the Scottish Special Housing Association was incorporated into Scottish Homes in 1988. Scottish Homes' strategy was to transfer its stock of over 60 000 dwellings and this has contributed to the major changes to the housing association sector in Scotland.

Leaving aside stock transfers, housing association activity is most significant in Greater London and especially in inner London. Some of the other differences between associations are important to note. The Housing Acts of the 1980s and arrangements for the 'Right to Buy' and transferable discounts have made the distinction between charitable and non-charitable associations important. This is a clear distinction between cooperative or mutual and non-mutual associations; and between stock transfer associations and others. Finally the objectives and focus of associations are not always 'general purpose' and, for example, some associations focus on the elderly, special needs, single people, provision of short-life housing, self-build housing or undertaking new initiatives. Increasing awareness of the problems faced by black people in housing and a desire by black people to control their own housing have led to the formation of associations catering exclusively for black people of various household types. Especially in housing action areas and general improvement areas housing associations and local authorities have worked closely together and this increases policy effectiveness. However it also highlights anomalies, with two parts of the public sector operating alongside one another, but subject to different financial constraints (and consequently to different standards) and with different methods of determining rents and different tenancy rights. Housing associations' image as small, local, community-based and responsive is under severe threat in this context. In the new environment following 1988 more attention has focused on the Housing Corporation, Scottish Homes and Housing for Wales.

The Housing Corporation was set up in 1964 but under the Housing Act 1974 it acquired a duty to register associations as fit to receive public funds and to monitor their subsequent performance. The period since 'has seen the evolution of a system which initially involved little more than the registration of housing associations, and some rather primitive financial controls, into a comprehensive machinery for auditing their performance on a variety of dimensions' (Day *et al.*, 1993: 8). The expansion of public funding has driven this development along with concern arising from scandals and revelations of inept handling of funds by housing associations in the late 1970s. Since 1989 the Housing Corporation's remit has been restricted to England. The new financial regime and other changes in legislation have altered the Housing Corporation's role and its approach has moved towards a comprehensive system of performance audit. The various supervisory functions – registration, monitoring and finance – have been brought together into a single performance audit division at regional level accountable to regional directors. This has increased the level of scrutiny of associations applying for registrations and has resulted in few new registrations (68 between 1990 and 1992). The Corporation's programme of inspection involves visits to associations, routine checks and emergency visits with greatest attention given to the large developing associations. Although this system appears generally to work satisfactorily, housing associations have various complaints, especially relating to regulations, policies on participation, problems of rents and affordability and criticism of management and administration even where outputs were satisfactory (see Day *et al.*, 1993).

In 1989 Scottish Homes assumed the statutory functions relating to registration and monitoring of housing associations in Scotland and in respect of the regulatory system has adopted most of the changes that are apparent for the Housing Corporation. However, Scottish Homes had other responsibilities as landlord in respect of properties previously managed by the Scottish Special Housing Association (SSHA). It also saw a need to establish a Scottish identity and develop an approach appropriate to the Scottish context. In particular, this has involved working with the community-based housing associations and cooperatives which have expanded rapidly in Scotland and had a major role in the regeneration of postwar housing estates, especially in the west of Scotland. These associations form some 27 per cent of Scotland's voluntary housing sector and the partnership area and community ownership programmes which fund them are major parts of the programme and expanded significantly in the early 1990s. The style of regulation developed has been one suitable for organisations which are new or lack experience and there has been no great pressure to make use of private finance. Because tenant involvement in these associations is strongly established there has also been less emphasis on tenant participation than in England.

Housing for Wales (Tai Cymru) was also established in 1989. As with Scottish Homes it has sought to establish a new independent image. The different structure of housing associations, different political culture and existing problems in the sector all influenced its early development. From 1999 Housing for Wales will cease to exist and will be absorbed within a new housing department of the Welsh Office. Ultimately the expectation is that it will become accountable to the Welsh Assembly.

Fragmented governance

The literature concerned with services provided by local government is inevitably concerned with the relationship between central and local government and how this operates in practice. However, in housing the early accounts of central–local relations need to be modified and complemented by an awareness of the increasingly important relationship between central government and the voluntary and private sectors.

Griffith, in the standard work on central–local relations in the early 1960s, described the philosophy of the then Ministry of Housing as *laissez-faire*:

> in that it leaves the local housing authorities to decide what is their local need and how far (if at all) it is to be met. (Griffith, 1966: 519)

The department had no machinery to discover whether programmes were realistic or reflected local needs:

> No one . . . looks to see whether local housing authorities are fulfilling their statutory obligations. And in many cases, the local housing authorities do not know whether they are doing so because of the inadequacy of the means of assessing housing needs. (Griffith, 1966: 518)

There were exceptions to this attitude and some of the department's activities were regulatory (control of standards, layout and design) or promotional (advisory material, research and development). The department was more inclined to encourage local autonomy and to restrict itself to exhortation and advice from other departments. A number of factors lie behind this. In particular, the development of public health provision in the nineteenth century was fraught with conflict over 'centralisation' and inspection and established a tradition of local autonomy reflected in the absence of clear housing duties for local authorities which could be referred to to indicate when they were failing to meet responsibilities.

Griffith observed that, unlike the Secretary of State for Education and Science, the Minister of Housing and Local Government had no statutory duty to ensure that the community was better housed. The department did not assume a national responsibility for housebuilding or the function of ensuring that local housing authorities were fulfilling their statutory obligations to provide housing to the extent that it was needed and therefore did not seek to exercise over local authorities the same amount of control as exercised by the department responsible for school building or the country's roads (Griffith, 1966: 289–90).

But the situation has changed over recent years. In 1969, Evelyn Sharp stated that the department had become increasingly interventionist because of perceived limitations of local authorities and 'political disagreement' (Sharp, 1969: 26). The reorganisation of the central department and the development of centralised policy-making with clearer intentions about resource allocation and policy direction has further extended this interventionism. Political disagreement has become more marked with the development of policies restricting discretion in relation to rent (under the Housing Finance Act 1972 and the Housing Acts 1980); with the introduction of cash limits and reductions in allocation of loan sanction for housing capital expenditure (through HIPs and Housing Plans); and with the reduction of discretion in relation to council house sales policy and rents.

The extension of central government's direct involvement was also evident in the development of policies with separate, top-sliced budgets with separate procedures for application and management. Inner City Policy and Comprehensive Community Programmes, Estate Action, Housing Action Trusts, City Grant and City Challenge are examples of such policies. What is involved is a fragmentation of procedures and control. Taken in conjunction with the impact of the Right to Buy, voluntary transfers of stock, the development of housing associations and tenant management organisations there has been a significant transfer of power from local government and the key framework for housing is no longer central–local government relations.

Bearing this in mind neither Griffith's *laissez-faire* view nor Cullingworth's similar bargaining view (Cullingworth, 1966: 62) of central–local relations in housing are any longer sufficient. The detail and complexity of controls and in particular of financial controls have increased. However ministerial controls and initiatives have not yet begun to eliminate sharp differences between local administrations in the tasks they face and the policies they adopt. The central–local government relationship is increasingly a regulatory and compulsory one and inevitably, it has tended to become a conflictual and political relationship.

In addition to direct scrutiny and even confrontation, central government has established other procedures to scrutinise local authorities. The most apparent of these is the system of audit. The Audit Commission for local authorities in England and Wales came into being in April 1983, following the Local Government Finance Act of 1982. The Commission appoints auditors to all local authorities in England and Wales. The auditors are required to satisfy themselves that each council's accounts are in order, that all expenditure has been in accordance with the law and that the council has made 'proper arrangements for securing economy, efficiency and effectiveness in its use of resources'. Although the Audit Commission is independent of central government and has been critical, for example, of the effect on local authorities of central government's block grant distribution system and arrangements for local housing strategies and planning, it is inevitably seen as a creature of central government and as reflecting central government's perspectives too closely. The literature on central–local relations distinguishes between partnership models and agent models (Rhodes, 1979). Partnership models are closer to Griffith's perspective and present local authorities and central departments as co-equals under Parliament. Local authorities have considerable discretion to design and implement their own policies. In agent situations – and it is generally accepted that there has been a movement away from partnership and towards these – local authorities implement national policies under the supervision of central departments and have little or no discretion. Recent literature also emphasises complexity, ambiguity and confusion in central–local relationships.

It may be argued that partnership models more nearly describe the relationships emerging in the 1980s between central government and the housing association movement or the private sector. As central government's relationship with local government has become more regulatory and conflictual and as it has become less inclined to use local authorities as the principal agencies for the development and implementation of housing policy, so it has become increasingly dependent on other agencies. Central government's relationship with various professions and the courts could be included in such a discussion. However it is with housing associations and building societies that it is easiest to identify a new corporatism.

The growth of home ownership in Britain has been significantly assisted by government policy and especially by taxation and subsidy. This support makes distinctions between 'public' and 'private' sectors of limited accuracy. The owner-occupied sector is state-subsidised and state-sponsored and has grown as part of public policy. Central government's cooperation and consultation with various private sector agencies, including builders, is a notable feature of this. However, it is in cooperation with building societies that the relationship is strongest. Closer working relations between government and building societies have been apparent at both central and local levels since the 1970s (Boddy, 1981). Harrison has stated that 'once a residual role had been mapped out for council housing, the building societies and the state could share an interest in the expansion of owner-occupation' (Harrison, 1984). But shared interest had gone beyond this. Other forms of privatisation of housing and housing management fit the ideological and fiscal aims of government and the interests of builders and building societies. Acquisition of council estates for refurbishment, whether in anticipation of subsequent letting or of sale, involves a further development of collaboration between government and the private sector. The Building Societies Act of 1986 made the involvement of the private sector in privatisation schemes which go beyond the expansion of owner-occupation possible on a much larger scale than before. It also provided the route for a continuing demunicipalisation, not just through the expansion of home ownership but also through a growing involvement of building societies in the provision of rented housing. The government has looked to societies to enable it to achieve national policy objectives and it has responded to building societies' needs – notably through legislation. Building societies have been encouraged to finance improvement in the private sector, refurbishment of council estates, council house sales and low-cost home ownership schemes. All of these policies have developed within a framework of general subsidy and favourable taxation conditions and special policies and projects. One view of these developments and of new legislation is that they form part of a depoliticisation of policy issues and a transfer of major policy decisions to a sphere of negotiation and brokerage between government and the industry. The high level of shared concerns around owner-occupation means that important policy conflicts will be resolved in this arena, rather than through public debate. Most recently policies relating to mortgage arrears, repossessions and reviving the home ownership sector have involved close collaboration between building societies and other lenders, the government and other housing bodies.

The contrast between the highly politicised and often overtly conflictual relations between central and local government and the cosy corporatism of government–private sector relations is striking. It has advantages but raises questions of autonomy and accountability. Hawes suggests that building societies have gained political importance in the process of restructuring and privatising housing and that a particular kind of corporatist relationship is involved. This is not the state intervention which brings capital labour and government together to direct the private sector of the economy. Nor is it adequately represented as a supportive intervention by government to sustain and improve the functioning of the market or a directive intervention by government to control and guide the private sector. Hawes suggests that the form of corporatist intervention is better seen as collaborative. He states: 'Those policies, although cloaked in the rhetoric of personal freedom, self-reliance and market forces, and reinforced by the wider ideology of priva-tisation, do, in fact, retain significant elements of intervention, subsidy and direction' (Hawes, 1986: 66).

Conclusions

Analysis of the administrative framework relating to housing must take into account substantial changes which have occurred in recent years. The key organisations involved in housing policy in the 1990s differ markedly from those of the 1970s and a more complex and fragmented pattern of control is involved. The building societies and other agencies involved in the home ownership market have a key role in managing housing consumption. While private landlords have declined further, the Housing Corporation, Scottish Homes and Housing for Wales are largely new organisations with expanded roles and budgets. Government offices in the regions in England and the regional dimension of housing policy have become increasingly significant in debates about policy especially with the increased reference to regeneration and the inclusion of major housing programmes in this approach. Sponsored bodies, non-departmental public bodies and executive agencies have become important in the housing field. They have grown in significance, as have private and voluntary organisations, as local authorities' housing role has declined. Housing associations have grown and changed with a different financial basis and with a new generation of stock transfer associations. Local authorities also operate within a tighter framework of central financial control, monitoring and scrutiny. All of this represents a shift in account-ability. The more limited role of local authorities means less direct account-ability of housing to the citizen. Appointed and nominated boards are accountable but the process can be obscure and confused. As a consequence of these changes the central issues for housing policy are now less about relationships between central and local government. Reference has been made earlier in this book to a variety of factors which would seem to reduce the autonomy and power of local housing authorities and increase the tendency for local authorities to become mere agents of the central state. Developments in the 1980s in relation to both rents and council house sales do involve central government laying down not just a framework for policy but details of policy content and procedure. Nevertheless considerable differences in policy objectives and in practice remain at local level. Even in relation to rents and council house sales, important variations remain. To this extent these changes have not produced a uniform and rational pattern of policy compatible with dominant centralised policy-making. However it might be argued that a dominant central bureaucracy would not in any event produce a uniform pattern of policy. If evidence of variation is not regarded as evidence of independence of action reference to direct and public conflicts over issues such as council house sales becomes more crucial. The ultimate evidence that the local state is not an agent of, or does not represent the same interests as, the central state lies in examples of obstruction, delay, creative circumvention and non-cooperation in relation to areas where central government places emphasis and priority and seeks to challenge functional divisions which have become well-established.

The role of the state in housing goes beyond central, local and regional government. The voluntary and private sectors have become increasingly important elements in housing policy. The financial dependency of a large group of the active housing association movement has left them more clearly as agents of the state – manipulated through the Housing Corporation and its equivalents. The autonomy and choice of associations could too easily be at the cost of jobs, and the corporatist relationship could be a directive one. In contrast, the relationship between the state and building societies and other financial institutions is more equal. In this case the state does not need just the organisational and managerial experience but the banking skills and funds which financial institutions can mobilise. But building society and banking activity in housing rests on a framework of state support and subsidy. The collaborative relationship between the state and the building societies and other parts of the private sector involves a major redrawing of the housing policy map. And the demutualisation of building societies is also significant. The corporate relationship between central government and the private and voluntary sectors has grown in importance. The centralisation of housing policy and decline in the role of local authority investment are part of this broader change in the administration and operation of housing policy.

One final point to note relates to the impact of membership of the European Union. In many areas of policy European legislation and regulation have become of major importance. While the European Commission has no competence in relation to housing and there is no likelihood of the development of a European housing policy, a range of policies have an indirect impact. Funds channelled through the EU have been used in relation to housing. This particularly relates to the housing component in economic regeneration and to policies related to the environment and community initiatives. One view is that the importance of EU policy and funding will increase and that local authorities and others will direct their energies towards European-level institutions to achieve policy changes perhaps in conjunction with similar organisations in other countries. Collective pressure across boundaries between regions and subregions may emerge as a mechanism to strengthen the role and impact of local government in relation to housing strategies as well as other areas of policy.

8

The Financial Framework

In the most general sense the financial framework consists of the various arrangements, combining market mechanisms and public policy measures, through which the costs of housing are met. The financial framework for housing reflects the fact that houses are expensive and durable, factors which have implications for both producers and consumers. There are different frameworks in place for each of the tenure categories in the British housing system, and each of them combines elements from the private market and public policy. The scope and complexity of these arrangements is such that it is inappropriate to attempt a comprehensive account in just one chapter. General introductions to housing finance are available elsewhere, for instance in the works by Aughton and Malpass (1999), Garnett, Reid and Riley (1991), Gibb, Munro and Satsangi (1999) and Hills (1991). This chapter has limited and specific aims, reflecting the themes of the book and concentrating on issues of central control and local autonomy. As previous chapters have shown, finance represents one of the main ways in which central government exercises control over the decisions and actions of organisations responsible for the delivery of housing services.

In aggregate housing finance involves huge flows of money, reflecting the high cost of housing, in terms of both its initial construction and the demands made on the incomes of consumers. The financial framework for housing includes major private sector institutions, such as the banks and building societies which provide much of the capital for private and public sector housing investment, as well as local government and voluntary organisations which are the main providers of rented housing. The financial institutions are driven by commercial considerations, and so market forces are an important part of any explanation of the operation of the financial framework. Also of central importance to the framework are the subsidies and tax reliefs provided by the Exchequer as governments seek to use finance as a means of achieving housing and other policy objectives.

Governments use financial devices to pursue a number of objectives, which can be summarised by saying that they wish to influence or control:

(a) the overall rate of investment in new building and renovation;
(b) the costs that fall to be met by households from their own resources;
(c) the tenure categories in which new building and renovation is concentrated;
(d) the overall pattern of owning and renting; and
(e) the aggregate level of public expenditure devoted to housing.

In the case of the private sectors the pursuit of these objectives is largely through the tax system and social security benefits, although some other subsidies are available. In relation to social rented housing central government has a more detailed and direct involvement in setting the framework for decisions about investment and pricing levels, hence the focus on these tenures in this chapter.

The next section looks at some of the key concepts which are necessary to the analysis of housing finance across all tenures. The focus then closes in on the current financial frameworks in local authority housing and the housing association sector.

Concepts in housing finance

Development and consumption finance

In thinking about housing finance it is necessary to distinguish between development finance and consumption finance. Development finance refers to the money which is needed to pay for the initial construction of housing, while consumption finance refers to the ways in which households meet the costs of buying or renting. The importance of this distinction arises from the high cost of housing in relation to incomes, and the differing interests of suppliers and consumers. Housing development requires large amounts of money to buy land and materials and to pay for the labour and machinery required for the construction of houses. Whether the builder or developer has sufficient money capital available or has to borrow it, the essential point is that, in order to finance future projects, it is normally necessary to realise the capital tied up in the newly built houses. In other words, the development process implies a short-term circulation of capital from money to property and back to money.

Housing consumption, however, generally requires a much longer-term circulation. The human need for housing means that consumers require access to a dwelling even though, in most cases, they cannot afford to buy outright, especially at the start of their independent adult lives. What consumers need is some method of spreading the cost of housing over a long period, thereby reducing the cost to an affordable proportion of regular income. In effect, the various tenure categories in Britain represent different approaches to cost-spreading, and the finance of housing consumption is concerned with the different ways in which households pay for their accommodation, and the forms of subsidy available to them.

Historically it was the role of the private landlord to facilitate the differing needs of builders and consumers. Landlords would typically buy dwellings from speculative builders, using their own or borrowed money, and then they would draw an income in the form of rents charged to tenants. In the twentieth century, individual home ownership, financed mainly by building society mortgages, and renting from local authorities have largely replaced private renting. Local authorities took over the task of providing new housing to rent, playing that crucial role of standing between the builder and the tenant. And now housing associations have taken over from local authorities as the main providers of new rented housing.

Capital and revenue

To understand the flows of money in housing provision and consumption, it is necessary to introduce another basic distinction: that between capital and revenue. This distinction is immensely important, but at the same time it is frustratingly arbitrary and vague (Hepworth, 1984: 9–11; Garnett, Reid and Riley, 1991: 5; Gibb and Munro, 1991: 68). Capital expenditure conventionally refers to the provision of durable assets, whereas revenue expenditure covers a range of recurring costs associated with the use of assets and the provision of services; thus the money raised to pay for the construction or modernisation of houses counts as capital, while the money used to pay the wages of housing management workers and to pay for routine repairs counts as revenue. Another important element of housing revenue expenditure is debt charges arising from borrowing for capital investment. In accounting terms, the convention adopted by the government is that items are counted as capital expenditure if the main benefits accruing from the expenditure are spread over a number of accounting periods (i.e. years), whereas items are counted as revenue if the benefits fall wholly within a single accounting period (DoE, 1988a: 19).

Although the capital–revenue distinction is fundamental it remains an accounting convention rather than a rigid framework. Thus, while capital expenditure is typically financed from borrowing, owner-occupiers normally borrow only a proportion of the purchase price of their home (using savings to make up the difference), and in the local authority sector in recent years the large-scale sale of assets, coupled with reduced levels of new building, has meant that a significant proportion of capital expenditure has been financed by receipts from sales. It is also possible, in any tenure, to meet the costs of capital expenditure directly from revenue income, without borrowing, and to use capital resources (either reserves or credit) to pay for expenditure which is normally met from revenue income (this is referred to as capitalised revenue expenditure). It is worth adding that just as capital expenditure can generate debt charges to be met from revenue income, so invested capital reserves generate interest which constitutes a flow of revenue income. Interest on receipts was a significant element of revenue income in some local authorities in the late 1980s, but its application to housing revenue expenditure was stopped by the Local Government and Housing Act 1989.

Affordability and subsidy

The term 'affordability' has entered the language of debate about housing in Britain only since the late 1980s, although the issue of what people could afford to pay for their housing has been at the heart of housing policy for decades. What brought the notion of affordability itself to the forefront was a combination of developments in the late 1980s. First, in the context of a housing policy which placed great emphasis on home ownership, the rapid increase in house prices relative to wages in 1987–9 raised questions about the affordability of mortgaged house purchase, especially among lower-income households in the regions with the highest prices (Bramley, 1990). Second, the government's deregulation of private sector rents, and in the housing association sector the shift to higher rents, supported by housing benefit, raised the issue of what proportion of income people could and should be expected to devote to meeting their housing costs. The debate has been notable for the lack of an agreed definition of affordability, and even the following attempt at a definition serves mainly to clarify the questions to be answered:

> Affordability is concerned with securing some given standard of housing (or different standards) at a price or rent which does not impose, in the eyes of some third party (usually government), an unreasonable burden on household incomes. A number of judgements and assumptions are made in putting the concept into practice, and, in broad terms, affordability is assessed by the ratio of a chosen definition of housing costs to a selected measure of household income in some given period. (Maclennan and Williams, 1990: 9)

The debate has not been helped by the government's refusal to state a clear position on affordability; the official line has been that it was for the market to set prices and private sector rents, and for housing associations and local authorities to set their own rents, although in April 1993 the Minister of Housing was reported to have revealed that for housing associations the DoE assumed 35 per cent of net income to be an affordable level of expenditure on rent (*Inside Housing*, 23 April 1993).

Another feature of the discussion has been the way it has centred on a very narrow definition of affordability, based on crude percentages of disposable income. In the case of rented housing this is more justifiable than in owner-occupation, where the assessment of affordability by reference to income alone ignores the possible impact of savings and intergenerational transfers. The National Federation of Housing Associations recommended a 20 per cent guideline, but others pointed out that the crucial figure was the amount of cash that tenants had left over after paying their rent (Randolph, 1993: 47). What has been missing from most contributions (for example, Cope, 1990; Ferguson and Wilcox, 1990; Gibbs, 1992) has been any discussion of the subjective element in affordability. However, Kempson (1993: 26–7) acknowledges that 'people differ in the way they allocate their money. Some choose to spend more on their housing and cut back on other expenditure; while others keep their housing costs low in order to spend more on other things. The higher the income the less need there is for such choices.' Whether 20 per cent or 40 per cent is affordable depends in part on the payer's perception of value for money, and factors such as the other demands on disposable income and the length of time that the expenditure is expected to remain at a given level. For example, owner-occupiers at the start of their housing careers might regard 40 per cent of income allocated to mortgage repayments as affordable, especially if they expect the amount to fall as a proportion of income, and if they anticipate making a capital gain. Tenants, on the other hand, are more likely to expect rent to increase as a proportion of income, and of course they have no access to any capital gain. Their view of what is affordable is, therefore, likely to be very different.

Whatever view is taken on the affordability debate, it is clear, as previous chapters have chronicled, that for 80 years various forms of subsidy have been used to reduce the housing costs borne by individual households. The concept of subsidy raises some interesting problems, involving debate about what counts as subsidy (Hills, 1991: 51–67) and the implications of different forms of subsidy for rent setting. On the question of definition, one approach is to measure subsidy in terms of money actually paid by national and/or local taxpayers to reduce the price paid by consumers. However some economists reject this cash-flow definition, arguing instead that the correct measure of subsidy is the difference between the actual price and the price that would be paid in a free market (Gibb and Munro, 1991: 3). Nevertheless official statistics and government accounts abide by the cash-flow definition, and that is the perspective adopted here, too.

Housing subsidies can be paid to either the provider or the consumer. In the former case the effect is to enable the provider to set prices or rents below what would be implied by costs or market conditions. The British council housing and housing association sectors illustrate different types of provider subsidy in action. In council housing subsidies were historically paid as fixed annual amounts per dwelling, representing a contribution to debt charges and enabling authorities to set rents at less than full cost, as discussed in Chapters 3 and 4. This reflected the wider policy of encouraging new building by local authorities and can therefore be referred to as investment subsidy (Malpass, 1992a): local authorities were entitled to subsidy for every new dwelling, irrespective of local rent levels. More recently (since 1972, apart from 1975–81) subsidy has been based on overall Housing Revenue Account deficits (actual or notional), reflecting a move away from investment towards a greater emphasis on subsidy as a lever on rents policy. Both investment and deficit subsidy are types of general housing subsidy, which is paid irrespective of the incomes of individual tenants.

General housing subsidy has also been important in the development of the British housing association movement. However, in this sector the main form of subsidy, Social Housing Grant (SHG), is paid as a capital sum at the time of construction. The principle governing it is to reduce the amount of remaining debt to a level which can be covered from rents set at levels which are in some broad sense affordable. Changes in the SHG regime are discussed in more detail later in this chapter, but it is appropriate to say here that, as in the local authority sector, these changes can be related in part to central government attempts to exert leverage on rents.

In the private rented and owner-occupied sectors a different approach to subsidy has tended to dominate; here assistance has been channelled directly to consumers, although there is historical precedent for the payment of subsidy directly to providers, in the period 1919–29, and more recently the tax relief available to investors in new private rented housing via the Business Expansion Scheme, 1988–93, represents a departure from established practice (Crook *et al.*, 1991b). For owner-occupiers there is a range of tax reliefs, on mortgage interest, capital gains and imputed rental income. It is also important to remember the availability of grants for repair and improvement work (Leather and Mackintosh, 1993). For purchasers of council houses and flats the discounts available under the Right to Buy have become significant (Forrest and Murie, 1988, 1990). Space does not permit a full discussion of all these forms of assistance (see Hills, 1991: ch. 12). However, a word on mortgage interest relief is appropriate: this is a form of assistance which is based on individual entitlement, so it counts as a consumer subsidy, but since 1983 it has been paid direct to mortgage lenders via the Mortgage Interest at Source (MIRAS) system (Hills, 1991: 195–200). An issue which has been debated in relation to mortgage interest relief is the extent to which, in the absence of any controls on prices, the benefits of relief are reflected in higher prices, indicating that the ultimate beneficiary of any subsidy may not be the person to whom it is paid or for whose benefit it is apparently intended (Gibb and Munro, 1991: 3).

The private rented sector has historically been unsubsidised, although improvement and repair grants have been available in various forms since 1949. It can be argued that rent control and regulation was effectively a subsidy to tenants imposed at the expense of landlords rather than the Exchequer. Since 1972 means-tested public assistance to private tenants has been available in the form of rent allowances, until 1982/3, and now housing benefit. This, however, raises another definitional problem, concerning the distinction between housing subsidy and income-related housing benefit. General subsidy refers to cash sums provided to bridge the gap between a landlord's housing expenditure and income from rents and other sources. General subsidy is indiscriminate, in the sense that it is distributed without regard to the income of individual tenants. Tax relief on mortgage interest, too, is a form of general subsidy in the sense that it is not targeted on those most in need of assistance. Tax relief is skewed in favour of the better off, more so until 1991 when relief was granted at one's marginal rate of tax rather than the basic rate. The two budgets of 1993 began the process of reducing relief below the basic rate of income tax, and Labour's first budget in July 1997 introduced a further cut to just 10 per cent.

Income-related assistance, on the other hand, represents an attempt to direct help to those who need it. General subsidy and income-related assistance are not mutually exclusive. Until 1972, all Exchequer housing subsidy to local authorities was distributed as general subsidy, but authorities were free to allocate assistance to tenants in ways which combined elements of general subsidy with income-related rent rebates. Only since 1972 has central government separated general subsidy from rebate assistance (Malpass, 1990). It can be convincingly argued that this separation should go further and that rent rebates should be seen as a form of income maintenance or social security, rather than a housing subsidy. After all, suppliers of goods and services do not normally tailor their prices to the specific incomes of individual customers. It is the role of the social security system to ensure that people on low incomes can afford to pay for the goods and services that they need, yet in the case of council housing local authorities have for many years operated as providers of a form of income maintenance. This situation was recognised in 1982, when the housing benefit scheme was introduced in succession to the old rent-rebate arrangements. Under the terms of the Social Security and Housing Benefits Act 1982, the local authorities continued to administer housing benefit, but responsibility within central government passed from the Department of the Environment to the Department of Health and Social Security (now the Department of Social Security).

The distinction between housing subsidy and income maintenance is important, not just in terms of classifying different aspects of social policy. It can be argued that the salience of housing benefit policy debates in the 1990s is a reflection of underlying deficiencies in the benefit system as a whole, resulting in a very high level of dependence on means-tested housing benefit. Housing subsidy is given to landlords to enable them to provide dwellings at affordable rents, while housing benefit is essentially a payment to tenants to enable them to pay the rent for their home. This is most clearly seen in the private rented sector where the rent charged is the full rent and housing benefit is explicitly given to tenants as a contribution towards their rent. In the council sector the situation is clouded by the fact that the local authority is both the landlord and the agent of the social security system and therefore housing benefit appears as a reduction in the rent charged to the tenant. The point to be established here is the conceptual distinction between housing subsidy and housing benefit, and the reason for emphasising the distinction is that it is fundamental to understanding the new regime for local authority housing finance, as will become clear later in this chapter.

Historic-cost pricing and current-value pricing

Having considered methods of subsidising housing consumption it is necessary to turn to the issue of rent setting. There is essentially a choice between variants of two basic approaches: historic-cost pricing and current-value pricing. The latter represents market or market-related approaches, while the former constitutes an alternative to the dominance of market ideas. The term 'historic-cost pricing' refers to the approach which has predominated in British local authority housing. In fact local authorities have adopted a variant known as pooled historic-cost pricing in which aggregate income from rents, subsidies and other sources is pooled in order to meet aggregate housing expenditure. This is a way of coping with inflation and avoiding wide differences between rents according to when houses were built. It means that the rents of older, cheaper houses are higher than is necessary to cover their debt charges and management and maintenance costs, but the rents of newer, more expensive houses are correspondingly lower than they would otherwise be. Theoretically the units within which pooling operates could be smaller or larger than individual local authorities: they could be estates within a local authority, or regional groupings of authorities. Indeed the entire national stock could be constituted as a single pool and the idea of national rent pooling has been discussed for some years, without ever gaining significant political support (Housing Centre Trust, 1975). Whatever the units of aggregation, historic-cost pricing in British public housing is essentially based on collective methods of accounting. This poses as separate questions the issues of the overall balance between rental income and subsidy, and the method of differentiating rents within and between localities. In the past, local authorities have enjoyed considerable autonomy in both respects, but Conservative governments in particular have shown increasing enthusiasm for current-value pricing, an approach which has serious implications for local autonomy.

Whereas historic-cost pricing starts from the aggregate rental income and works down to the individual rent, current-value pricing tends to be conceived the other way up: the starting-point is the rents of individual dwellings and the aggregate income is merely the sum of all the individual rents. In general this approach has implications for rent and subsidy levels, and for the relationship between central and local government. Historic-cost pricing has the advantage of relating rents to expenditure, thereby minimising reliance on means-tested benefits. There are various versions of current-value pricing. For instance, the fair rent system, introduced in the private sector in 1965 and in the housing association sector in 1972, based rents on moderated market rents, aiming to be fair to both landlord and tenant. A feature of the fair rent system was that rents were set by an independent Rent Officer Service, which removed from the landlord any real control of the rents charged.

Another variant of current-value pricing is capital value rents, as advocated by the Inquiry into British Housing in 1985 (NFHA, 1985). Here the proposal was that all rented housing in all sectors should have rents set to provide a return on capital at a standard rate of 4 per cent of the current value.

The common feature of different versions of current-value pricing is that they are much more closely aligned to the market than is historic-cost pricing. This has three main implications: (i) rents tend to be higher; (ii) subsidies are directed towards individuals in the form of income-related assistance; and (iii) for local authorities it means that they have less discretion in rent fixing. There are some difficulties associated with the application of current-value pricing in social rented housing. For instance, the assessment of property values is problematic, and the justice of relating rents to values is questionable – if property values rise in an area then owner-occupiers benefit in terms of a capital gain, but for tenants in the same area the effect would be higher rents with no access to any capital gain. Another issue which has arisen in the use of property values in the assessment of rent increases under the Local Government and Housing Act 1989 is that in some areas rents are considerably above the level implied by capital values (Malpass, 1992b: 24–5; Malpass, Warburton, Bramley, and Smart, 1993). There is also the question of what happens when capital values fall; rent reductions seem very unlikely.

Public expenditure and private finance

The final set of concepts to be considered in this section refers to public expenditure and private finance. It is not the intention to embark on a detailed discussion of the definition of public expenditure (Gibb and Munro, 1991: ch. 3), but it is necessary to identify the meaning of the term 'private finance' in relation to public expenditure. A development of recent years has been the growth of 'private finance' for housing association investment, and it is important to be clear how this differs from the funds which local authorities have traditionally raised from private investors for their programmes of housing investment. When local authorities were building up their stocks of houses they borrowed a large proportion of the capital they required directly from private sources and the balance was borrowed indirectly via the Public Works Loans Board. All this money counted as public expenditure, and the loans were secured against the local authorities' revenue-raising powers rather than the value of the assets created.

In the case of housing associations, the whole of their development programme supported by Housing Association Grant counted as public expenditure until 1987 when the Treasury agreed to the concept of 'mixed funding', whereby borrowing from private sources no longer counts as public expenditure. The idea of mixed funding was adopted as the basis of the new capital finance regime for housing associations in the Housing Act 1988. The advantage of mixed funding is that more dwellings can be produced for a given level of public expenditure since only the grant element counts under this heading. However, accompanying the Treasury concession on public expenditure was the imposition of the condition which required that private lenders should have no more security than for normal private sector loans.

What was new about private finance was that housing associations had not previously borrowed directly from private lenders, and that such lending would not count as public expenditure. However, local authorities, which had long experience of borrowing from private sources, were not given the public expenditure concession.

This section has outlined some of the key concepts in housing finance as a prelude to examination of the current frameworks operating in relation to social rented housing.

The local authority framework

The capital side

This section outlines the system introduced by the Local Government and Housing Act 1989, which has been in operation in England and Wales since April 1990.

Local authorities borrow money on a regular basis for a variety of budgetary reasons and they normally operate a single account, the consolidated loans fund (or equivalent), from which individual projects are financed. This means that, although housing capital costs are conventionally repaid over 60 years, the actual borrowing can be organised quite differently, according to changing circumstances. The money for each project may be borrowed from the consolidated fund over a 60–year period, but borrowing by that fund from external sources may be over much shorter periods. This illustrates how housing capital is in a sense indistinguishable from, and integrated with, other local authority programmes.

Local authorities raise capital for housing projects from a variety of sources, but the main sources are borrowing (or equivalent credit arrangements) and capital receipts from the disposal of assets. Until 1980, the overwhelming proportion of housing capital was obtained by borrowing from private investors, either directly or via the Public Works Loans Board. Local authorities can raise mortgages, they can borrow from the Stock Exchange by issuing loan stock, or they can issue local bonds (Hepworth, 1984: ch. VII).

The other major source of capital for housing, asset sales, was insignificant before the introduction of the council tenants' Right to Buy in 1980. Since that time huge amounts of money have been received by local authorities: between 1981/2 and 1987/8, local authorities in England and Wales raised about £17 billion by the sale of capital assets, of which £12.5 billion came from the sale of houses and flats (DoE, 1988a: 2). However, the pattern of receipts varies considerably across the country and the authorities with the greatest need to spend have tended not to be the authorities with the greatest amounts of capital receipts (Forrest and Murie, 1988: ch. 6).

Until the mid-1970s, local authorities enjoyed considerable freedom to determine their own housing capital expenditure levels. If their proposals met the requirements of the prevailing rules on costs and standards, then central government approval for borrowing ('loan sanction') was virtually automatic. However, since then central government has become increasingly interventionist in local authority finances in general, including, inevitably, capital expenditure on housing. Chapters 4 and 5 have referred to the introduction of the Housing Investment Programme system in 1977/8, but this has to be seen in the context of a wider system of controls on local authority capital expenditure and the use of capital receipts introduced in the Local Government, Planning and Land Act 1980.

From the point of view of both central and local government, the 1980 system did not work satisfactorily, and in 1986 the government published proposals for change in a Green Paper, *Paying for Local Government* (Great Britain, 1986). Reaction to these proposals led to further work and a consultation paper was published in July 1988 (DoE, 1988a).

The 1980 system was seen to suffer from four main problems. First, it failed to bring about capital expenditure at local level which was consistent with public expenditure plans as a whole.

Second, the 1980 system created a distribution of capital spending power which did not match the need for expenditure. This was partly due to the way that capital receipts tended to be greatest in areas with least need to spend, and vice versa, and partly because of the fact that the government had failed to foresee that restrictions on the use of capital receipts did not prevent authorities carrying forward the unused part from one year and spending the permitted proportion in the next year, and so on until all the money was spent; this became known as the cascade effect.

The third main problem associated with the 1980 system was, from the point of view of central government, that it did not prevent local authorities from undertaking capital expenditure outside the framework of the legislation.

The fourth problem was that because of the other problems the government had resorted to frequent changes of primary legislation, producing an uncertain implementation environment.

In responding to these features of the 1980 system, the government took into account four objectives:

1.   to provide effective government influence over aggregate levels of local authority capital expenditure and borrowing;
2.   to bring about a distribution of capital expenditure which reflects national and local needs;
3.   to promote the government's aim of reducing the size of the public sector by asset sales and efficient asset management; and
4.   to provide a sound basis for local authorities to plan their capital programmes with confidence. (DoE, 1988a: 11)

The system outlined in the 1988 consultation paper, and enacted in Part IV of the Local Government and Housing Act 1989, was primarily concerned with controlling the use of credit by local authorities, as distinct from total expenditure. The 1989 Act system brought together under one heading borrowing and all other credit arrangements which have the same economic effect as borrowing. There are two other sources of finance for capital projects:

1.   government grants or contributions from third parties (which might be other local authorities).
2.   local authorities' own resources, including approved proportions of capital receipts and revenue contributions (in the case of housing projects, revenue contributions must come from HRA income).

Each year individual local authorities are given a 'credit approval' which places a limit on credit arrangements. This basic credit approval (BCA) may be supplemented by special credit approvals (SCAs) issued by ministers to particular authorities in the light of circumstances during the year. It is important to note that because capital expenditure is not ring-fenced the BCA is a single amount covering all services. However, each authority is also given a specified amount which represents the maximum figure for housing capital expenditure which will be subsidisable within the Housing Revenue Account (HRA). Authorities are free to spend more of their BCA on housing, and to debit the debt charges to the HRA, but such expenditure would result in higher rents rather than higher subsidy.

The Exchequer provides specified capital grants (SCGs) (as distinct from annual contributions towards debt charges) in respect of certain local authority housing activities in relation to the private sector, including renovation grants, area improvement and slum clearance. There may also be situations in which an authority receives capital grants from another local authority. This might arise where a housing authority has obtained a large capital receipt from the sale of its entire housing stock and wishes to finance services in its area provided by the county council.

The third main element of capital finance for housing is capital receipts from the sale of assets. The 1989 Act empowers the Secretary of State to specify an amount for receipts taken into account (RTIA) when calculating basic credit approval levels. The system also provides for a proportion of capital receipts to be set aside for debt redemption or for the financing of future commitments. The proportion of housing receipts that local authorities can spend is 25 per cent, and 75 per cent must be used for debt redemption or future commitments. In the case of non-housing capital receipts, 50 per cent may be spent on new investment.

Local authorities were not actually required to use accumulated receipts to repay outstanding debts, and in practice many of them did not. This led to arguments for the release of accumulated receipts, said to amount to some £5 billion, and on taking office the new Labour Government announced a capital receipts initiative which consisted of the equivalent of phased release of receipts via the issuing of SCAs.

The 1989 Act system effectively replaced the HIP mechanism, but the term 'HIP' lives on in the context of the annual distribution of 'HIP allocations'. Each year every authority is given a HIP allocation which consists of an annual capital guideline (ACG) plus an allocation for the private sector programme, the SCG. The ACG is broadly the amount available to be spent on the public sector stock (although authorities have discretion to use ACG resources to support the private sector programme and/or non-housing capital expenditure).

The total amount of capital expenditure which may be financed by borrowing, the BCA, is the sum of the SCG and the ACG, less a figure for receipts taken into account:

$$BCA = (ACG - RTIA) + SCG$$

The impact of the 1989 Act capital control system varies from place to place, but it is clear that the intention was to give central government much tighter control over local authority expenditure and that this has been broadly achieved. It has removed much of the flexibility which local authorities enjoyed and exploited in the 1980s, and as Malpass *et al.* (1993: 45–6) have shown, the amount spent by local authorities on capitalised repairs fell dramatically between 1987/8 and 1991/2. Despite the temporary relaxation of the rules affecting new receipts, the application of capital receipts to the redemption of debt represents a severe restraint of capital programmes in many areas, but it also has the effect of reducing debt charges falling on the HRA. On the other hand, the elimination of the cascade effect places considerable pressure on rents to support continued expenditure on maintaining and refurbishing the existing council stock. In overall terms it is clear from research on the implementation of the 1989 Act (Malpass *et al.*, 1993) that the new capital control system has had more impact on local authorities than the new regime for the revenue side.

The revenue side

Turning now to questions of housing revenue finance, the first point to note is that, unlike capital, the Housing Revenue Account (HRA) is kept quite separate from other local authority programme areas. On the expenditure side of the HRA, loan charges historically constituted the largest single item, although since the redefinition of the HRA in 1990 expenditure on management and maintenance and on rent rebates is greater (DoE, 1993: 86). During the 1980s, authorities were free to make surpluses on their housing operations and a growing number of HRAs came to include expenditure items representing transfers to the general rate fund (now the general fund).

On the income side of the HRA, the pattern has changed considerably over the years, but the main items have been rents, Exchequer subsidies and rate fund contributions. The latter were compulsory under all Housing Acts between 1919 and 1952 (except the 1923 Act), and throughout the period 1919–90 (except 1972–4) authorities enjoyed the power to make discretionary rate fund contributions. Some authorities, for reasons of high costs or local political preference, established a tradition of substantial levels of rate fund contribution, but by the 1980s, in most areas, contributions were either zero or close to it. The composition of Exchequer assistance has changed in response to a policy shift away from general subsidy towards means-tested assistance (Malpass, 1990).

In terms of central–local relations, the key issues on the revenue side of local authority housing finance revolve around the level of rents, the level and methods of distribution of subsidy and the amount of local autonomy in relation to rents and subsidies. Since central government is the main provider of financial assistance to council housing, it clearly has a close and legitimate interest in how the level of assistance is fixed and how the benefits are distributed amongst authorities and tenants. At the local level, the two key factors influencing subsidy are the scale of investment (both past and present) and the rents policies of local authorities. At the same time, subsidy policy can be used to influence investment and pricing policy at the local level. The interaction between central and local policies is extremely complicated, reflecting past exercise of autonomy at local level, as well as contemporary policy differences (Malpass *et al.*, 1993).

In the early 1980s, the government brought about a fundamental restructuring of local authority rents and subsidy policy, resulting in a major redistribution of assistance from general subsidy into rent rebates (housing benefit). In the short term this produced a sharp increase in the real level of rents, but it also had two other outcomes which became important reasons for further change. First, large numbers of authorities lost all general housing subsidy (but not rent-rebate subsidy) and their HRAs moved into actual or notional surplus, thereby raising the issue of who was to control the size and use of such surpluses. For the years 1982–90 this question was effectively resolved by lobbying by the Association of District Councils in late 1981, the result of which was that the Secretary of State agreed to concede local control of surpluses. More than 25 per cent of authorities in England and Wales quickly acquired the habit of transferring HRA surpluses into the general rate fund. Central government was thus in the position of contributing growing amounts of rent-rebate subsidy to authorities whose HRAs were in surplus and, arguably, not in need of as much subsidy as they were receiving.

The second relevant outcome of the 1980 subsidy system was that aggregate rate fund contributions to HRAs soon came to exceed Exchequer subsidy, something which had never happened before. Local authorities had become the major suppliers of 'indiscriminate' (i.e. non-means-tested) assistance, but in fact most authorities made either no rate fund contribution or just a very small payment. During the 1980s, London authorities generally accounted for around 75 per cent of total rate fund contributions and, since nearly all of the largest contributors were Labour-controlled authorities, this became a reason for the government's proposal, announced during the 1987 general election campaign, to ban all rate fund contributions.

It was in July 1988 that the government issued a consultation paper outlining its proposals for a new financial regime covering local authority rents and subsidies (DoE, 1988b). The consultation paper contained a critique of the 1980 system in which reference was made to the multiplicity of sources of subsidy (housing subsidy, rent-rebate subsidy, rate support grant and rate fund contributions) and the diverse pattern of assistance across the country. The government's point here was essentially that it was not in full control of the flow of Exchequer resources into HRAs and that as a result of local decisions actual and notional HRAs were moving out of alignment. The second element in the critique was that the 1980 system had produced distortions in the incentives to efficiency and good management. It was argued that the freedom to make unconstrained rate fund contributions provided a cover for inefficiency in housing management. The same sort of argument was applied in reverse in relation to authorities generating surpluses in the HRA, when it was stated that, 'It is essential that those surpluses should not be available to be used as a cushion for bad practices and inefficiency' (DoE, 1988b: 5). The stated objectives of the new regime were that it should be simpler, fairer and more effective. A simpler system, it was said, should produce subsidy arrangements which work in a more intelligible way and give consistent incentives. Fairness was referred to in relation to the balance between tenants and council tax payers, and between tenants in different areas. And an effective system would direct available resources to areas of need, and provide an incentive for good management.

The new regime, effective from April 1990, is essentially a modified version of the 1980 system. Subsidy continues to be based on the notional deficit on the HRA in each local authority, and each year the Secretary of State issues figures for the assumed changes in rent income and management and maintenance (M & M) expenditure. However the new regime incorporates three important changes:

1. the 'ring-fence' around the HRA, preventing contributions from the general fund (referred to as rate fund contributions before 1990) and discretionary transfers into the general fund;
2. a redefinition of what counts as the deficit on the HRA; and
3. differentiation of increases in rents and M & M expenditure.

At one level the ring-fencing provisions are straightforward, and have been effective in preventing councils from making discretionary payments between the HRA and the general fund. However, the issue of what should be properly charged to a 'landlord account' has been much harder to resolve and the DoE has broadly left authorities to continue with previous practice. The important point about the ring-fence is that central government now controls the whole of the subsidy required to bridge any HRA deficit and can therefore manipulate the deficit itself.

The other provisions of the new regime are a little more complicated. The 1989 Act effectively redefined what counts as the HRA deficit; whereas the old system's measure of deficits was based on unrebated rents the new system works on rebated rents, which massively increases the measure of deficit and gives central government much more leverage on rent levels – the greater the deficit the greater the subsidy and therefore the greater the scope for subsidy withdrawal, with consequent pressure on rents.

The 1989 Act introduced a major innovation in the form of the HRA subsidy, which combines general housing subsidy and rent-rebate subsidy. Together they make up the gap between notional expenditure and notional income from rebated rents and other sources. The rent-rebate element is always a positive amount, but if income, including the rebate element, is deemed to exceed expenditure then the housing element is negative and is netted off against the rebate element. By 1992/3 nearly three-quarters of English and Welsh authorities were in the position where their total HRA subsidy was reduced in this way, and a handful (nine) had no HRA subsidy at all (CIPFA, 1992). And by 1994/5 notional HRA surpluses in England exceeded total housing subsidy and began to make increasing contributions towards the cost of housing benefit. Current expenditure plans suggest that by the end of the century surpluses will account for more than 30 per cent of the cost of housing benefit for council tenants (DoE, 1997: 29).

Turning to the differentiation of determinations of changes in rents and M & M, the underlying reason for a new approach was that standard determinations (as applied in the 1980s) failed to take sufficient account of variations in local circumstances. The problem, however, is to find ways of differentiating the determinations accurately and fairly across the country. To achieve this goal requires the collection and analysis of large quantities of data, on a scale and with a degree of sophistication which has not been achieved in the past and which is not readily achievable even now.

In the case of rents, the 1988 consultation paper said only that 'rents should generally not exceed levels within reach of people in low-paid employment, and in practice they will frequently be below market levels' (DoE, 1988b: 5). The government had two objectives in relation to council rents: first, to raise average rents in all areas in real terms, and second, to move towards a situation where council rents vary in a way which reflects the sorts of variations found in the private sector. It is important to say that the policy is not explicitly that the rent for each house should be directly related to its capital value. In determining guideline rent *increases* the DoE (now the DETR) takes into account differences in capital values in each local authority area, and it remains for the local authority itself to set the rents of individual dwellings. The method employed is based on a process which begins with the capital value of each authority's stock expressed as a fraction of the total value of all council dwellings in the country. If an authority's stock is worth, say, 1 per cent of the total, then it would be expected to produce 1 per cent of the total rent income in the whole country. This gross amount, divided by the number of dwellings, would give an initial indication of the average increase (or decrease) for the year. The next stage involves a percentage increase reflecting the Secretary of State's view of how much rents generally should rise in the year, followed by a further amount to cover inflation.

However, applying this methodology to the established pattern of rents would have produced some huge increases in some places, and some similarly large decreases elsewhere. In order to keep rent increases down to politically acceptable levels in high-value areas, and to prevent actual rent reductions in low-value areas, the system includes a damping mechanism. Each year a figure is set for the national aggregate amount to be raised in rents, and guideline increases are contained within upper and lower limits set to generate this aggregate figure. Thus, the upper and lower limits are tied together: the higher the upper end of the range, the lower the bottom limit, but if the upper limit is set at a modest level then the lower limit is dragged up, in order to generate the required amount overall. The pattern of guidelines is shown in Table 8.1.

Table 8.1 *Rent assumptions, 1990/1 to 1997/8*

	1990/1 £	1991/2 £	1992/3 £	1993/4 £	1994/5 £	1995/6 £	1996/7 £	1997/8 £
Minimum guideline increase								
England	0.95	1.38	1.20	1.50	1.50	1.82	0.67	0.48
Wales	1.05	1.41	1.13	1.25	1.50	1.82	0.92	0.63
Maximum guideline increase								
England	4.50	2.50	4.50	3.00	2.90	2.82	1.17	0.98
Wales	3.15	2.50	3.40	2.75	2.90	2.82	0.92	0.94
Average guideline rent								
England	23.06	24.90	27.31	29.43	31.60	33.88	34.63	35.36
Wales	23.48	25.31	27.37	29.17	31.30	33.58	34.50	35.23
	%	%	%	%	%	%	%	%
Inflation assumption	5	6	4.5	2.75	2.5	3.25	2.75	2.0
Real increase								
England	5	2	5	5	5	4	0	0
Wales	2	2	4	4	3.5	4	0	0

Sources: DoE and Welsh Office.

The effect of this system in operation over several years has been to widen the differences between notional rents in high- and low-value areas, between the north and south of England. Authorities which have had the minimum guideline each year were assumed to raise rents by a total of £9.20 between April 1990 and April 1997, whereas authorities with the maximum were assumed to increase rents by £22.37. Most northern authorities have been given the minimum guideline rent increase each year while authorities receiving the maximum guideline each year have been concentrated in the south. In practice most authorities have increased rents by more than the guidelines, especially in London, and so the government has been able to make significant progress towards its objective of greater rent variation across the country.

For several years the Conservative government pursued a policy of average guideline rent increases above the rate of inflation, but then in 1995 a change of policy was indicated (DoE, 1995: 27), implying a move towards increases in line with inflation. This new policy was implemented in April 1996 and 1997, and re-enforced by subsidy penalties for authorities which increased rents by more than their guideline amount.

On the issue of management and maintenance, the government's intention was similarly to move towards a more uniform system, with differential M & M allowances related to differences in the age and type of stock in each area, taking account of geographical factors. The approach was to determine an overall national amount to be spent on M & M, and then to distribute allowances related to authorities' relative need to spend. In the first year a suitable mechanism was not in place and the basis of calculation was essentially a rolled-forward version of the old system. But since 1991/2 the DoE has developed a method, based on stock characteristics, of calculating target allowances for spending on repairs and maintenance, and for management. Each authority has an allowance, derived from actual expenditure in previous years, and a target allowance, based on stock characteristics. The implementation problem has been to bring the two into line with each other.

As with rents, the established pattern of expenditure across the country differed significantly from the target allowances produced by the government's computer: some were spending much less than their target allowance, while others were spending far more. The approach, therefore, has been to increase the allowances of low-spending authorities, bringing them closer to their targets (giving them incentives to increase actual spending), and to rein back the high spenders. Increases in allowances have been confined to those authorities whose allowances were below their targets, while authorities with allowances above their targets have seen their allowances frozen or even decreased in cash terms. In 1996/7 and 1997/8 the aggregate amount was frozen in cash terms, which meant that any increase for low spenders could only be achieved by decreases for the rest.

The final point to make on the current system is to draw attention to the way in which the assumed real increases in rents have tended to exceed the assumed real increases in M & M expenditure, thereby resulting in withdrawal of subsidy. In this sense the government is the agent of disrepair in the public sector, to the extent that it assumes that a proportion of extra rent income will go to the benefit of the Treasury in the form of lower subsidy, rather than to the benefit of tenants in the form of improved housing services.

The housing association framework

The purpose of this section is to outline the framework for housing association finance based on the Housing Act 1988. The Act introduced changes affecting both capital and revenue, and although it is convenient to discuss them separately it is important to remember that they are two sides of one system: changes on the revenue side, such as the deregulation of rents, have to be understood in relation to changes on the capital side. Although the focus of this section is the current system it is necessary to make some reference back to the old system, but for a more detailed comparison see Cope (1990: 81–138).

The growth of the housing association movement since 1974 has been based on the Housing Association Grant (HAG) (since the Housing Act, 1996, this has been replaced by Social Housing Grant – SHG), which is a capital grant paid to associations on new development schemes in order to reduce outstanding loans to levels generating affordable rents. From 1974 to 1989 HAG was calculated at the point when schemes were completed and ready for occupation. The local rent officer service would set fair rents for newly completed dwellings and this would provide a basis for working out how much debt could be serviced, after making allowance for management and maintenance costs. Typical HAG rates were 80 per cent or more. Despite the generosity of the HAG system some associations were eligible for a revenue subsidy, Revenue Deficit Grant, if their income failed to meet their approved outgoings (Hills, 1991: 119–20).

The generosity of the grant regime combined with the effect of inflation on rents meant that, at least with respect to their post-1974 stock, associations were more likely to be in surplus than deficit. From 1980 onwards there was therefore a requirement that associations paid surpluses into a Grant Redemption Fund, the benefits of which accrued to the Treasury.

The old framework was not only financially generous to associations, it also effectively provided a risk-free environment (Randolph, 1993: 149), in which the Housing Corporation in practice underwrote the full costs of new developments. However, in September 1987 the DoE produced a consultation paper on the financing of housing associations (DoE, 1987), in which it outlined proposals for changes designed to introduce market disciplines to the work of associations, and to raise rents towards market levels.

The objectives of the new regime were to increase the volume of rented housing that associations could produce for a given level of public expenditure, and to create new incentives to associations to deliver their services in the the the most cost-effective way (DoE, 1987: 1). These objectives implied continuation of the mixed funding system which was introduced on an experimental basis in 1987, and a shift from capital grant to means-tested housing benefit; the phrase that was used at the time was that housing benefit would 'take the strain' of higher rents.

The policy of mixed funding for new development was implemented through existing powers, but important changes affecting the type of tenancies offered on new lettings and the rules affecting rent setting, which were necessary for the success of mixed funding, required legislation. Proposals for the introduction of new-style tenancies for new lettings, with rents outside the fair rent system, were contained in Part I of the Housing Act 1988; Part II dealt with other matters relating to housing associations.

The capital side

The scale of capital expenditure by housing associations is effectively controlled by the government, which determines, through the Approved Development Programme (ADP), the amount of money available for the Housing Corporation to distribute in the form of grant. The ADP, agreed annually by the Secretary of State, sets the framework under which the Housing Corporation allocates capital resources to housing associations, including the basis on which the capital programme is shared between regions and between categories of expenditure. The government also determines the proportion of development costs covered by grant. Thus the rate of growth in the housing association sector is very sensitive to government policy, albeit mediated through the Housing Corporation. The Corporation is in practice a vehicle for the implementation of government policy, with little capacity to pursue its own objectives.

There are a number of key features of the capital finance regime which has been in operation since April 1989:

1. In order to shift an element of risk on to associations themselves the amount of grant payable on any new development scheme is set at the outset rather than at the point of completion; this reverses the previous procedure and means that associations bear responsibility for containing

development costs, knowing that any increases will not be reflected in higher grant.

2. Grant is now also paid at a much earlier stage in the development process than was previously the case, an innovation which caused major cash-flow problems in 1990/1 during the transitional period from the old to the new regime.

3. Mixed funding is now the norm for new housing association developments; this means that the balance of development cost not covered by grant is required to be raised from private investors and does not count as public expenditure. Again there is a risk element involved, to the extent that the private finance element is not underwritten by the Housing Corporation or the Treasury, and therefore associations are exposed to the requirements of the private lenders. The risk element is increased by the fact that there is no possibility of claiming Revenue Deficit Grant on post-1989 mixed funded schemes – all costs have to be met out of the association's own resources, which effectively means rents or reserves.

4. Grant is paid as a percentage of development costs at a level which is set annually, and which has been subject to downward pressure since the start of the new regime; in 1989/90 the rate was set at an average of 75 per cent, but by 1998/9 it had been reduced to 54 per cent. The actual grant rate received by most associations is well below this headline rate, however, as a result of a government decision to distribute grant competitively. Associations which can bid at less than the nominal grant rate can expect to receive higher allocations. But to do so they have to increase efficiency and/or contribute from their own reserves or from new capital receipts. The nominal grant rate varies from the national average and is calculated by reference to total cost indicators (TCIs), which relate to costs of different types of development in different areas, and the grant rate specified for each district.

5. Schemes developed since 1989 do not qualify for major repairs grant and associations are required to make provision for the cost of such repairs out of their own resources; the recommended way of accumulating resources for this purpose is to invest in a sinking fund annually a percentage (0.8–1 per cent) of the estimated rebuilding cost of the property. The effect of this sort of forward planning is arguably to increase rents, at least in the early years, and associations have had to consider the balance between affordability and longer-term provision for repairs. Some have chosen to delay the start of sinking funds until schemes are several years old.

6. The Corporation assumes that associations raise their private funding in the form of low-start deferred interest loans, implying a lower level of grant to produce affordable rents than would be required using conventional loans. In practice, however, associations are free to raise

loans on any prudent basis, and many, especially the larger ones, have tended not to borrow on low-start terms.

The revenue side

On the revenue side of the system the Revenue Deficit Grant continues to exist but is now payable only in exceptional circumstances. This reflects the shift towards making associations more self-reliant and is a demonstration to the Treasury that private loans are not underwritten by public funds. The grant redemption fund has been replaced by the rent surplus fund (RSF), which continues the same function of removing income surpluses arising from the pre-1989 stock; the new arrangements, however, allow associations to keep 100 per cent of surpluses, although 80 per cent has to be set aside to pay for major repairs and only 20 per cent can be used at the discretion of the associations.

Turning to questions of rent setting, the 1988 Act represented a major departure from established practice in the housing association sector. By introducing assured tenancies for new lettings from 15 January 1989 the Act began the process of phasing out the fair rent system and ushered in an era in which associations are now responsible for setting their own rent levels on an increasing proportion of the stock. The 1987 consultation paper referred to the government's intention to keep grant rates at levels which would allow associations to set 'sensible rents that are attuned to the means of their prospective tenants', and went on to say that 'In general, the government would expect associations to be able to set their rents for newly provided dwellings significantly below the free market level' (DoE, 1987: 4). The debate about the affordability of housing association rents has hardly moved on since that time, largely because the government and the Corporation have steadfastly refused to give clear guidance on what the term means. This can be explained in terms of the government's commitment to the market mechanism and its reluctance to interfere in the relationship between associations and their private financiers.

Many associations had no experience of rent setting, and since 1974 the rent officer service had set the rents of all HAG-funded dwellings. Associations therefore came to the issue of rent setting for the first time in the context of uncertainty about how the new private finance arrangements were going to work and what implications they would have for rents. In the event rents of new stock rose rapidly and the NFHA set up a system for monitoring rents, known as CORE (continuous recording of rents). Randolph (1993: 45–6) reports that rents for newly built dwelling rose by 104 per cent between the second quarter of 1988 and the same period in 1991, at a time when prices generally rose by just 26 per cent. During this period fair rents rose in line with inflation. Rents of new lettings continued to outstrip inflation; a ministerial answer in May 1993 indicated that rents of new housing association assured tenancies (including relets of existing dwellings) rose by 18 per cent in 1990, 17 per cent in 1991 and 15 per cent in 1992 (Hansard, 27 May 1993).

Rising rents accentuated problems of affordability for tenants and increased the cost of housing benefit borne by the Treasury. This led to a change of policy similar to that which was introduced in the local authority sector, and in 1995 the government announced proposals for a rent formula based on a specified percentage above or below inflation (RPI $+/- X$). This approach did not meet with the approval of the lenders and the government dropped the idea, but it did proceed with plans to make associations compete for grant on the basis of the rents they proposed to charge as well as the amount of grant required. Under the new Labour Government the policy was developed by the adoption of 'benchmark' rent levels for each local authority area, with the general expectation that associations wishing to win grant allocations should bid at rents in line with these levels. In addition, the rate of increase of rents of existing dwellings is to be constrained by the expectation that each association's total annual rent bill will not increase by more than 1 per cent above inflation. The question of rent control is of considerable concern to housing associations and their lenders; it runs counter to the strategy introduced in 1989, and resort to control has to be seen in the context of the continuing absence of reform of the housing benefit system – it is easier to control rents than to reform housing benefit.

Conclusion

This chapter has attempted to introduce the subject of housing finance by looking at some of the basic concepts and conceptual distinctions, the key policy issues and the specific provisions of the Local Government and Housing Act 1989. It was argued that an understanding of housing finance required an initial grasp of concepts such as capital and revenue, the distinction between general subsidy and means-tested assistance, and different approaches to pricing. Later discussion has confirmed the value of a clear conceptual grounding because it has been shown that contemporary policy developments represent a departure from established conventions. For instance, whereas the norm in the past was that capital expenditure was funded from borrowing, and revenue income was used to service debt charges, under the 1989 Act authorities are required to use capital receipts to pay off old debt and are encouraged to meet capital expenditure from revenue income. This represents a reversal of what has been regarded as the appropriate way to manage public housing finance.

Earlier in this chapter a distinction was drawn between historic-cost pricing and current-value pricing. How does the 1989 Act system relate to these basic categories? The underlying preference seems to be for current-value pricing, since this is closest to the market, but the 1989 Act system does not require authorities to set prices in accordance with current values. However it is clear that historic-cost pricing has been abandoned, in the sense that the cost of providing council housing is no longer the benchmark for fixing overall rent income. The new regime in fact combines current-value and historic-cost approaches; the introduction of 'Right to Buy' valuations as a way of differentiating rent increases prefigures a system in which rent levels themselves reflect current values, but from the local authority perspective the income received will be limited to the cost of provision. In other words, the new regime suggests a situation in which tenants pay rents set by current values but the authority receives only enough income to cover costs, any excess income being, in effect, creamed off by central government.

This raises a third example: the way in which the new regime ignores the important distinction between housing subsidy and housing benefit. By rolling together deficit subsidy and rent-rebate subsidy into the new HRA subsidy, the government capped its liability to meet the costs of housing benefit at a level where the notional HRA is in balance. This is effectively the same as paying housing benefit in full but requiring authorities to repay HRA surpluses to the Treasury. The distinction between housing subsidy and housing benefit is one which previous Conservative governments have done much to establish, notably in 1972 and 1982, but the principle was abandoned in 1989. Why? The answer lies in the complexity of central–local relations and the new regime represents another attempt to centralise the benefits of rising council rents, after the failure of the 1980 system.

Underlying the analysis presented in this chapter is a policy approach to housing finance in which emphasis is placed on the importance of the relationship between central- and local-level agencies. Finance provides one of the most significant ways in which the centre can influence local decisions and, although this has always been the case, the conclusion to emerge from discussion of the 1989 Act is that the government was primarily concerned with asserting its dominance over local authorities. The controls over capital expenditure represent a real reduction in local autonomy and seem certain to herald a period of much reduced investment in council housing. If local authorities are to sustain maintenance expenditure at levels approaching those that were possible in the 1980s, they will have to draw more heavily on revenue income from rents, at a time when they will have less control over the rate of increase in rents as a result of subsidy changes. Councils are artificially constrained in their ability to provide satisfactory standards of housing services, and tenants are entitled to perceive the new financial regime in terms of reduced value for money. The better-off tenants see themselves contributing towards the rebates of the less well off, aware that, if they buy their homes, they will not only escape that burden but also become entitled to subsidy themselves (via tax relief on mortgage interest). The new financial regime thus emerges as a policy informed more by wider considerations to do with the further residualisation of council housing, and having little to do with a principled reform of housing finance.

Similarly the government has reformed housing association finance in a way which reflects its determination to direct the course of future developments. The 1987 White Paper may have referred to housing associations as part of the 'independent' rented sector but it is clear that they are in fact closely controlled by policy considerations, reflecting their dependence on public expenditure, whether in the form of capital grant or housing benefit. Affordability has been seen by associations as a key issue in the early 1990s but they have not been able successfully to challenge the government's policy of bearing down on grant levels. The whole affordability debate has been pursued against a background of government refusal to face up to the challenge of defining credible and coherent criteria for affordability. The lack of logic in the situation is highlighted by the way in which the local authorities and housing associations are working with two quite different approaches to affordability: local authorities are expected to set rents by reference to capital values whereas housing associations are expected to think in terms of rents as a proportion of income.

Housing finance in Britain continues to require fundamental reform if it is to be both equitable and efficient. There has been no shortage of change in recent years, but it has not obviously been driven by a coherent understanding of what is required in order to achieve a fairer and more efficient system. Attempts to put forward rational, comprehensive reform packages have met with little interest and much hostility from ministers driven more by a combination of party ideology and short-term economic imperatives.

9

The Policy Process

In earlier chapters, it was suggested that housing policy could be understood in terms of intervention designed to respond to and accommodate the restructuring of housing provision as patterns of need, demand and supply alter over time in a changing social economic and political context. In this and subsequent chapters, attention shifts to an analysis based on the notion of the policy process, in terms of how policies are determined, implemented and evaluated. The purpose of the present chapter is to review the main perspectives on the policy process, and to begin to apply these to housing, while succeeding chapters deal in more detail with aspects of policy-making, implementation and evaluation respectively. One of the objectives of this chapter is to indicate that policy processes are more complicated than is implied by the model of policy-making, implementation and evaluation, and this approach is adopted merely as a convenient way of presenting the material.

In looking at how policies are made and carried out, it is important to bear in mind the limits imposed by the wider context, and to remember that, although there are real decisions and real choices to be made, the nature of those decisions and the range of choices is largely determined by the framework of capitalist social relations. A further relevant consideration is the influence of history to the extent that the issues to be resolved and the range of available options are both affected by what has happened in the past. As Hogwood (1987: 5) says:

> because parties alternate in office or individual parties change their emphasis . . . government as the party in office may have a stated purpose and intentions which are substantially different from what the government as a whole set of organisations engaged on delivering public policies is actually doing. The bulk of policy delivery at any given time reflects the political priorities and legislation of previous governments.

Policy analysis

'Policy analysis' has been defined as 'finding out what governments do, why they do it and what difference it makes' (quoted in Ham and Hill, 1993: 4).

The subject developed as an independent area of academic study, mainly in the United States in the 1950s and 1960s, although interest has subsequently grown in Britain and some significant contributions to policy analysis debates have been produced by British writers (see Guide to Further Reading, p. 000). A number of distinct theoretical approaches have emerged (a good way into the debates is provided by Hill, 1993). Two of the most influential contributors to the development of policy analysis were the Americans Herbert Simon and Charles Lindblom. Simon's rational model is often contrasted with Lindblom's incremental view of policy-making (Hogwood and Gunn, 1984: 43). Simon was associated with commitment to the idea that planned, rational policies could be achieved, although he recognised the limits to fully rational decision-making in the real world. Lindblom was far more sceptical about the potential of planning and is best known for coining the phrase 'muddling through' to describe the way in which policy-makers cope with the realities of their position (Lindblom, 1959). He was associated with the idea that muddling through led to incremental changes in policy.

Both Simon and Lindblom went beyond the analysis of actual policy action to engage in debate about how such action ought to be conducted, and in policy analysis it is important to distinguish between descriptive and prescriptive models. The former seek merely to describe what normally happens in practice, while the latter represent attempts to set out what ought to happen. Descriptive models are of assistance to students of policy processes to the extent that they provide some indication of what to expect and look for, whereas prescriptive models might be a very poor guide to reality. Prescriptive models, on the other hand, are helpful to people actually engaged in policy activity, providing them with a framework in which to operate.

Rational approaches to the policy process tend to assume that there is a logical sequence of events, in the sense that, for instance, deciding what to do would logically precede action designed to put decisions into action. Both Simon and Lindblom outlined rational models of policy-making, based on a series of stages in the policy process, although Lindblom in particular then went on to develop a critique of rationality in policy processes. In the words of Hogwood and Gunn (1984: 52), 'Lindblom goes far beyond identifying the limits to rationality . . . and often seems to delight in demonstrating how real-life policy-making stands rationality on its head.'

In the British literature Hogwood and Gunn (1984) are exponents of the rational approach and it is appropriate to consider their model:

1. Deciding to decide (or agenda setting);
2. Deciding how to decide;
3. Issue definition;
4. Forecasting;

5. Setting objectives and priorities;
6. Options analysis;
7. Policy implementation;
8. Evaluation and review;
9. Policy maintenance, succession or termination.

Items 1–6 in this list can be grouped together as the policy-making process, and it is a common feature of such models that policy-making, or deciding what to do, is broken down into more stages than implementation. However the implementation process may be just as complex and equally worthy of closer analysis. Linear versions of the rational model can also be criticised for implying that the policy has a clear beginning and ending, when in reality it is much more likely that change and information generated by action will lead to reappraisal of the original problem and objectives, leading to further policy-making and implementation. Thus it may be more useful to adopt a circular model, such as the one proposed by Smith (1976) (see Figure 9.1).

Whether the models be linear or circular, there is the further, and much more serious, criticism that the rational view of the policy process is of little value as a guide to what actually happens, although it may be useful as a prescriptive tool, suggesting what *should* happen.

Much of the early policy analysis literature concentrated on the policy-making stages, with little attention being given to implementation (Gunn, 1978: 1), but the situation changed after the publication in 1973 of a seminal study by Pressman and Wildavsky (1973). Entitled *Implementation*, the book was a study of how employment creation policies established in Washington failed to deliver the expected number of new jobs in Oakland, California. Pressman and Wildavsky not only stimulated greater interest in implementation studies, they also came to represent the so-called 'top-down' approach, inspiring the development of an alternative, 'bottom-up' perspective.

The Pressman and Wildavsky approach was both top-down and rational, being based on the assumption that, as they put it, 'a verb like "implement" must have an object like "policy"' (1973: xiv); this meant that policy must exist first in order for implementation to occur. They argued that the explanation for the gap between Washington's policy and achievements on the ground lay in the number and quality of the links between actors and agencies at different points in the implementation chain. Their thesis was essentially that if the links in the chain were not characterised by close understanding and cooperation then the gap between intention and outcome would tend to widen as the number of links increased. They coined the term implementation deficit to describe this gap. Implicit in the top-down perspective is the idea that policy-making and implementation are, and should be, separate activities; the top-down view is a denial of a policy-making role for lower-level actors in the policy process, which leads to the conclusion that if outcomes fail to match intentions then, as Ham and Hill

Figure 9.1   *The circular model of the policy-making process*

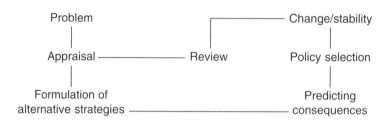

Source: Adapted from Smith (1976).

(1993: 113) put it, 'the top should get a better grip on the situation'- a prescription which has ominous implications for local government.

The rational, top-down view of policy has a certain common sense appeal; it seems at first as if policy must precede action, and we are used to the idea that policy is determined at the top, whether it be in government or business. Political parties competing for power at central and local government levels put forward their policies, but it is understood that implementation rests upon the actions of salaried officials, and the very term 'civil servant' implies a hierarchical relationship in which policy is made by politicians at the top and implemented lower down.

However, a challenge to this taken-for-granted view emerged in another influential American book, Michael Lipsky's *Street-Level Bureaucracy* (1980). Lipsky used the term 'street-level' bureaucrats to include a range of public service workers who work directly with the public (in a sense Lipsky was echoing the British debate about the role of urban managers (see Pahl, 1975). Lipsky's thesis was that

> the decisions of street-level bureaucrats, the routines they establish, and the devices they invent to cope with uncertainties and work pressures, effectively *become* the public policies they carry out . . . [and] that public policy is not best understood as made by legislators or top-floor suites of high-ranking administrators, because in important ways it is actually made in the crowded offices and daily encounters of street-level bureaucrats. (1980: xii)

Lipsky did not engage in direct debate with Pressman and Wildavsky, but his work was influential amongst those who did. Although Pressman and Wildavsky made a major contribution to the extent that they drew attention to the need to study the complexities of implementation, their formulation attracted criticism from writers who identified a number of weaknesses. Successful top-down policy requires (i) a clear understanding of what is to be achieved, (ii) access to the resources needed to achieve that goal, (iii) the ability to marshal and control those resources, and (iv) the capacity to communicate with and control others who are essential to policy action. Critics have pointed out that policies are often not clearly defined and set out in terms that implementers can work from. There are good reasons why politicians may not want to spell out exactly what their policies are; to do so may be to court conflict with, rather than gain cooperation from, the implementing organisations, and to provide too much detail about policies may be to make the work of critics easier when performance fails to match up to intentions (Hogwood and Gunn, 1984: 52). Criticism of the top-down perspective emphasises the ambiguity of policies and the complexity of policy processes. Ham and Hill (1993: 104), for instance, argue that policies are sometimes 'quite deliberately made complex, obscure, ambiguous or even meaningless'. They refer also to the possibility of some policies having only a symbolic standing; this means that their expression reflects political necessity or correctness, but that there is little real intention to commit the resources needed for their achievement.

Even when there is a high level of commitment the bottom-up critique of the top-down approach is that there is no clear dividing line between policy-making and implementation:

> Policy cannot be regarded as a 'fix' but more a series of intentions around which bargaining takes place and which may be modified as each set of actors attempts to negotiate to maximise its own interests and priorities. Interests and pressures may alter over time in relation to changing circumstances and in response to the way that the continuing activities of the organisational environment impinge on the 'outside world'. Thus it becomes difficult to identify a distinct and sequential 'implementation process' which starts with the formulation of policy and ends with action. Rather, it is appropriate to consider implementation as a policy/action continuum in which an interactive and negotiative process is taking place over time, between those seeking to put policy into effect and those upon whom action depends. (Barrett and Fudge, 1981: 24–5)

The emphasis in the bottom-up approach is on complexity, ambiguity, negotiation and compromise (Barrett and Hill, 1986). It is not a simple inversion of the top-down approach, and indeed Ham and Hill (1984: 100) explicitly accept much of the top-down agenda. The crucial differences are that the bottom-up approach rejects the idea that policy can be expected to be clearly established in advance of implementation, and that it accepts and incorporates a policy-making role for implementing agencies. Both perspectives accept that in practice policy is shaped and reshaped during implementation, but they differ in their prescriptions; implicit in the top-down view is that it is possible, and desirable, for the top to get a tighter grip on implementation, whereas the bottom-up writers make a virtue out of accepting the policy-making role of implementers. The people on the ground, delivering services, require some degree of autonomy and discretion in order to carry out their tasks, and to add some interest to their jobs. It can also be argued that the top can never have complete knowledge of all local circumstances, but that local knowledge is precisely what street-level bureaucrats do have, thereby making them best-placed to determine policy in specific situations.

According to the bottom-up perspective, policies are often ambiguous and tend to change over time, which means that in the absence of clear instructions implementers have to make policy decisions. In addition lower-level actors and agencies have their own interests, priorities and policy agendas which they seek to pursue. Thus policy is inevitably modified as it is negotiated into action.

Top-down approaches to the policy process, epitomised by Pressman and Wildavsky, were seriously challenged by their bottom-up critics, but Marsh and Rhodes (1992) have argued that the bottom-up approach also has its deficiencies. They suggest that there is a tendency to overestimate the amount of street-level discretion and to underestimate legal, financial and organisational constraints (Marsh and Rhodes, 1992: 7). They also point out that criticism of the top-down model can be overstated, arguing that some policies do have clear objectives and that policy decisions are made which do structure the decision-making environment of local level actors. Marsh and Rhodes are particularly strong in their contention that the Thatcher governments in Britain in the 1980s were driven by a commitment to a top-down method of operation, and that it was this commitment to what Marsh and Rhodes see as an inappropriate and ill-considered model which helps to explain the failure of many Thatcherite policies (1992: 9).

The important point here is that to take a bottom-up view is not to deny that policy often comes from the top; rather, it is to provide an explanation of why these policies are likely to be resisted or modified as they are put into action. Top-level actors are clearly not the only stakeholders in the policy process.

The policy process in housing

So far this chapter has looked at policy analysis in very general and conceptual terms and it is appropriate now to raise the question of the extent to which these general perspectives apply to housing. Are there reasons to believe that housing is in any sense peculiar or distinctive in the way that policy processes work themselves out? It is worth remembering in this context that much of the literature is based on American research which, because of the nature of public policy in the United States, draws very little on housing examples. Lipsky's American work, for instance, makes little or no reference to housing and may be contrasted with the British work by Pahl and others interested in urban managerialism, which draws heavily on research in housing. The general point here is that attempts to theorise about policy processes are likely to be influenced by the particular public services chosen to provide research material. Policy processes are likely to reflect, to some extent, the particular content and context of decisions. Housing policy is different from other public services because of the emphasis on high cost, continuing need and fixed location. The work of the street-level bureaucracy in housing is different from, say, social work because in housing the service is tied so closely to the fixed capital assets tied up in the houses, which cannot be easily or quickly changed, whereas in social work the emphasis is different with much more weight on interpersonal relations. Another contrast would be with education, where the social base of the service is wider and officials are often dealing with middle-class parents with choices.

A key organising theme of this book is that in housing central government has a leading role in making policy but implementation is largely the responsibility of local authorities, housing associations and other agencies. However, as Chapter 1 has acknowledged, these implementing agencies are also active policy-makers. The policy-making role of local government is axiomatic: elections provide an opportunity to choose between different policies, not just different styles of implementation. In a sense the British system of government, with locally elected councils, incorporates a bottom-up approach to policy, to the extent that the policy-making role of lower levels is recognised and institutionalised. Indeed, much of British housing policy has developed on the basis of a permissive, rather than coercive, legislative framework set up by central government to give local authorities powers to devise and operate local level policies. Chapters 2–5 illustrated how the structure of policy has reflected the relative autonomy of local authorities and how their freedom to determine local policies has been eroded over recent years. In the simplest terms it is tempting to think of central government as the top and local authorities and housing associations as the bottom. But of course it is not as simple as that. In constitutional terms, Parliament represents the top in the policy process, although Richardson and Jordan (1979) argue that Parliament itself plays little direct role in the policy process. They refer to the notion of policy communities, consisting of representatives from government departments, professionals and interest groups, which determine much of the detail of policy.

An example of a policy community at work is provided by the making of the new financial regime for local authority housing, which was incorporated in the Local Government and Housing Act 1989. Ministers, led by the then Secretary of State for the Environment, Nicholas Ridley, were keen to remedy the deficiencies of the 1980 subsidy system and to move towards a more market-related pricing system in council housing. A small team of senior civil servants, working with ministers, devised a set of proposals which were unveiled in a brief consultation paper (DoE, 1988b). This was followed by the establishment of a working party which brought together civil servants and representatives of the local authority associations (including association staff and specialist advisers). This working party continued to meet on a regular basis throughout the time that the Local Government and Housing Bill was going through its various parliamentary stages. A series of detailed papers were prepared for the working party, by both civil servants and local authority representatives, and considerable progress was made in developing the detail of the new system. It is not unreasonable, therefore, to see the working party as a kind of parallel policy-making forum, providing the experts with an opportunity to flesh out the bare bones of the system outlined in the Bill before Parliament. To the extent that the working party represented a policy community it also displayed the conflicts which are often found even in the closest communities. The way in which policy communities are constituted to some extent reflects the administrative culture of the central government department concerned; Wilkes (1987) has suggested that the DoE has a culture which emphasises negotiation and cooperation with local government, in contrast to some other departments.

The identity and location of the bottom of the policy process is more difficult. In terms of constructing a chain of agencies on whom successful policy action depends, local authorities and housing associations are clearly key players towards the bottom of the chain, but they in turn depend upon a range of other actors and agencies for the provision of goods and services. And as the contract culture develops and spreads so more providers are organisations separate from the authority or association (indeed, in the era of the enabling local authority housing associations are a category of independent organisation upon which councils depend for the achievement of local housing strategy goals).

Given that local authorities and housing associations have a policy-making role of their own it is important to remember that there is a 'top' to be identified at this level too. Elected councillors and management committee members constitute this lower-tier top, and the top-down or bottom-up debate can be conducted at this level.

On the question of where policy ideas come from, the top-down approach regards the top as their source, while the bottom-up view is that they exist at all levels and are the subject of negotiation in the policy action process. However, it is worth making the point here that there are several examples of housing policy ideas which have emerged from the local level and have been subsequently taken over by central government and returned to the localities in a top-down way. The sale of council houses is the clearest example of a local initiative (pioneered in Birmingham; see Murie, 1975) which was turned into a leading plank of government policy. A more recent example is the large-scale voluntary transfer of council housing stocks to housing associations set up for the purpose; this emerged as a local-level response to different central government proposals in the Housing Act 1988 giving tenants the right to opt for new landlords. But where do local-level ideas come from? This issue is discussed more fully in Chapter 10, and here it is sufficient to note that in local government and housing associations policy ideas and proposals are just as likely, if not more likely, to emerge from officers as from the formal policy-makers, the committee members.

Reference has already been made to the way in which central government tends to formulate policy but leaves implementation to local government and other organisations. However, in some areas of policy Whitehall civil servants are actively and continually engaged in aspects of implementation. Again the financial regime for local authority housing introduced in 1990 provides an example. Malpass *et al.* (1993: 28) have argued that the new financial regime amounted to a system which was designed to be operated by central government on an annual basis, and that in this sense it differed from policies such as the Right to Buy. In the latter case once the legislation was put in place the role of the centre was largely confined to monitoring and policing local authority compliance. In relation to the 1989 Act financial regime, however, central government departments are responsible for a crucial set of inputs each year. Initially each year the DoE has to negotiate its budget with the Treasury, and this provides the context within which decisions are then made about changes in guideline rents and management and maintenance allowances (see Chapter 8). In addition the DoE officials have to process local authority subsidy claim forms during the year. The system in operation has been described as 'hideously complicated' by one of the DoE officials responsible for its implementation (Malpass *et al.*, 1993: 37).

There are also examples of central government involvement in implementation as a way of transcending local authority opposition. The attempt to introduce Housing Action Trusts (HATs) is one such example, where ministers sought to impose what they saw as a solution to the problems of run-down estates (Karn, 1993). The HATs experience also shows how sometimes implementation can be thwarted not by the street-level bureaucracy but by the very people who were ostensibly the beneficiaries of the policy, the tenants. Woodward (1991) chronicles and analyses the successful campaign by tenants in Tower Hamlets to prevent the imposition of a HAT in the borough.

Even in cases where central government is closely involved in implementation the local level retains a policy-making role to some extent, although how far it can be exercised is constrained by the policy instruments adopted by the centre. The term 'policy instruments' has been used in different ways. Bevan's view of local councils as plannable instruments (see Chapter 6) finds an echo in the suggestion by Cullingworth (1979: 1) that local authorities, new towns, housing associations, building societies and so on were the 'instruments of housing policy'. However, it is perhaps more common now to think of policy instruments as distinct from institutions; instead policy instruments are wielded by institutions and are the mechanisms through which policy action is carried forward. Acts of Parliament, government circulars and statutory instruments are types of general policy instrument used by government to establish its policies. But these sorts of general instruments are vehicles for the delivery and enforcement of more specific policy instruments, such as subsidies, rent controls and tax reliefs.

Governments adopt a variety of approaches to the implementation of housing policy, according to their commitment to the particular policy, the type of policy involved and the agencies responsible for implementation. Government policies are pursued via instruments which can be classified as prohibitive, coercive, permissive or incentive. A government which is deeply committed to a particular policy is more likely to use coercive or prohibitive measures, forcing, say, local authorities to sell their houses, or preventing them from disposing of capital receipts. A lower level of commitment would suggest the use of permissive legislation, such as that allowing large-scale voluntary transfer. Where a government wishes to pursue an objective through the private sector then incentive measures are generally used, as in the case of the tax breaks offered to investors in private rented housing via the Business Expansion Scheme. Incentive-based instruments are also used in the public sector, as in the example of the discounts offered to council tenants through the Right to Buy. In this case incentives to tenants are combined with mandatory requirements on councils.

The general point here is that the study of implementation requires consideration of policy instruments because of the extent to which the instruments deployed are likely to reflect the nature of the policy objectives and the way in which implementation proceeds. Where governments are committed to particular objectives, and where they anticipate less than full cooperation from local-level agencies, then it is likely that they will deploy policy instruments which draw the centre more into the implementation process. And where governments seek to work through the private sector then they will use instruments which rely on creating incentives for private institutions to act in ways which help to achieve policy objectives.

Barrett and Hill (1986: 39) refer to the way in which conflicts of interest have influenced policy and the development of services, quoting the power of doctors as a significant factor shaping both the NHS and the way that policy is framed. In housing, too, it is possible to argue that the power of local authorities has been a powerful influence on the way that central government has sought to secure its policy goals and the extent to which those goals have been achieved. Local authorities have jealously defended their autonomy from central government (even as it has been eroded), and successive governments have tended to rely on permissive, incentive and leverage devices to carry housing policy into practice. Thus, in the past councils were allowed rather than instructed to build houses; they were given subsidy incentives to encourage them to build, and the subsidy system was used to apply leverage on rents (Malpass, 1990).

The outcome of the exercise of local autonomy over many years has been that local housing authorities now vary considerably, not just in terms of the numbers of houses they own but also in their administrative styles and structures and, most significantly from the point of view of central government, their financial circumstances. This latter point is important to the extent that the government wishes to use financial leverage devices in order to ensure that its policy objectives are translated into local-level outcomes. The variation in financial circumstances at local level means that it is very difficult for the centre to achieve consistency of outcomes without adopting very complex policy inputs. A simple, uniform policy laid upon a highly uneven surface is likely to be received differently in different places and to produce very different outcomes; but a complex policy, designed to take account of the unevenness of the policy surface, poses severe problems for central government which can never have perfect knowledge of local circumstances.

Governments can be expected to anticipate implementation problems, in the form of both resistance by those upon whom action depends and unexpected consequences when policies fail to work in the way that was intended. Study of the policy process requires consideration of the extent to which policy is designed to take account of these different sorts of implementation problems (Ingram and Schneider, 1990; May, 1991). In housing policy governments sometimes know from the start that particular policies will be highly unpopular with some or all of the agencies required to carry them out. In such cases the legislation can be framed in a way which permits action to be taken against defaulting agencies. In the Housing Finance Act 1972, for instance, the government gave itself powers to impose an increasingly severe range of penalties on local authorities which failed to comply with the requirements of the transition to higher 'fair' rents (Skinner and Langdon, 1974). And in the Housing Act 1980, the government again gave itself powers to act against authorities which tried to delay or prevent the implementation of the Right to Buy (Forrest and Murie, 1985).

However, threats and penalties can backfire on the government, as in the 1972 Act when the government was challenged by a small local authority, Clay Cross, in Derbyshire. High court action, the imposition of a commissioner to take over the functions of the council and the final disqualification of the entire council all provided opportunities for the council to publicise its campaign of opposition, and can be seen as making the government look rather foolish as it called on the might of the legal system to crush resistance by a small group of working-class elected representatives (Malpass, 1992c). Lessons were clearly learned from the Clay Cross experience, because in the Housing Act 1980, the government again sought large increases in rent but this time it adopted a different strategy towards local authority resistance.

The 1980 subsidy system denied local authorities any opportunity for public defiance; instead of threatening authorities with penalties if they did not comply with the policy the Act left it to local authorities to decide their own rent levels but, crucially, it contained mechanisms which enabled central government to apply powerful financial leverage on authorities. As a device to overcome implementation problems the subsidy system in the 1980 Act was far more elegant and effective than the administrative–judicial mechanism in the 1972 Act. This is an example of what Ingram and Schneider (1990) refer to as a smarter statute, in the sense that the legislators devised a framework which increased the probability of the centre achieving its policy objectives, even in the face of concerted opposition from local authorities.

Rents policy also provides illustrations of how governments deal with the problem of unforeseen consequences and changing circumstances. The Housing Finance Act 1972 was an example of legislation which was inflexible. The Act contained details of the cash amounts by which rents would rise each year, and so any changes to those amounts would have required new primary legislation. Rising inflation meant that, had the Act not been repealed for political reasons, it would have needed amendment to enable rents to rise fast enough to catch up with fair rents. In the Housing Act 1980 and in its successor, the Local Government and Housing Act 1989, the government adopted an enabling strategy, which means that the legislation itself did not specify rent increases but establishes powers for the Secretary of State to do so in the circumstances prevailing at the time.

It is important to remember that local authorities, housing associations and the other organisations on whom policy action depends do not necessarily see their role in terms of implementing government policy. They have their own objectives, which may depart from those of the government in significant ways; this is obviously the case in local authorities controlled by parties opposed to the government, but it also applies to housing associations which cherish their independence from government. Housing associations are heavily dependent on central government, but government policy is increasing their reliance on private finance, which means that they are subject to commercial pressures, and there is always the potential for market forces to come into conflict with public policy objectives. Any organisation which has to survive in a business environment is likely to give priority to survival rather than government policy when conflicts arise.

In some cases central government policy will be received as simply one of a set of constraints on local-level policies. Faced with a flow of policies from the centre local-level agencies can adopt different tactical responses, which can be summed up as: ignore, comply, avoid or exploit. Legislation which is permissive or which relies on incentives is most easily ignored. Sometimes policy can be avoided or evaded, most easily perhaps when its impact can be predicted and there is time to take action before it takes effect; an example would be the way that local authorities used up capital receipts in 1989/90 in advance of regulations which reduced the level of useable receipts. An example of evasion is the way that some authorities minimise their obligations towards homeless people by the way they interpret the rules on intentionality. Exploitation of policy occurs when implementing agencies go beyond compliance with the letter and spirit of legislation. The clearest examples arise in situations when legislation is found to provide unintended opportunities for action, such as the wording of the Local Government, Planning and Land Act 1980, which allowed local authorities to spend virtually all of their capital receipts instead of the restricted proportions intended by the government.

Implementation at the local level varies according to the type of policy involved. The implementation of area improvement policies, for instance, is very different from the implementation of rents policies. In the latter case it is clear that if a local authority approves a rent increase of a certain amount for all tenants then that increase will be applied from the specified date and there is no officer discretion involved in implementation. However, in the case of area improvement, a decision by a local authority to improve a particular area is just the beginning of a complex implementation process in which officer discretion is likely to play a significant part in determining the pace and overall success of the policy. Area improvement is a good example of a type of policy which requires considerable negotiation amongst a large number of interested parties if it is to succeed. It is likely to involve negotiation amongst different professional groups within the authority, and between the authority and the multiplicity of actors and agencies in and beyond the area to be improved. In order to implement the policy officials have to negotiate with different property owners, some of whom may be absentee landlords and not easy to contact, and who may not share the authority's policy aspirations. A number of housing associations and the Housing Corporation are also likely to be involved. Finally improvement to the physical fabric requires the involvement of financial institutions, builders and materials suppliers. Putting together a programme of improvement work based on mobilising all these interests can be a formidable implementation task, of a quite different order from increasing council house rents. The point to be made here, then, is that local-level implementation needs to be understood in terms of the particular policies being put into effect.

Turning to the question of evaluation, it is clear that the great majority of policies fail to some extent (Marsh and Rhodes, 1992: 9), but assessment of just how far policies have failed, and why, can be very difficult, not least because of the tendency, noted earlier, for objectives not to be clearly stated in a form which permits outcomes to be compared with intentions. A major problem for evaluation studies is the difficulty of establishing a direct causal link between policy action and observable events. The term 'outcomes' is commonly used in this context but it implies a causal link which may not be present. In housing a relevant example would be the suggestion that the rate of home ownership in Britain is a reflection of housing policy, but it is arguable that home ownership would have grown irrespective of government policies designed to encourage it, and attributing a particular proportion of its growth to particular factors is very difficult (Saunders, 1990: 29–41). In more general terms it is easier to say when policies have failed completely than it is to measure their success. Where there is no identifiable outcome resembling stated policy objectives then the policy has clearly failed, but when policy objectives appear to have been achieved to some extent it is difficult to be sure that the cause was policy action itself. There is also the issue of whether policies can be fairly judged in terms of short-term effects or whether a longer period is necessary in order to assess their full impact (Marsh and Rhodes, 1992: 5). This is a question which has been raised in relation to the right time-scale for the assessment of housing estate design and layout; there are numerous examples of schemes which have won design awards when they were first built but which have later proved to be unpopular with tenants.

Policies fail for different reasons, and it must be remembered that some policies, those with solely a symbolic purpose, are never intended to be implemented. Sometimes performance fails to match intentions because the objectives are not shared by those responsible for implementation, or because they are unaware of what the objectives are. In either case, if implementers have their own objectives and priorities to which they are more or less committed then clearly outcomes will depart from top-level intentions. In some circumstances policies fail because of poor policy design, and examples from housing policy have been referred to above, or because the policy was ineptly implemented. A sports analogy is appropriate here: a golfer may hit the ball into a bunker because the wrong club was chosen for the shot, or because, although the right club was chosen, the shot was poorly executed. A task for policy evaluation is to distinguish between these explanations, for the implications for action are very different. Ingram and Schneider (1990) argue that policy analysis should provide information to enable policy-makers to frame legislation which has a good chance of being successfully implemented. They suggest that different types of policy instrument should be considered according to the level of support for the policy, the level of information available about the policy area, and the level of commitment among implementing agencies. The choices that are made, however, will reflect a top-down or bottom-up orientation.

Policy evaluation can be conducted in relation to criteria other than explicit or implicit policy objectives. Policies can be evaluated against value-for-money criteria, and in recent years British governments have commissioned a series of housing research projects designed to assess the value of policy initiatives. Policies can also be evaluated in terms of their overall impact – in answer to the question of who benefits. This last perspective is the one which underlies Chapter 12.

Conclusion

This chapter has sought to introduce the main perspectives on the policy process and to begin to apply them to housing. What emerges from this is a view of policy which acknowledges many of the bottom-up criticisms of the conventional top-down approach. It has been argued here that the British system of government, with directly elected local councils, institutionalises a policy role for the local level, and that therefore policies have to be negotiated into practice. In addition, other implementing agencies, such as housing associations, are independent bodies with their own values and priorities, and are subject to commercial pressures which also mean that central government cannot take it for granted that its housing policies will be straightforwardly translated into action on the ground.

The existence of separate tiers of government highlights the need to recognise that the top-down or bottom-up debate can be conducted at each level. It is not unreasonable to see housing policy as being subject to a process of repeated reinterpretation. Ideas which may come from or be taken up by ministers are worked on by civil servants and others in the Whitehall policy community, before being passed back for political approval and legitimation. Central government policy outputs, often in the form of legislation, are then passed down to local authorities and housing associations, where there is a process of analysis and reinterpretation, leading up to local political decisions which provide the framework for another reinterpretation as policies are negotiated into practice by the street-level bureaucracy.

10

Local Policy-Making

This chapter is concerned with policy-making in local authorities and housing associations. In terms of an interest in policy-making the key feature shared by councils and associations is that each is made up of two quite distinct groups: both have unpaid committee members who carry formal responsibility for policy decisions, and salaried officials whose primary formal responsibilities are to advise their committees and to carry out agreed policy. Chapter 9 put forward a view of the policy process which suggested that policy-making and implementation are not best understood as separate and sequential phases. However, for present purposes of understanding how members and officers relate to one another it is appropriate to focus on policy-making as a distinct activity.

The first part of the discussion looks at some of the evidence on roles and relationships in fairly general terms and then the second part goes on to a more focused consideration of some examples of housing policy-making. There is a considerable body of literature on British (mostly English) local government and good accounts are to be found in, for instance, Gyford *et al.* (1989), Stoker (1991) and Barron *et al.* (1991). Important and revealing research was carried out in the mid-1980s for the Widdicombe Committee of Inquiry into the Conduct of Local Authority Business (Widdicombe, 1986), and Gyford *et al.* (1989) reports directly on work carried out for the committee.

Much of the research on local government has been carried out by political scientists whose main interest tends to be the structures, relationships and processes of government rather than particular programme areas such as housing. The prolonged assault on local government by the Thatcher governments gave rise to a number of studies of central–local relations and local responses to central government policy (Boddy and Fudge, 1984; Goldsmith, 1986; Blunkett and Jackson, 1987; Lansley, Goss and Wolmar, 1989; Cochrane, 1993). There also emerged a literature looking at new styles of management in local government (Hoggett and Hambleton, 1987; Laffin, 1989; Farnham and Horton, 1993). Little of this work deals with housing in a direct way, and of particular relevance to this chapter is the noticeable shortage of good recent accounts of housing policy-making at local level.

As for housing associations, there is much less research-based literature available, and the way that these organisations work remains largely unexplored and unknown territory. An understanding of housing associations cannot be inferred from a reading of the local government literature. It is not safe to assume that what applies in local government will also apply in associations; there are distinct and important differences, which are partly to do with differences in scale and scope but which are primarily due to the non-elected nature of housing association committees. Most housing association committee members are not politicians in the same sense that local councillors are, but they are inevitably involved in politics with a small 'p', to the extent that housing associations are concerned with the distribution of scarce resources. Committee work is therefore likely, at least sometimes, to resemble the sort of planning, plotting, alliance-building and brokerage of deals which is the stuff of politics in local government.

Roles and relationships in local government

Who is involved in deciding local housing policy, and how do they stand in relation to one another? Legally it is the elected representatives who are responsible for the policy of a local authority, but it is now generally accepted that although they may be the decision-takers they are not the only decision-makers; the full-time salaried officials are also heavily involved in formulating policy proposals which eventually become policy decisions as a result of formal voting by elected members in committees and in the full council, and the officers must be seen as a highly significant set of actors in the policy-making process. Beyond the town hall are political party organisations, some of whose activists have an interest in local government and its policies, and there are various interests, including those primarily related to consumption issues (tenants, council tax payers) and those primarily related to production issues (builders, suppliers, unions). These various interests may or may not be organised and represented in the policy-making process. To develop an adequate understanding of the making of housing policy it is necessary to include reference to all potential participants, and to probe well beyond the 'cultural clichés' (Dearlove, 1973: 229) which purport to describe roles and relationships in local government.

The elected representatives

For the councillor who aspires to an active role in housing policy it is necessary to secure a place on the relevant service committee. (Until recently virtually all housing authorities had a housing committee, but current trends in public sector management involve a shift towards smaller numbers of committees, sometimes covering more than one service area (see Elcock,

1993: 151).) However, getting onto the right committee may not be easy, either because of competition for places or because of the power of patron- age, vested in the leadership. Nevertheless, for the unsuccessful, and for those who wish to contribute to the policy of committees other than those on which they sit, there are opportunities provided by the private meetings of the party group of councillors. In councils organised into parties it is normal practice for each party group to meet together on a regular basis, to determine which way the whole group will cast their votes in the full council meeting, and there may also be wider-ranging policy meetings. These opportunities notwithstanding, the right to speak is not the same as the right to be heeded, and a number of writers have drawn attention to the subtle (and not so subtle) ways in which rank-and-file members are typically controlled by the development of behavioural conventions and political pressure.

Dearlove, for instance, in his study of the ruling Conservative group in Kensington and Chelsea in the early 1970s, found that newly elected members were expected to adopt a quiet and passive role, until they had become adequately socialised into the role of Tory councillor, and had learned to accept existing policy. He went on to say that 'the silence rule is not in itself of critical importance, but it is a means of restricting contribu- tions until new councillors have learnt to respect the established pattern of commitments and the ethos of the authoritative councillors' (Dearlove, 1973: 147.) David Green (1981) reported at length on his participant observation of Newcastle City Council and its Labour group. In looking at the difficulties faced by the councillor wishing to influence policy through the Labour group, he employs Gyford's notion of three roles open to members: policy initiation, policy scrutiny and policy acceptance. Green found that the Newcastle Labour group as such did not play a significant part in policy initiation (Green, 1981: 51) and neither did the all-Labour Policy and Resources Committee of the council: 'The ineffectiveness of this committee meant that outside the mainline committees systematic thinking either about key issues of the present or about future problems was not taking place among majority party councillors' (Green, 1981: 55). 'Policy scrutiny' means the examination of proposals that have been initiated elsewhere, and again Green found that the Newcastle Labour group devoted very little time to this activity. At their regular pre-council meetings to consider reports on the agenda for the full council the group normally raced through the business in a 'highly perfunctory manner'. Members who tried to intervene or raise debate were, he says, given every indication that this was not approved behaviour. The conclusion drawn by Green from this case study is that 'The group acted principally as a receiving shop, serving to legitimise decisions which, in reality, had been taken elsewhere' (Green, 1981: 62). Thus the individual councillor could not, on this evidence, expect to use his or her position as a group member to influence policy decisions.

Backbench councillors may also experience difficulty in using their position as ward representatives as a way of pursuing important issues. Green suggests that the power of the party leadership is such that pressure can be exerted on the rank and file to toe the party line and to consider party policy rather than ward matters. On this topic Davies comments that, 'The councillor who persistently acts as an ombudsman for his Ward very soon provokes irritation and is eventually simply frozen out of all the patterns of information-flow and the perpetual "brokerage" that constitutes the political aspect of local government' (Davies, 1975).

Councillors, then, vary not only in their attitude towards policy-making, but also in their capacity to influence policy according to their position in the party hierarchy. Green has highlighted access to information as a key factor in differentiating between, in particular, the committee chairman (with very good access) and the backbenchers (with very limited access) (Green, 1981: 145).

The officers

If the hierarchical structure of party groups is important in determining who has influence on policy decisions, then the much more overtly hierarchical bureaucratic organisation of the administrative branch of the local authority must be expected to display this tendency even more markedly. Direct involvement with policy-making is concentrated at the level of chief officers and their senior colleagues although, as Chapter 9 has discussed, officers much nearer to the street level can have an influence over policy through the way it is translated into action.

However it is also true that officers at lower levels in an organisation may sometimes exercise influence on policy because of the dependence of chief officers on the flow of information upwards through the departmental hierarchy. This is especially relevant in the large urban authorities where a chief housing officer, responsible for a stock of perhaps 50 000 dwellings and a total staff of 1000, must inevitably rely on subordinates to keep him or her briefed on the current situation. The development of research and policy units in the larger authorities institutionalises a policy role for certain officers below the top levels.

Departmental chiefs do not, however, have only the influence of their own staff to consider. They must also operate in negotiation with other chief officers, amongst whom the head of finance can be expected to have considerable influence over the budgets and policies of individual programme areas. (This is a local-level manifestation of the point made in Chapter 1 about the importance of the Treasury in shaping housing policy at national level.) The development of the modern local government service has entailed the increased involvement of salaried professionals in specialised functional departments, giving rise to the possibility of professional as well as departmental conflicts over policy matters. There is, moreover, variation between departments in terms of size and share of the total budget, which is associated with differences in status and power among chief officers (Stanyer, 1976: 122–3). The growth of corporate management notwithstanding, policy-making should be seen as a process of interdepartmental bargaining (Malpass, 1975). When policy is being formally debated in chief officers' committees, or when particular decisions are being haggled over by senior officials, some will be in a better position than others to ensure that their view prevails, that their departments secure desired areas of responsibility, or that especially unattractive tasks fall elsewhere. Each occupational group has its view of the world and how it should be, usually based on a fairly coherent professional belief system, and so the lines of cooperation and conflict are quite clearly drawn and known in advance. In order to preserve its ability to cope with the everyday problems that it faces, and to pursue its longer-term aims, each group can be expected to promote its preferred version of the facts.

The public

The final category to be considered is the general public in the local authority area. Under this heading are included individual electors, political parties (at ward and constituency levels), loose informal and ephemeral groups organised around a particular issue, more permanent and formally constituted pressure groups, and commercial interests. What roles do all these very different groups play in influencing housing policy? What opportunities are open to them? The inequality found among councillors and officers in relation to policy-making is even more obvious among individuals and groups in the general public beyond the confines of the town hall.

A particularly interesting and important group with a close interest in local housing policy are council tenants. Some writers have argued that the structure of public sector housing has always excluded the interests of tenants (Birchall, 1992: 163), but the construction of large council estates gave tenants as voters a means of holding the authority to account and recent evidence suggests that a majority of authorities now have some sort of mechanism for direct participation of tenants in decision making affecting their estates (Cairncross *et al.*, 1993). Council tenants, however, do not necessarily identify a common collective interest and divisions on class and racial lines may be seen to undermine their capacity to formulate coherent demands and to pursue these to a successful conclusion (Cairncross *et al.*, 1993). Nevertheless there are numerous examples of tenants acting together to influence policy-making as it affects their estates. Particularly effective in this respect were the tenant-led campaigns to thwart the imposition of Housing Action Trusts in 1989/90 (Woodward, 1991; Karn, 1993).

The literature on local politics in Britain contains quite widespread agreement that the likely effectiveness of different sorts of interest groups is based on the nature of the relationship that they are able to establish with local councillors. Dearlove (1973) found that in Kensington and Chelsea councillors tended to regard outside groups as either helpful or unhelpful to the authority. They reacted more positively to the helpful groups, because these were seen to be furthering the interests of the authority itself by their actions, or their demands were contained within the general scope of existing policy – they were not a threat to the status quo. In the case of such groups it was possible for them to establish good and close working relationships with the authority, as a result of which they could expect to attain their objectives by working through the 'proper' channels. The 'proper' channels were considered by councillors to be approaches through elected members, and other methods based on generally quiet, unobtrusive and informal methods of communication. On the other hand, groups seen as unhelpful by councillors were those that existed for purposes not wholly approved by the authority, or that levelled demands at the council that could not be met within established policy. Dearlove found that councillors were much less responsive to these groups, and the normal channels of communication were consequently not open to them. In this situation they were forced into using 'improper' methods, such as demonstrations, sit-ins and publicity campaigns. However, to resort to such tactics left these groups open to the charge that they were irresponsible and to be condemned for not using the proper channels.

Newton (1976) came to similar conclusions in Birmingham, and so too did Saunders (1980) in Croydon. Newton, for instance, notes the close and often friendly relations between the council and established groups that are respectable, reliable and responsible. For them, business can be conducted at 'friendly lunch-time meetings or official subcommittee meetings', whereas groups that lack this close relationship have to adopt different, more visible tactics. He suggests that organisations such as tenants' associations are viewed with scepticism or even hostility, which cuts them off from the local authority. 'Organisations of this kind are faced with a classic political dilemma – either they become more moderate to gain acceptance with decision-makers, or else they preserve their policy but remain relatively powerless' (Newton, 1976: 86–7). Saunders found that the politicians in Croydon emphasised the importance of the proper ways of going about attempts to influence the authority. He, however, stresses more than the other writers the social class differences between pressure groups as a factor determining access to policy-makers. He identifies the principal categories in Croydon as the working class on the council estates and older declining private neighbourhoods, the middle class in the suburban areas and the town-centre business interests. According to Saunders' analysis the working-class groups have little alternative but to use the 'improper' channels of public protests, whereas for the more privileged groups the doors are wide open and they have no need to demonstrate their views in public (Saunders, 1980: 223).

An important conclusion to emerge from this analysis is that publicly visible campaigning might well be a sign of weakness and failure in an organisation, and conversely a lack of visible activity cannot be regarded as a sign of impotence. Pressure groups vary in the resources that they can deploy against a local authority in terms of time, manpower, expertise and money, but perhaps the most valuable resource is a close relationship with the authority. In any case it is necessary to take account of the influence exerted by outside organisations in the study of local authority policy-making.

Relations between members and officers

Few people would any longer defend the view that councillors make the policy and that officers merely offer technical advice and carry out instructions. Although this notion has obvious political appeal in certain circumstances, and can be a convenient defensive stance for officials, it is analytically misleading to say the least. Councillors have the authority of elected representatives who have been empowered to carry out the responsibilities of the council on the basis of statements put before the electorate. Although in reality most voters may not know what was promised at the election, and councillors may not do what they said they would do, they nevertheless confront the officers as duly elected representatives. The officers, on the other hand, can claim the authority of experts. The increasing specialisation and professionalisation of posts within local government has resulted in the strengthening of expertise as a justification or basis of authority. Two forms of rationality meet in local government: the political rationality of the elected members and the bureaucratic–technical rationality of the officers. A decision that is right politically can be viewed by the officers as technically quite wrong, and vice versa, and it has been suggested that officers sometimes see their role in terms of 'saving councillors from themselves' (Corina, 1977: 24). As Gyford (1976: 39) says:

> To those schooled in a profession, especially one with a fairly high technical content, it is hard to admit that a proposal which is apparently right on technical grounds can be dismissed on 'mere' political grounds. The notion that there are objectively correct solutions to problems lies at the heart of much professional education . . . Thus it is all too easy for professional officers to believe that their own views are both correct and in the public interest, and that they are moreover self-evidently so.

Relations between councillors and officers can be seen as negotiated, in the sense that the distribution of power between the two groups in the process of town hall decision-making is only more or less fixed. The idea of negotiated relationships allows for considerable variation of influence from decision to decision, and policy to policy. It also allows for the existence of an elite of senior councillors and officers who may sometimes operate as a team; Saunders (1980: 224), for instance, has suggested that his research in Croydon revealed the chief officers and political leaders to be 'close allies'. Councillors and officers are not, however, necessarily equal partners in such teams, nor are they equally matched as adversaries. First it is important to take into account the inherent advantages held by the officers because of their position as both full-timers and experts. Councillors, on the other hand, are usually part-time, with other work to do as well, and they are generally not especially knowledgeable about the complexities of local government finance or the detailed problems of, say, running a large housing department. The officers can exercise power not only in the way that they present material to a committee for decision, but also in their ability to control what comes up for decision. That is, they can present a case to a committee in such a way that there is only one possible decision, and they can also decide what is on the agenda, so that some relevant matters may never appear as issues at all. This invisible use of power can be very important in practice, and is certainly of great interest theoretically (Bachrach and Baratz, 1970: ch. 1).

Councillors are in a weak position in relation to the officers, because in addition to their status as part-timers they also have to participate in activities at ward level. A further problem for the elected representative is that he or she is dependent upon periodic reselection and reelection, which requires some party political activity. Thus, whereas the officer comes to policy-making unencumbered by other demands, the councillor comes as someone who also has a full-time job to do, a series of constituents' problems to resolve and a political role to play in the local party.

However, second, it is necessary to remember that not all councillors are equal. Some councillors have power and influence because they hold particular positions within their party group or as chairs of main committees. Committee chairs are in a good position to develop close relationships with their chief officers, and the chair–chief officer relationship has been seen as a key axis of power in local government. The idea of an elite of political leaders and chief officers has been widely accepted in the literature, although this perspective has been challenged by Stoker (1991: 90). Some councillors, especially long-serving committee chairmen, do acquire considerable knowledge and skills in areas such as housing. It is also increasingly common for the political leaders in the larger authorities to be virtually full-time politicians. Thus some councillors are in a good position to negotiate from strength with the officers, and this is the basis of the alliance within the member–officer oligarchy. It is common for the political leaders to represent safe seats, in which it is not so necessary for them constantly to cultivate their support. The point here is that, given this model of officer–member relations within the town hall, it is possible to predict how different councillors will regard interest groups in their wards and more generally. The model can be extended to include outside groups and forces participating in policy-making. Opposition members, backbenchers in the majority party and anyone in a marginal seat may be expected to pay more attention to ward matters, as a way of consolidating support and dealing with potential electoral dangers. As Davies (1975) has pointed out: 'It is of the essence of intra-ward politics to be able to claim credit for everything and to permit no rivals for public esteem . . . So the one thing elected representatives cannot permit (let alone encourage) are movements over which they have little or no influence.' Councillors generally have an interest in keeping politics in their ward quiet and undemanding because of the demanding nature of their role within the town hall. It may often be useful to a councillor to be able to refer to, or draw upon, pressure-group support in a particular negotiation, but unhelpful groups have nothing to offer the councillor save problems. Arguments about constructive conflict, the value of wide political debate and the need to involve the broad body of the electorate in local politics are unlikely to appeal to the overworked councillor struggling with his or her colleagues and the bureaucracy.

Policy-making in housing associations

It must be acknowledged at the outset that policy-making in housing associations is an area which has been widely neglected during the expansion of housing studies in recent years. Research has tended to concentrate on the impact of government policy on aspects of development (Randolph, 1993) and finance (Hills, 1991), to the neglect of issues of how policies within associations are decided and the role of voluntary committees in determining policy. Housing associations are not required to employ staff (and a third of registered associations in 1992 had no employees at all (Housing Corporation, 1992a: 47)), but they must have a management committee of unpaid voluntary members. This section looks at what is known about housing association committees and their role in policy-making.

The published literature specifically on housing association committees amounts to little more than three items, a study of six associations in 1983 (Platt *et al.*, 1985), a report of a survey of associations in 1984 (Crook, 1985) and a report of a postal questionnaire sent to individual committee members in 1988 (Kearns, 1990). Given this situation it was decided to carry out a small piece of research specifically for this chapter and the following discussion draws on a number of interviews with committee chairs and directors of Bristol-based associations in the summer of 1993.

It is important to establish that although local authorities and housing associations are similar in that they both have unpaid committee members who have a policy-making and monitoring role, they are also different in significant ways, and an understanding of how associations work, in terms of committee activities and policy processes, cannot be inferred from a reading of the local government literature. The most obvious difference is that whereas local councillors are elected on a universal adult suffrage, housing association committee members are elected from among the members of the association itself. Association memberships are generally very small, and even some of the biggest associations have shareholding memberships which hardly exceed the number of places on the management committee. Crook (1985: 4) found that over two-thirds of associations had fewer than 50 shareholding members. This is the origin of the often-used phrase 'self-perpetuating oligarchies' to describe housing association committees. Most local councillors are required to fight contested elections every three or four years, but contested elections are rare in housing associations; in Crook's (1985: 5) survey only 7 per cent of associations reported contested elections. Indeed it is much more likely that associations have to look for people to fill vacancies rather than having to choose between rival candidates. Kearns (1990: 42) found that 61 per cent of members were recruited by direct invitation from either the chair or director of the association, and that only 6 per cent made a direct approach on their own behalf. Only 4.6 per cent were proposed or elected by a tenants' group. People elected to a housing association committee are required to stand for reelection every three years, but as sitting members they are entitled to reelection without nomination, and if there are more vacancies than nominations then it is very difficult for them to be removed.

A second difference is that local government is openly political, and almost always party political, whereas housing association committees are not. One of the Bristol chairs interviewed for this chapter had served on his committee since 1974 and claimed not to know the political leanings of the other members. He described the committee as apolitical. In local government people are elected as representatives of particular wards, and there is no expectation that they have any special expertise, but in housing associations the Housing Corporation requires committees to have 'the capacity, commitment and experience to direct their association' and to have 'an appropriate range of skills' (Housing Corporation, 1992b: 10). These skills are taken to include legal, financial, management and property development expertise. Thus in this sense a housing association is more like a board of directors than a local authority housing committee. Housing association committee members sit as individuals with particular skills and experience rather than as representatives of groups of people, and therefore the authority of their contributions to policy debates resides in their standing as experts rather than their status as elected representatives. Associations are now officially encouraged to have tenants on their committees, and they are perhaps more likely to define their role in terms of representing the interests of tenants as a whole, but they are usually appointed rather than elected and therefore lack the authority provided by an electoral mandate.

Another consequence of the way that housing association committee members are recruited is that they are essentially a collection of individuals, whereas local authority committees are generally made up of party groups. This means that in local government there are built-in alliances, and usually a built-in majority on each committee. The fact that the outcome of debate in a housing association committee cannot be taken for granted may be seen as a distinct strength, but whatever view is taken it is clearly the case that the two types of committee are very different as a result. This is not to say that politics, with a small 'p', are absent from the work of housing association committees; nor, indeed, should it be assumed that party politics are absent, but they are more likely to remain muted and implicit.

Platt *et al.* (1985: 6) classified association committees as either active or passive:

> Active committees are those which set policy and monitor performance and in which the majority of members contribute to meetings. Passive committees are those which act as a sounding board for the officers and in which only the chairman or a minority of members contribute.

The authors claimed that their interviewees were well able to allocate their own associations to one or other of these categories. In the Bristol interviews the sounding board metaphor was also understood and accepted as an important role of the committee, even where it was seen to be active rather than passive.

In two of the Bristol associations the directors were quite open about saying that policy ideas often came from them, and that they saw themselves as leading the committee. In a third association, run on quite different principles, with the staff group constituted as a non-hierarchical collective, the staff interviewees reported that the committee had itself initiated the idea of a major policy review, and the impression was gained that the staff were having to adjust to a more active and assertive set of committee members.

On the question of where power lies in housing associations, little evidence emerges from the work of Crook, Kearns and Platt *et al.*, although Platt *et al.* (1985: 18) say that only one of the six associations that they looked at lived up to the expectation that the committee should determine policy, set objectives and monitor performance. The impression given by the comments of officers interviewed by Platt *et al.* is that they saw themselves as carrying the weight of policy work, and in the Bristol interviews, too, there were suggestions that the committees have to be pushed into addressing the bigger policy issues. In the Bristol interviews the question of power was raised by reference to the idea which emerges from the local government literature that the chair-chief officer relationship is often the key axis of power. In the collective association it was denied that such an axis could emerge, and in the others it was not seen as an accurate description. One chairperson said that he would try to avoid the situation where he and the director held all the power.

In another association the director referred candidly to the potential for tensions to emerge between the committee and senior staff. In a period of rapid change imposed by central government one source of tension would be different responses to outside pressures which require some associations to consider their position. For example, associations with an established inner city base and a well-developed public service ethic might be expected to disagree internally about how to respond to Housing Corporation pressures to adopt a more businesslike approach and to compete with other associations for developments on suburban and rural greenfield sites. There are different ways of dealing with situations of this kind. One obvious way is to schedule the subject as a main agenda item at a management committee meeting; this at least gets the issue out in the open, but carries the risk that damaging conflicts and splits will emerge, either within the committee or between it and the officers. The opposite strategy is to ensure that the issue does not get discussed at all, or at least not in a head-on way, until the ground for a consensus has been prepared by careful informal lobbying. The point to draw out here is that if committee members rely on the director to set the agendas for their meetings then they hand over to that person the power to decide what gets discussed, and with it the power to decide what gets decided. In such situations, chief officers who want to avoid conflict or the risk of decisions that they do not personally or professionally agree with can keep contentious issues off the agenda.

The lack of good empirical evidence on how housing associations work makes it difficult to come to firm conclusions about their policy-making processes, but given energetic and committed senior staff, and/or a close working relationship between the director and chair, it is difficult to see that ordinary voluntary committee members have much effective power to determine housing association policy.

Policy-making in action

The purpose of this section is to focus in on examples of different approaches to the study of policy-making in housing organisations. Previous editions of this book have drawn on accounts of different approaches, and the intention now is to supplement those examples with some up-to-date research carried out specifically for this chapter.

The kinds of questions to be considered in the analysis of policy-making include:

- Who is involved?
- Where does the power lie?
- What are the processes for reaching decisions?
- What determines which ideas are accepted and which rejected?
- What determines the boundaries of the policy-making debate?
- What are the values underpinning policy, and whose values are they?

One approach to generating some answers to these questions is to concentrate on the details of how particular decisions are produced. This can be very difficult to do because of the problems of gaining access to private or informal, non-minuted, meetings. However, in a short article about the redevelopment of one street of cottages in Sunderland in the early 1970s Norman Dennis (1973) was able to overcome these barriers and to give an insider's view since he was a member of the ruling Labour group on the Sunderland Housing Committee at the time. Much of the value of this little story lies in the scarcity of such accounts in relation to housing policy. Central to Dennis's approach is the proposition that to understand how power is being exercised it is necessary to stay close to the details of what actually happens. The key players in the drama included the council officers who put forward plans for demolition of the street, councillors, including the local ward members, and local residents. Dennis's account shows how the officers' report was processed through various stages, including the private meetings of the party group, to which researchers do not normally have access. He is able to illustrate the importance of party groups in local political processes by setting group meetings in the sequence of committee meetings, and showing how group decisions should (but do not always) determine the decisions made by committee or full council. In this example group meetings are shown to provide important opportunities for decisions to be challenged. He shows, for instance, how ward members were able to secure a second chance to pursue the decision they wanted by persuading the Labour group to refer back the Housing Committee report which was on its way to the full council for approval. He also shows that even when battles appear to be won nothing should be taken for granted, and how the influence of determined officers can overturn decisions which councillors are in the process of making.

However, the Duke Street story is more than an account of the frustrations of being a backbench councillor, for it also covers the contributions of local residents in the struggle for power. The story illustrates the way that decision-making can gather pace from an initial report by an officer to other officers, through committee and group discussion, employing 'normal procedures', to more 'coercive' attempts by residents to influence the council by resorting to the media, and ward councillors similarly resorting to publicly visible tactics such as tabling deliberately embarrassing questions to the committee chair at the council meeting. The fact that Dennis's study refers to decisions about slum clearance in the early 1970s does not reduce the relevance or value of his insights about policy-making in local government.

Another approach to the analysis of policy-making in housing is provided by Malpass's work on the redevelopment of the Byker area of Newcastle (Malpass, 1977, 1979, 1980). Again the fact that this research refers to events which are now quite distant in time should not detract from their relevance in terms of policy-making. In contrast to the previous example the Byker study was concerned with generating an explanation based on a longitudinal analysis of policy development in a much larger area over a long period of time, from the early 1950s to the late 1970s. Over such a long time there are opportunities for priorities to be revised, for opposition to emerge and fade away, for political control to change (both locally and centrally), and for economic conditions to alter. The longer-term perspective of the Byker study draws attention to policy-making as an incremental process in which problems and objectives are gradually refined and redefined. Various themes and goals are woven together, not necessarily neatly or coherently, as new goals emerge and new solutions are promoted by a succession of dominant individuals and groups.

Essentially what happened in Byker was that an initial, 1950s' approach based on slum clearance contained proposals for redevelopment on a relatively small scale. This was later overtaken by a 1960s' concern for large-scale urban redevelopment, which swept up the whole neighbourhood into clearance plans. Local opposition to this coincided with a shift in local political control and the emergence of the idea that local communities could and should be protected from the ravages of large-scale redevelopment. Thus it was that some 15 years after the beginning of planning for the redevelopment of the area, and four years after the beginning of demolition, it was decided to make a new start, with new consultant architects brought in to devise a plan for community-based redevelopment.

By the late 1960s the commitment to retain the community by offering local rehousing, for those who wanted to stay had become a highly visible component of policy, but it was additional to rather than a replacement for other, preexisting, commitments. The Byker example shows how policy-making can be a sort of sedimenting process in which new layers are laid on top of the old without replacing them. As a relatively late addition, retaining the community was supported by much less accumulated commitment within the authority than was enjoyed by the slum clearance and comprehensive redevelopment approaches. These earlier policies had priority over retention of the community because of the commitment to them. The higher priority of physical redevelopment resulted in the community being retained only in so far as it was compatible with the fulfilment of these goals. That is, they were only marginally affected by the addition of the objective of retaining the community, but its definition was severely limited in practice by their priority. Nevertheless, in terms of the politics of policy it is important to remember the utility of the high public visibility of the policy of retaining the community. It is not surprising that, once it was established as a popular policy, retaining the community continued to be supported publicly by councillors of both main parties. Despite what was actually being done as a result of the priority attached to earlier policy decisions, they repeatedly stressed their earnest desire to retain the community spirit in Byker by providing local rehousing. The sincerity of these statements is not in question; the point is that higher priority was attached to goals which conflicted with the community orientation.

More generally, this study suggests an incremental or sedimentary view of the policy process, in which over time new goals can be added, although this process may lead to the development of incoherent and incompatible objectives. It suggests that commitment varies from policy to policy, and that commitment can be the basis for ordering the priority of objectives and resolving conflicts between them. High-commitment primary objectives will, other things being equal, stand more chance of being attained than lower-commitment secondary objectives. However, secondary objectives may be highly popular with the public and will therefore be given high visibility by the authorities to gain support for their overall policy.

The studies of Duke Street and Byker are examples of research on different time-scales, both looking at how local authorities formulated policies to tackle locally defined problems; another approach to the study of local policy-making is to look at situations where the local-level actors are faced with new central government policies which require local responses. The two examples to be considered here include the case of council house sales in Norwich following the Housing Act 1980, and Bristol's response to the introduction of City Challenge in 1991. In the Norwich case the city council was openly opposed to the newly introduced Right to Buy, and in the City Challenge study Bristol's position was one of grudging acquiescence, tinged with hostility among some senior councillors.

The Norwich case study, which draws on work by Forrest and Murie (1985), is an example and consequence of increased central intervention and part of the process of nationalisation of housing policy affecting the behaviour of central and local government. For 50 years Labour had been the dominant party on the city council and as a result there had been no history of selling council houses under pre-1980 powers. The introduction of a statutory Right to Buy was therefore seen by Norwich's controlling group as hostile legislation, to which it was impossible not to respond in some way.

In this situation, the development of policy in Norwich initially involved three major elements. First, councillors chose to delay consideration of the provisions contained in the Housing Bill. Only when further delay would weaken the council's ability to safeguard the council stock were the details considered. Second, the consideration of the Bill focused on exemptions and other loopholes in the legislation which could be used to minimise the impact of the legislation on local service provision. Third, the council through its officers began to consider the new administrative systems which needed to be set up.

In contrast to some other examples of local resistance to central government (Skinner and Langdon, 1974; Malpass, 1992c), there was no question of non-compliance with the law, but a situation developed from early on which from one perspective (the local authority) could be seen as a reasonable and studied response to an aggressive piece of legislation, but from another (central government) could be viewed as calculated intransigence. The city council was very slow to take action to implement the requirements of the Act, although the leader of the council responded to the view that Norwich was purposely dragging its feet by arguing that the admittedly slow rate of progress was a combination of staff shortages and the overall pattern of priorities.

Towards the end of February 1981, Norwich received a letter from the DoE detailing complaints from two tenants about 'apparent lack of progress'. This was to be the first of many such letters detailing tenants' complaints over lack of progress. This barrage of tenants' complaints appears to have been encouraged by the local Conservative Party, which held public meetings on the subject, and Conservative Party Central Office, by a series of articles which appeared in the local press and by more frequent questions in Housing Committee by Tory members concerning overall progress on sales.

Under the Housing Act 1980, the use by the Secretary of State of powers of intervention hinged on proof of households experiencing unreasonable delays in buying their dwellings, rather than on the 'reasonableness' of the council in deciding its overall system of priorities. The encouragement to tenants to 'put pen to paper', therefore, was of more than symbolic value. A 'dossier of despair' from tenants was not just 'more likely' to bring action from the government: it was a legal precondition for intervention.

There followed a series of letters between ministers and the civil servants and the city council, in which the government expressed its mounting irritation with the slowness of action on the Right to Buy in Norwich, and the city defended its actions. Essentially the argument was about reasonableness: ministers were concerned about what they saw as the unreasonably slow rate of progress in Norwich, and the city argued that the government's expectations were unreasonable for an authority with no previous experience in this area of housing. In an environment where the council was being urged to contain staffing levels the council had to balance the demands of the Right to Buy provision against 'other no less compelling demands on its resources'. The main points of disagreement between Norwich and central government were matters of priorities and not of non-compliance with the law.

Whilst for ministers the Right to Buy was a high-profile policy demanding a high priority in its implementation, for Norwich there were more pressing concerns, particularly in a period of fiscal constraint. There was certainly, and quite explicitly, a lack of enthusiasm for sales among Norwich councillors. But what was being argued was not a defiance of the law, but a resistance to central attempts to determine the pattern of allocation of resources and the order of priorities. If other authorities chose to put the sales policy at the top of their priorities, as many did, that was (presumably) perfectly reasonable, provided it was the outcome of local democratic processes and not the product of central diktat. What was worse was the setting of priorities by a central government which was at the same time severely limiting the resources available to meet the full range of statutory obligations. From the point of view of ministers, Norwich were acting unreasonably and were clearly politically opposed to a policy which had a mandate at national level. Westminster was the supreme power and the sale of council houses was one of the major electoral promises of the Conservative Government.

A meeting in September between Norwich and the Minister for Housing and Construction covered the major areas of disagreement. Norwich refused to agree to a timetable which satisfied ministers. The target ministers were demanding was regarded as unrealistic and would involve unacceptable neglect of other, more important areas of housing. The council significantly changed its approach and set a higher target for processing applications. Ministers insisted on a higher rate of sales and the Norwich response was not considered sufficient. Norwich had considered the implications of intervention and the additional costs involved in trying to accede to ministerial demands. They took advice on their legal position in October.

Norwich maintained their position that a number of steps had been taken to comply with the wishes of the DoE and they were being perfectly reasonable in the circumstances. But, as Heseltine remarked, 'it was also necessary . . . to take into account tenants and other local authorities. The council's rate of progress were not comparable to others'. It was his responsibility 'to achieve the objectives of the Act'.

It was apparent that the only means of escape for Norwich was to agree to the use of the District Valuer to speed up the processing of applications. But Norwich had moved as far as they were prepared to go. Following this meeting, the Secretary of State issued a notice of intervention. The outcome was that one of the Secretary of State's representatives became responsible for the administration of the sale of council houses in Norwich between December 1981 and May 1985, when the notice of intervention was withdrawn. Norwich challenged the intervention in the High Court and the Court of Appeal but once the courts had decided in favour of the Secretary of State, the city council decided to cooperate fully with him. The DoE set up its office within the council buildings.

Norwich officers during the period of intervention were still involved in implementation and discussion of policy, but clearly the responsibility for local policy-making had changed. It should however, be borne in mind that, for the DoE, the action in Norwich probably had its greatest impact (and this was no doubt the intention) in demonstrating political will and encouraging others, rather than in achieving results for Norwich tenants.

Local policy-making in relation to council house sales in Norwich is an account of responses to legislation and central government scrutiny. Even in an area where detailed legislation applied the council had a range of crucial decisions to make to determine how it carried out its responsibilities. In this case, the political pressures determining action involved central government and 'opposition-led' and orchestrated tenant representations passed to central government. The role of central government is more prominent than in the other case-studies, where there is a greater danger of underestimating the direct or indirect control of central government on local policy-making. The full account of the Norwich case also emphasises the importance of legal advice and of the courts in determining what policy would emerge. Judgements about finance, staffing and priorities were also involved. Policy-making in one area is not insulated from other developments nationally or locally. At the local level, the environment of financial restriction operating at the time no doubt strengthened arguments against increasing the staff commitment to this policy. The degree of central involvement in the Norwich case understandably raised questions about the role of local authorities and the purpose of local administration. The Secretary of State's representative remains an unusual feature of local policy-making, although this and other ways of centralising policy have become more evident in legislation. At one level, the council house sales story is one of central government aims replacing local government's in local policy-making. The commitment of central government to their policy stance was unusually high and envisaged detailed intervention. For local government, policy-making involved a succession of compromises and concessions. The ultimate attempt to resist further encroachment on local control was defeated, although in the aftermath of legal action the decision to cooperate was crucial.

The final example to be considered in this chapter concerns the production of Bristol's responses to the government's City Challenge initiative in 1991 and 1992. The account presented here draws on interviews with key actors carried out specifically for this chapter (see also Oatley *et al.*, 1993). City Challenge was introduced as a way of making authorities compete for resources which had previously been allocated within other programmes (including HIPs and the Housing Corporation ADP). It was technically an aspect of urban policy rather than housing, but housing resources were incorporated, and in the Bristol case there was a considerable housing element to the extent that two large peripheral housing estates were the geographical focus of the bid.

In 1991 Bristol was one of 15 cities invited by the government to bid for resources under the City Challenge initiative. The following year the scope was widened to include invitations to all 57 urban programme authorities. During the months preceding the first round of City Challenge staff in Bristol Housing Services had been in discussion with officials at the regional office of the DoE about a substantial Estate Action bid for the peripheral estates of Hartcliffe and Withywood, and from the Bristol point of view City Challenge seemed to be in effect a development from these discussions. But City Challenge was much wider and more ambitious than Estate Action, since it involved more than housing and required competing authorities to show that their bids included partnerships with the private sector and local community organisations. In the case of Bristol (and other non-metropolitan areas) it was also necessary to involve the county council. An important element of City Challenge was the inclusion of high-visibility 'flagship' projects, designed to have a clear demonstration effect on urban regeneration. Another important feature was the competitive nature of the initiative – authorities were asked to submit bids in the knowledge that some would fail and therefore receive no funds at all from the City Challenge budget.

City Challenge was launched in the last week of May 1991 and authorities were given a very tight timetable of six weeks for the preparation and submission of their bids. How did Bristol respond? There were several key decisions to be made: whether to accept the invitation to bid, which part of the city to choose, who should lead the bid preparation, how the process should be conducted, what should go into the bid and how the bid should be presented.

The first three of these issues were resolved quickly and without wide debate or consultation. The invitation was addressed to the city council and it was senior politicians who decided that the invitation would be accepted, albeit without enthusiasm. The city received very clear messages from the regional office of the DoE that the Hartcliffe and Withywood area should be selected for the initiative, reflecting both the fact that discussions had already begun about how to lever in more resources to the area and the DoE's perception of this area as 'something special' among deprived peripheral estates. All the local authority officers and members interviewed about City Challenge were agreed that in 1991 there was effectively no consideration of other areas after the DoE had made its view clear. In the context of the first round bid the third decision stemmed directly from the second: given the choice of Hartcliffe and Withywood and the previous discussions between Housing and the DoE, it was logical to see City Challenge in terms of a housing-led exercise. Housing Services was also the only city council service with an established presence in the Hartcliffe and Withywood area.

A team of officers was established to work up the bid, under the leadership of one of the two area housing managers. Somewhat paradoxically the team was located in offices in the city centre, five miles from the estates. The task before the hastily assembled team was a severe test of their professional and political skills as they faced up to producing a bid which was technically credible, politically acceptable (to both the Labour leadership of the city council and Conservative ministers), and effectively packaged and presented. The task was made more difficult by the pressure to involve business and community interests, in a city where there was not a well-established history of partnership between the council and the private sector. A really crucial factor here was that the major industrial site adjacent to the Hartcliffe and Withywood estates was the former Wills tobacco factory, owned by the Hanson Trust and vacant since 1989. Credible proposals for the site were seen to be necessary for a successful bid, but Hanson proved to be particularly distant and difficult to deal with.

In terms of the local politics of City Challenge, the officers were working not only with both Bristol and Avon councillors, but also with the knowledge that the leadership of the Bristol Labour group were much less enthusiastic about City Challenge than the ward members representing Hartcliffe and Withywood itself. The local ward members (all Labour) naturally saw City Challenge as a way of getting more resources into their area and therefore supported the idea, but the leadership took a different view, based on objections to the principle of competitive bidding for resources and to the humiliation of being seen to dance to a Tory government tune. They objected to the resources being tied not to proven need but to particular ways of tackling that need; the government was not only seeking to tell local authorities how much money they could spend but also insisting that it be spent in certain ways, designed to elevate the profile of the private sector. In Bristol there was also pressure to include within the bid certain projects (such as a ring road and increased tenure diversification) to which the city council leadership was opposed. Another factor in City Challenge which was opposed by at least some leading Labour members in Bristol was the implied requirement for successful bidders to set up an implementation structure outside direct municipal control. Local politicians who had opposed the establishment of the Bristol Urban Development Corporation in the late 1980s could not be expected to accept willingly a further erosion of their power and influence.

The production of the first-round bid involved the officers in a period of intense effort, and for the two area housing officers the task was made more difficult by the requirement on them both to provide the housing element of the bid and to coordinate the whole exercise. In the time available, and given the lack of established relationships with the business sector in the city, it proved difficult to involve either the private sector or community interest groups in any meaningful way. In this sense City Challenge exposed the difficulties of the two local authorities in working cooperatively with each other and with the private sector.

City Challenge also exposed the lack of clearly established political structures to guide and validate decisions. There were informal meetings between the bid team and the chief executive, and meetings involving Labour councillors. The local ward members were particularly active in steering the bid in acceptable directions, but the influence of less directly involved senior councillors should not be underestimated. The emphasis, however, was on informal meetings rather than on formal reports to committees, via the Labour group. The Labour group on Bristol City Council appears to have had no discussion of City Challenge, despite the importance of the initiative in terms of both its implications for policy-making and the sums of money involved (£37 million over five years).

City Challenge bids were not merely submitted to the DoE; in the first round they were presented to ministers in person at events staged in the various cities. In Bristol it was decided that the presentation and explanation of the bid would be led by an official from the Planning Department, partly to demonstrate that the bid was not just about housing. There were no councillors involved in the presentation, and this was apparently taken as an indicator of the lack of political commitment to the bid and to the City Challenge approach.

Bristol's bid in the first round of City Challenge failed to secure funding. The letter informing the city of the decision referred to lack of vision in the proposals for the Wills site, and the scope for greater involvement of the private sector in the strategic management of the programme. The letter also stated that the wider impact of the bid for Bristol had not been fully demonstrated, important transport links to other areas needed further development and greater diversification of tenure needed to be considered. These reasons are given here to indicate both the extent of government involvement in determining the content of City Challenge programmes, and to draw attention to the difficulties for the city in putting together a second-round bid: on the one hand the future of the Wills site depended on the stance taken by a multinational business conglomerate, over which Bristol City Council could hope to have little influence, and on the other the reasons for the first failure covered several sticking points for the political leadership in the city.

The first-round decisions were announced in July 1991, and although it was generally expected that there would be a second round little was done in Bristol to keep going any momentum established in the first round. There was some discussion, generated by officials, of whether a bid based on a different area of Bristol would stand more chance of success, but there was no political support for this and active resistance from Hartcliffe and Withywood councillors. Sticking with Hartcliffe and Withywood was seen as the only viable option, despite the difficulties of producing a bid capable of winning within the ground rules set by the government.

It was not until the beginning of 1992 that steps were taken to establish a team, just ahead of receipt of the invitation to bid. This time the timetable was a little longer and the Bristol response was more securely grounded, organisationally if not politically. A senior officer from the city chief executive's office was placed in charge of bid preparation, and the chief executives of both Bristol and Avon provided support in terms of releasing staff for the duration. The team worked from a base in Hartcliffe itself and greater efforts were made to involve both the private sector and the local community. Some private sector representatives were particularly active in the second round. The establishment of a steering group (including representatives of the private sector, the local community, the two councils, Bristol's two universities and the MP for Bristol South) demonstrated the partnerships involved.

As an exercise in policy-making it appears that the second-round bid benefited from the experience of the previous year, and from the longer time-scale available. There were, for instance, regular weekly briefings for the ward councillors. It was felt that the first-round bid had been 'too housing-led', hence the decision to have the second team managed by a planner from the chief executive's office, and the strategy of altering the balance within the bid itself.

However, while it was possible to improve the organisational and partnership aspects of the process there remained serious obstacles to a successful bid, and in the event the second-round bid did not attract government financial support. Three main factors underlying Bristol's repeated failure in City Challenge can be identified, and they are all to do with the way that influence over policy-making can be exercised by actors who are not actively engaged in the process, or whose refusal to become involved has a negative effect. First, given the emphasis on private sector partnerships and economic regeneration within City Challenge it was inevitable that the Wills site would play an important part in the Bristol bid. What seems to be demonstrated very clearly by the experience of both rounds is that it is easy enough to involve local and regional capital in projects of this kind but that big multinationals have the financial strength to defy central and local government, and to put their own interests above those of the local economies and communities in which parts of their empires are located. Had Hanson chosen to cooperate by selling the site at a realistic price then the bid would have been much enhanced, but the price demanded was too high for any of the City Challenge players to match.

Second, the stance of leading Labour councillors in Bristol was critical in the sense that it determined the boundaries within which officers could negotiate proposals. A firm veto on issues such as tenure diversification, the ring road and the establishment of separate boards or companies to manage a successful bid meant that the officers were left to produce a bid without much realistic chance of success in terms of its content. Indeed, there is evidence to support the inference that Labour group leaders had privately decided that they had to be seen to be participating in City Challenge but that they would stick to their principles rather than compromise enough to enable the production of a bid with a good chance of success in the competition. (At that stage they probably thought they could rely on a Labour victory in the 1992 general election and a return to policies more to their liking.) It might then be argued that this was the real policy-making process and that everything that came after was effectively just going through the motions. Whatever the accuracy of this inference it serves as a reminder that the visible parts of policy-making processes are not necessarily the most important.

The third factor was that in addition to the problems with the content of the bid, the lack of enthusiasm amongst leading Bristol councillors was known and understood by DoE civil servants and their ministers. The reliance on officers to present both bids was seen as significant, as was the fact that particular councillors, well-known to the DoE, chose to distance themselves from the bids. In this sense the bids lacked political credibility with the government.

Conclusion

This and the previous chapter have been concerned with four main issues. The first was the nature of the policy process, and it was suggested that, although it is tempting, and useful up to a point, to think in terms of a rational sequence of stages, reality is not so simple. Therefore more sophisticated or flexible models are necessary as a guide to understanding what actually happens. The Duke Street story illustrated how local authority decision-making does not always conform to the formal rules of procedure, and the Byker study demonstrated most clearly the way in which policy-making in practice can deviate from normative expectations and highlighted the artificiality of the distinction between policy-making and implementation as sequential stages. The second issue was the question of who is involved in policy-making at the local level. The thrust of the argument was the need to differentiate not only between councillors, officials and outside interests, but also to recognise that, for instance, some councillors are much more influential in policy-making than others. The same is true of officials and interest groups. It was also suggested that, while councillors and officials can be shown to operate on different bases of authority which can generate conflict between them, it is important to consider the powerful position created by committee chair–chief officer alliances. More generally, corporate management may create or exacerbate a situation in which an authority is dominated by an elite of political leaders and chief officers working together as a team; as a result backbench councillors in particular may find themselves cut off from a policy-making role.

The third issue was the structure and content of local housing policy and two points were made. *New* policy is relatively rare in the day-to-day routine of local government. Once an allocation policy, for example, is established, it tends to run on without a lot of policy-making activity, although it is appropriate to refer to the notion of policy-making as an incremental process, a sort of fine-tuning of the system, which is not incompatible with the observation that major policy decisions are infrequent events. Such decisions may be more frequent in certain areas of policy and it was suggested that there are five broad categories within local housing policy. The value of this observation is that it draws attention to the fact that policy-making consists of several distinct sorts of decisions.

Finally, having looked at the questions 'Who makes policy?' and 'What does it consist of?', the next question was 'How is it done?' Four examples were presented from what is a surprisingly thin coverage of policy-making in the very large number of local housing studies. The four examples were chosen to illustrate different approaches to the problems of how policy is determined; each has its strengths and weaknesses. Dennis's microscopic analysis has the capacity to show how formal procedures and informal conventions operate in practice, but the danger is that the values and actions of individuals assume undue significance. If, as he rightly says, it is important to stay close to the details, it is equally important to avoid being submerged by them. The terms within which policy-making takes place are, after all, largely imposed from outside, by the economy and central government policy constraints. The approach of the Byker study of policy-making over a long period takes into account a wider perspective, but it is open to the charge of retrospective rationalisation. To look at policy-making through direct participation is to avoid this problem, but participant observers are rarely impartial and there is an inevitable risk of attributing policy change to the intervention of the pressure group concerned. A further problem with this approach is that it can only be utilised to investigate policy-making where there is open conflict and organised interest group activity. Studies of this kind tend to deal with the influence of working-class groups, often in slum clearance or improvement areas. Other important policy issues are much less well-documented because of the absence of organised protest.

The approach in the Norwich case comes closer to a participant observer study. A shorter policy history was fully documented because it resulted in litigation. The documentation involved identified the arguments and considerations presented at the time rather than after the event. In addition, interviews with key actors enabled a closer reconstruction of events than is usual. The resulting account is more heavily dependent on material from the local authority but provides the fullest available account of central–local government conflict in the housing sphere. While it provides a detailed blow-by-blow account of how policy was determined, the nature of the case compared with the Duke Street story highlights the role of central government and of strategic housing, staffing and other issues. The case study of policy presented here does not attempt to assess questions of 'whose interest' and broader questions of the nature of accountability, the role of the judiciary or the broader structural or ideological determinants of action taken by central or local government.

All the approaches described here are concerned with how decisions are made and how policy is produced. What is lacking is a way of looking at non-decision-making and the management of the public agenda. It is important to know how issues arise and are resolved, but it is equally important to know how issues do not arise. So far, little work in this area has been carried out, no doubt for good methodological reasons.

11

From Policy to Practice: The Management of Housing

As was argued in Chapter 10, the tendency to equate policy decisions with action or to assume that policy decisions are translated into action without being changed by it is not an adequate representation of the way policy is made or implemented. In this sense implementation is not best conceived as the translation of policy into a number of consequential actions but rather policy and implementation are closely interactive elements in a single process. At any one time policy is likely to be influencing action and action influencing policy. If for this reason alone, a picture of policy-making in housing which referred solely to the way political statements on objectives, programmes and intentions are arrived at would be misleading. The policy itself is still being developed and changed as action is undertaken. Indeed the discussion in Chapter 10 illustrates how misleading it would be to refer to initial policy statements in developing an understanding of policy.

Rather than looking at policy and how it develops and changes, the intention of this chapter is to start at the other end of the policy–action relationship and consider examples of the way policy is carried out. At one level this may be assumed to be a consideration of unproblematic, technical, administrative processes established to make policy work. However, following the discussion in Chapter 10, the starting-point in this chapter is that actions taken to 'make any single policy work' could be of widely differing kinds and the action adopted has important implications. Decisions in relation to 'action' or implementation as distinct from, say, target or objectives setting, will often have more than a marginal impact on the consequences of the policy–action process.

The variety of policies and policy objectives involved in housing policy creates some problems in generalising about the policy–action process in housing. Some problems derive from shortcomings in policy formation itself – lack of clarity of objectives or identification of resources to meet objectives. However there are some prior factors which need to be taken into account. This is not a reference to the broad social and structural constraints which affect every policy area, but is rather a reference to fundamental conflicts in and between policies. Cullingworth (1973) has stated that

> In no field more than housing is there such a multiplicity of possible objectives and such a wide range of techniques available for meeting them. One important implication of this is that the potential for conflict between different housing policies is large much to the embarrassment of successive governments. (1973: 39–40)

Cullingworth went on to quote Donnison's illustration of this:

> A policy of housing those in most urgent need may conflict with a policy of replacing the worst houses, and both may conflict with a policy for stimulating demand through subsidies directed to those who are most likely to be persuaded by such help to build or buy homes for themselves: different people will benefit from the pursuit of each of these objectives. An attempt to keep pace with the housing needs of expanding industrial centres may conflict with an attempt to revive poverty-stricken regions. A policy designed to improve productivity in the building industry may not be best suited for eliminating unemployment in the building trades. A policy designed to eliminate rent controls and create a 'free market' in housing may conflict with the need to avoid inflation of living costs and wages. Every country's housing policies contain the seeds of several such conflicts, for housing is so central a feature of the economy and the way of life it supports that many of the competing aspirations at work in society gain some expression in this field. (Donnison, 1967: 86)

While this comment is largely directed at general policy objectives concerning central government, the general perspective is equally applicable to policies pursued at a local level. In a policy area where conflicts are so significant the policy–action process is likely to be affected. Conflicts which affect policy objectives will not disappear once these objectives have been determined. Rather such conflicts are likely to be constantly addressed and readdressed through particular cases and in individual decisions. Those involved in implementation are likely to be faced with judgements which derive from broader conflicts. They are involved in a constant resolution of such conflicts at a practical level.

The significance of policy conflicts which characterise housing is most apparent when implications for the nature of the policy process are considered. The most widely referred-to models of the policy process are based on ideas of negotiating consensus. Barrett and Fudge (1981) refer to a group of writers who 'see bargaining as a specific form of negotiation which takes place in a context of shared purpose or in recognition of the need to work together' (1981: 22). Alternative conceptualisations present bargaining and negotiation as a struggle for control of self-determination rather than as a means of resolving conflict. But what relevance do these models have to a policy area characterised by conflicts which are unresolved and remain as shared conflicts rather than being translated into shared objectives? 'Negotiation' in such an environment is likely to be concerned with control or to be collaboration to sustain the impression of clarity of shared objectives. Self-preservation in this environment may require negotiation. Organisations with different objectives and interests will set these aside where it is mutually beneficial to do so.

While it is important to acknowledge conflicts which are at the heart of housing policy and conflicts between and among the major public and private sector institutions operating in housing, any more particular account of the operation of policy requires some distinctions to be drawn between different relationships and different policies. It is helpful to distinguish between policies primarily concerned with production and those concerned with consumption. Apart from any theoretical or economic distinction, housing policies in these areas involve very different clients and outputs. Production policies involve relatively uncomplicated quantitative targets and outputs and the most important relationships are between the customer and contractor – between different corporate bodies involved in a financial or commercial relationship. Potential users of dwellings are rarely involved in key decisions. Consumption policies may differ in significant ways. Objectives in rationing are more complex, including explicit consideration of social objectives – of who benefits and who loses. Measures of performance on policy targets are not all easily quantifiable but involve notions of equity and standards of service. Finally, the most important relationship is between supplier and service-user – the service-user being an individual or household client often in a dependent situation. The relationship is governed not by financial and commercial factors but by political priorities affecting the legitimacy and priority of claims and involving notions not only of efficiency and economy but also of need, merit and fairness. An ideological element is present in establishing a relationship which retains the client's confidence in the fairness of the system and the prospect of ultimate benefit.

The other dimension of policy involves organisational responsibility. Thus, for example, central government's only normal involvement in policy implementation is through other organisations – local authorities, new town development corporations, the Housing Corporation, building societies and so on. Local authorities or housing associations operate in a more mixed way. In some cases local authorities operate directly through parts of their own organisation (direct labour departments, technical services, lettings staff, and so on.). In other cases they will buy in external services on a contract basis (consultant architects, construction firms, estate agents, contract cleaners). In a further set of cases local authorities seek to achieve their policy objectives by mobilising or orchestrating the activities of other agencies. This latter role is referred to variously as an enabling or strategic role. In each of these three types of relationships the policy–action process is influenced by different factors. In the first case it is affected by intraorganisational bargaining and conflict. The housing department may have to cope and negotiate with other local authority departments which it cannot coerce. The nature of corporate management, relationships between chief officers, relationships with chief executive and treasurer and the roles played by councillors, committee chairmen and council leaders are all likely to affect how far 'housing' policy is modified through compromises and trading. In some (few) cases the political weight behind housing policy may enable a command or coercive style of negotiation. In other cases a bargaining process may involve deferring to other departments over design, layout or details of schemes.

In what is referred to above as contract relationships, many intraorganisational issues may remain. Before entering into negotiation with autonomous organisations, different interests within the local authority will be involved in a process of negotiation to arrive at agreement over what, as contractor, the local authority is seeking to buy. The negotiation between contractor and customer is then one which has a financial basis and compromises and trade-offs reflecting the different interests of contractor and customer are made by both parties.

In the third – enabling or devolved – relationship referred to above, organisational arrangements have an additional element. While a financial relationship may be involved, the local authority is seeking more than is acknowledged through payment. It is often seeking to persuade or enable autonomous organisations to direct their own resources in ways they otherwise would not. Thus, for example, local authorities may seek through loans and grants to persuade housing associations to put organisational and financial resources into particular areas; may seek through policy, verbal and legal guarantees to persuade building societies to lend 'down-market'; or may seek through disposals of land, package and partnership arrangements to persuade private builders to undertake starter homes or build-for-sale projects using their own capital and without drawing on the local authority to finance the project. The relationship here is one which involves trade-offs, but where the compromise may be greater on the part of the local authority which is the dependant in the relationship.

The management of housing

This chapter focuses on these issues in relation to the management of housing consumption. One of the reasons for focusing on this is that housing management has become a key area in policy debate. A caricature of much of this debate would be that housing management is an activity exclusive to the social rented housing sector and that there is a crisis in housing management in the local authority sector. This chapter is concerned with offering a broad consideration of these issues, drawing on recent evidence and concluding with some comments on the implications of this for the discussion of housing policy and practice.

At the outset it is important to clarify what is meant by the management of housing, and who carries it out. The clearest distinction in this context is the one that has already been made between production and consumption. Once the process of development and housing construction is completed there are a series of basic activities which are carried out to arrange and organise the use and exchange of those dwellings. It is these activities which are referred to here as the management of housing. In brief they involve processes which pass the dwelling into use by a household, which determine and secure payment for that use, which maintain and repair the dwelling, which determine the various other aspects of the environment within which the dwelling is used (such as rights, conditions and quality of a range of services associated with use of the dwelling and secured by payment for use) and which determine exchanges of dwellings or terminate their use. A distinction may also usefully be made between day-to-day or street-level management and longer-term strategic management.

These basic activities occur in all dwellings and tenures. Households which have owned dwellings for generations may not be involved in all of these processes but organise some of them. In this case the basic activities are the responsibility of the individual household and it may be possible to refer to self-provisioning or self-management. In the more general case with tenants or home owners there are formal relationships with other organisations whose activities and decisions affect the use of the home and autonomy within it. If the basic activities are involved generally is it appropriate to use the term 'management' for them? This term describes a process through which resources are converted into a system designed to achieve certain organisational goals. Management embraces planning, organising, controlling and implementing processes to achieve these goals. While the picture which the term 'management' conjures up is one of managers or bureaucrats operating in complex organisations, management equally operates in mutual organisations, families or households. How individuals set about achieving objectives in relation to housing involves management, albeit of a different scale and type, in just the same way as when a large bureaucracy sets about achieving objectives in relation to housing.

In this sense home owners manage their housing. They are involved in decisions about the basic activities outlined above. One perception would be that home owners have control and autonomy and manage their homes to achieve their own shorter-term and strategic objectives, while tenants are managed by others in the context of the short-term and the strategic interests and objectives of their landlords. In reality the picture is less polarised between tenures, and variations in autonomy, power and control exist in each. In the case of tenants, ownership rests with a landlord. However the landlord is constrained by statute. Tenants have legal rights, although these may not be so easy to enforce. In addition, custom and practice may mean that landlords seek support or approval from tenants and exercise their landlord role in a way which is responsive and accountable to tenants. A continuum is easily constructed from the worst types of exploitative and violent private landlordism through participative management approaches to forms of management cooperative or community leasehold. The ends of this continuum have little in common.

In a similar way the image of home owners as autonomous, independent managers of housing with control over their environment obscures reality. Ownership status is of importance but is rarely absolute. Where owners have an outstanding mortgage, the mortgagor has important rights in relation to the property. These can relate to use and mortgage deeds have traditionally contained clauses relating to subletting. More importantly, loss of autonomy relates to failure to meet mortgage payments. The possibility and practice of repossession are demonstrations of the limits on the autonomy of home owners. In this situation the mortgagor–mortgagee relationship has considerable similarities with that of landlord and tenant. The same is true for home owners of leasehold property or those owning mobile homes. In the latter case the site owner has considerable powers to change sites and fees charged for plots. A significant number of home owners have bought leases and a landlord retains responsibilities for certain services, repairs and maintenance. Under the new legislative arrangements introduced in 1993 for leasehold enfranchisement, these home owners may join together to take over these functions but even then they will be provided in common. In any event home owners are dependent on services provided by those managing blocks of flats and may have limited control over management. A similar situation may apply where warden and related services are provided in sheltered housing built for sale. In both of these cases there can also be limited control over the charges that are levied. The homeowner is subject to this management rather than being the sole manager. Again, it is more accurate to talk of a continuum of management arrangements among home owners. This would have, at the one end, dependent and potentially exploitative relationships and, at the other, arrangements in which the homeowner has considerable autonomy as manager.

Even in the latter category and even where owners remain in houses which they own outright, there is an active management task in relation to repairs and maintenance. Managing this task may involve contractual arrangements with builders or mortgage arrangements to fund the activity. The demand for support and assistance in carrying out this aspect of management is evident in the use made of agency services provided by local authorities and voluntary organisations. Such services are particularly directed at and used by low-income households and older people (Leather *et al.*, 1985). In one of the few attempts to examine systematically how home owners manage their homes, Malpass, Garnett and Mackintosh (1987) interviewed low-income home owners in inner-city Bristol. The high cost of maintenance and refurbishment was identified as the main disadvantage of home ownership and lack of savings and low incomes appeared to be the major factors inhibiting maintenance work. Shortage of funds also helped to explain why 84 per cent of owners had not commissioned an independent structural survey before buying their house, despite the risks involved in an area of older housing subject to subsidence. While other work has referred to finance in this context, this Bristol study refers to other resources affecting the management of maintenance and refurbishment. These include time, knowledge, skills, contacts, enthusiasm, confidence and resilience. Whether and how maintenance work was carried out was affected by all of these factors.

All of these comments suggest the need to examine how the management of housing is carried out in practice, rather than to make assumptions based on tenure labels. The point applies with even more force where tenure forms are more clearly mixed, as with shared ownership or rental purchase schemes and where the provision of caretaking, warden or other services is involved. In the expanding sheltered housing for sale sector charges and terms related to warden and other services may cut across the apparent security and autonomy associated with home ownership.

Home owners who are leaseholders in blocks of flats can be dependent on a landlord or landlord's agent for the provision of a range of services. As previously rented mansion blocks and, more recently, council-owned flats have been sold to home owners so the very different position of leasehold home owners has become apparent. Considerable evidence is available about the management of such blocks of flats. The management problems in these blocks are particularly severe in home owners' views in older, mixed-tenure London blocks owned by property companies or overseas owners and where there have been one or more changes in ownership. New leasehold blocks outside London and owned by residents' companies present fewer problems. Blocks purpose-built for private renting before 1939, subsequently sold and now of mixed tenure, also present problems. The report of the Nugee Committee on *The Management of Privately-Owned Blocks of Flats* (1985) emphasised that living in flats gives rise to problems, and financial and other obligations of a different character from those which accompany living in houses, and these problems are not necessarily solved or even eased by a change in the form of tenure under which the flat is occupied. Some of the dissatisfaction with the management of blocks stemmed from 'the lack of control by those who have to pay for the management on the way their money is spent and some from an insufficient appreciation of the provisions of the present law, which are designed to bring the quality of management in all blocks closer to the highest professional standards'.

The report commented:

The skills needed to manage a block of flats so as to maintain it in a proper condition at economic cost and with sensitivity to the expectations of the tenants must not be under-estimated. It is regrettably apparent that many of the traditional landlords who owned residential property and managed it to the highest standards have withdrawn from active management of such property and in some cases from ownership of it altogether. Furthermore, there are reputable firms of managing agents who have previously undertaken the management of residential property but who are now no longer prepared to do so.

The withdrawal of many reputable managing agents from the field is closely related to their increasing difficulty in satisfying tenants as a body. (paras 6.6 and 6.7)

In some cases, residents in these properties did not know their landlord's name and difficulties in relation to this arose where the properties had changed hands several times in quick succession and where the landlord was based overseas. One of the main areas of complaint by residents against landlords and managing agents concerned excessive delay in carrying out maintenance work or repairs or in responding to requests for action. A related area of complaint concerned excessive delays in responding to reasonable requests for information. This was a frequently made complaint against managing agents. Leases and service charge agreements did not always provide a clear and positive basis for action. How these blocks were managed is affected by the nature of managing agents and landlords. These agents and landlords, as in the case of private landlords, have different orientations and characteristics which determine how they implement their housing management.

The management of leasehold properties has been the subject of later research. A study published in 1991 (Thomas *et al.*, 1991) was based on interviews with owners and tenants in leasehold flats. This indicated that leaseholders (whether home owners or renters) rarely had a full understanding of the concept of leasehold and its implications; that leases

were written in a way which gave rise to difficulties with interpretation and implementation both raising leaseholders' expectations and allowing unscrupulous managing agents and landlords to evade their duties; that leaseholders found it difficult to ascertain their rights where they wished to take action against the managing agent or landlord; that taking legal action to solve problems was not always appropriate; and that some disputes over leasehold management occur because the property management profession practices without formal guidelines or controls.

The problems faced by home owners in relation to management of leasehold properties have been an important influence on the development of leasehold enfranchisement. The Leasehold Reform, Housing and Urban Development Act 1993 conferred new rights on certain leaseholders related to collective acquisition of the freehold of the premises they live in.

Managing agents and private owners of mixed-tenure mansion blocks are clearly managers of home owners. Other agencies manage other aspects of home ownership. The exchange professionals – solicitors, estate agencies, building societies and others – are deeply involved when home owners buy and sell property. They act as gatekeepers and play a major role in search and information activity. One striking role for management of home ownership arises where home owners fall into arrears with mortgage repayments. The way that creditors manage arrears is then an important aspect of housing management. Some detailed accounts of policy implementation exist for building societies (Ford, 1988a; 1988b). The explanations which emerge from this research come remarkably close to those put forward to account for the way that social landlords implement their housing management roles.

The focus of attention in both home ownership and the private rented sector has tended to be on access and ownership rather than on management. The view that management just happens or that variations in management are not important aspects of these tenures does not stand up, however. Some other illustrations related to this are appropriate. Accounts of the management of housing by private landlords focus in particular on decisions relating to rent and to investment and disinvestment. While decisions over these matters have been subject to a wide range of legislation, landlords have retained considerable room for manoeuvre and operate in very different ways. They may operate on the edge of or outside the law. Harassment and illegal eviction to gain vacant possession of properties either in order to relet at higher rent levels or in order to sell are well documented (Milner Holland Report, 1965; Francis, 1971). More recently it also became clear that a high proportion of lettings by private landlords have been made outside the Rent Acts (GLC, 1984). Landlords also make use of various devices to create licences or holiday lettings in order to avoid or evade the more stringent regulation of other lettings. How landlords respond to regulation will reflect a number of aspects. Initially, it is important to acknowledge that public regulation of the sector will vary. The operation of regulations relating to rent restriction, multiple occupation, house condition and other environmental health matters and to harassment and eviction will reflect the policies, resources and practices of those responsible for administering such regulations.

Some of the variation in the way private landlords manage their properties in order to achieve their objectives is a response to forms of public control or regulation. However in this, and in their general behaviour, all private landlords do not behave in the same way. Landlords have different resources, characteristics and orientations which influence their objectives and responses to constraints and opportunities. One recent study of private landlords in Britain distinguishes between six types of landlords of residential property: traditional landlords, employer landlords, informal landlords, investor landlords, commercial landlords and financial landlords (Allen and McDowell, 1989). These types have different orientations to the rented housing market. For example, for traditional landlords the activity of letting property is not a straightforward commercial activity, but is modified by a service ideology. The potential economic return is only one element in decisions. Employer landlords who are concerned especially to provide accommodation for employees (perhaps those working outside the normal working day, say in hotels) are not motivated by rental income yield. Indeed higher rental yields can only be achieved by increasing wages. In contrast to these groups, investor landlords with long-term or inherited property ownership seek a rate of return from letting property, while commercial landlords treat housing as a commodity and are involved in repeated buying and selling to realise capital – making money from letting property is a secondary, incidental and short-time activity.

Each type of private landlord has a particular orientation to the market and so a propensity to act in a particular way, depending on how they evaluate their property holdings, their sources of finance, their assessment of future gains and their knowledge and awareness of the political and social climate. Their actions also depend on national economic, demographic and housing policy factors. Landlords have different reactions to vacancies in their properties – whether they sell the property, refurbish or relet, who they let to, at what rent and on what legal basis.

The social rented sector: initial perspectives

There is a substantial literature on housing management in the social rented sector in Britain. Much of this refers to the work of early housing reformers, and especially Octavia Hill, in establishing basic principles of housing management. In practice there have been two differing and at times conflicting views about how the functions should be organised. The approach associated with the Octavia Hill tradition has involved managing collective housing provision through individual casework and small-scale management units. This social approach dates from the 1860s and 1870s when Octavia Hill pioneered the management of social housing provision by measuring the worthiness of individual tenants to various grades of tenancies. This tradition was perhaps continued during the growth of municipal housing in the 1930s when the Women Housing Estate Managers tried to bring some of the notions of modern social work into their activities. Thus there has developed a view which has seen housing management in terms of dealing with individuals and family units. More recently those belonging to this tradition have supported tenant management and/or involvement, for example through the Department of the Environment's Priority Estates Project. This has concentrated on directing resources to problem estates, consulting tenants, securing cooperation between various agencies, and carefully monitoring the results. A development of this view can be seen in the efforts that have begun to measure the views and aspirations of tenants and in the trend towards decentralisation of housing management in many local authorities during the 1980s.

The other tradition in housing management – the 'contractual approach' – can perhaps be linked to the growth of municipal housing in the 1920s. Here the emphasis has been on bureaucratic distance and on the application of fixed and ascertainable rules. One of the fullest guides to practice of this sort was set out in 1981 by the Housing Research Group of the City University (Legg *et al.*, 1981). After looking at procedures and outcomes in local authority housing departments, that research team put forward a number of proposals which included better information provision, and target and performance indicators for a number of housing functions. Much recent discussion about housing management has been in terms of the effort to set up clear and easily ascertainable rules and criteria for performance, such as the length of letting intervals, the level of rent arrears compared with the size of rent rolls, and rates of filling housing voids.

The Audit Commission's study of housing in 1984/5 referred to 97 per cent of local authorities in England and Wales. It concluded:

> Very few authorities operate in exactly the same way. Some have a highly centralised housing department; others are almost entirely decentralised. Some have all the housing functions under the direct control of a chief housing officer; others operate with the financial aspects outside the housing department, under the treasurer, yet others have no separate housing organisation at all, typically with the treasurer in control of the management of all council housing. (Audit Commission, 1986: 14)

The study identified 12 small housing authorities with no separate housing department (and an average stock of less than 4000). In 108 authorities (average stock below 8000) the treasurer was responsible at least for rent collection, rent accounting, rent arrears recovery and housing benefit. Of the 129 authorities with more than 10 000 dwellings, 65 per cent had some form of area-based management (on average 7200 dwellings per area).

The Audit Commission's view (1986: 15) was that 'a unified housing function is much to be preferred'. It is less confusing for tenants and involves clear managerial responsibility and accountancy. However consolidated, that management would only make sense if the quality and training of staff were appropriate and the Commission expressed concern about levels of professional knowledge and management skills.

The wide differences in the ways the housing service is organised and housing departments are structured are illustrated in other ways. The Audit Commission's study of rent collection (1984) suggested that seven London boroughs had adopted decentralised area-based organisation. In the metropolitan districts the pattern was reversed, with 30 decentralised and seven centralised. The 30 largest shire districts were more evenly split between centralised and decentralised. This pattern should be considered in the light of trends towards decentralisation. Separating responsibility for different functions (lettings, maintenance, rent accounting, for example) is not regarded as an effective or efficient way of organising the housing service. Various different groups were urging the merits of decentralisation – with various different objectives. Among these objectives are improvement of service, accountability, distribution of services and raising political awareness. Inevitably where decentralisation has proceeded different considerations have determined the emerging pattern. Whether the housing service has been decentralised on its own or as part of a more general decentralisation of services, physical considerations (such as size of area, definition of neighbourhood boundaries, location, design and access of offices), organisational considerations (range of services, role of other agencies, role of neighbourhood officer, relationship to chief executive and so on) and issues of relative power of centre and locality are involved.

Evidence on the organisation of housing management in England and Wales enables some comparison between local authorities and housing associations. Local authorities have statutory duties, for example, in relation to homelessness and housing benefit administration. Housing associations are not required to undertake these. Local authorities responding to a national survey carried out in 1987 indicated that they were responsible on average for 32 functions, while housing associations named 27 (Centre for Housing Research, 1989). Housing associations usually had the full range of their management tasks under their direct control. However this does not mean that they were devoid of problems of divided responsibility. In local authorities a number of tasks were commonly carried out in departments other than housing. This was especially the case in smaller authorities. Of the 135 authorities responding to the national postal survey in England, housing benefit payments to private sector tenants were the responsibility of a department other than housing in 67 per cent. The equivalent figures for other functions most commonly carried out by other departments were as follows: carrying out repairs, 66 per cent; computer services, 59 per cent; housing benefit payments to council tenants, 55 per cent; performance review, 44 per cent; rent accounting, 40 per cent; rent collection, 31 per cent; repair administration, 29 per cent; sales to sitting tenants, 28 per cent.

The organisation of housing management differed substantially between local authorities and housing associations and within each type of organisation. Size of stock, geographical coverage, numbers of staff, staff skills, training and motivation differed considerably. Housing associations tended to be smaller, with higher levels of cost and staffing per unit. About one-third of local authorities operated with area offices and reduced the scale of operation in this way. A few local authorities of all sizes (12 per cent of the total sample) had what they defined as neighbourhood offices below area office level. The average number of staff in such offices was three and the average number of dwellings managed about 1000. This was twice the average number of dwellings covered by housing association area offices. The most likely functions to be decentralised by local authorities to a more local level were rent collection, rent arrears recovery, arrears prevention, repairs reporting, pre-inspection of repairs, post-inspection of repairs and estate management. The large local authorities were far more likely than the small authorities to decentralise functions.

The functions most likely to be completely centralised were rent account-ing, housing benefit administration, homelessness administration, allocation policy, making up the capital programme, house sales and back-up functions such as computing, training, research and performance review. Those least likely to be fully decentralised were rent collection and repairs collection, but these were still fully centralised in more than half the authorities.

The reasons for adopting decentralised structures and the form and effect of decentralisation vary considerably, and relate to particular histories and geographies. The general characteristics of housing organisations presented for England in 1989 are reproduced in Table 11.1. The considerable differences in the attributes of housing organisations are emphasised in this summary. However the detailed evidence in studies carried out in England and Wales emphasises variation and change. The evidence cautions against assuming that particular categories or organisations will necessarily carry out functions or perform in a particular way. The widely held view that smaller landlords are more efficient and effective managers is not disproved by these data. However, where smaller landlords operate in areas of high demand with good-quality housing, they cannot be easily compared with landlords operating in very different environments and with different resources. It is also clear that large landlords can, and do, achieve high standards of performance. Furthermore, larger landlords have a capacity to respond more effectively to certain problems, including homelessness.

In discussing the factors which influence policy implementation in differ-ent housing organisations it is also important to refer to different systems of accountability. One of the most significant differences between local autho-rities and housing associations is in their accountability to committees of elected councillors and to appointed management committees respectively. While the former arrangement conforms with notions of formal democracy, some criticisms are voiced in terms of undue 'political interference'. While there are undoubtedly examples of such interference, say, to give an advantage to particular individuals in the allocation of housing, this is evidence of bad practice rather than an inevitable consequence of the form of accountability. There are those who argue that the less clear and certainly less democratic systems that operate in housing associations are to be preferred to the ultimate control of housing by elected members. One glaring

Table 11.1 *Summary of organisational characteristics*

Characteristic	Metropolitan councils	District councils	National/ regional housing associations	Local housing associations
Coverage of functions	Comprehensive	Fragmented	Comprehensive	Comprehensive
Scale of estate management	Large	Medium	Small	Small
Job satisfaction of staff	Average	Average	High	Average
Staff morale	Average	Average	Low	High
Proportion of qualified staff	Many	Few	Many	Few
Management control of performance	Little	Little	Extensive	Little
Extent of tenant participation	High	Low	High	Low
Perceptions of tenants' views	More positive view of service than tenants	Accurate perception of tenants' views	More critical view of service than tenants	Accurate perception of tenants' views
Housing management costs	Average	Low	Average	High

Source: Adapted from Centre for Housing Research (1989: 30).

contrast lies in the fact that management committees of housing associations often have little or no contact whatever with tenants themselves.

Organisations are not static. Current policies for housing associations involve a faster rate of growth, a more robust and commercial attitude to attract private finance for development, and a different pattern of monitoring and supervision. These pressures change organisations, their practices and policy implementation. For Wales it has been argued that the differences between housing associations and local authorities in terms of management procedures or organisational forms can be attributed less to any conscious policy or management style than to size and age (Clinton *et al.*, 1989). Housing associations originally set up to cover special needs but beginning to take on a generalist role have to confront new tasks of a sort which in the past have only been carried out by local authorities. They do not find that they can deal with them in a way that is entirely different from local authorities, and in any case they nearly always have to rely on the same fund of experience, with managers drawing on what they had learned while working in local authorities.

It is not possible to read off from organisational characteristics how services are managed and implemented. Superficially similar organisational arrangements may be implementing different policies and working to different formal rules and priorities. Even where this source of variation is not substantial, they are likely to be operating in a different context with different housing stocks and financial and other resources and dealing with tenants and applicants with different characteristics and needs. They are likely to be experiencing the effects and tensions of change in different ways. Finally, the practices which evolve in implementing policies will reflect all of these pressures and ways of coping with them. Which department a service is organised in, whether management is carried out in a unified or fragmented department, where there is some local or neighbourhood office structure, will all have an effect on practices which emerge. Interdepartmental rivalries, confusion over responsibilities and conflicting or competing demands will all affect implementation, but how they affect it will vary and be influenced by other factors. In local authorities, declining stock and investment programmes have an impact on both organisation and practice. In housing associations, pressures of growth and change may be equally severe.

Following the legislation of 1988 and the expanded role of housing associations, these organisations have undergone significant changes. In order to raise funds on the private market the asset base of societies has also been important and some amalgamations of societies have occurred in order to develop a stronger base and take advantage of private sector borrowing. Under the new financial arrangements, smaller associations which wish to develop are operating at a disadvantage on a number of fronts and whether they carry out new development or turn to development agreements with other, larger, associations remains to be seen (Randolph, 1993). In general, the pressures for change in housing associations since 1988 are likely to lead towards a more homogeneous housing association sector relying on large-scale production to the detriment of small-scale, one-off and specialist development (Randolph, 1993). An associated outcome linked also to high rents, less desirable tenancy rights than exist in the local authority sector and the way nominations from local authorities affect the profile of tenants is leading to a concentration of poorer people in the sector. The long-term outcome of these developments may mean that housing associations in the future will be regarded as much less effective landlords, will be faced with more problems, and will bear a less favourable comparison with other landlords than has been shown in the past.

Any consideration of the implementation of housing management cannot assume that organisational arrangements any more than formal policy will determine implementation. There is a need to look in more detail at the way implementation is carried out. The appropriate level for analysis is in relation to specific functions. In what follows, general processes are illustrated through discussion of the operation of allocation policies in local authority housing.

Implementing allocation policies

The implementation of housing management policies by local authorities and housing associations is, then, influenced by a wide range of factors. Detailed accounts of how different functions are performed become accounts of coping with a range of often conflicting pressures. Perhaps the clearest accounts of such pressures relate to those affecting housing allocation policies in the local authority sector. A variety of research evidence has shown how households with low incomes or low bargaining power tend to be housed in the least popular dwellings in the council sector. The Cullingworth Report (1969) commented that

> the underlying philosophy seemed to be that council tenancies were to be given only to those who 'deserved' them, and that the 'most deserving' should get the best houses. Thus, unmarried mothers, cohabitees, 'dirty' families and 'transients' tended to be grouped together as 'undesirables'. Moral rectitude, social conformity, clean living and a 'clean' rent book on occasion seemed to be essential qualifications for eligibility – at least for new houses.

Subsequent research evidence has shown that this pattern survives even where the intention of policy is to avoid discrimination. As has been shown in earlier chapters, local housing authorities have built up considerable stocks of dwellings to rent. These properties vary in terms of age, size, design, location, standards and desirability. The number of these properties available for letting at any time will be determined by the number of new (newly built or acquired) lettings and vacancies occurring in the existing stock (relets). The normal situation facing local authorities is for demand for its properties to exceed supply. A large number of households apply and wait for accommodation. In a market situation, price rises would result from excess demand and rationing by price would occur. Price differentials would also develop between different parts of the council housing stock. The least popular dwellings would be cheaper to rent. In local authority housing, rationing according to price is not regarded as appropriate and other criteria apply. The local authority is involved in rationing and seeks to establish criteria and processes which enable it to cope with demand and also sustain belief that the system operates fairly. For a considerable period, debate in this area has focused on who gets council housing and therefore on residential and other exclusions. However, allocation and transfer policies also determine who gets what housing – who gets the most desirable and the least desirable dwellings. In this context, the impact of the implementation of allocations and not just of formal rules affecting eligibility is of greater interest.

Whereas allocation policy (as distinct from action) is concerned with formal rules and establishing a framework for the operation of discretion (point schemes, priorities and so on), it is rarely concerned with matching properties and households. Matching, while it operates within the policy limits and other constraints, is an area where the individual allocating officer translates personal and organisational perceptions into policy action. In some cases, decisions about who should get the worst houses are directly influenced by policies towards 'unsatisfactory tenants' or 'problem families'. However there are other factors in the implementation of allocation policies which affect this issue. In analysing policy action in this area, debate has resolved around the relative importance of officer discretion and of structural factors affecting the supply of housing and administrative action. Earlier work, for example, focused on the role of housing visitors and emphasised their role in 'grading' applicants for council housing (Damer and Madigan, 1974).

The role of housing visitors and 'grading' has been seen by some researchers to explain why the worst council housing tends to be allocated to low-income, black, single-parent and large families. Housing visitors' cultural and social perceptions lead these households to be classified as only suitable for poor property and, consequently, it is only such property which will be allocated to them. The role of the housing visitor is perhaps the most thoroughly discussed part of the implementation process in housing allocations. But interpretation of the importance of the role of the housing visitor illustrates the tendency for analysis of implementation processes to focus on actors involved rather than on the whole process and to attribute a degree of influence or autonomy which is deduced from the outcome of the policy rather than detailed analysis of the policy–action process.

Other contributions have attempted to identify other influences on matching and allocation, and to counter the view that local housing officials operate as independent or at least semi-autonomous managers, establishing and operating procedures such as 'grading' which derive from personal and professional values and an ideology built around notions of the deserving and undeserving poor and good and bad tenants.

The research literature has increasingly complemented reference to administrative and professional discretion such as 'grading' with references to shortages and supply factors which heavily constrain allocation. The emphasis on shortage links with issues of production as well as consumption, and widens the consideration away from housing management or housing itself and towards broader economic and political processes which determine levels of housing investment, the organisation of housing and patterns of need and demand.

While 'grading' in certain circumstances is an explicit process bound to lead to allocation of certain perceived types of household to certain categories of dwelling, this can only be the most important element where housing allocators have some choice and flexibility in matching supply and demand on a day-to-day basis. English (1979), referring to his research in Clydeside, stressed bargaining power and the ability to wait for more popular accommodation, either through urgency of need or rules governing the number of offers made, rather than other factors, and concluded: 'the allocation system was not responsible for what was happening, but merely passively reflected differential demand' (1979: 115).

More recent research in Nottingham, Hackney and Tower Hamlets (Simpson, 1981; Phillips, 1985; CRE, 1984) similarly emphasises problems of 'matching' in situations of high demand, limited supply and variation in popularity of properties. The different bargaining power of clearance or other decant cases and social-need priorities, the homeless, transfer applicants and general waiting-list applicants means that households moving through different routes obtain different types of dwelling irrespective of other characteristics. In addition, the way that discretion is exercised at various points affects patterns of allocation.

The evidence shows the way in which policies which are intended to be equitable tend to channel different groups of households towards different parts of the council stock. Accounts of this process start with discussions of eligibility for council housing. For those not excluded on residential, tenure, household structure or other grounds, practice and procedures relating to grading of properties, offers and refusals, areas of choice and the fit which is considered appropriate between dwelling and household size determine which queue or queues are long and move slowly. Ability to wait in these queues is likely to differ. Applicants' ability to delay (or bargaining power) may be limited because they are in an application category which has restrictions on refusals (this is common for those who are homeless) or their existing circumstances make them unwilling or unable to wait. Those with least bargaining power tend to be in the queues for the least desirable property and tend to be the least able to wait for better properties, even in such a queue. They will tend to join the fastest-moving queues which have fewer of those with more points or priority ahead of them in the queue. In this way, rather than one queue or waiting-list operating, there are separate queues or markets for particular parts of the stock. Those with more bargaining power can compete for better housing and those with less bargaining power compete in the lowest-demand sectors. Queues move at different rates and queues for the most desirable and shortest-supply accommodation are slowest to progress. Those desperate for rapid rehousing have little chance of obtaining this unless they join the fastest queues and accept offers of properties from these.

The way in which discretion is exercised does not lead households with similar needs to be treated with the degree of equity which the formal presentation of policy generally implies. The evidence of a succession of studies suggests that discrimination on racial and other grounds not 'intended' in policy is widespread. The way that needs and preferences are recorded, the availability of information, language barriers, prejudgements and stereotyping of applicants, the process of offering and viewing properties and a variety of working assumptions, goals and attitudes affect the outcomes of policy. These factors, while operating within and affected by supply-and-demand constraints, cannot be explained away by such constraints and are the products of other social and economic processes.

In the mid-1980s, the effects of very low rates of new building by councils and an accumulating loss of relets associated with council house sales seriously affected the supply of dwellings available for letting in some areas. At the same time, economic, social and housing market changes led to a general increase in homelessness and sustained the demand for council housing. The implementation of allocation policies changed significantly as a result of these factors, irrespective of any changes in allocation policy as such. Nevertheless local authorities coped with the changing circumstances in different ways. One emerging feature in metropolitan areas was the increasing use of bed and breakfast hotels to provide 'temporary' (but often of lengthy duration) accommodation for homeless households. Certain categories of homeless households have statutory rights under homeless persons legislation (introduced in 1977, consolidated in the Housing Act 1985 and amended by the Housing Act 1996). This legislation always left substantial room for different local interpretations and rates of acceptance. When accepted, homeless persons were also treated in widely different ways and often in a less favourable way than other households seeking housing. It has been common practice to deny homeless households more than one offer of accommodation. A refusal of accommodation can be regarded as evidence of intentional homelessness and as removing any obligation on the council to provide housing. The legislation makes such practices possible, and leaves the homeless with very little power to 'bargain' for better housing as well as little capacity to wait. The likelihood of their being offered and accepting properties which those with more bargaining power and capacity to wait have rejected is reflected in evidence about where the homeless are housed. While the likelihood of such outcomes is affected by the context of supply and demand, it is also affected by policy (and especially attempts to monitor and counter such tendencies) and by the practice of those involved in implementing policy. Under the legislation of 1996 the duty placed on local authorities to provide permanent accommodation for those accepted as homeless and in priority categories was removed and the scope for different treatment was increased.

Where homeless households include greater proportions of, for example, black people or of women, these processes may form only part of a pattern of discrimination. The evidence on allocation processes indicates that certain groups are likely not only to be disadvantaged by processes applied to all households, but to be affected by specific discrimination. Various studies of race and allocations have consistently drawn attention to this (Phillips, 1985).

The importance of policy implementation and practice rather than formal housing policies and expressions of preference is demonstrated by a study of Birmingham's allocations policy in the late 1970s (Henderson and Karn, 1987). In Birmingham the ideal of equal treatment of all races was not achieved in allocations in a number of respects. In spite of the relaxation of residential qualifications which had previously been the greatest hindrance to households from minority ethnic groups, it remained more difficult for Asians and West Indians to qualify for housing. This was mainly because of less favourable treatment of owner-occupiers, unmarried cohabiting couples and joint families. In addition, Asians and West Indians appear to have had to accumulate more points to be allocated to older housing and (for West Indians) to flats, and to have had their area preferences met less often than white households. The transfer system exacerbated rather than moderated the unequal pattern of initial allocations. The explanation for these patterns may have related to unwillingness to offer a wide range of choice of estates (in the expectation that offers of housing would be refused), to the disproportionate allocation of flats to one-parent families and to the nature of interviews with applicants.

Henderson and Karn concluded from this research that

> it was the attitude of whites towards living in the inner city and older parts of the middle-ring which was by far the most powerful element in producing the growing segregation of West Indians and Asians in those areas. The strong preference of whites for the suburbs produced a tendency for inner city vacancies to be offered to West Indians or Asians because housing officers expected white applicants to reject such property. This means that when Asians and West Indians have moved into council houses they have largely moved out of the middle ring and towards the inner city estates, whether or not their preferences would have predicted such a move. (1987: 273)

This study argued that underlying processes and causes of discrimination are likely to be repeated in a similar or modified form in all housing authorities in Britain. This is because they are not a product merely of formal allocation policies. Nor are they primarily a consequence of a housing department having in its employ particular racially or socially prejudiced individuals. Rather they are products of the day-to-day working practice of a housing department. Discriminatory practices are a product of the normal structure of allocations within a much wider pattern of competition for scarce resources in society.

Within the Birmingham Housing Department certain features of the system were crucial to discriminatory outcomes. The first was described as a dual allocation system. The duality consisted of the different interests and modes of operation of officers responsible for allocation control on the one hand and for management of the stock in area offices on the other. Because of Birmingham's size the duality of interest was reflected in identifiable practices by different officers. In a smaller authority a single officer may well perform both functions and find him/herself torn between two conflicting sets of interests.

The structure of the allocation system in Birmingham consisted of two sets of interrelated processes (including both formal policies and informal working practices). These formed a complex unity essential for the operation of the system. The process of allocation of properties consisted of filling vacant properties. In doing this it was important for allocation controllers to make offers which would lead to allocations and so minimise the void rate (the number of properties vacant) and the loss of rent income. Thus the attempt was to match people with properties they were likely to accept and so achieve a quick turnaround of the void and minimise loss of rent income. In order to achieve this it was important to avoid matching properties considered to be undesirable or in poor condition with applicants who were thought likely to be 'choosy' or 'respectable' and unlikely to accept such properties. It was also part of the logic then that those who were 'disreputable' or less choosy or more desperate could be matched with such properties because they would accept them.

Alongside this process the second element of the dual allocation process involved management officers who were concerned to minimise problems on estates. They sought to protect themselves and their colleagues from the conflict and aggression and from the time-consuming duties which they saw as resulting from certain types of tenants or mixes of tenants in the properties for which they were responsible.

As a consequence of this interest, area officers intervened in order to overturn potential offers made by allocation control, in an attempt to check the movement of particular sorts of tenants into and around their 'patch'. Decisions to veto potential offers to particular applicants seemed to affect predominantly those who were seen to be 'disreputable' and therefore as far as officers were concerned were likely to constitute actual or potential 'problem' families. In particular area officers were likely to have a far greater interest than allocation control did in eliminating allocations of 'disreputable' tenants to 'respectable' areas. Allocation control was likely to minimise these because it tended to reserve such areas for the 'choosy', but a number would inevitably slip through. This was partly because allocation control had only limited information on each applicant, partly because officers had to attempt to meet people's area preferences and partly because such a letting was not in itself a problem as far as speed of allocation was concerned. Area officers were also sensitive to offers of housing in 'rough' areas to 'respectable' families because these too could produce management problems, in terms of complaints and requests for transfers. Such offers were, however, less crucial to area officers than to allocation control with its overriding concern about void rates.

So area officers used their power to 'block' allocations and to put in 'bids' for applicants to assert their interests when these ran contrary to the interests of allocation control. The end product of the combination of the two parts of the system was, however, a much more complete matching of the 'respectable' tenant to the 'respectable' estate than either part of the system would have produced on its own. By organising the desperate and the 'disreputable' into the groups that received the least attractive offers, the system managed to classify on social grounds even those applicants about whom there was relatively little information.

All of this involves a process in which categorisation of people and property as 'suitable' is crucial. In practice such categorisation was not based on good information, was highly subjective and related to images of types of applicant and images of estates and streets. These images grow out of the wider society rather than the housing allocation process. Many of the codes and images have their origins in social differences which are reflections of the class structure of society and others have a specifically racial origin. In this stereotyping process working-class people come to be informally categorised as (broadly) 'respectable' or 'disreputable'. Middle-class people are by definition considered 'respectable'.

The superimposition of codes results in the informal designation of people as 'respectable' or 'disreputable' and so the codes became progressively invested with official status as the application progressed through the allocations system. As a result, those codes became a basis on which images and stereotypes were constructed or confirmed and then became important grounds on which applicants were categorised for allocation purposes. Such categorisations were necessary for the allocations system to be able to discriminate between different claims for housing. The structure of the allocations system was such that it depended on the penetration of positive and negative codes and stereotypes which could be mobilised to effect 'suitable' housing allocations. What constituted a 'suitable' housing allocation reflected the contradiction of interests between different parts of the dual allocation system. It suggests that policy outcomes reflect a series of implementation actions and the coping strategies and judgements required to complete housing management tasks. Only by changing the context and constraints faced by allocators – say by accepting a higher void rate and the costs associated with it – would the outcomes and the costs of these outcomes be susceptible to change.

This picture of policy implementation in one local authority and in one housing management function applies more generally. The processes involved will exist in other organisations and in relation to other functions. At one level it highlights the need to take action on the supply side of housing to produce more and better housing and upgrade low-demand housing. Variations in quality of housing will remain, however, and review of other conflicting priorities is also crucial. These factors and a clear commitment to equal opportunity policy are essential and changes in staffing and training can only be expected to have an impact in such a context.

In the housing circumstances of the 1990s these general processes are affected by other factors. With little new local authority building, applicants for housing are likely to be offered a relet or a nomination to a housing association. In 1991/2 in England, more than one in five lettings to new tenants by social landlords were by housing associations. These were more likely to be lettings of new dwellings but to involve higher rents and assured tenancies with fewer rights than would apply in a local authority house – including no Right to Buy. In deciding whether to offer or accept such lettings, managers and applicants will include consideration of affordability. Where households are entitled to housing benefit, higher rents present no immediate difficulty (although the longer-term poverty trap problem may prove severe). Thus the channelling of low-income homeless households towards housing association properties is likely to be significant. Households who can wait are often likely to prefer a property with a lower rent and with the Right to Buy and managers are likely to categorise households according to whether they are likely to be able to afford a housing association rent or to accept nomination. High levels of homelessness imply a large number of applicants who are unable or unwilling to wait for a better offer. Within this framework the channelling of households towards different parts of the social rented stock will remain systematic and will continue to reflect aspects of supply and demand, and the interaction of pressures on both applicants and allocators.

Conclusions

Policy–action in housing management is the product of a variety of influences and constraints. Social, historical and investment processes determine the broadest constraints of demand and supply. Constraints which arise from legislation and government regulation, from the clarity or lack of clarity of objectives and from organisational arrangements and culture are all important. It is inappropriate to imply that formal policy-making or setting of objectives is the critical element. Equally the formal organisational arrangements for departmental responsibility, decentralisation or staffing and training arrangements do not determine the way in which policy is translated into action. Other factors are of crucial importance. The urban manager and the managed both cope with an environment which they do not control and both cope in ways which reflect the variety of pressures placed upon them. The practices which emerge may start as coping strategies but become necessary for management and are invested with a different official status.

What actually happens through policy–action is the product of the interaction of these factors and the differential power of those involved. These outcomes in turn begin to frame the perceptions and attitudes of those involved. For example, Byrne (n.d.) and Damer (1974) describe the historical factors leading to prejudiced management and client views of estates. Who estates were built for and initially allocated to forms part of the perception of these estates and reputation is developed and sustained by subsequent actions by applicants and by housing and other officials. These perspectives on urban managers, implementation and policy–action have mainly been illustrated in this chapter in relation to allocation policies. While this discussion demonstrates how difficult it is to change this situation, it is clear that neither organisational nor formal policy changes will deal with the underlying processes. Indeed the same kinds of processes exist in all organisations carrying out housing management. This was most clearly illustrated in relation to building societies' management of mortgage arrears. However the management of housing in other areas and in all tenures involves the same range of factors interacting to determine how policy is implemented.

12

Evaluating Housing Policies

Whatever the explicit or implicit aims of policy, and whatever processes of implementation are involved, the assessment of the outputs of policy are important. In the literature on social policy, evaluations have focused on the distributional impacts of policies on who benefits and who loses and on how these patterns of benefit relate to stated objectives and the language employed to justify policies. Who benefits and who loses as a result of policy not only indicates whether the objectives of the policy concerned are being met. Evaluation of policy also involves consideration of whether there are other unintentional consequences of policy, whether there are wider effects of policy which bring the policy concerned into conflict with other policies and objectives. Furthermore housing policies characteristically involve a multiplicity of objectives. As was argued in Chapter 11, these objectives are often in conflict.

Recent debates about the outputs of housing policy have separately referred to economy, efficiency and effectiveness. This has particularly been used in evaluation of aspects of housing management. The major debates about housing management in recent years have related to the role of local authorities in housing and the problems associated with council housing, especially in large urban areas. The management of council housing has been subject to much closer scrutiny in recent years.

The Audit Commission's analysis (1986) of local authority housing management rested on economy and efficiency measures. Economy measures involve identifying costs and the 'economy' practised is indicated by the price per unit paid for inputs. However landlords who perform well in economy terms by paying less for, say, staff or office space (even in terms related to the size of stock) will not necessarily be operating efficiently or effectively. Assessing efficiency involves measuring outputs as well as inputs. It involves relating costs to measures of service provision. This is likely to provide a more relevant guide to performance for consumers than economy measures do. However measures of efficiency involve measuring outputs which are often complex. In addition to volume of service or output, consumers will be concerned with dimensions of quality. Issues of direction and distribution of service can also be seen as measures of quality too often ignored in simple output measures. The identification of effectiveness involves moving beyond economy and efficiency to embrace these issues of quality of service and to relate to the actual objectives and intentions of policies and concern with wider repercussions and unintended outputs.

The most general evaluations of the effects of local housing policy have concerned who benefits from council housing. Although council housing has been seen as a way of improving the housing conditions of lower-income households in the past, the poorest households have often continued to live in the worst housing in the privately rented sector. The generally accepted view of the interwar period is that, while Exchequer subsidy encouraged local authorities to build, it was not sufficient, in view of attitudes to rate subsidies, to bring down rents to a level where they were within the capacity of those with the lowest incomes (Bowley, 1945). Marian Bowley's conclusion on much of the interwar period was that

> the market for local authority houses was largely confined to a limited range of income groups, that is, in practice, the better-off families. The working-class families who benefited most directly from subsidies were the relatively small group of about half a million families who were among the best-off. (1945: 129–30)

The development in the 1930s and again in the 1950s of active slum clearance policies involved local authorities in housing the poorer as well as more affluent slum-dwellers. Perhaps because of this development, there must be some doubt about how far council tenants' incomes differed from those in the private rented sector. Indeed Schifferes states that 'council tenants were only marginally better off than private sector tenants. A sample of 1939 tenants showed an average wage of about £3 a week, only slightly higher than the national average of £2.65 and skilled working-class trades predominated' (Schifferes, 1976); and Parker (1967) refers to 'the prevalence of low and largely undifferentiated working-class incomes'. In this sense, while council housing may have selected out the 'respectable' working class, this does not imply a wealthy section of the population.

Since 1945, and with the continuation of slum-clearance programmes, the social selectiveness of council housing has continued to change. As the private rented sector has contracted and the most affluent have been attracted into owner-occupation, and as local authorities have increasingly selected tenants on the basis of need, irrespective of rent-paying ability, so the proportion of lower-income households who are council tenants has increased. To this extent (and bearing in mind the variable quality of council housing and evidence referred to in Chapter 11 concerning who gets the worst housing) local authorities have developed a service which has come to be the major provider of housing for working-class and lower-income households. This development, however, raises the question of how far council housing should be available to anyone who prefers to rent, rather than to only a section of that group and to those who are unable to buy. While the clearer social role of council housing conforms to notions of channelling subsidy and housing resources to those in need or to those most vulnerable in the housing market, it also raises concern about stigmatisation and segregation. As council housing begins to cater more clearly for the 'disadvantaged', so disadvantaged households are more clearly identifiable through tenure status and so the reputation of council housing is changed in a way which further speeds the process towards a welfare role. While this may be regarded as a problem in itself, it is undoubtedly exacerbated if there is a decline in quality of accommodation, level of subsidy, terms on which subsidy is obtained (means-tested rather than general assistance), style of management, quality of repair and maintenance services and opportunities for mobility and choice. Under these circumstances the welfare role develops fewer eligibility characteristics with more affinity to a poor law service than to a high-standard social service concerned to redistribute resources. In this context, any general evaluation of council housing would need to address these questions.

While slum clearance policies undoubtedly resulted in a physical improvement in the housing stock, policy evaluation in this area raised a variety of wider issues. Concern about the economic costs, social disruption and the destruction of stable communities was increasingly referred to in connection with clearance policies. While such policies did succeed in improving the physical quality of dwellings, they had other effects. Residents in areas identified for clearance themselves began to oppose policies designed to provide them with modern high-quality properties because of the full impact of the policy (see, for example, Dennis, 1970). Two particular issues arise from this example. First, the impact of policies differs in different localities according to the nature both of dwellings and communities being affected and of dwellings being offered in replacement. Second, the question of *when* to evaluate policy is a crucial one. Communities disorganised and disrupted following slum clearance may subsequently be re-established and the symptoms of disorganisation may decline. A study by Coates and Silburn (1980) in Nottingham reports a follow-up of households rehoused from slum clearance in the early 1970s. In 1976, only a quarter of the sample of original residents were still living in St Ann's. Over 50 per cent had been rehoused in large council estates – mostly in the district they preferred. However one in four had accepted a house in a district that was not their first choice and some households did not feel that their new house or neighbourhood was an improvement. These included the small group of former owner-occupiers, some of the most elderly households, whose dislike stems from problems of adjustment or inappropriate housing. Less predictable, larger families who were still cramped for space had not experienced as great an improvement in their housing conditions as some others. While most households had moved to better housing and most approved of the change, there was a small group who were dissatisfied. In this context, and related to work in London by Young and Willmott (1957) and concern with the effects of clearance on communities, Coates and Silburn emphasise the continuing strength of the extended family in council housing following the redevelopment of St Ann's.

There are a range of considerations which can be introduced into evaluation. The reasons why certain procedures may be adopted and, indeed, why certain interests choose to participate, involve benefits through income, employment or profit from the process. Benefits from housing production accrue variously to landowners, developers, builders, building professionals and providers of finance for building. And it may be argued that housing programmes are most appropriately evaluated in terms of employment generation – if only because the building process is so labour-intensive. In practice, the economic impact of programmes has influenced decisions on them and it would be blinkered to evaluate housing policy only in terms of whose housing opportunities are changed, or of supply changes.

In the remainder of this chapter, examples of evaluation of housing policy are presented. The examples illustrate different aspects of evaluation and different policies used (the sale of council houses, voluntary transfers and housing management).

The sale of council houses

The social impact of the sale of council houses has been the subject of a number of studies in recent years. The earliest studies were carried out in Birmingham and referred to discretionary sales carried out under powers conferred by the Housing Act 1957 (Niner, 1975; Murie, 1975). Subsequent studies have shown a remarkable consistency with the earliest studies in terms of who buys and what properties have been sold. However the changing framework of policy and the evidence from a wider range of local authorities has added considerably to this picture.

In the period 1967–78, some 14000 dwellings were sold in Birmingham. Examination of these sales shows that the properties sold were not a cross-section of all council properties in the city. The effect of council house sales was to change the age structure of the stock. Explanations of this involve a number of factors. The types of property at some stage excluded from sale (especially flats and one-bedroom bungalows for the elderly) were mainly postwar dwellings. More important, property types which proved difficult to sell (particularly flats) were mainly built after the war, while prewar dwellings were predominantly houses with gardens, which proved most easy to sell. Third, the ability to buy was not universal and tenants able and wishing to buy may have been more concentrated in older property. Finally, the financial arrangements for sale, including discount and fixing sale price, were more likely, both because of tenant characteristics and the relationship between construction cost and valuation, to inhibit purchase of more modern (more expensive) dwellings. Thus a policy to extend an even-handed opportunity to buy immediately accumulated important differentials because of the varied nature of the commodity and of consumers.

The age and property-type differences affecting sales are linked to another important dimension of the way the policy of council house sales worked out in practice. This was the tendency for sales to be unevenly spread geographically. Inevitably, different property types built or acquired at different times tend to be located in different areas of the city, reflecting the spatial pattern of growth of public housing, and differential rates of sale result in clear patterns with few sales in inner-city flatted estates and more in outer suburban estates of houses with gardens.

A survey of 193 sitting tenants who bought their council dwellings in Birmingham between 1968 and 1973 gives a picture of which tenants benefited directly from the council's policy of selling dwellings:

> There is a wide variation in the households buying council houses but they are clearly not drawn equally from all tenant groups. Neither the youngest nor the oldest heads of household are fully represented among purchasers. The age groups 30–59 are over-represented among purchasers. At the same time older small households are considerably under-represented among purchasers. Small adult households, large families and larger households are over-represented. Age and family cycle factors are clearly linked and are related to the tendency for purchaser households to have more than one wage earner.
>
> Roughly 50 per cent of households had two or more wage earners and only four per cent had no full-time wage earner – a factor which clearly excluded the aged and may imply that few in relatively insecure jobs or without jobs are council house purchasers. Seven households had more than three persons in full-time work and in one case eight members of the household were in full-time work. Very small and very large households were under-represented among purchasers. Households of between two and four persons account for two-thirds of purchasers but only slightly over one-half of all tenants. Purchasers were also considerably more likely to have dependent children than council tenants in general. (Murie, 1975)

Family cycle factors, however, are not a sufficient explanation of which tenants bought their houses. Purchasers have higher incomes and are more likely to be in non-manual and skilled manual jobs than tenants in general. In addition, it appears that newer tenants are under-represented among purchasers, a large group of whom had moved into their present dwelling through exchange or transfer.

The evidence does not support the contention that Birmingham's sales policy extended owner-occupation principally to groups who could not gain access through the private market. Purchaser households were in general better off than other local authority mortgagors – in addition, purchasers are in most cases willing to forgo other expenditures in order to become owners. What apparently prevents purchasers from becoming owner-occupiers through the private market is an immobility which appears to reflect household and housing situation. In satisfying their housing demands, purchasers have preferred to forgo tenure status for other benefits (Murie, 1975: 126).

Another view of this evidence is that while, in theory, purchasers could have become owner-occupiers through another route, in practice they would not do so unless the council led them into owner-occupation. In that sense the policy did reach a group who otherwise would not have become owner-occupiers. One element in this is the high quality of accommodation these households had use of. To obtain comparable accommodation in the private sector would have required very considerable expenditure. To this extent council house sales did extend an opportunity which otherwise could only have been realised at great expense. The age composition of purchaser households would probably exclude some from receiving mortgages of the necessary size. In some cases, age and income factors would probably prevent purchasers from becoming owners through any other process. This factor is a 'consequence' of the lending policies of local authorities, building societies and other agencies. To this extent some purchasers are excluded. Council house purchase may offer the only possibility of changing tenure and at the same time maintaining housing facilities, and providing the new opportunities associated with owning. It may be argued, however, that a package of housing services of this type is available to few. Rather than extending a choice to a deprived group, council house sales may be seen as having added to the privilege of a highly selected group. The characteristics of purchaser households suggested that a continuation of the policy of council house sales would have had the effect of 'creaming off' a distinct group and reducing the social diversity in council-owned dwellings. Considerations of this type do not provide any 'conclusive' evidence, but their importance cannot be discounted.

As outlined in Chapter 5, the Housing Act 1980 altered the arrangements for the sale of council dwellings. A 'Right to Buy' replaced the discretionary powers operating previously. The Right to Buy at the same time provided higher discounts, a right to a mortgage and a set of common procedures for implementing sales. The ability of local authorities to exclude properties from sale was minimal. Evidence on the purchasers of council houses in the early years of the Right to Buy is available for Birmingham and other areas. The characteristics of council tenants purchasing their housing in Birmingham in 1979/80 did not differ substantially from those buying between 1968 and 1973 or from the national profile of purchasers. The consistency, for example, in age and family cycle position of purchasers suggests that the policy, rather than catering for a pent-up demand, benefits a succession of households as their circumstances change. The higher discounts available to those with longer periods of tenancy appeared to have increased the proportion of elderly purchasers, but the largest group of purchasers continued to be in the middle stage of the family life cycle. One of the implications of 'recruitment' of new purchasers as family cycle and family circumstances change is a higher overall level of sales than some commentators predicted. The impact of relets and issues of segregation arising from differential rates of sale by estate or area or property type (flats continued to be much less likely to be sold) become more important. The impact of the policy on non-buyers is also crucially affected by what other developments are taking place and affecting the supply of lettings and opportunities to transfer.

National figures show that flats continued to be very poorly represented among sales (some 4 per cent of sales compared with 30 per cent of the stock) even though the Right to Buy fully extends to them. Only after 1986, with the much higher rates of discount associated with flats, did sales of these dwellings increase but they remained under-represented among sales up to 1993. Sales were particularly popular in semi-detached, three-bedroomed houses. The conclusions from a national survey in England in 1985/6 suggest that buyers under the Right to Buy are remarkably similar to those buying at earlier stages. Thus:

> RTB purchasers were predominantly middle-aged, usually married, often with a grown-up family and including more than one wage earner. Manual skilled workers were over-represented amongst buyers and so, too, were white collar workers. The survey findings further revealed that the middle-aged and large adult households were, as tenants, not only more likely than other tenant households to have an above-average income but they were also more likely to occupy desirable accommodation. Thus, it would appear to be the fortuitous combination of ability to pay with occupancy of an attractive property which has contributed to the over-representation of these household groups amongst buyers. In summary, the survey findings were in broad agreement with those of earlier studies of council house sales concerning the socioeconomic characteristics of buyers. (Kerr, 1989)

The more recent evidence on purchasers of council houses shows a similar pattern. However, comparisons between different localities indicate that the significance and effects of a common policy (with limited scope for variation in implementation) are very different. For example, the costs of purchase vary considerably between authorities; the value of discounts also varies considerably; there is a consistency in terms of age of principal earner, emphasising the life cycle effect; the incomes of council tenants do not vary as substantially as do sale prices and the ratio of purchase price and income varies considerably; in some areas low valuations mean that the cost of buying is below that of renting – a factor which affects reasons for and attitudes to buying. A national policy has important different local effects in terms of who benefits and whose opportunities are damaged. Some of this variation derives from local housing market and policy background and some from the way that the sales policy itself operates.

Any assessment of the social effects of the sale of council houses involves more than the households who bought as sitting tenants. The longer-term effect of sale is to increase the stock of dwellings allocated through market processes and to reduce those allocated through bureaucratic and needs-related processes. The effects of this are more difficult to assess, but the questions can be easily posed: are the dwellings allocated through market processes allocated to households who are similar to those who were previously tenants or who are being allocated to vacant council dwellings through application or transfer procedures? If so, then the loss of relets of vacancies for allocation is unimportant – the same households achieve the same housing through a different route. But if the households are different, the policy clearly redistributes opportunity in favour of those who can buy and to the disadvantage of those who cannot. There is some evidence which enables this to be assessed (Forrest and Murie, 1990b). A comparison of the characteristics of purchasers of former council houses with those of early sitting-tenant purchasers shows that the new purchasers are younger and at an earlier stage in the family cycle. Sitting tenants who purchase their council dwellings tend to be middle-aged, with a fairly large family growing up. Those who buy on resale are younger, with no family or with one or two very young children. The purchasers of former council houses are more directly comparable with first-time buyers generally than with new council tenants and include a high proportion of previous home owners. Many households would not have been allocated dwellings on grounds of need.

There are now data which enable a fuller evaluation of Right to Buy sales which refer to the longer-term and wider impact of council house sales. This evidence is from a national study of over 3000 dwellings which were bought under the Right to Buy and have since changed hands that has been completed for England (Forrest and Murie, 1994). This study also involved tracing some 450 vendors of former council homes to identify where they had moved after leaving their former council home.

The most striking result of this research is that the majority of purchasers of former council homes (51 per cent) were home owners at their previous address. Former council homes represent an important addition to the stock of dwellings available to first-time buyers but more than half of purchasers are moving within the owner-occupied sector – typically from smaller terraced houses or flats. Former council homes as a whole cannot be said to be at the bottom end of the owner-occupied market.

In terms of their occupational backgrounds, those moving into former council homes are not dramatically different from those moving out on resale. In other words, there is not a striking middle-class incursion into areas which were formerly exclusively council-owned and managed. However, this is because RTB purchasers are disproportionately from white-collar and skilled manual backgrounds compared to the council tenant population as a whole. Both RTB purchasers and resale purchasers have very different characteristics from council tenants in general and new tenants in particular. Purchasers of former council homes are to some extent a younger version of those moving out – young couples and small families at an early stage of the family life cycle with heads of household in professional, managerial and skilled manual employment. They are an employed, economically active group of households, often with multiple earners. There is an absence of low-income households, unemployed persons, previously homeless persons and other less advantaged groups.

Higher-income households are more heavily represented among purchasers of higher-priced former council dwellings. This also related to regional differences. In higher-demand areas with higher house prices more former council homes are bought by previous owners and by those in higher-status, white-collar employment. It appears that in southern areas with higher housing demand there is a wider market for former council homes and a narrower valuation gap between such dwellings and their nearest market equivalents. Where house prices are relatively low, former council homes serve a more localised, working-class market. The price differentials among former council dwellings reflect general regional price differentials. Former council homes are more expensive in the South than in the north of England. Within areas, those in rural locations tend to be more expensive as are those dwellings which are less obviously ex-council.

Research which has sought to indicate the impact of the sale of council houses shows a remarkably consistent pattern in terms of properties sold and who buys them. Especially in a period of rising house prices the gainers are clear and represent a cohort of council house tenants whose achieved housing status qualifies them for an option not available to other households. The losers in this process are not so easily identified individually. They are members of later cohorts who find that the declining supply and range of choice in council housing increases waiting time, restricts their choice or means that they will not obtain a house at all. In addition to these considerations and concerns about social segregation, the research illustrates two other issues. First, the characteristics and impact of the policy relate to other developments occurring alongside. The significance of council house sales for the supply of housing to rent depends on what is happening elsewhere. The coincidence of high sales alongside low rates of new building has had an adverse effect but this has also to be seen in the context of the flow of relets associated with the existing stock. Other elements of the evaluation relate to what has been happening to rents and dwelling prices. The nature and extent of advantages to individuals depends on these contextual factors as well as on the policy itself. The second issue illustrated by the evaluation of council house sales relates to time-scale. Sales of properties change the occupiers' tenure status but, in the short term, very little else. What happens on resale is more significant with issues of social and neighbourhood change. Over time the consequences of sales will have different dimensions and are also likely to relate to questions of repair and maintenance and to house condition.

Research completed in 1998 offers some final important perspectives on the Right to Buy. Eighteen years after its introduction the policy operates in a housing market with a different structure and different financing. The council stock is different and is less attractive relative to other tenures. The population of council tenants has also changed with fewer households in the middle age groups which have most favoured purchase. This reflects the impact of the Right to Buy itself but also of decisions of tenants who can do so to move out of the sector. The evidence from more recent sales suggests that more council house buyers are buying to enable them to move on rather than to secure the home they are attached to. Consistent with this is the fact that these purchasers are younger (Jones and Murie, 1998).

This may well indicate that the Right to Buy is now a mature policy operating in a system already transformed by its early impact. The Right to Buy has changed the system and has been changed by it – with its relevance and appropriateness reduced. At the same time as the policy has matured it has become more complex. It is no longer a simple uniform policy offering a new and straightforward package.

Successive pieces of housing legislation have changed the details of the operation of the Right to Buy. However, the relevance and the nature of the Right to Buy have also been changed by other developments in housing policy over the period in which it has operated. There are some obvious examples of policies which relate directly to the Right to Buy. The introduction of the Rent to Mortgage scheme in 1993 offered an alternative route for lower-income tenants to become home owners. The policy has been largely ineffective with the numbers of households exercising this right remaining extremely small. Nevertheless, such changes have complicated the alternative routes to home ownership. The same point can be made about the variety of policies developed to promote home ownership. The Right to Buy has not been the only way of accessing the opportunities provided by home ownership.

A different agenda has been concerned with the rights of council tenants themselves. The tenants' charter, introduced in the 1980 housing legislation, has been followed up with different approaches to tenants' rights and the encouragement of ways of increasing the involvement of tenants in the management of their housing. In 1987 there was a major policy shift which became embodied in the Tenants' Choice legislation of the 1988 Housing Act. This legislation provided tenants with the opportunity to change landlord and although it was made little use of, the large-scale voluntary transfer procedures which were largely based on this have been effective. In over fifty local authorities there is no longer a council housing sector as the council stock has been transferred to housing associations. While the Right to Buy has remained on the statute book, additional policies and opportunities have emerged. The Right to Buy is no longer the only measure providing tenants with opportunities to review their relationship with their landlord. The development of housing association provision and large-scale voluntary transfers has begun to change the tenancy rights of those previously in the council sector. New tenants in these organisations are assured tenants who do not have the Right to Buy.

New arrangements for housing association tenants contained in the 1996 housing legislation provide the opportunity for purchase grants. These arrangements, as with a number of portable discount schemes operating previously, provide tenants with opportunities to buy dwellings other than those of which they are a sitting tenant. The Right to Buy has itself become more complicated and is operating in a more complex policy environment. The option which it offers of purchase as a sitting tenant may not always be as attractive as the option offered through other schemes, of purchasing a property elsewhere or of placing stronger demands on landlords to improve services. Over this period the council housing sector has become more differentiated. In some places, whether or not there have been large-scale voluntary transfers, resources generated through capital receipts or otherwise have enabled sustained investment to improve the quality of the housing stock. In other areas the restrictions on capital expenditure have starved the sector of investment and there is a massive backlog of disrepair. In these largely urban areas the council estate of the late 1990s is less attractive than that of the late 1970s. Changes in the financial regime for council housing have altered the sector in other ways. The shift from bricks-and-mortar subsidies towards housing benefit subsidy, in a period of increased social and economic inequality, has contributed to the residualisation of the sector. An increased proportion of tenants are those on low incomes, with limited immediate prospects of buying a house through the Right to Buy or any other scheme.

In this context the relevance of the Right to Buy to the needs of tenants is less apparent than it was in 1979.

Voluntary transfers

The evaluation of recent developments in housing policy can be further highlighted with reference to an evaluation of large-scale voluntary transfers (Audit Commission, 1993). This report adopted a similar structure for evaluating the transfer option to one previously adopted for council house sales (Murie, 1975). In deciding whether to bid for a place in the Large Scale Voluntary Transfer programme it argued councils should consider the effect on a number of stakeholders:

- existing tenants;
- new tenants;

- the local authority and its council tax payers;
- central government. (Audit Commission, 1993: 3)

In considering the tenants' viewpoint the paper refers to three groups of tenants:

1. existing tenants who are usually given a rent ceiling guarantee for the early years of the transfer and have their Right to Buy preserved;
2. new tenants who will gradually become the majority as tenancies turn over and who do not have these guarantees and rights;
3. tenants of additional dwellings which are built with funds arising as a result of the transfer.

The advantages of the transfer differ for these groups with the clearest disadvantage for the second group, especially in view of the considerable increase in rents experienced by new tenants. Both new and existing tenants benefit from catch-up repairs and improvements to the housing stock. The general conclusion of this study referring to other stakeholders is that the balance of advantage will vary between transfers:

- Local authority general funds will gain more than they lose, particularly in the early years, but the gain will be eliminated as the Housing Benefit (HB) costs of rising rents impact upon the general fund.
- New tenants will pay more in rent but will have the benefit of earlier repairs. They will also pay more to finance new social housing.
- Existing tenants will gain in the early years since they will be protected from increases in guideline rents for local authority housing rents.
- Lenders will make their profit with considerable loan security as there are a number of steps that could be taken in an emergency should the association run into difficulties.
- The Public Sector Borrowing Requirement (PSBR) shows an initial gain but the government's revenue costs rise as the cost of HB grows. (Audit Commission, 1993: 10)

The effectiveness of housing management

The debate about housing management in Britain has been dominated by stereotypical images of different types of landlord. If much of the early antagonism to private landlordism was based on images of the exploitative landlord the more recent debate has been dominated by critiques of local authority housing management. These critiques imply variously that local authorities are inherently and inevitably bad managers and that the involvement of local politicians and local political considerations is inimical to good management, that local authorities as landlords are responsible for too large a stock or that the 'monopoly' control over rented housing is incompatible with efficiency (see, for example, Henney, 1985; Coleman, 1985; Power, 1987). While some presentations suggest reforms and good practice which would make local authorities good landlords, others imply that only changes in ownership and control would improve management.

Most of this discussion rests on assertion rather than analysis. There are indeed problems in evaluating these types of proposition. These problems arise because no two organisations operate in the same environment and subject to the same constraints and with the same opportunities. More crucially it may be argued that some critiques start from a fundamentally false position. This is the assumption that the key element determining the nature and effectiveness of housing management relates to staffing and organisational attributes. Alternative causal explanations could be offered. For example, financial arrangements, dwelling stock characteristics or household needs and resources may be more fundamental to whether a particular management regime is effective. Because the British housing system has not operated with the same financial framework for all landlords and because of the different histories of landlords and local communities, this possibility would caution against expecting patterns of management to be associated with landlord type. If patterns do relate to landlord type they are likely to do so only in the most general terms and any such relationship would also be likely to relate to some other factor.

One example of this is the study of local authorities' performance in housing management carried out by the Audit Commission (1986) and the attempt to rank authorities in terms of how good their management is. The study lacks any comparison with the management performance of private landlords or of other social landlords and lacks the evaluation of users' attitudes which would be essential to develop a perspective on effectiveness. Furthermore the basic methodology used does not represent a systematic research design. As with much of the debate, there is little attempt to set management performance in a context of changing and varied tenant characteristics, stock characteristics or the process of residualisation. It is easier to manage good-quality properties in attractive locations and to satisfy older people. Neither the task nor the resources of local authorities are the same throughout the tenure.

A more recent study of empty public sector properties in Scotland (Murie, Wainwright and Anderson, 1994) emphasises the significance of differences in demand and in stock characteristics as well as the impact of other policies and objectives. Bearing these cautions in mind various recent analyses of housing management raise important issues about housing management. Studies in England and Wales (Centre for Housing Research, 1989; Clinton *et al.*, 1989) demonstrate that the services delivered by both local authorities and housing associations vary considerably, as measured in different ways. They also demonstrate that the organisational arrangements made to deliver services vary, policies vary, the resources and needs vary. Categorical statements about whether one kind of landlord is better than another, or one set of organisational arrangements work better than another, are not supported by this evidence.

As the Glasgow University study of housing management in England states:

> The identification of 'effectiveness' builds upon 'economy' and 'efficiency' measures. It also requires an understanding of the quality and success of service provision. 'Effectiveness' relates to over-all indicators of organisational performance such as the proportion of housing offers which are accepted or the proportion of repairs completed within given time targets. The number of unambiguous indicators of this kind which can be constructed from data available to associations and authorities is, however, relatively restricted. Other indicators which have been used in this context, such as the tenant transfer rate or the vacancy rate (Audit Commission) suffer from the serious limitation that they depend as much, or even more, on the context being managed as they do on management effectiveness. (Centre for Housing Research, 1989)

The Audit Commission itself recognised that the intended outputs of policies reflect the different priorities set by local authorities. They are also affected by financial constraints emanating from central government. Other factors such as the age structure of the tenant population, demographic growth and the ease of access to other tenures affect the volume and nature of demand and turnover. These are contextual factors with consequences for costs and outputs. They are not within the local authority's control and if they are not taken into account could distort the impression of the local authority's own performance.

The effectiveness of housing management is, then, difficult to measure. Some measure of consumer satisfaction is a desirable element. But even in this, the results may not reflect management performance alone, or even principally. For example, the results could be related to differences in policy aims, the quality of accommodation, the extent to which dwelling types and location can be matched to demand, waiting-list trends, the level of maintenance service and so on.

In this sense, discussion of effectiveness has to be checked in terms of the potentially different interests of different groups. Tenants' views are more likely to emphasise the quality of service as well as costs and are less likely to be impressed by cost considerations irrespective of the quality of outputs. It is also true that there are likely to be differences in assessment of effectiveness between tenants and applicants and between tenants in different types of locality and of dwellings. As is suggested below, some of the evidence on tenant satisfaction shows that it is dwelling type rather than management style factors which dominate.

The task of identifying the effectiveness of housing management is complex and judgement is required for at least three reasons: incompleteness of data and problems of isolating and attributing costs to single services in an interlinked system; the different valuations placed on different patterns reflecting different objectives and conceptions of effectiveness; and problems in measuring the value or quality of service. These cautions apply equally to the recent research for England and Wales. Both studies place more emphasis on tenant perceptions of effectiveness than the Audit Commission has done. However, interpreting these data presents difficulties. It is all too easy to compare the views of the population of council tenants (or tenants of particular types of council) with those of housing association tenants (or tenants of particular types of housing association) and to explain differences by the landlord category.

However, other factors intervene. If, say, there are major property or demographic differences between the households in different landlord categories, the explanation for different responses may lie in these areas, rather than landlord category. As the Welsh study indicated, high levels of dissatisfaction with housing and the housing service among both housing association and council tenants were expressed by similar groups. Those not working, larger households, those with children, those neither newly allocated nor very long resident were more likely to be dissatisfied. For housing association tenants, property features were important. For council tenants, being housed other than from the waiting-list was important, as were issues connected with the type of neighbourhood. Dissatisfactions over repairs were common in both tenures, as were concerns about facilities available to children. Those tenants expressing lower levels of dissatisfaction were, in both tenures, likely to be either retired or in full-time work, small (one-person) households, those who had had major improvements carried out since they moved in, those who had not recently reported repairs, and those with a low demand for involvement in management.

What this suggests is that most forms of dissatisfaction are not easily resolved by 'better management'. Better repairs and major improvement programmes could be expected to reduce dissatisfaction. But for housing associations some features of their stock are likely to remain sources of dissatisfaction, however well-managed. In these cases, dissatisfaction would derive from the property irrespective of who the landlord was. The second important point is that the relationship between variables shows how it is possible to falsely identify good management performance. They imply that by (carefully) selecting certain types of tenants a landlord could achieve higher levels of satisfaction than would apply where a different tenant population experienced the same management system. To the extent that housing associations have housed more uniform populations, proportionately fewer families with children, and people from a waiting-list (rather than as homeless or under other statutory obligations), they have a more 'management-friendly' task. The traditional role and statutory duties of local authorities have not enabled them to select the easiest-to-manage tenants (and it is not suggested here that they should). Housing associations' development programmes have similarly left them with some properties which have less satisfactory standards and may increasingly result in higher levels of tenant dissatisfaction. This may be exacerbated in the future if housing associations generally take on a greater role in housing families with children and in housing the homeless. In both tenures the problems are affected by the reduced scope for transfer and exchange. For both types of landlord the changing role implies a more difficult task in achieving higher rates of tenant satisfaction. It is misleading to associate management performance with landlord type or even management inputs and to ignore the independent influence of other factors which may be temporarily or coincidentally associated with a particular landlord organisation.

The Glasgow study for England presents aggregate percentages for categories of organisation. From these data local housing associations emerge with the highest percentage of tenants who are very or quite satisfied with their dwelling (Centre for Housing Research, 1989: 37). However such a result must be treated with care. When the scores for individual organisations are considered, the three local housing associations record 84 per cent, 80 per cent and 72 per cent. The four shire district local authorities record 83 per cent, 82 per cent, 74 per cent and 67 per cent. The variation and overlap in tenant satisfaction within either category (local authority and housing association) is emphasised in the analysis of the Welsh tenant survey. In neither the Welsh nor the English studies are the 'best' and 'worst' landlords, as indicated by tenant surveys, consistently the same.

The general implications of this are that all landlord organisations perform unevenly. None fall down in every respect and none perform well in every respect. Not only is it unwise to start with a view that tenants' satisfaction can be assumed from whether their landlord is a local authority or a housing association, but also it cannot be assumed that those landlords perform evenly in terms of different aspects of the service they deliver. Assessment of management performance involves measuring outputs rather than making assumptions based on type of landlord. And direct measures of tenants' and applicants' views are important in measuring effectiveness: where comparisons are made between organisations, sensitivity to differences in properties and the population involved is important.

Just as important as the immediate position is whether performance is improving or deteriorating. The pressures and changes affecting some housing associations will make it impossible for them to continue to operate in the way that they have in the past. Some of these pressures increase the likelihood that they will become more like local authorities in certain respects. At the same time some local authorities are changing their services and developing some of the attributes which have been regarded as peculiar to housing associations.

The Wales study suggests that local authorities are more formal in their approach to the delivery of housing services and, partly as a consequence, achieve better results on a number of important measures of service delivery. The housing associations operate with higher costs and with a closer relationship with their tenants. Indeed there are many aspects of housing management where housing associations are able to provide a more informal and supportive service. Local authorities seemed to be more efficient over arrears and voids, where a strong financial accountability issue emerged. In contrast to this perspective is the evidence that local authorities were more likely to undertake repairs which were the responsibility of tenants, while the associations were more likely to enforce tenant obligations.

It is suggested that higher management allowances have encouraged associations to adopt more staff-intensive approaches to housing management. Local authorities operate with more formalised procedures and routines and may actually spend more time processing and checking on repairs or allocations. Whether that is necessary or whether resources could be diverted to areas where client contact could be enhanced is unclear. Equally, as associations grow, it is likely that more time and resources will be given to procedures and the question is whether this will diminish accessibility to clients.

The analysis of cost variations in the study of housing management in England took differences in context into account. It tentatively concluded that, while housing associations performed better in certain areas:

> They also incurred considerably greater expenditure than did councils. The twelve per cent better performance on repair speed may well have been worth the additional 30 per cent of resources expended. But was the 11 per cent superiority on allocation really worth the additional 82 per cent of expenditure? A less ambiguous case was arrears prevention and recovery where a 65 per cent positive differential in spending by associations was related to a 31 per cent poorer performance on arrears prevention and recovery. (Centre for Housing Research, 1989: 120)

In terms of effectiveness:

> the highest 'effectiveness status', in the tenants' view and better images in the tenants' eyes, were secured at resource levels fifty per cent greater than in 'moderately highly rated' landlords. But the tenant scores separating these two categories represented only a five to ten per cent improvement on the indicators used. The question remains as to whether a ten per cent improvement was worth an additional fifty per cent spending. (Centre for Housing Research, 1989: 120)

The evaluations of housing management summarised in this section suggest that who the landlord is is less important than what the landlord does and whether it is responsive to the interests of tenants and applicants. And what the landlord does cannot be read off from landlord type. Consequently, evaluating performance involves systematic monitoring and scrutiny and developing a methodology for measurement in relation to specific aspects of the service such as voids or arrears. Much of the current discussion in housing refers to developing systems of performance measurement which would act as triggers for further investigation or as 'can-openers' which are useful in promoting further enquiries to explain performance variation. The implication of developing the use of such measures is that they do lead to such further enquiries – routinely for any 'bad' performers. The implication is also that such further enquiries should be open and that there should be participation in them by tenants' organisations.

Conclusions

The examples referred to in this chapter demonstrate problems in evaluating policy. Issues of definition, identification of the influence of context and of indirect or wider policy impacts complicate apparently simple assessments. In relation to council house sales, it is important to identify who directly benefits and to consider the fact that there is a tendency for the better off and the better-housed to benefit most from such schemes. However issues of wider- and longer-term impact involve consideration of what properties are released or of who benefits on resale. There are also important substitution effects. Finally, housing policies do not take place in a vacuum. A changing social and economic environment – demographic change, unemployment and social polarisation – may serve to change the significance or selectivity of a policy where the policy itself does not change. Equally, the impact of one policy is crucially affected by what other policies are occurring. Thus the sale of council houses operates alongside a range of other policies, including those determining the supply of new lettings and those determining allocations and quality of service. In the period of discretionary sales prior to 1980, more council houses were being built than sold. In any one year the effects of sales were more than offset by new building. In the 1980s, sales exceeded new council building and dominated the changing nature of local housing markets. Any evaluation of sales would still need to be set in a context of other changes. Council house sales have not developed as part of a sensitive strategy to achieve certain ends, and any attempt to relate sales to notions of need has largely been abandoned. Nevertheless it makes little sense to ignore the changing context in which they occur in assessing who benefits or whose housing opportunities are damaged. Equally, the outputs from housing management are affected by a range of influences. Evaluating housing management could be misleading if it assumes that the type of landlord is of key importance, but that identification of tenants or stock or the wider context is of only academic interest. Equally important is how evaluations deal with time-lags and change and whether they take sufficient account of whether performance is improving or deteriorating.

The longer-term impact of the sale of council houses has become more important in the 1990s. The discussion of the loss of relets emphasises that such a loss is slow and cumulative. Few tenants who buy would have moved out and left a property available for reletting in the short term. The cumulative loss of relets will be affected by the age and mobility of households involved. Over a longer period the normal void rate of some 4 per cent will apply, and over a period of 25 years the loss of relets will at least equal the number of properties sold.

In addition to the loss of housing opportunity for households on the waiting list, the sale of council houses directly reduces the housing opportunities of existing council tenants. The extent of this loss depends on the scale of reshuffling through transfers and mutual exchanges. But every new or vacant dwelling available in the public sector enables more than one household to move.

A policy presented as a way of extending individual rights and opportunities emerges as a selective and partial policy affecting a much wider population than those who do succeed in buying. The policy has much wider consequences and implications than were considered relevant in developing the policy. It is important not to attribute to a single policy effects which are the result of a much wider set of public and market activities. Nevertheless the policy can be evaluated in terms of who benefits and who loses, and can be assessed within the context of other developments. While the policy implications of such evaluation will be a matter of political judgement, the identification of the wider consequences resulting from policy intervention requires some conscious and systematic evaluation, without which any understanding of what the policy does is likely to be limited.

The issues in relation to housing management are different. The evaluation of policy does not end with assessing who obtains housing, but embraces the quality of service received as a tenant. Some of this relates to economy and efficiency, but broader evaluation of effectiveness, especially relating to tenants' own views of the service they receive, are crucial elements of evaluation. As indicated in a number of studies, the resulting picture does not conform to certain stereotypes and implies attention to continuous monitoring and performance measurement, rather than assuming that changes in ownership and various types of reorganisation will ensure better performance. This chapter has concentrated on who benefits in terms of individual households and demographic groups, and on consumption aspects of housing.

A fuller analysis would refer in addition to the interests served in the processes of production and exchange of housing, and would acknowledge benefits to producers, financiers and exchange professionals. Thus the expansion and contraction of municipal housing programmes since the First World War can be seen as a response to the requirements of the building industry as much as to the needs of consumers. Current low-cost home ownership initiatives and proposals for the privatisation of estates must also be seen in this perspective. Where housing policy has been used as an economic regulator, or is related to Treasury estimates of what the country can afford, the assessment of who benefits must be in terms of the aims and objectives of the broader economic policies involved and whose interests are served. The ways in which policies and problems are presented and, for example, the positive endorsement of home ownership through the policies discussed in this book also operate in the interests of the home ownership industry.

13

New Labour: New Directions for Housing Policy?

The outcome of the general election of May 1997 provided a convenient point from which to look back over housing policy during 18 years of Conservative government, and Chapter 5 has identified the main themes and outcomes of this period. It is also appropriate at this point to review housing policy over the twentieth century as a whole, but it is equally necessary to try to look forward to what seems likely at this stage to be at least a two-term Labour government, taking us well into the twenty-first century.

The evidence discussed in previous chapters has emphasised the dynamism of the housing system, driven by a combination of economic growth, market forces and policy action. Taking the twentieth century as a whole, the pattern of housing tenure has been transformed and there have been massive changes in the quality and quantity of housing available. For more than half the century the housing problem was seen in terms of gross overall shortages, poor quality and the gap between the price of decent accommodation and the amount that could be afforded by a significant proportion of the population. The dominant policy responses were subsidised new building and slum clearance.

Clearly policy has had an impact on the quantity, quality and tenure of housing, and on the distributional issues of who gets what housing. However, the extent to which changes can be attributed to housing policy as such should not be overstated. For instance, for many years the growth of home ownership took place in the absence of positive policy action. It was argued in Chapter 1 that the long-term restructuring of housing tenure should be seen as the modernisation of the housing market. In the restructuring process, which necessarily took many years, local authority housing played an important, but changing, role. Whereas local authorities developed a housing service that provided mainly for the better-off groups within the working class, over a prolonged period they have been gradually, but increasingly vigorously, encouraged towards a quite different position, providing for a growing proportion of the least well off. This residualisation of the council sector is an important reminder that tenure categories change over time, not just in size but also in terms of what they stand for and what they do in the housing system. Council housing has been transformed from a position in which successive governments saw it as a necessary part of any attempt to solve housing problems into one where it has come to be seen as very much part of the problem to be tackled.

It is worth remembering in this context that the administrative framework has also changed considerably over time, and even where there appears to be continuity there is change: local authority housing services are now delivered by very different organisations from those which first developed large-scale housing in the 1920s. The same is true of the housing associations and mortgage lenders which also have deep historical roots. Modern housing organisations have been substantially changed by policies, forces and trends over the past 25 years, particularly since the reorganisation of local government in 1974/5 and the incorporation of housing associations within the scope of mainstream policy following the Housing Act 1974.

Taking a long view highlights change, but it also allows patterns of continuity to show up. In this context it is important to remember that change and continuity are not opposites – it is possible to identify continuities in the direction of change, and changes of policy mechanism designed to deliver continuing policy objectives. For many years after the formative period of 1915–19 housing policy consisted essentially of measures prompted by shortage and poor quality: rent control in the private sector, and slum clearance and new building by local authorities. It was not until the 1960s that the most positive policies emerged to encourage the growth of owner-occupation and of housing associations. For a considerable period after 1915, amounting altogether to two-thirds of the century, housing consumption in Britain was shielded from the full effects of market forces: rent control and housing subsidies meant that tenants generally paid less than full market rents, while owner-occupiers benefited from mortgage interest tax relief and rates of interest kept below the market rate by the building societies' cartel agreement. In more recent years measures have been introduced to reduce regulation and to free the market, a process which Whitehead (1991) has characterised as an attempt to move housing policy from a needs base to an affordability base. Central to this project has been acceleration of the long-established trend away from general housing subsidies towards income-related forms of assistance. Further aspects of continuity which have been referred to in earlier chapters include the consensus on high levels of new building for 25 years after the Second World War, the growth of broad-based support for owner occupation since the early 1950s, and the expansion of local authority housing up to 1980.

The end of housing policy?

In the past, when shortages were endemic, 'housing policy was about estimating housing needs, setting quantitative output targets, boosting housebuilding, especially in recessions, raising the average physical condition of the stock, removing substandard housing, and pursuing the goal of a decent home for every household' (Kleinman, 1996: 175). For the great majority of people in Britain housing conditions are now much improved compared with the start, or even the middle, of the century. It can be argued that the fact that the majority of households are reasonably well and securely housed has had an impact on the politics of housing, and it is certainly true that at the two British general elections in the 1990s housing was barely debated, indicating that none of the main parties saw it as a potent issue. Housing has slid down the order of political priorities, leading some people to question whether this decline is terminal (Bramley, 1997). Housing has been diminished and marginalised, to the extent that it is no longer the sort of portfolio that ambitious young politicians would see as providing a good opportunity to make a name for themselves.

When housing is debated it is in terms quite different from those of earlier decades. Different formulations of the problem lead to different policy prescriptions. In this sense, housing policy, as it was understood until well into the second half of the twentieth century, has come to an end. In the early 1980s, for example, Donnison and Ungerson (1982: 287) argued that 'Most housing problems are really problems of unemployment, poverty and inequality'. This sort of perspective lends support to the idea that improvements in housing can be achieved via other programme areas, chiefly social security and economic regeneration, and Bramley (1997: 403) suggests that with the decline of 'formal' housing policy it is possible to identify elements of housing-related policy action in a number of areas. In a similar vein Kleinman (1996) argues that (in Britain in particular, but also in France and Germany) housing policy has collapsed, or split into two quite distinct sets of concerns. On the one hand, the needs of the relatively well-housed majority can be addressed through measures designed to maintain a stable, efficient and effective housing market, together with policies intended to produce steady economic growth. This is mainly about sustaining the continued expansion of owner-occupation. 'Other aspects of housing policy,' argues Kleinman, 'for example, homelessness, social housing provision, means-tested housing allowances, are provided to a minority of the population, a minority which is increasingly segregated or at least differentiated from the majority in terms of its location, its ethnic group or its household type' (1996: 175). He goes on to point out that the policy measures directed to the needs of the minority 'relate to concentrations of poverty, associated with economic restructuring and social disintegration. These are not fundamentally bricks-and-mortar issues, or even about housing management and housing finance. They are increasingly about social dysfunction, about the collapse of communities, about the impacts of mass unemployment and poverty on everyday life' (177). This points to the complexity of the problems to be dealt with, and to the conclusion that it is no longer sufficient to think in terms of simply building houses. The implication is that in order to make any impact on complex problems it is necessary to devise broadly-based responses, seeking to address issues of housing, employment and social dysfunction together.

Kleinman also refers to the way in which the housing problem has come to be seen as no longer a national issue but a series of local and special needs, accompanied by a shift from mass to individual solutions. This can be linked to post-Fordist analyses of the welfare state, which refer to the transition from large-scale, centralised bureaucracies delivering standardised products and services to much more flexible, fragmented and decentralised structures (Burrows and Loader, 1994). This approach, which links developments in the welfare state to broader changes in the underlying economy, not only helps to anchor understanding of housing policy but also highlights the extent to which policies are shaped by forces beyond the direct control of any particular government. In this sense the fragmentation of social rented housing in the 1980s and 1990s can be seen as more than a reflection of Thatcherite and post-Thatcherite animosity to Labour-led local authorities.

Post-Fordist analysis reinforces the conclusion that housing policy in the way that it was manifested in much of the post-1945 period has indeed come to an end, but it is a line of argument that should not be taken too far. In particular, on the question of fragmentation it is important to remember the point that has been made throughout this book in relation to the multiplicity of local housing authorities (particularly before reorganisation in 1974/5), and the relatively loose control exercised over them by central government in the past. And in relation to the contemporary social policy agenda, it is important not to lose sight of the housing dimension to strategies designed to tackle social exclusion and economic regeneration. Not all housing problems have been solved, nor can measures to tackle these problems be subsumed within other programmes. There is still a need for considered policy action designed to tackle a range of housing problems, albeit that to be effective such action often needs to be carefully coordinated with other intervention. Indeed it can be argued (and has been in Chapter 6 above) that housing is so important in the way that it influences access to a variety of essential public services and job opportunities that a coherent housing policy should be regarded as a necessary precondition of a redistributive welfare state. Instead of accepting the end-of-housing-policy thesis, therefore, there is a case for a much stronger emphasis on housing as the basis for social and economic regeneration.

A new housing crisis

In 1979 and throughout most of the 1980s housing worked well for the Conservative Party in electoral terms, but although many individual households undoubtedly benefited from aspects of housing policy, the longer-term impact of 18 years of Tory rule has been a legacy of intractable problems facing the Labour Government. There is an acknowledged need for very large volumes of investment in new and improved housing over the years up to 2016, mainly to accommodate an expected increase of 4.4 million households and to modernise the existing stock. Most of the new houses will be in the owner-occupied sector, although there remain major question marks over the supply of land and the location of large amounts of new housing. Indeed in public debate about housing supply the dominant issue is not so much how to ensure that sufficient homes are provided to accommodate the projected increase in households, but where any houses that are built will be located; discussion has degenerated into a battle between urban and rural interests. In the social rented sectors there are also land supply and locational issues, but they tend to be overshadowed by problems of finance and affordability.

Among the most far-reaching changes since 1979 have been the growth of owner-occupation and the decline of council housing. Both were claimed as great achievements by the Conservatives, but they also pose challenges to be tackled over the coming period. In the case of owner-occupation the chief problems arise from the tendency to instability in the British housing market, and the growing numbers of owners on low incomes facing difficulties in managing their repair and maintenance responsibilities. A rising proportion of low-income home owners are elderly people, and increasingly they are owners who have little or no experience of renting. Unless the image of renting can be improved they are likely to want to remain as owners if possible. The rapid growth of home ownership among people on lower incomes, coupled with the impact of interrupted earnings during recessions and as a result of the 'flexible' labour market, means that in the future there are likely to be more home owners who enter retirement carrying mortgage debt and living in houses already showing cumulative signs of inadequate maintenance over many years.

Another aspect of this problem concerns the changes and cuts affecting grant aid for the repair and modernisation of older houses. The need for investment in older properties tends to be greatest in inner city areas, including those areas with the highest proportions of minority ethnic households. Failure to recognise the continuing need to invest in inner-city renewal is likely therefore to include a discriminatory element. The problem of the condition of the owner-occupied housing stock is one that cannot be ignored, and which can be expected to increase up to and beyond the millenium.

The decline of council housing is associated with three distinct problems. First, the gradual elimination of investment in new council houses since 1980, coupled with the impact of the Right to Buy, has meant that households needing to rent have increasingly had to turn to either housing associations (which have not been able to expand output sufficiently to make up for the decline in the council sector) or private renting (where, since 1989, rents have been rising rapidly as a result of deregulation). Second, the Right to Buy has stripped out the best and most attractive of the council stock, leaving councils with dwellings that are the most expensive to maintain and renovate to an acceptable standard, at a time when capital resources have been cut severely. Third, the increasing proportion of council tenants who are outside the labour force has been associated with corresponding concentrations of poverty, deprivation and social exclusion in the sector, further reducing the ability to pull in resources.

For decades local authorities were able to work on the assumption that there was unmet demand for rented housing, and the only effective limits to growth were availability of land and capital. But now, especially in some parts of the north of England, there is increasing evidence to suggest that there is a potentially very serious problem of lack of demand for council housing, leading to abandonment and demolition of expensive assets. Part of the explanation for this situation must be the way in which 18 years of ministerial denigration of council housing has had the cumulative effect of undermining the image of the sector, turning it into the tenure of last resort. In the past there was always a certain amount of differentiation amongst council estates, and problems of difficult-to-let dwellings have been recognised for at least 25 years, but as residualisation intensifies and the image of council housing as a whole declines there is a danger that it will become increasingly difficult to recruit tenants, except amongst groups with least choice.

In the other tenures, housing associations have grown rapidly from a small base in the period since 1989, but their stock in 1996 was still only a quarter the size of the remaining council sector in England and Wales. Associations have faced steep cuts in the Housing Corporation's capital programme since 1992/3, and although collectively they have been very successful in attracting large amounts of private finance, their ability to go on developing is limited by the diminishing amount of unmortgaged equity in the stock. Associations with significant numbers of older rehabilitated houses in inner-city areas have been exposed to some very difficult choices by withdrawal of grant aid for major repairs to existing stock. This has highlighted the tension between the social role of associations and the expectations on them to behave in a business-like way. Commercial logic might point to a disposal of run-down inner-city stock, while social commitment to such areas implies heavy investment in stock regeneration, even though increases in rental income cannot be expected to cover expenditure. It was governments in the 1970s which deliberately brought housing associations in as partners to the local authorities in housing action areas, but it is the associations that are now left with the responsibility from which government has walked away.

Private renting has expanded since 1988 as a result of the Business Expansion Scheme (now discontinued) and the impact of the housing market recession, but few people now expect private renting to make much of a contribution to meeting the need for new affordable rented housing over the next couple of decades.

A further pressing problem facing the government is that the housing finance arrangements inherited from the Conservatives are unsustainable, but very difficult to reform. The area in most urgent need of attention is the housing benefit system, where expenditure has spiralled, and where high expenditure is failing to produce desirable outcomes, especially in relation to the poverty trap affecting households of working age. In the late 1980s the Conservatives deregulated private renting and introduced measures to raise the real value of both local authority and housing association rents. Housing benefit was to 'take the strain', but ministers took fright at the rapid increase in the total bill (which in 1997/8 exceeded £10 billion, in England alone (DoE, 1997: 31)). Measures were introduced to limit benefit entitlement and to cap rent increases by social landlords. At issue is not just the aggregate expenditure on housing benefit but also the fact that the current system provides up to 100 per cent of actual rent, and is subject to a punitive rate of withdrawal as income rises, generating severe disincentives to go from benefit into work. There is a case for saying that much of the attention given to the rising cost of housing benefit is misplaced in the sense that it is only exposed to criticism because of deficiencies in the wider benefit system. A social security system which relied less on means-testing and which incorporated an element for housing costs in basic scale rates would not have such a high headline figure for housing benefit. Alternatively, an income tax system which exempted people on low earnings would also lessen the problems of the poverty trap.

On the related issue of rent levels in the social rented sectors, there is a good case for some rationalisation designed to reduce or remove the differentials between equivalent dwellings owned by councils and housing associations. The problem here is how to achieve such a rationalisation; if local authorities were to raise their rents towards the levels charged by associations then the affordability of their rents would be reduced, whereas if associations reduced their rents to local authority levels then their business plans would be damaged.

Building a new housing policy

In May 1997 a Labour government took office for the first time for a generation. An overall majority of 179 made it secure for a least one five-year term, and attempts to speculate about housing policy development over the foreseeable future can be built on the assumption of Labour in power. The new government inherited a situation that was very different from that which faced the last incoming Labour Government in 1974. Apart from social and economic change over the intervening period, four successive election victories had given the Conservatives the opportunity to stamp their own ideological imprint on housing, as discussed in Chapter 5.

In thinking about the future it is much easier to be confident about the problems to be tackled than about the solutions that the government will adopt. The room for manoeuvre for any government is limited, by the actions of its predecessor, the nature of the housing system itself and the wider national and international economic framework. Treaty commitments within the European Union and competitive forces in the global economy have a powerful constraining effect on public expenditure, and in any case some areas of the housing system are easier to reform than others. For instance, it is very difficult to make much impact on the overall quality of the housing stock in the short term. Similarly, new building programmes are difficult to crank into action quickly, especially in the case of local authorities, which have seen their landbanks reduced and their development staff dispersed. It is easier to make an immediate impact in areas such as rents and subsidy policy, or in relation to the rights of homeless people.

However, the new government has shown no sign of wanting to make radical changes to housing policy, nor any willingness to tolerate the sorts of increases in public expenditure that would be necessary to relaunch a substantial council house building programme. For the foreseeable future, at least, it is reasonable to expect considerable continuity with policies established under the Conservatives. In Opposition the Labour Party had made a number of clear statements about aspects of its housing policy, which was remarkable in view of the party's strategy of avoiding definite commitments. There was a pre-election pledge that compulsory competitive tendering of local authority housing management had no future, a commitment to release local authorities' accumulated capital receipts and a promise to restore the rights of homeless people to the position obtaining before the Housing Act 1996. However, one important issue on which Labour's Opposition Treasury team had refused to give ground was the reform of the public spending conventions, to the frustration of the housing lobby, which had identified the public spending borrowing requirement (PSBR) as a major barrier to further much-needed housing investment (Hawksworth and Wilcox, 1995).

Once in office Labour introduced a series of over a hundred comprehensive spending reviews across the board, including housing. In the meantime, the new government rapidly back-pedalled on CCT, allowing existing tendering schedules to go ahead as planned, but proposing in future to introduce a new regime based on the notion of 'best value', without the compulsory element. On capital receipts, within months of taking office the government introduced a 'capital receipts initiative' which amounted to the first tranche of released resources, adding £900 million to local authority capital programmes over two years. And on homelessness the government gave local authorities discretion in the way they interpreted the Act, but a year after the general election there was no sign of primary legislation on homelessness or any other housing policy measures.

The results of the comprehensive spending review (CSR) were revealed in July 1998, in a carefully staged series of Ministerial announcements. Although most public attention focused on the large sums of additional spending allocated to health and education, the announcement of much smaller amounts for housing was generally well received by commentators and providers alike. The headline figure was the provision of £3.6 billion to be spent by local authorities over three years on the renovation of their housing stock. Taken together with the capital receipts initiative announced in 1997 this effectively fulfilled the election pledge to release the £5 billion of accumulated receipts. Coming after years of significant cuts in resources this was obviously very welcome, but there are a number of caveats that must be entered. First, the aggregate cost of outstanding repairs needed by local authority dwellings (officially acknowledged to be £10 billion in England alone) is far greater than the resources being released; second, after five years of Labour government overall annual capital spending on housing will. remain below the levels achieved by the Conservatives in the early 1990s; and third, the Housing Corporation's capital programme is to remain static in real terms, at a quarter of the level of 1992–3.

The CSR was essentially a spending review, rather than a policy review, although some clear lines of thinking did emerge, such as the emphasis on renovation rather than new building in the social rented sectors. On the issue of stock transfers, where the Tories had published proposals requiring that councils transferred their houses to other landlords, Labour has continued to support transfers without insisting on them. In a pamphlet on the future of local government, Tony Blair (1998) made it clear that in his view there could be no return to the model of local authorities as comprehensive service providers. The future, as he saw it, lay in local authorities developing stronger and more effective partnerships with a range of non-municipal providers, which suggests that in relation to housing provision policy will continue along the route started under the Conservatives. It is less clear what will happen in relation to the really big issue of housing benefit reform. So far this has proved to be just as puzzling to Labour as it had been to the Conservatives. It is not just that there has been no sign of action – there has been no indication that the government knows what to do. The same is true of rents in the social rented sectors.

Moving on from an assessment of the Labour's first year in office to the question of where housing policy might go in future, the following is more a set of proposals than a forecast of what the government will do. As a start there are four general points to be made:

1. Reforms that are narrowly based and/or tenure-specific are very unlikely to be sufficient to the task of resolving the problems of housing in Britain beyond the end of the twentieth century. Thus further investment is necessary, but not enough; it needs to be combined with reforms in management practices and arrangements for subsidy and assistance.

2. Outmoded distinctions between public (bad) and private (good) must be abandoned in favour of policies designed to ensure that everyone is guaranteed a decent home at a price they can afford, irrespective of whether they are buying or renting. Mass home ownership, embracing large numbers of low-income households, should not be seen as a cheap option in terms of public expenditure. To ensure that housing conditions for low-income owners do not deteriorate, it is necessary to provide financial and other forms of assistance to help meet running costs in addition to interest charges.

3. Reforms must be located at both central and local levels. Local authorities, even in partnership with the private sector, cannot be expected to solve all the housing problems in their area without corresponding changes in central government policy. Equally, changes in national policy will not be effective without appropriate and complementary practices at local level. Problems which manifest themselves at the local level are not necessarily susceptible to resolution at that level. For instance, management responses to run-down estates are bound to have only a limited impact unless central government makes sufficient resources available and also abandons the residualist approach to public housing.

4. Housing policy is in itself inadequate to the task of tackling current housing problems. The point here is that, although it is obviously important to devise and implement good housing policies, it is also necessary to locate housing in the wider economic context, and to recognise that a prosperous economy, with lower levels of unemployment, is almost a necessary precondition of sustained improvement in the housing situation.

It is important to break away from narrowly conceived tenure-based strategies. Rejection of the doctrinaire privatisation policies of the Conservative governments of 1979–97, however, need not imply commitment to large-scale authoritarian municipal landlordism. On the contrary, what is required is an approach which embraces a plurality of tenure arrangements, ensuring that the necessary investment takes place and that appropriate housing services are available to all consumers. From this point a number of others naturally follow.

Remembering what was said earlier in the chapter about fragmentation and complexity, local authorities should be encouraged to develop their strategic role. The emphasis on complexity implies recognition of differences in circumstances from place to place, and acceptance that standard, centrally determined solutions cannot be relied upon to deliver desired outcomes in every locality. This strengthens the case for different partnerships and strategies for individual localities. The fragmentation of responsibilities across a range of municipal, voluntary and private sector organisations also points to the need for effective coordination by local authorities. However, they need to be given the combination of powers, expertise and finance to permit them to implement their strategies with a good chance of achieving real progress. In this connection it is appropriate to mention here the potential for variation in policy and practice arising from devolution to Scotland and Wales, and the development of a stronger regional planning and governance framework in England.

The notion of complexity embraces recognition of the need to devise broad-based approaches, bringing together public, voluntary and private sectors to tackle problems on a range of fronts simultaneously. Problems that are identified in terms of particular areas of housing cannot be effectively tackled by narrowly conceived bricks-and-mortar or management-based strategies. In the same way, to the extent that problems of poverty, unemployment, crime, drug-taking, ill health and educational under-achievement are spatially concentrated, they have a housing element. As Murie and Nevin (1997: 5) have argued:

> housing must play a fuller part in regeneration activity and should not be left as a marginal backdrop where key decisions are left to the market and based simply on price signals. It is too important in terms of health gain and the security and well-being of households, as well as in its contribution to local economic regeneration.

A further point on local authorities as strategic enablers is that it is necessary to break out of the constraining effect of annual financial settlements for both local authorities and housing associations. Proper local housing strategies require planners to be able to take a rather longer-term view, and sensible spending decisions require the freedom to move resources freely across financial years.

Finance is at the heart of housing policy, and without access to reasonable amounts of capital it is very difficult to make any headway. Although in the past local authorities were allowed to borrow for capital projects without detailed restrictions imposed by the centre, over the past 25 years they have been increasingly constrained. In recent years a great deal of debate has focused on the question of what counts as public expenditure, and, as mentioned above, there is widespread support within housing circles for the abandonment of the PSBR, which is seen as imposing unnecessarily constraining rules. However, so far the new government has not shown any real sign of moving to the widely favoured alternative, the general government financial deficit (GGFD). There is a very strong case for finding a framework that would allow more capital investment in social rented housing, but in the meantime local authorities will have little choice but to press ahead with stock transfers to housing associations or local housing companies (LHCs).

Mechanisms such as local housing companies, which take council housing outside the constraints of the PSBR while allowing the elected local authority to retain influence over management and development, probably represent the shape of things to come. There are grounds for believing that LHCs (or other similar models) should not be seen as simply a device for escaping the PSBR but as a means of offering real advantages in terms of their ability to engage more effectively in local economic regeneration and involve tenants more directly in control. Indeed it can be argued that they represent the basis for a resurgent, growing and vibrant public housing sector for the twenty-first century.

However, whether social renting is successful in the future depends to a large extent on what is done about rents, benefits and subsidy policy. The effect of policies in recent years has been to raise the real value of rents and to trap tenants who cannot afford to move from benefit into low-paid work. Measures taken to cap rent increases and to contain the growth of housing benefit have also had the effect of creating difficulties for social landlords struggling with rising costs. The need for a thorough review of rents and subsidy policy is recognised to be urgent, but solutions are difficult to achieve without either increasing expenditure or creating problems for tenants. Priority needs to be given to the search for an approach to subsidy that allows social landlords to continue to develop, and to set rents at levels that permit tenants to move easily into work. There is a degree of agreement that the move towards means-tested assistance has gone too far, and a return to higher levels of general subsidy would be welcomed. An outstanding issue to be addressed in the reform of housing benefit concerns the position of owner-occupiers on very low incomes. They remain outside the scope of the existing system, although their entitlement to assistance with mortgage interest was substantially reduced under the Conservatives.

Finally, it has been suggested above that housing policy, at least in the short term, is likely to be characterised more by continuity than change. However, on the evidence of the past 18 years, it is clear that if Labour remains in office for more than one term then it does have the opportunity to bring about real change. It is too early to say with any confidence whether Labour has a vision of a housing system for the twenty-first century, or how it would intend to realise such a vision.

Guide to Further Reading

The volume of literature concerned with housing in Britain has grown enormously in recent years, and there is now also an expanding body of comparative work. This guide to further reading identifies important books which are readily accessible, and lists them under a series of headings which reflect an attempt to cover the scope of housing studies. In using this guide, however, it is important to remember that classifications of this kind are inevitably arbitrary to some extent, and the headings used here do not represent watertight categories: books are mentioned under the most appropriate heading, and some appear more than once.

Reference should also be made to the various journals which regularly publish on housing issues. Academic journals include: *Housing Studies, Urban Studies, Policy and Politics, Journal of Social Policy, Area*, and *International Journal of Urban and Regional Research*. Professional journals include: *Housing Review, Roof, Housing, Inside Housing, Social Housing, Agenda*, and *Housing Today*.

The Council of Mortgage Lenders publishes a quarterly, *Housing Finance*, which contains articles on private housing and a mass of valuable statistics on mortgages and house prices. This journal continues the series previously published as the *Building Societies Bulletin*.

In addition, organisations such as the Institute of Housing, CHAS and Shelter regularly produce useful pamphlets and other publications on housing topics. Academic institutions such as CURS (Centre for Urban and Regional Studies, University of Birmingham), SPS (School for Policy Studies, University of Bristol), the Department of Urban Studies at the University of Glasgow, and the Centre for Housing Policy, University of York, publish working papers and occasional papers on housing and related issues.

A useful addition to the housing literature is the book by Douglas Robertson and Pat McLaughlin (*Looking into Housing: A Practical Guide to Housing Research*, Chartered Institute of Housing, 1996). This fills a gap for students planning dissertations and practitioners with research projects to carry out.

The housing system

P. Balchin's *Housing Policy: An Introduction* (Routledge, 3rd edn, 1995) provides a useful complement to *Housing Policy and Practice,* including as it does chapters on investment and the housebuilding industry as well as the main housing tenures. A new book edited by Balchin and Rhoden (*Housing: The Essential Foundations*, Routledge, 1998) provides an up-to-date introduction to the field, as do *Social Housing: An introduction* (Longman, 1998), by Stephen Harriott and Lesley Matthews, and *Housing and Public Policy*, edited by Alex Marsh and David Mullins (Open University Press, 1998). An excellent summary of developments over the last quarter of the twentieth century is provided by John Hills in the second edition of *The State of Welfare*, edited by Glennerster and Hills (Oxford University Press, 1998). Mary Smith's *Guide to Housing* (Housing Centre Trust, 3rd edn, 1989) offers a wide-ranging but largely uncritical survey of the housing system in Britain, including contributed chapters on Scotland and Northern Ireland (but not Wales). It is unfortunate that *Housing Policy* (Penguin, 1982) by D. Donnison and C. Ungerson is now out of date and out of print. There are a number of other general books which are now of largely historical value only: A. Murie, P. Niner and C. Watson, *Housing Policy and the Housing System* (Allen & Unwin, 1976); J. B. Cullingworth, *Essays on Housing Policy* (Allen & Unwin, 1979); S. Lansley, *Housing and Public Policy* (Croom Helm, 1979). Similarly dated but still potentially useful are the three parts of the *Technical Volume* which accompanied the Green Paper (*Housing Policy: A Consultative Document*, HMSO, 1977). These contain discussions and statistical data on all the main tenures, and can be updated by reference to the regular statistical series such as *Housing and Construction Statistics* (which appear quarterly and in an annual volume covering the last 10 years). *Report of the Inquiry into British Housing* (NFHA, 1985) contained much valuable material and interesting, if contentious, interpretation. (See also the two accompanying volumes of *Evidence and Supplement* and the *Second Report*, 1991.)

During the 1980s, alternatives to the dominant perspective on housing were developed by, for instance, the Labour Housing Group, which published *Right to a Home* in 1984 (Spokesman). This was followed up by pamphlets from the LHG, such as *Manifesto for Housing* (1985) and *A Housing Vision for the 1990s* (1988). A later collection of essays by LHG members was edited by Jane Darke (*The Roof Over Your Head*, Spokesman, 1992).

Meanwhile right-wing academics also made their contributions, among them P. Minford, P. Ashton and M. Peel, *The Housing Morass* (IEA, 1987)and J. Black and D. Stafford, *Housing Policy and Finance* (Routledge, 1988). In this context it is appropriate to mention Alice Coleman's highly influential *Utopia on Trial* (Hilary Shipman, 1985). The book presents a popularised account of research on council flats in London, and amounts to a polemic against public housing. Whereas Coleman located the housing problem in the public sector, the collection edited by P. Malpass clearly set out a wider perspective on housing in the mid-1980s: *The Housing Crisis* (Croom Helm, 1986).

A book which is distinguished by its explicitly theoretical objectives is Jim Kemeny's *Housing and Social Theory* (Routledge, 1992).

A valuable reminder of the differences within the British housing system is provided by the book edited by Hector Currie and Alan Murie on *Housing in Scotland* (Chartered Institute of Housing, 1996).

The history of housing and housing policy

The best general introduction to housing problems and policy responses up to 1914 is still E. Gauldie's *Cruel Habitations* (Allen & Unwin, 1974), which should be read in conjunction with J. N. Tarn's *Five Per Cent Philanthropy* (Cambridge University Press, 1973) and J. Burnett's *A Social History of Housing 1815–1985* (David & Charles, 2nd edn, 1985). See also M. Daunton, *A Property Owning Democracy?* (Faber, 1987) for a short account of the history on housing in Britain. There continues to be interest in the housing management work of Octavia Hill, and the best modern biography is by Gillian Darley (*Octavia Hill: A Life*, Constable, 1990); enthusiasts should also consult the very useful edition of Hill's essays and letters to her fellow workers, edited by Robert Whelan (*Octavia Hill and the Social Housing Debate*, Institute of Economic Affairs, 1998).

A very useful addition to the literature is the collection of articles edited by John Goodwin and Carol Grant, *Built to Last? Reflections on British Housing Policy* (Shelter, revised edition, 1997). Another useful collection of essays, conceived to commemorate the centenary of the passing of the Housing of the Working Classes Act 1890 is *A New Century of Social Housing*, edited by Lowe and Hughes (Leicester University Press, 1991). Patrick Nuttgens' book based on his television series, *Home Front* (BBC, 1989), covers a lot of ground in a very accessible form, in contrast to the massive historical survey of housing policy by Alan Holmans, *Housing Policy in Britain: A History* (Croom Helm, 1987). This is immensely thorough within the areas covered, but it gives little attention to the years before 1914 and stops in the late 1970s, and it is not an easy read.

More advanced students of nineteenth-century housing should refer to D. Englander's excellent study of *Landlord and Tenant in Urban Britain, 1838–1918* (Clarendon Press, 1982) and M. Daunton's *House and Home in the Victorian City* (Edward Arnold, 1983).

More focused studies are provided by A. Wohl's major work on housing and poverty in London, *The Eternal Slum* (Edward Arnold, 1977) and A. Jackson's *Semi-Detached London* (Allen & Unwin, 1973) which looks at suburban housing development. Michael Harloe's massive comparative study of social housing in Europe and the USA (*The People's Home?*, Blackwell, 1995) can be profitably read just for its British content.

M. Swenarton, *Homes Fit for Heroes* (Heinemann, 1981) and L. Orbach, *Homes for Heroes* (Seeley, Service, 1977) between them give a good account of the key events during and just after the First World War, but reference should also be made to the papers in J. Melling (ed.), *Housing, Social Policy and the State* (Croom Helm, 1980); these cover the period from about 1885 to 1939 and are based on local case studies, with, in most instances, a strong theoretical content. The interwar period is dealt with in M. Daunton, *Councillors and Tenants: Local Authority Housing in English Cities, 1919–1939* (Leicester University Press, 1984). This includes four local case-studies and is rich in fascinating historical detail.

Two important but difficult-to-obtain studies dealing with housing policy between the wars are M. Bowley's *Housing and the State* (Allen & Unwin, 1945) and J. R. Jarmain's less well-known *Housing Subsidies and Rents* (Steven, 1948). Their work has been drawn upon by subsequent writers such as A. Nevitt, *Housing, Taxation and Subsidies* (Nelson, 1966), R. A. Parker, *The Rents of Council Houses* (Bell, 1967) and S. Merrett, *State Housing in Britain* (Routledge & Kegan Paul, 1979), who are all concerned with post-1945 developments as well. Nevitt's book is now of limited value and Parker's book has been superseded by P. Malpass, *Reshaping Housing Policy: Subsidies, Rents and Residualisation* (Routledge, 1990). Merrett's book is still the most comprehensive and authoritative historical account of the development of public housing.

A number of writers have provided historical studies of particular issues within a narrow period of time. For example, K. Banting has looked at private sector rent policy in the years after the Conservatives' 1957 Rent Act, and the process that led to Labour's response, the 1965 Rent Act, in *Poverty, Policy and Politics* (Macmillan, 1979). A rather different approach is represented by books that look at the longer-term history of a specific component of policy. In this category it is appropriate to mention J. English, R. Madigan and P. Norman's *Slum Clearance* (Croom Helm, 1976), the first part of which contains a very useful historical review. P. Dunleavy's *The Politics of Mass Housing in Britain 1945–1975* (Clarendon Press, 1981) examines the growth and decline of support for building high flats. E. Gittus also has a useful chapter on this phenomenon in her *Flats, Families and the Under Fives* (Routledge & Kegan Paul, 1976).

Local authority housing

As already mentioned, Stephen Merrett's *State Housing in Britain* (Routledge & Kegan Paul, 1979) remains a basic text, but a number of other writers have subsequently been attracted to the problem of explaining the changing character of council housing. Stephanie Cooper, *Public Housing and Private Property* (Gower, 1985), dealt with the period 1970–84, and concentrated on issues of sales and rents and subsidies. Anne Power, on the other hand, focused on housing management in *Property Before People* (Allen & Unwin, 1987). A larger-scale study of housing management in the council and housing association sectors in England was carried out by a team at the Centre for Housing Research in Glasgow: *The Nature and Effectiveness of Housing Management in England* (HMSO, 1989). The Audit Commission also produced reports of investigations of local authority housing practices: *Managing the Crisis in Council Housing* (1986) and *Improving Council House Maintenance* (1986). A new book on housing management is that by Martyn Pearl (*Social Housing Management: A Critical Appraisal of Housing Practice*, Macmillan, 1997).

Ray Forrest and Alan Murie continued their work on the sale of council houses, publishing *An Unreasonable Act?* (SAUS, 1985) and *Selling the Welfare State* (Croom Helm, 1988). The first of these studies concentrates on the issues raised by the conflict between central government and Norwich City Council, while the second is more wide-ranging, drawing on case studies in a number of authorities. The continuing story of sales is carried forward in *Reviewing the Right to Buy*, by Alan Murie and Colin Jones (Policy Press, 1998). Another key aspect of policy in the public sector in the 1980s was rents and subsidies, which was discussed by P. Malpass in *Reshaping Housing Policy* (Routledge, 1990).

Reference to Alice Coleman's *Utopia on Trial* has already been made, and it should be read in conjunction with the collection of papers edited by N. Teymur, T. Markus and T. Woolley (*Rehumanising Housing*, Butterworths, 1988). The papers presented here were originally prepared for a conference called in response to the attention given to Coleman's research. Another book to focus on problems in the public sector is F. Reynolds, *The Problem Housing Estate* (Gower, 1986).

In a different vein, a number of writers have speculated about trends in public housing. For instance, in the early 1980s the collection edited by John English looked at *The Future of Council Housing* (Croom Helm, 1982). This was followed by *Public Housing: Current Trends and Future Developments*, edited by D. Clapham and J. English (Croom Helm, 1987). David Clapham then produced a short book speculating on the end of council housing as it currently exists: *Goodbye Council Housing?* (Unwin Paperbacks, 1989). The book by P. Willmott and A. Murie, *Polarisation and Social Housing* (Policy Studies Institute, 1988) considers trends in the social composition of housing tenures, and compares the situations in Britain and France. A valuable addition to the literature is *The Eclipse of Council Housing* (Routledge, 1993) by Ian Cole and Robert Furbey.

Owner-occupation

Owner Occupation in Britain (Routledge, 1982), by S. Merrett, with F. Gray, provides a thorough analysis but is not so accessible as the earlier *State Housing in Britain*.

M. Ball has made a major contribution to housing studies in the 1980s, but his *Housing Policy and Economic Power* (Methuen, 1983) is also heavy going for readers new to the subject. However Ball produced a useful summary of his ideas, including proposals for reform, in *Home Ownership: A Suitable Case for Reform* (Shelter, 1986).

One of the issues to emerge in the 1980s was that of low-income home ownership and this attracted the attention of a number of researchers: P. Booth and T. Crook (eds) *Low Cost Home Ownership* (Gower, 1985) present papers on a range of related issues. V. Karn, J. Kemeny and P. Williams report research on home ownership in inner Birmingham and Liverpool in *Home Ownership in the Inner City* (Gower, 1985); in *A Foot on the Ladder?* (SAUS, 1984), R. Forrest, S. Lansley and A. Murie provide an evaluation of the government's low-cost home ownership initiatives.

Two substantial contributors are Peter Saunders, *A Nation of Home Owners* (Unwin Hyman, 1990), which reports research on the experience of and attitudes towards home ownership in three English towns, and Ray Forrest, Alan Murie and Peter Williams, *Home Ownership: Differentiation and Fragmentation* (Unwin Hyman, 1990), which offers a different interpretation based on a range of evidence. On the building societies, Martin Boddy's *The Building Societies* (Macmillan, 1980) remains a useful starting point. An account written with an insider's knowledge and perspective is provided by M. Boleat, *The Building Society Industry* (Allen & Unwin, 1983). A more detached and critical view is given by T. Gough, *The Economics of the Building Societies* (Macmillan, 1982). See also D. Hawes, *Building Societies – The Way Forward* (SAUS, Occasional Paper, 26, 1986). None of these books, however, gives an account of the major changes affecting building society activity in the second half of the 1980s. There remains an important gap in the literature on this subject, which is only partly filled by M. Boddy's article, 'Financial Deregulation and UK Housing Finance', *Housing Studies,* 4 (2) (1989), but see also the chapter by Kearns and Stephens in *Ownership, Control and Accountability* (P. Malpass (ed.), Chartered Institute of Housing, 1997).

The collection by J. Doling, J. Ford and B. Stafford, *The Property Owing Democracy* (Avebury, 1988) provides a valuable focus on mortgage arrears. Valuable research on the experience of home owners is reported in *Home Owners on New Estates in the 1990s* by Ray Forrest, Tricia Kennet and Philip Leather (Policy Press, 1997).

Private rented housing

The best and most thorough account of the private rented sector is Michael Harloe's *Private Rented Housing in the United States and Europe* (Croom Helm, 1985). There are a number of other books on this subject, which continues to attract scholarly attention despite its continuing decline: J. Doling and M. Davies, *The Public Control of Privately Rented Housing* (Gower, 1984); P. Kemp (ed.), *The Private Provision of Rented Housing: Current Trends and Future Prospects* (Gower, 1988); C. Whitehead and M. Kleinman, *Private Rented Housing in the 1980s and 1990s* (University of Cambridge, 1986); P. Kemp, *The Future of Private Renting* (University of Salford, 1988). The last-named volume has a very useful discussion of the deregulation of private renting and proposals for reform.

A rather different approach to the private rented sector is presented in J. Allen and L. McDowell, *Landlords and Property* (Cambridge University Press, 1989). This book is not as up to date as its date of publication would imply, but it does provide an interesting analysis of the different types of private landlordism, based on research in two London boroughs. Another book based on empirical research in London is *Cities, Housing and Profits* by C. Hamnett and B. Randolph (Hutchinson, 1988).

Housing associations

The best available book providing a general introduction to housing associations, their structure, organisation and role in the British housing system is *Housing Associations: Policy and Practice,* by Helen Cope (Macmillan, 1990). The descriptive and legalistic tome by C. V. Baker, *Housing Associations* (Estates Gazette, 1976) is seriously out of date. There is a useful pamphlet by John Hills, *The Voluntary Sector in Housing: The Role of British Housing Associations* (LSE, Welfare State Programme, No. 20, 1987). The forthcoming book by Peter Malpass, *Housing Associations and Housing Policy* (Macmillan, 1999) will provide a more thorough historical perspective than has been available hitherto.

Housing conditions and urban renewal

Housing and the Urban Environment by Barry Goodchild (Blackwell, 1997) may prove to be a valued successor to *Introduction to Urban Renewal* (Hutchinson, 1982) by M. Gibson and M. Langstaff, and A. Thomas's *Housing Urban Renewal* (Allen & Unwin, 1986). See also *The State of UK Housing* by Philip Leather and Tanya Morrison (Policy Press, 1997).

Women and housing

One of the first books to focus on this topic was *Women and Housing* (Housing Centre Trust, 1980) by M. Brion and A. Tinker. Brion later published *Women in the Housing Service* (Routledge, 1995). A good starting-point is Chapter 5 in G. Pascall, *Social Policy: A Feminist Analysis* (Tavistock, 1986) or Section 11 in *Women and Social Policy* (Macmillan, 1985) edited by C. Ungerson. Sophie Watson and Helen Austerberry, *Housing and Homelessness: A Feminist Perspective* (Routledge, 1986) carried the analysis forward, and Watson has continued with *Accommodating Inequality: Gender and Housing* (Allen & Unwin, 1989), a book which draws on Australian experience. An influential contribution to debates about women and housing comes from D. Hayden, *Redesigning the American Dream* (Norton, 1984). The more recently published book by Marion Roberts, *Living in a Man Made World* (London: Routledge, 1991) is a valuable addition, as is *Housing Women* (Routledge, 1994), edited by Rose Gilroy and Roberta Woods.

Finance

For many years there was a distinct lack of good housing finance books, but now the situation is much better. *Unravelling Housing Finance* by John Hills (Clarendon Press, 1990) is probably the best, although its coverage is not as comprehensive as the books by David Garnett, *Housing Finance* (CIH, 3rd edn forthcoming), or Gibb and Munro, *Housing Finance in the UK: An Introduction* (Macmillan, 1991, 2nd edn forthcoming). Beginners might prefer to start with Henry Aughton's *Housing Finance: A Basic Guide* (Shelter, 4th edn, 1994; new edition forthcoming). For a highly useful digest of up-to-date statistics, with accompanying commentary, see Steve Wilcox's *Housing Finance Review* (annually from the Joseph Rowntree Foundation).

The issue of housing finance reform has been on the political agenda in one form or another for many years, but for present purposes the Green Paper of 1977, *Housing Policy: A Consultative Document* (HMSO, Cmnd 6851), is probably a good starting-point. In practice, governments have tended to focus on the rented sectors, particularly local authority housing. For an account of the course of rents and subsidies policy since 1945 see P. Malpass, *Reshaping Housing Policy* (Routledge, 1990). However there is a literature which examines the arguments for, and the forms of, wider-ranging reform of housing finance, such as M. Warburton, *Housing Finance: The Case for Reform* (CHAS, 1983); A. Walker, *Housing Taxation: Owner Occupation and the Reform of Housing Finance* (CHAS, 1986); I. Kelly, *Heading for Rubble: The Political Need for Housing Finance Reform* (CHAS, 1986). The NHFA *Report of the Inquiry into British Housing* (1985) put forward a detailed proposal for across-the-board reform. The AMA outlined a proposal for universal housing allowance in *A New Deal for Home Owners and Tenants* (1987) and later published *Housing Tenure and Finance* (1990) which looked at further possibilities for reform. John Hills suggested a subsidy system for rented housing which would overcome party political differences in *Twenty First Century Housing Subsidies* (LSE, 1988) and M. Ball outlined a ten-point plan for reforming owner-occupation (*Home Ownership: A Suitable Case for Reform,* Shelter, 1986).

On the issue of housing benefit, Peter Kemp's *The Cost of Chaos* (SHAC, 1984) provides a good indication of the early problems with the scheme. See also Kemp's edited collection, *The Future of Housing Benefits* (Centre for Housing Research, 1986). Looking to the future, J. Hills, R. Berthoud and P. Kemp provide stimulating papers in *The Future of Housing Allowances* (Policy Studies Institute, 1989).

Comparative housing studies

A feature of the development of housing studies has been the emergence of considerable interest in comparative work, breaking away from the Anglocentric approach of the past. As long ago as 1967, D. Donnison's *The Government of Housing* (Penguin) contained a strong comparative element, which was carried forward into *Housing Policy* (D. Donnison and C. Ungerson, Penguin, 1982). Other pioneers in the field were B. Heady, *Housing Policy in the Developed Economy* (Croom Helm, 1978); J. Kemeny, *The Myth of Home Ownership* (Routledge, 1981); and R. Duclaud-Williams, *The Politics of Housing in Britain and France* (Heinemann, 1978). Later works included the collection edited by M. Wynn, *Housing in Europe* (Croom Helm, 1984), and *Polarisation and Social Housing,* by P. Willmott and A. Murie (PSI, 1988), in which they compare the British and French experience. A particularly valuable contribution to this field was made by Michael Harloe in *Private Rented Housing in the United States and Europe* (Croom Helm, 1985). He later joined M. Ball and M. Martens to write *Housing and Social Change in Europe and the USA* (Routledge, 1988).

Recent additions to the field include the five-country survey by Anne Power, *Hovels to High Rise: State Housing in Europe Since 1850* (Routledge, 1993), and the collection edited by Graham Hallett, *The New Housing Shortage* (Routledge, 1993). The most detailed historical study is that by Michael Harloe (*The People's Home?*, Blackwell, 1995), but also very useful is Mark Kleinman's *Housing, Welfare and the State*, which reviews policy in Britain, France and Germany. An addition to this increasingly popular area of work is *Comparative Housing Policy* by John Doling (Macmillan, 1997).

There is an extensive literature on housing in the third world, but useful starting-points would be *Self-Help Housing. A Critique* (edited by P. Ward, Mansell, 1982) and *People, Poverty and Shelter* (edited by R. Skinner and M. Rodell, Methuen, 1983).

Contemporary issues

Under this last heading it is appropriate to cite a number of works already referred to. For instance, on the question of the way forward for council housing, the works by Coleman, Power, Clapham and Forrest and Murie are highly relevant. And on housing and social change Peter Saunders's book, *A Nation of Home Owners* (Unwin Hyman, 1990) is an important contribution, certain to generate debate.

An issue of continuing topicality is relations between central and local government, and there is a long list of books to be cited, beginning with Barrie Houlihan's *Housing Policy and Central–Local Government Relations* (Avebury, 1988). Others include: *Local Government and Urban Politics* (W. Hampton, Longman, 1987); *Democracy in Crisis* (D. Blunkett and K. Jackson, Hogarth Press, 1987); *The Politics of Local Government* (G. Stoker, Macmillan, 1988); *The Politics of Local Expenditure* (K. Newton and T. Karran, Macmillan, 1985); *The Future of Local Government* (edited by I. Stewart and G. Stoker, Macmillan, 1989); *The Changing Politics of Local Government* (J. Gyford, S. Leach and C. Game, Unwin Hyman, 1989); and *Councils in Conflict* (S. Lansley, S. Goss and C. Wolmar, Macmillan, 1989).

For work on contemporary housing policy there are two edited collections, by Peter Malpass and Robin Means, *Implementing Housing Policy* (Open University Press, 1993) and by Johnston Birchall, *Housing Policy in the 1990s* (Routledge, 1992). The Joseph Rowntree Foundation produces a regular flow of work analysing contemporary issues, and the *Findings* series provides short accounts of all projects funded by the Foundation. Two good examples of recent outputs from Rowntree work are *Local Housing Companies: New Opportunities for Council Housing* by Steve Wilcox (JRF, 1993) and *Building for Communities: A Study of New Housing Association Estates* by David Page (JRF, 1993). Another example of research funded by the JRF but not published by them is the study of the implementation of the 1989 housing finance regime for local authority housing by Malpass, Warburton, Bramley and Smart (*Housing Policy in Action*, SAUS, University of Bristol, 1993).

The DoE also commissions and publishes a considerable amount of research on current policy. Examples include *Evaluating Large Scale Voluntary Transfers of Local Authority Housing*, by Mullins, Niner and Riseborough (HMSO, 1992) and *The Scope for Compulsory Competitive Tendering of Housing Management*, by Baker, Challen, Maclennan, Reid and Whitehead (HMSO, 1992). The new government has expressed support for empowerment of tenants and in this context it is appropriate to mention two books on this topic: Cairncross, Goodlad and Clapham (*Housing Management, Consumers and Citizens*, Routledge, 1996) and the collection edited by Cooper and Hawtin (*Housing, Community and Conflict*, Ashgate Gower, 1998).

An excellent collection of essays dealing with the key issues of the mid-1990s and beyond is *Directions in Housing Policy* (Paul Chapman Publishing, 1996) edited by Peter Williams. Another collection of essays, this time on the contemporary issue of governance, was brought together by Peter Malpass (*Ownership, Control and Accountability*, Chartered Institute of Housing, 1997).

Bibliography

Achtenburg, E. P. and Marcuse, P. (1986) 'The Causes of the Housing Problem', in Bratt, Hartman and Meyerson (1986).

Addison, P. (1977) *The Road to 1945* (London: Quartet).

Allen, J. and McDowell, L. (1989) *Landlords and Property* (Cambridge University Press).

Anderson, I., Kemp, P. and Quilgars, D. (1993) *Single Homeless People* (London: HMSO).

Anderson, K. and Wainwright, S. (1993) 'Moving on Tenant Rights', *Housing*, pp. 28–9.

Archbishop of Canterbury (1985) The Report of the Archbishop of Canterbury's Commission on Urban Priority Areas, *Faith in the City* (London: Church House Publishing).

Ashford, D. (1981) *Policy and Politics in Britain* (Oxford: Basil Blackwell).

Ashworth, W. (1954) *The Genesis of Modern British Town Planning* (London: Routledge & Kegan Paul).

Association of Metropolitan Authorities (AMA) (1980) *Housing in the Eighties* (London: AMA).

—— (1982) *Building for Tomorrow* (London: AMA).

—— (1983) *Defects in Housing*, Parts 1–3 (London: AMA).

—— (1985) *Capital Controls in Local Government in England* (London: HMSO).

—— (1986a) *Managing the Crisis in Council Housing* (London: HMSO).

—— (1986b) *Improving Council House Maintenance* (London: HMSO).

Audit Commission (1984) *Bringing Council Tenants' Arrears under Control* (London: HMSO).

—— (1986) *Managing the Crisis in Council Housing* (London: HMSO).

—— (1993) *Who Wins? Voluntary Housing Transfers*, Occasional Paper No. 20 (London: HMSO).

Aughton, H. (1990) *Housing Finance: A Basic Guide*, 3rd edn (London: Shelter).

Aughton, H. and Malpass, P. (1994) *Housing Finance: A Basic Guide*, 4th edn (London: Shelter); 5th edn due late 1999.

Bachrach, P. and Baratz, M. (1970) *Power and Poverty* (Oxford: Oxford University Press).

Balchin, P. (1989) *Housing Policy: An Introduction* (London: Routledge).

Ball, M. (1983) *Housing Policy and Economic Power* (London: Methuen).

—— (1986a) 'Housing Analysis: Time for a Theoretical Refocus?', *Housing Studies*, 1 (3) pp. 147–65.

—— (1986b) *Home Ownership: A Suitable Case for Reform* (London: Shelter).

—— (1988) *Rebuilding Construction* (London: Routledge).

Banim, M. and Stubbs, C. (1986) 'Rethinking the Terms of Tenure: A feminist critique of Mike Ball', *Capital and Class*, 29, pp. 182–94.

Banting, K. (1979) *Poverty, Policy and Politics* (London: Macmillan).

Barker, B. (1983) 'The Operation of the Labour Party in Bristol', Working Paper, 27 (Bristol: School for Advanced Urban Studies, University of Bristol).

Barker, P. (ed.) (1984) *Founders of the Welfare State* (London: Heinemann).

Barrett, S. and Fudge, C. (eds) (1981) *Policy and Action* (London: Methuen).

Barrett, S. and Hill, M. (1986) 'Policy Bargaining and Structure in Implementation Theory: Towards an Integrated Perspective', in Goldsmith (ed.) (1986).

Barron, J., Crawley, G. and Wood, T. (1991) *Councillors in Crisis: the Public and Private Worlds of Local Councillors* (London: Macmillan).

Bassett, K. and Short, J. (1980) *Housing and Residential Structure: Alternative Approaches* (London: Routledge & Kegan Paul).

Biffen, J. (1979) Chief Secretary to the Treasury, quoted in the *Daily Telegraph* (25 September).

Birchall, J. (ed.) (1992) *Housing Policy in the 1990s* (London: Routledge).

Birrell, D. and Murie, A. (1980) *Government and Politics in Northern Ireland* (Dublin: Gill & Macmillan).

Blair, T. (1998) *Leading the Way: A New Vision for Local Government*, (London: Institute for Public Policy Research).

Blunkett, D. and Jackson, K. (1987) *Democracy in Crisis* (London: Hogarth Press).

Boaden, N. (1971) *Urban Policy Making* (Cambridge: Cambridge University Press).

Boddy, M. (1980) *The Building Societies* (London: Macmillan).

—— (1981) 'The Public Implementation of Private Housing Policy', in Barrett and Fudge (eds) (1981).

Boddy, M. and Fudge, C. (eds) (1981) 'The Local State: Theory and Practice', Working Paper, 20 (Bristol: School for Advanced Urban Studies, University of Bristol) pp. 24–37.

—— (1984) *Local Socialism?* (London: Macmillan).

Boleat, M. (1986) *The Building Society Industry*, 2nd edn (London: Allen & Unwin).

Bowley, M. (1945) *Housing and the State 1919–1944* (London: George Allen & Unwin).

Bramley, G. (1990) *Bridging the Affordability Gap: Report of Research on Access to a Range of Housing Options* (Birmingham: BEC Publications).

Bramley, G. (1997) 'Housing Policy: A Case of Terminal Decline?', *Policy and Politics*, vol. 25, no. 4, pp. 387–407.

Bramley, G. and Murie, A. (1983) *Housing Allocation in Hackney*, SAUS, unpublished.

Bramley, G., Leather, P. and Murie, A. (1979) 'Housing Strategies and Investment Programmes', Working Paper, 7 (Bristol: School for Advanced Urban Studies, University of Bristol).

Bratt, R., Hartman, C. and Meyerson, A. (eds) (1986) *Critical Perspectives on Housing* (Philadelphia: Temple University Press).

Brett, C. E. B. (1982) 'Housing in Northern Ireland', *Housing Review* (May–June) pp. 75–6.

Brown, M. and Baldwin, S. (1978) *The Year Book of Social Policy in Britain 1977* (London: Routledge & Kegan Paul).

Bryant, R. (1979) *The Dampness Monster: A Report of the Gorbals Anti-dampness Campaign* (Glasgow: Scottish Council of Social Service).

BS News (1986) Building Societies Association, *Building Society News*, 6 (3) (March).

Burch, M. and Wood, B. (1983) *Public Policy in Britain* (Oxford: Martin Robertson).

Burrows, R. and Loader, B. (1994) *Towards a Post-Fordist Welfare State?* (London: Routledge).

Byrne, D. S. (n.d.) 'Problem Families: A Housing Lumpen-Proletariat' (University of Durham).

Byrne, D. and Damer, S. (1980) 'The State, the Balance of Class Forces and Early Working Class Housing Legislation', in *Housing, Construction and the State, Political Economy of Housing Workshop.*'

Cairncross, L., Clapham, D. and Goodlad, R. (1993) 'The Social Bases of Tenant Organisations', *Housing Studies*, 8 (3) (July), pp. 179–93.

Cantle, T. (1986) 'The Deterioration of Public Sector Housing', in Malpass (ed.) (1986).

Centre for Housing Research (1989) *The Nature and Effectiveness of Housing Management in England* (London: HMSO).

Chartered Surveyor Weekly (1988) (18/25 August).

CIPFA (1992) *Housing Revenue Account Statistics 1992* (London: CIPFA).

Clinton, A. *et al.* (1989) *The Relative Effectiveness of Different Forms of Housing Management in Wales* (Cardiff: The Welsh Office).

Cmnd 9513 (1985) *Home Improvement: A New Approach* (London: HMSO).

Coates, K. and Silburn, R. (1980) *Beyond the Bulldozer* (University of Nottingham).

Cochrane, A. (1993) *Whatever Happened to Local Government?* (Buckingham: Open University Press).

Cockburn, C. (1977) *The Local State* (London: Pluto Press).

Cole, I. and Furbey, R. (1993) *The Eclipse of Council Housing* (London: Routledge).

Coleman, A. (1985) *Utopia on Trial* (London: Hilary Shipman).

Coleman, D. and Salt, J. (1992) *The British Population* (Oxford: Oxford University Press).

Collins, C. A., Hinings, C. R. and Walsh, K. (1978) 'The officer and the councillor in Local Government', *Public Administration Bulletin*, 28 (December), pp. 34–50.

Commission for Racial Equality (1984) *Race and Council Housing in Hackney*.

Committee of Public Accounts (1979) Session 1978–79, Housing Associations and the Housing Corporation, HC 327 (London: HMSO).

Community Development Project (1976) *Whatever Happened to Council Housing?* (London: CDP Information and Intelligence Unit).

—— (1977) *The Poverty of the Improvement Programme* (London: CDP).

Conservative Party (1979) *Conservative Party Manifesto 1979* (April) (London: Conservative Central Office).

—— (1987) *The Next Moves Forward* (London: Conservative Central Office).

Conway, M. and Knox, C. (1990) 'Measuring Housing Effectiveness: A Case Study in Customer Evaluation', *Housing Studies*, 5 (4) (October), pp. 257–72.

Cope, H. (1990) *Housing Associations: Policy and Practice* (London: Macmillan).

Corina, L. (1975) *Local Government Decision Making*, Papers in Community Studies, 2 (York: University of York) .

—— (1977) *Oldham CDP: Assessment of its Impact and Influence on the Local Authority*, Papers in Community Studies, 9 (York: University of York).

Crook, A. (1985) *Strengthening Committees* (London: National Federation of Housing Associations).

Crook, A., Kemp, P., Anderson, I. and Bowman, S. (1991a) *Tax Incentives and the Revival of Private Renting* (York: Cloister Press).

—— (1991b) *The Business Expansion Scheme and Rented Housing* (York: Joseph Rowntree Foundation).

Cullingworth, J. B. (1966) *Housing and Local Government* (London: George Allen & Unwin).

—— (1973) *Problems of an Urban Society, Vol. 2, The Social Content of Planning* (London: George Allen & Unwin).

—— (1979) *Essays on Housing Policy* (London: George Allen & Unwin).

Cullingworth Report (1969) Ninth Report of the Housing Management Sub-Committee of the Central Housing Advisory Committee (Chairman J. B. Cullingworth), *Council Housing Purposes, Procedures and Priorities* (London: HMSO).

Damer, S. (1974) 'Wine alley: the sociology of a dreadful enclosure', *Sociological Review,* 27, no. 2, May, pp. 221–48.

—— (1980) 'State, Class and Housing: Glasgow 1885–1919', in Melling (1980).

Damer, S. and Madigan, R. (1974) 'The Housing Investigator', *New Society* (25 July).

Darley, G. (1990) *Octavia Hill: A Life* (London: Constable).

Davies, B. (1968) *Social Needs and Resources in Local Services* (London: Michael Joseph).

Davies, J. G. (1975) 'Whose Grass Roots? Citizens, Councillors and Researchers', in Leonard (ed.) (1975).

Day, P., Henderson, D. and Klein, R. (1993) *Home Rules Regulation and Accountability in Social Housing* (York: Joseph Rowntree Foundation).

Dearlove, J. (1973) *The Politics of Policy in Local Government* (Cambridge: Cambridge University Press).

—— (1979) *The Reorganisation of British Local Government* (Cambridge: Cambridge University Press).

Dearlove, J. and Saunders, P. (1984) *Introduction to British Politics* (London: Polity Press).

Dennis, N. (1970) *People and Planning* (London: Faber & Faber).

—— (1972) *Public Participation and Planners' Blight* (London: Faber & Faber).

—— (1973) 'Half Beating City Hall: the Duke St Story', *New Society* (4 October).

—— (1975) *'Community Action, Quasi-Community Action and Anti-Community Action',* in Leonard (ed.) (1975).

Department of the Environment (1971) *Local Government in England Government Proposals for Reorganisation,* Cmnd 4584 (London: HMSO).

—— (1976) *Housing Policy,* Cm 6851 (London: HMSO).

—— (1980) *Appraisal of the Financial Effect of Council House Sales* (London: DoE).

—— (1982) *English House Condition Survey 1981,* Part 1 (London: HMSO).

—— (1985) *An Inquiry into the Condition of the Local Authority Housing Stock in England* (London: DoE).

—— (1987) *Finance for Housing Associations: The Government's Proposals* (London: DoE).

—— (1988a) *Capital Expenditure and Finance: A Consultation Paper* (London: DoE).

—— (1988b) *New Financial Regime for Local Authority Housing in England and Wales: A Consultation Paper* (London: DoE).

—— (1993) *Annual Report 1993,* Cm 2207 (London: HMSO).

—— (1995a) *Our Future Homes: Opportunity, Choice and Responsibility,* Cm 2901, (London: HMSO).

—— (1995b) *More Choice in the Social Rented Sector,* (Consultation paper linked to the Housing White Paper, Cm 2901) (London: DoE).

—— (1997) *Annual Report 1997,* Cm 3607 (London: HMSO).

Department of the Environment for Northern Ireland (1996) *Building on Success* (Belfast: HMSO).

Department of Social Security (1992) *Households Below Average Income* (London: HMSO).

DETR (1997) *Building Partnerships for Prosperity* (London: HMSO).

Doling, J. and Davies, M. (1984) *Public Control of Privately Rented Housing* (London: Gower).

Donnison, D. (1967) *The Government of Housing* (Harmondsworth: Penguin).

Donnison, D. and Ungerson, C. (1982) *Housing Policy* (Harmondsworth: Penguin).

Draper, P. (1977) *Creation of the DoE, CSD* (London: HMSO).

Dunleavy, P. (1980) *Urban Political Analysis* (London: Macmillan).

Dunleavy, P. and O'Leary, B. (1987) *Theories of the State: The politics of liberal democracy* (Basingstoke: Macmillan).

Edwards, M. *et al.* (eds) *Housing and Class in Britain* (Political Economy of Housing Workshop).

Elcock, H. (1986) *Local Government,* 2nd edn (London: Methuen).

—— (1993) 'Strategic Management', in Farnham and Horton (eds) (1993).

English, J. (1979) 'Access and Deprivation in Local Authority Housing', in Jones (ed.) (1979).

English, J., Madigan, R. and Norman, P. (1976) *Slum Clearance* (Beckenham: Croom Helm).

Ermisch, J. (1984) *Housing Finance: Who Gains?* (London: Policy Studies Institute).

Farnham, D. and Horton, S. (eds) (1993) *Managing the New Public Services* (London: Macmillan).

Ferge, Z. and Miller, S. M. (eds) (1987) *Dynamics of Deprivation* (London: DoE) (London: Gower).

Ferguson, A. and Wilcox, S. (1990) *Rent Setting and Affordability* (Coventry: Institute of Housing).

Finnegan, R. (1980) 'Housing Policy in Leeds Between the Wars', in Melling (ed.) (1980).

Foot, M. (1973) *Aneurin Bevan, Vol. 2, 1945–60* (London: Davis Poynter).

Ford, J. (1988a) *The Indebted Society* (London: Routledge).

—— (1988b) 'Managing or Mismanaging Building Society Mortgage Arrears', *Housing Studies,* 3 (1).

Ford, J. and Wilcox, S. (1992) *Reducing Mortgage Arrears and Possessions* (York: Joseph Rowntree Foundation).

Forrest, R. (1980) 'The Resale of Former Council Houses in Birmingham', *Policy and Politics,* 8, pp. 334–9.

Forrest, R., Gordon, D. and Murie, A. (1996) The Position of Former Council Homes in the Housing Market, Urban Studies.

Forrest, R., Murie, A. and Gordon, D. (1996) *The Resale of Former Council Homes* (London: HMSO).

Forrest, R. and Murie, A. (1976) *Social Segregation, Housing Need and the Sale of Council Houses* (Birmingham: CURS, University of Birmingham).

—— (1983) 'Residualisation and Council Housing: Aspects of the Changing Social Relations of Housing Tenure', *Journal of Social Policy,* 12 (4) pp. 453–68.

—— (1984a) *Monitoring the Right to Buy 1980–1982* (Bristol: SAUS, University of Bristol).

—— (1984b) *Right to Buy? Issues of Need, Equity and Polarisation in the Sale of Council Houses* (Bristol: SAUS, University of Bristol).

—— (1985) *An Unreasonable Act? Central–Local Government Conflict and the Housing Act 1980,* SAUS Study, 1 (Bristol: SAUS, University of Bristol).

—— (1988/1990) (2nd edn 1990) *Selling the Welfare State* (London: Routledge).

—— (1990a) *Residualisation and Council Housing: A Statistical Update* (Bristol: SAUS, University of Bristol).

—— (1990b) *Moving the Housing Market* (Aldershot: Avebury).

—— (1994) 'Home Ownership in Recession', *Housing Studies,* 9 (1).

Forrest, R., Lansley, S. and Murie, A. (1984) *A Foot on the Ladder* (Bristol: School for Advanced Urban Studies, University of Bristol).

Foster J and Hope T (1993) *Housing Community and Crime: The Impact of the Priority Estate Project* Home Office Research Study no.131 HMSO.

Foster, S. (1992) *Mortgage Rescue: What Does It Add Up To?* (London: Shelter).

Francis Report (1971) *Report of the Committee on the Rent Acts*, Cmnd 4609 (London: HMSO).

Fraser, D. (1979) *Power and Authority in the Victorian City* (Oxford: Basil Blackwell).

Garnett, D., Reid, B. and Riley, H. (1991) *Housing Finance* (Coventry: Institute of Housing and Longman).

Gauldie, E. (1974) *Cruel Habitations* (London: Allen & Unwin).

Gerth, H. H. and Wright Mills, C. (1984) *From Max Weber* (London: Routledge & Kegan Paul).

Gibb, K. and Munro, M. (1991) *Housing Finance in the UK: An Introduction* (London: Macmillan).

Gibb, K., Munro, M. and Satsangi (1999) *Housing Finance in the UK: An Introduction*, 2nd edn (London: Macmillan).

Gibbs, J. (1992) *Rent Levels, Rent Structures and Affordability* (Coventry: Institute of Housing).

Gilbert, B. B. (1970) *British Social Policy 1914–1939* (London: Batsford).

Gill, O. (1977) *Luke Street: Housing Policy, Conflict and the Creation of the Delinquent Area* (London: Macmillan).

Gittus, E. (1976) *Flats, Families and the Under Fives* (London: Routledge & Kegan Paul).

Goldsmith, M. (ed.) (1986) *New Research in Central–Local Relations* (London: Gower).

Grant, C. (ed.) (1992) *Built to Last: Reflections on British Housing Policy* (London: Shelter).

Great Britain (1949) *Selection of Tenants and Transfers and Exchanges*, 3rd Report of the Housing Management Sub-Committee of the Central Housing Advisory Committee (London: HMSO).

—— (1955) *Residential Qualifications*, 5th Report of the Housing Management Sub-Committee of the Central Housing Advisory Committee (London: HMSO).

—— (1961) *Homes for Today and Tomorrow* (Parker Morris Report) (London: HMSO).

—— (1965) *The Housing Programme 1965–70*, Cmnd 2838 (London, HMSO).

—— (1969) *Council Housing: Purposes, Procedures and Priorities*, 9th Report of the Housing Management Sub-Committee of the Central Housing Advisory Committee (London: HMSO).

—— (1971) *Fair Deal for Housing*, Cmnd 4728 (London: HMSO).

—— (1977a) *Housing Policy: A Consultative Document*, Cmnd 6851 (London: HMSO).

—— (1977b) *Housing Policy: Technical Volume Part I* (London: HMSO).

—— (1977c) *Housing Policy: Technical Volume Part III* (London: HMSO).

—— (1986) *Paying for Local Government*, Cmnd 9714 (London: HMSO).

—— (1987) *Housing: The Government's Proposals*, Cm 214 (London: HMSO).

Greater London Council (GLC) (1984) *Private Tenants in London: The GLC Survey 1983–84* (GLC).

Green, D. (1981) *Power and Party in an English City* (London: Allen & Unwin).

Griffith, J. A. G. (1966) *Central Departments and Local Authorities* (London: Allen & Unwin).

Gunn, L. (1978) 'Why is Implementation So Difficult?', *Management Services in Government* (November).

Gyford, J. (1976) *Local Politics in Britain* (Beckenham: Croom Helm).

Gyford, J. and James, M. (1983) *National Parties and Local Politics* (London: Allen & Unwin).

Gyford, J., Leach, S. and Game, C. (1989) *The Changing Politics of Local Government* (London: Unwin Hyman).

Hall, S., Nevin, B., Beazley, M., Burfitt, A., Collinge, C., Lee, P., Loftman, P., Riseborough, M., Sibljanin, A. (1998) *Competition, Partnership and Regeneration: Lessons from Three Rounds of the Single Regeneration Budget Challenge Fund* (Birmingham: CURS, University of Birmingham.

Ham, C. and Hill, M. (1984, 1993) *The Policy Process in the Modern Capitalist State* (London: Harvester Wheatsheaf).

Hampton, W. (1987) *Local Government and Urban Politics* (London: Longman).

Harloe, M. (ed.) (1977) *Captive Cities* (London: Wiley).

—— (1978) Chapter 3 in Brown and Baldwin (eds) (1978).

—— (1985) *Private Rented Housing in the United States and Europe* (Beckenham: Croom Helm).

—— (1995) *The People's Home* (Oxford: Blackwell).

Harrison, M. (1984) *Corporatism and the Welfare State* (London: Gower).

Hawes, D. (1986) *Building Societies – The Way Forward* (Bristol: SAUS, University of Bristol).

Hawksworth, J. and Wilcox, S. (1995) *Challenging the Conventions* (Coventry: Coventry Institute of Housing).

Heiser, T. (1992) Interview on BBC Radio, *Analysis,* 24 May.

Henderson, J. and Karn, V. (1987) *Race, Class and State Housing* (London: Gower).

Henney, A. (1985) *Trust the Tenant: Devolving Municipal Housing* (London: Centre for Policy Studies).

Hepworth, N. (1984) *The Finance of Local Government,* 7th edn (London: Allen & Unwin).

Heseltine, M. (1979) House of Commons, Hansard, col. 407 (15 May).

Hill, M. (1976) *The State, Administration and the Individual* (London: Fontana).

—— (1983) *Housing Benefit Implementation from Modified Ideal to Complex Reality* (Bristol: SAUS, University of Bristol).

—— (ed.) (1993) *The Policy Process: A Reader* (Brighton: Harvester Wheatsheaf).

Hill, M. and Bramley, G. (1986) *Analysing Social Policy* (Oxford: Basil Blackwell).

Hills, J. (1991) *Unravelling Housing Finance: Subsidies, Benefits and Taxation* (Oxford: Clarendon Press).

Hills, J. (1997) *The Future of Welfare* (York: Joseph Rowntree Foundation).

HM Treasury (1981) *The Government's Expenditure Plans 1981–82 to 1983–84,* Cmnd 8175 (London: HMSO).

—— (1984) *The Government's Expenditure Plans 1984–85 to 1986–87,* Cmnd 9143 (London: HMSO).

—— (1990) *The Government's Expenditure Plans 1990–91 to 1992–93,* Ch. 8, 'Environment', Cmnd 1008 (London: HMSO).

Hoggett, P. and Hambleton, R. (eds) (1987) *Decentralisation and Democracy*, Occasional Paper 28 (Bristol: School for Advanced Urban Studies, University of Bristol).

Hogwood, B. (1987) *From Complacency to Crisis* (Oxford: Oxford University Press).

Hogwood, B. and Gunn, L. (1984) *Policy Analysis for the Real World* (Oxford: Oxford University Press).

Hole, J. (1866) *The Homes of the Working Classes* (London: Longmans, Green).

Holmans, A. (1993) The Changing Employment Circumstances of Council Tenants in DoE *Homing in England* (London: HMSO).

Holmans, A. E. (1997) *Housing, Family and Working Lives*, U of Warwick.

House of Commons (1980) *First Report from the Environment Committee, Session 1979–80. Enquiry into Implications of the Government's Expenditure Plans 1980–81 to 1983–84 for the Housing Policies of the Department of the Environment* (London: HMSO) HC 714.

—— (1981a) *Third Report from the Environment Committee, Session 1980–84, Department of Environment's Housing Policies: Enquiry into Government's Expenditure Plans 1981–84 and the updating of the Committee's First Report for the session 1979–80 (London: HMSO)*.

—— (1981b) *Second Report from the Environment Committee Session 1980–81, Council House Sales*, vol. 1, HC 366–1 (London: HMSO).

Housing Centre Trust (1975) *Evidence to the Housing Finance Review* (London: HCT).

Housing Corporation (1992a) *Housing Associations in 1992* (London: Housing Corporation).

—— (1992b) *Performance Criteria* (London: Housing Corporation).

Ingram, H. and Schneider, A. (1990) 'Improving Implementation through Framing Smarter Statutes', *Journal of Public Policy*, 10 (1) pp. 67–88.

Institute of Housing (1981) *Annual Review 1980* (Coventry: Institute of Housing).

Jackson, P. (ed.) (1985) *Implementing Government Policy Initiatives: The Thatcher Administration 1979–1983* (London: Ripa).

Jones, C. (ed.) (1979) *Urban Deprivation and the Inner City* (Beckenham: Croom Helm).

Jones, C. and Murie, A. (1998) *Reviewing the Right to Buy* (Birmingham: CURS, University of Birmingham).

Jones, C. and Stevenson, J. (eds) (1983) *The Year Book of Social Policy in Britain 1982* (London: Routledge & Kegan Paul).

Karn, V. (1993) 'Remodelling a HAT', in Malpass and Means (eds) (1993).

Kearns, A. (1990) *Voluntarism, Management and Accountability* (Glasgow: Centre for Housing Research, University of Glasgow).

Kellas, G. and Madgwick, P. (1982) 'Territorial Ministries: The Scottish and Welsh Offices', in Madgwick and Rose (eds) (1982).

Kemeny, J. (1987) 'Toward a Theorised Housing Studies: A Counter Critique of the Provision Thesis', *Housing Studies*, 2 (4) pp. 249–60.

Kempson, E. (1993) *Household Budgets and Housing Costs* (London: Policy Studies Institute).

Kerr, M. (1989) *The Right to Buy* (DoE, HMSO).

Klein, R. (1984) 'Edwin Chadwick', in Barker (ed.) (1984).

Kleinman, M. (1991) 'Housing and Urban Policies in Europe: Towards a New Consensus?', paper presented to the Housing Studies Association Conference, Oxford (September).

Laffin, M. (1989) *Managing under Pressure: Industrial Relations in Local Government* (London: Macmillan).

Lambert, J., Paris, C. and Blackaby, B. (1978) *Housing Policy and the State* (London: Macmillan).

Lansley, S. (1979) *Housing and Public Policy* (Beckenham: Croom Helm).

Lansley, S., Goss, S. and Wolmar. C. (1989) *Councils in Conflict* (London: Macmillan).

Leather, P. (1983) 'Housing (Dis)Investment Programmes', *Policy and Politics*, 11 (2) pp. 215–27.

Leather, P. and Mackintosh, S. (1993) 'Housing Renewal in an Era of Mass Home Ownership', in Malpass and Means (eds) (1993).

Leather, P. and Murie, A. (1986) 'The Decline in Public Expenditure', in Malpass (ed.) (1986).

Leather, P. *et al.* (1985) *Review of Home Improvement Agencies* (London: DoE).

Lee, P. and Murie, A. (1997) *Poverty, Housing Tenure and Social Exclusion* (Bristol: Policy Press).

Lee, P., Murie, A. and Gordon, D. (1995) *Area Measures of Deprivation* (Birmingham: CURS, University of Birmingham).

Legg, C. *et al.* (1981) *Could Local Authorities be Better Landlords? An Assessment of How Councils Manage Their Housing* (Housing Research Group, The City University).

Leonard, P. (ed.) (1975) *The Sociology of Community Action,* Sociological Review Monograph, 21.

Lindberg, L. and Alford, R. (eds) (1975) *Stress and Contradiction in Modern Capitalism* (Lexington: Lexington Books).

Lindblom, C. (1959) 'The Science of "Muddling Through"', *Public Administration Review,* 19.

Lipsky, M. (1980) *Street-Level Bureaucracy: Dilemmas of the Individual in Public Services* (New York: Russell Sage).

McCulloch, D. (1980) 'How the AMA Fought – and Improved – the Housing Bill', *Municipal Review* (October).

McGivern, W. (1989) 'Building a Better Belfast', *Housing Review,* 38 (1) (January–February), pp. 22–4.

McLennan, G., Held, D. and Hall, S. (1984) *The Idea of the Modern State* (Buckingham: Open University Press).

Maclennan, D. and Williams, R. (1990) *Affordable Housing in Britain and America* (York: Joseph Rowntree Foundation).

Madgwick, P. and Rose, R. (eds) (1982) *The Territorial Dimension in UK Politics* (London: Macmillan).

Malpass, P. (1975) 'Professionalism and the Role of Architects in Local Authority Housing', *RIBA Journal,* 81 (6) (June), pp. 6–29.

—— (1977) 'Byker: Community-Based Renewal', *Roof,* September.

—— (1979) 'Myth, Magic and the Architect', *Architects' Journal,* 9 and 16 May.

—— (1980) 'The Architect and the Community', *Housing,* December.

—— (1984) 'Octavia Hill', in Barker (ed.) (1984).

—— (ed.) (1986) *The Housing Crisis* (Beckenham: Croom Helm).

—— (1990) *Reshaping Housing Policy: Subsidies, Rents and Residualisation* (London: Routledge).

—— (1992a) Investment Strategies', in Grant (ed.) (1992).

—— (1992b) 'Housing Policy and the Disabling of Local Authorities', in Birchall (1992).

—— (1992c) 'The Road from Clay Cross', in Grant (ed.) (1992).

Malpass, P. and Means, R. (1993) *Implementing Housing Policy* (Buckingham: Open University Press).

Malpass, P. and Murie, A. (eds) (1990) *Housing Policy and Practice,* 3rd edn (London: Macmillan).

Malpass, P., Warburton, M., Bramley, G. and Smart, G. (1993) *Housing Policy in Action: The New Financial Regime for Council Housing* (Bristol: School for Advanced Urban Studies, University of Bristol).

Malpass, P., Garnett, D. and Mackintosh, S. (1987) 'Home Ownership and the Management of Maintenance', in Spedding (ed.) (1987).

Marsh, D. and Rhodes, R. (eds) (1992) *Implementing Thatcherite Policies* (Buckingham: Open University Press).

Marx, K. and Engels, F. (1967) *The Communist Manifesto* (Harmondsworth: Penguin).

May, P. (1991) 'Reconsidering Policy Design: Policies and Publics', *Journal of Public Policy,* 11 (2) pp. 187–206.

Melling, J. (ed.) (1980) *Housing, Social Policy and the State* (Beckenham: Croom Helm).

Merrett, S. (1979) *State Housing in Britain* (London: Routledge & Kegan Paul).

—— (1986) 'Capital Controls and Housing Expenditure', *Housing Review,* 35 (1) (January–February), pp. 14–15.

Miller, M. (1979) 'Garden City Influence on the Evolution of Housing Policy', *Local Government Studies* (November–December).

Milner Holland Report (1965) *Report of the Committee on Housing in Greater London* (London: HMSO).

Murie, A. (1975) 'The Sale of Council Houses', Occasional Paper, No. 35 (Birmingham: CURS, University of Birmingham).

—— (1983) *Housing Inequality and Deprivation* (London: Heinemann).

—— (1985) 'What the Country Can Afford? Housing under the Conservatives', in Jackson (ed.) (1985).

—— (1989) *Lost Opportunities? Council House Sales and Housing Policy in Britain 1979–89* (Bristol: School for Advanced Urban Studies, University of Bristol).

—— (1992) *Housing Policy in Northern Ireland: A Review* (Centre for Policy Research, University of Ulster).

Murie, A., Niner, P. and Watson, C. (1976) *Housing Policy and the Housing System* (London: Allen & Unwin).

Murie, A., Wainwright, S. and Anderson, K. (1994) *Empty Public Sector Dwellings in Scotland* (Scottish Office).

Murie, A. and Nevin, B. (1997) *Beyond a Halfway Housing Policy: Local Strategies and Regeneration* (London: Institute for Public Policy Research).

Newton, K. (1976) *Second City Politics* (Oxford: Oxford University Press).

NFHA (1985) *Report of the Inquiry into British Housing* (London: NFHA).

—— (1991) *Inquiry into British Housing: Second Report* (London: NFHA).

Niner, P. (1975) *Local Authority Housing Policy and Practice* (Birmingham: CURS, University of Birmingham).

Norman, P. (1975) 'Managerialism: A Review of Recent Work', in Conference Paper 14, *Proceedings of the Conference on Urban Change and Conflict* (York, Centre for Environmental Studies) (London: Centre for Environmental Studies).

Nugee Committee (1985) *Report of the Committee of Inquiry on the Management of Privately-Owned Blocks of Flats* (London: HMSO).

O'Higgins, M. (1983) 'Rolling Back the Welfare State: The Rhetoric and Reality of Public Expenditure under the Conservative Government', in Jones and Stevenson (eds) (1983).

Oatley, N., Lambert, C., Malpass, P. and Bolan, P. (1993) 'Issues in the Evaluation of City Challenge: The Failed Bids', paper presented to the ESRC Seminar, Urban Policy Evaluation (Cardiff) (September).

Offe, C. (1975) 'The Theory of the Capitalist State and the Problem of Policy Formation', in Lindberg and Alford (eds).

Orbach, L. (1977) *Homes Fit for Heroes: A Study of the Evolution of British Public Housing 1915–21* (London: Seeley, Service).

Page, D. (1993) *Building for Communities* (York: Joseph Rowntree Foundation).

Pahl, R. (1975) *Whose City?,* 2nd edn (Harmondsworth: Penguin).

—— (1977) 'Managers, Technical Experts and the State: Forms of Mediation, Manipulation and Dominance in Urban and Regional Development', in Harloe (ed.) (1977).

Painter, M. J. (1980) 'Policy Coordination in the Department of the Environment 1970–1976', *Public Administration,* 53 (Summer).

Parker, R. A. (1967) *The Rents of Council Houses* (London: Bell).

Phillips, D. (1985) *What Price Equality?* (London: GLC).

Platt, S., Powell, J., Piepe, R., Paterson, B. and Smyth, J. (1985) *Control or Charade* (Portsmouth: Portsmouth Polytechnic).

Political Economy of Housing Workshop (1976) *Housing and Class in Britain* (London: PEHW).

Pooley, C. G. (ed.) (1992) *Housing Strategies in Europe, 1880–1930* (Leicester: Leicester University Press).

Power, A. (1987) *Property Before People* (London: Allen & Unwin).

—— (1993) *Hovels to High Rise: State Housing in Europe since 1850* (London: Routledge).

Power A (1987) *The PEP guide to Local Housing Management: Vol 1, The PEP Model* Department of the Environment.

Prescott-Clarke, P., Allen, P. and Morrissey, C. (1988) *Queuing for Housing: A Study of council Housing Waiting Lists.* HMSO.

Prescott-Clarke, P., Clemens, S. and Park, A. (1994) *Routes into Local Authority Housing* HMSO.

Pressman, J. and Wildavsky, A. (1973) *Implementation* (Berkeley: University of California Press).

Randolph, B. (1993) 'The Reprivatisation of Housing Associations', in Malpass and Means (eds) (1993).

Ravetz, A. (1974) *Model Estate: Planned Rehousing at Quarry Hill, Leeds* (Beckenham: Croom Helm).

Rex, J. and Moore, R. (1967) *Race, Community and Conflict* (Oxford: Oxford University Press).

Rhodes R. A. W. (1979) *Central–Local Government Relationships* Report of an SSRC Panel of Research Initiatives Board (London: SSRC).

Richards, Janet (1981) 'The Housing (Homeless Persons) Act 1977: A Study in Policymaking', Working Paper, 22 (Bristol: School for Advanced Urban Studies, University of Bristol).

Richardson, J. and Jordan, A. (1979) *Governing under Pressure: The Policy Process in Post-Parliamentary Democracy* (Oxford: Martin Robertson).

Ridley, N. (1988) Speech to Institute of Housing Conference (17 June), DoE News Release.

Robson, B., Bradford, M., Dean, I., Hall, E., Harrison, E., Parkinson, M., Evans, R., Garside, P., Harding, A., Robinson, F. (1994) *Assessing the Impact of Urban Policy* (London: HMSO).

Saunders, P. (1975) 'They Make the Rules', *Policy and Politics,* 4 (1) pp. 31–58.

—— (1979) *Urban Politics* (London: Hutchinson).

—— (1980) *Urban Politics: A Sociological Interpretation* (Harmondsworth: Penguin).

—— (1981a) *Social Theory and the Urban Question* (London: Hutchinson).

—— (1981b) 'Notes on the Specificity of the Local State', in Boddy and Fudge (eds) (1981).

—— (1986) Contribution to discussion, *Environmental Planning D: Society and Space,* 4.

—— (1990) *A Nation of Home Owners* (London: Unwin Hyman).

Schifferes, S. (1976) 'Council Tenants and Housing Policy in the 1930s', in Political Economy of Housing Workshop, *Housing and Class in Britain.*

Sharp, Evelyn (1969) *The Ministry of Housing and Local Government* (London: Allen & Unwin).

Simpson, A. (1981) *Stacking the Decks* (Nottingham and District CRC).

Skinner, D. and Langdon, J. (1974) *The Clay Cross Story* (Nottingham: Spokesman).

Smellie, K. B. (1969) *A History of Local Government*, 4th edn (London: Allen & Unwin).

Smith, B. (1976) *Policy Making in British Government* (Oxford: Martin Robertson).

Smith, M. (1989) *Guide to Housing*, 3rd edn (London: Housing Centre Trust).

Spedding, A. (ed.) (1987) *Building Maintenance Economics and Management* (London: Spon).

Spicker, P. (1985) 'Legacy of Octavia Hill', *Housing* (June), pp. 39–40.

Stanyer, J. (1976) *Understanding Local Government* (London: Fontana).

Stewart, J. and Stoker, G. (1989) *The Future of Local Government* (London: Macmillan).

Stoker, G. (1988) *The Politics of Local Government* (London: Macmillan).

—— (1991) *The Politics of Local Government*, 2nd edn (London: Macmillan).

Swenarton, M. (1981) *Homes Fit for Heroes* (London: Heinemann).

Tarn, J. N. (1973) *Five Per Cent Philanthropy* (London: Cambridge University Press).

Thatcher, M. (1979) House of Commons, Hansard, col. 407 (15 May).

Thomas, A., North, C., Spencer, L. and Ward, K. (1991) *The Landlord and Tenant Act 1987: Awareness, Experience and Impact* (London: HMSO).

Townsend, P. (1987) 'Poverty in Europe', in Ferge and Miller (eds) (1987).

Treasury (1981) *The Government's Expenditure Plans 1981–82 to 1983–4*, Cmnd 8175 (London: HMSO).

Waldegrave, W. (1987) 'Some Reflections on Housing Policy', Conservative Party News Service (19 May).

Walker, R. (1985) *Housing Benefit* (London: Housing Centre Trust).

White, J. (1981) *Rothschild Buildings: Life in an East End Tenement Block, 1887–1920* (London: Routledge & Kegan Paul).

Whitehead, C. (1983) 'Housing under the Conservatives: A Policy Assessment', *Public Money* (June).

Whitehead, C. and Kleinman, M. (1992) *A Review of Housing Needs Assessment* (London: The Housing Corporation).

Widdicombe (1986) *The Conduct of Local Authority Business*, Report of the Committee of Enquiry into the Conduct of Local Authority Business, Cmnd 9797 (London: HMSO).

Wilcox, S. (1993) *Housing Finance Review 1993* (York: Rowntree Foundation).

—— (1997) *Housing Finance Review 1997/98* (York: Joseph Rowntree Foundation).

Wilding, P. (1972) 'Towards Exchequer Subsidies for Housing, 1906–1914', *Social and Economic Administration*, 6 (1) pp. 3–18.

Wilkes, S. (1987) 'Administrative Culture and Policy Making in the Department of the Environment', *Public Policy and Administration*, 2 (1).

Williams, P. (1978) 'Urban Managerialism: A Concept of Relevance?', *Area*, 10.

—— (1982) 'Restructuring Urban Managerialism: Towards a Political Economy of Urban Allocation', *Environment and Planning A*, 14, pp. 95–105.

Willmott, P. and Murie, A. (1988) *Polarisation and Social Housing* (London: Policy Studies Institute).

Wohl, A. (1977) *The Eternal Slum* (London: Edward Arnold).

Woodward, R. (1991) 'Mobilising Opposition: The Campaign Against Housing Action Trusts in Tower Hamlets', *Housing Studies*, 6 (1) (January), pp. 44–56.

Young, G. (1991) 'Our Shared Commitment', *Roof* (November–December).

Young, M. and Willmott, P. (1957) *Family and Kinship in East London* (London: Routledge & Kegan Paul).

Younis, T. (1990) *The Study of Implementation* (Aldershot: Dartmouth).

Index